Cambridge International AS Level

Modern Europe 1774–1924

Nicholas Fellows
Mike Wells
Series editor: Dr Jo Edwards

Endorsement indicates that a resource has passed Cambridge International Education's rigorous quality-assurance process and is suitable to support the delivery of their Cambridge International AS History: Modern Europe, 1774–1924. However, endorsed resources are not the only suitable materials available to support teaching and learning, and are not essential to achieve the qualification. For the full list of endorsed resources to support this syllabus, visit www.cambridgeinternational.org/endorsedresources

Any example answers to questions taken from past question papers, practice questions, accompanying marks and mark schemes included in this resource have been written by the authors and are for guidance only. They do not replicate examination papers. In examinations the way marks are awarded may be different. Any references to assessment and/or assessment preparation are the publisher's interpretation of the syllabus requirements. Examiners will not use endorsed resources as a source of material for any assessment set by Cambridge International Education.

While the publishers have made every attempt to ensure that advice on the qualification and its assessment is accurate, the official Cambridge International AS Level History: Modern Europe, 1774–1924 specimen assessment materials and any associated assessment guidance materials produced by the awarding body are the only authoritative source of information and should always be referred to for definitive guidance.

Our approach is to provide teachers with access to a wide range of high-quality resources that suit different styles and types of teaching and learning.

For more information about the endorsement process, please visit www.cambridgeinternational.org/endorsed-resources.

Third-party websites and resources referred to in this publication are not endorsed.

Acknowledgements

Every effort has been made to trace all copyright holders, but if any have been inadvertently overlooked, the Publishers will be pleased to make the necessary arrangements at the first opportunity.

Cambridge International Education material in this publication is reproduced under licence and remains the intellectual property of Cambridge University Press & Assessment.

Third-party websites and resources referred to in this publication are not endorsed.

Although every effort has been made to ensure that website addresses are correct at time of going to press, Hachette Learning cannot be held responsible for the content of any website mentioned in this book. It is sometimes possible to find a relocated web page by typing in the address of the home page for a website in the URL window of your browser.

Hachette UK's policy is to use papers that are natural, renewable and recyclable products and made from wood grown in well-managed forests and other controlled sources. The logging and manufacturing processes are expected to conform to the environmental regulations of the country of origin.

Orders: please contact Hachette UK Distribution, Hely Hutchinson Centre, Milton Road, Didcot, Oxfordshire, OX11 7HH. Telephone: +44 (0)1235 827827. Email education@hachette.co.uk Lines are open from 9 a.m. to 5 p.m., Monday to Friday. You can also order through our website: www.hachettelearning.com

The authorised representative in the EEA is Hachette Ireland, 8 Castlecourt Centre, Castleknock Road, Castleknock, Dublin 15, D15 YF6A, Ireland

ISBN: 9781036008949

© Nicholas Fellows and Mike Wells 2025

First published in 2025 by

Hachette Learning,

An Hachette UK Company

Carmelite House

50 Victoria Embankment

London EC4Y 0DZ

www.hachettelearning.com

Impression number   10 9 8 7 6 5 4 3 2 1

Year   2028 2027 2026 2025

All rights reserved. Apart from any use permitted under UK copyright law, no part of this publication may be reproduced or transmitted in any form or by any means, electronic or mechanical, including photocopying and recording, or held within any information storage and retrieval system, without permission in writing from the publisher or under licence from the Copyright Licensing Agency Limited. Further details of such licences (for reprographic reproduction) may be obtained from the Copyright Licensing Agency Limited, www.cla.co.uk

Cover photo Shawshots / Alamy Stock Photo

Illustrations by Newgen Publishing UK

Typeset in Newgen Publishing UK

Printed and Bound in Great Britain by Bell & Bain Ltd, Glasgow

A catalogue record for this title is available from the British Library.

Contents

Introduction	iv
Overview	ix

CHAPTER 1 France, 1774–1814

1 What were the causes and immediate consequences of the 1789 Revolution?	2
2 How and why did France become a republic by 1792?	17
3 How well was France governed in the period 1793–99?	31
4 What caused the rise and fall of Napoleon Bonaparte?	46
Study skills	65

CHAPTER 2 Liberalism and nationalism in Germany, 1815–71

1 What were the causes of the revolutions of 1848?	72
2 What happened during the 1848 revolutions, and what were their consequences?	89
3 Why was Bismarck appointed as Minister President of Prussia, and what were his aims in the period up to 1866?	105
4 How and why was the unification of Germany achieved by 1871?	119
Study skills	132

CHAPTER 3 Russia from autocracy to revolution, 1881–1924

1 What challenges faced the Tsarist regime between 1881 and 1894?	138
2 What were the causes and outcomes of the 1905 Revolution up to 1914?	156
3 How and why did the Bolsheviks seize power in October 1917?	171
4 How were the Bolsheviks able to consolidate their power up to 1924?	190
Study skills	205
Glossary	210
Further reading	214
Index	216
Photo credits	220

Introduction

This book is designed to support your understanding of the key themes, events, and people significant to Modern Europe between 1774 and 1924, specifically in France, Germany, and Russia. Cambridge International AS Level History (syllabus code 9489 or 9981) offers an education in understanding the changes that characterised the period. The book has been endorsed by Cambridge Assessment International Education and is listed as an endorsed textbook for students studying the syllabus.

This introduction gives you an overview of:
- the content you will study for the European Option: Modern Europe 1774–1924
- the structure of the syllabus
- the different features of this book and how these will aid your learning.

1 What you will study

From 1774 to 1924, Europe went through a period of great change. In France, the old political system was overthrown in a revolution, followed by years of war. In the nineteenth century, the map of Europe and the balance of power changed, especially with the rise of Germany as a nation-state. In the twentieth century, Russia saw the Tsarist government overthrown and replaced by the world's first communist government under Lenin and his Bolshevik party. These changes altered the borders and future of Europe.

This book covers the following topics post-1750:
- Chapter 1 examines the causes of the French Revolution and how it developed, and also how Napoleon was able to emerge and establish his empire.
- Chapter 2 traces the growth of liberalism and nationalism in Germany between the years 1815 and 1871. This covers the attempts to unite states and how this eventually led to a powerful and united Germany.
- Chapter 3 covers the overthrow of the tsar, a series of revolutions, and how Lenin and the Bolshevik Party eventually built a Soviet system.

2 Structure of the syllabus

The information in this section is based on the Cambridge International Education syllabus. You should always refer to the appropriate syllabus document for the year of examination to confirm the details and for more information. The syllabus document is available on the website: www.cambridgeinternational.org.

Cambridge International AS Level History will be assessed through two papers: a Historical Sources Paper and an Outline Study.
- Paper 1: For Paper 1, you need to answer one two-part document question on one of the options given. You will need to answer both parts of the question you choose. This counts for 40 per cent of the AS Level.
- Paper 2: For Paper 2, you need to answer two two-part questions from three of the options given. You must answer both parts of each question you choose. This counts for 60 per cent of the AS Level.

These topics rotate year-on-year. One topic is assessed on Paper 1, and the two remaining topics are assessed on Paper 2.

Assessment questions

For Paper 1, there will be two parts to each question. For part (A) you will be expected to compare two sources on one aspect of the material. For part (B) you will be expected to use all the sources and your knowledge of the period to address how far the sources support a given statement.

For Paper 2, you will select two questions from the options on Europe 1774–1924. There will be two parts to each question. Part (A) requires an explanation of causes, and part (B) requires you to consider and weigh up the relative importance of a range of factors. You will need to answer both parts of each question you choose.

Key concepts

The syllabus also focuses on developing your understanding of a number of key concepts, and these are also reflected in the nature of the questions set in the examination. The key concepts for AS History are as follows:

Cause and consequence

The events, circumstances, actions, and beliefs that have a direct causal connection to consequential events and developments, circumstances, actions, or beliefs. Causes can be both human and non-human.

Change and continuity

The patterns, processes, and interplay of change and continuity within a given time frame.

Similarity and difference

The patterns of similarity and difference that exist between people, lived experiences, events, and situations in the past.

Significance

The importance attached to an event, individual, or entity in the past, whether at the time or subsequent to it. Historical significance is a constructed label that is dependent upon the perspective (context, values, interests, and concerns) of the person ascribing significance and is therefore changeable.

The icons above appear next to questions to show where key concepts are being tested and what they are.

Command words

When choosing the two essay questions, keep in mind that it is vital to answer the actual question that has been asked, not the one that you might have hoped for. A key to doing well is understanding the demands of the question. Cambridge International AS Level History uses key terms and phrases known as command words. The command words are listed below:

Command word	What it means
Compare	Identify similarities and differences, and support your choice with relevant evidence.
Explain	Set out how and why something happens, supported with relevant evidence.

Questions may also use phrases such as these:
- How far do you agree?
- To what extent?

Answering assessment questions

It is important that you organize your time well during an assessment. In other words, do not spend too long on one question and leave yourself short of time Before you begin a question, take a few minutes to draw up a brief plan of the major points you want to make and your argument. You can then tick them off as you make them. This is not a waste of time as it will help you produce a coherent and well-argued answer. Well-organized responses with well supported arguments and a conclusion will score more highly than responses that lack coherence and jump from point to point.

Whoever reads your answers will focus on what you have done right, rather than what you have done wrong.

Answering source questions

For questions that ask you to compare two sources, you should be able to:
- make a developed comparison of the two sources
- identify both similarities **and** differences in the evidence that the two sources provide about a particular issue
- use contextual knowledge and source evaluation to **explain** the similarities and differences.

For questions that ask you to analyse more than two sources, you should be able to:
- identify whether the sources support or challenge the statement in the question
- use source content to explain how each source supports or challenges the statement
- use your contextual knowledge to help you understand and analyze the sources
- recognize nuance in the sources where appropriate.

A well-written answer for a source question should:
- evaluate the sources to reach a supported judgment as to how far the sources support the statement.

If you are writing a timed essay about sources where you cannot choose a question to answer, you may find it helpful to:
- spend ten minutes reading the sources carefully
- identify the key terms and phrases in the question so that you remain focused on the actual question
- underline any quotations you will use to support your arguments.

Answering essay questions

For questions that ask you to explain causes, you should be able to:
- consider two or three relevant causes and explain how they were factors
- support each cause with relevant and accurate evidence
- make links between the factors.

For analytical essay questions, you should be able to:
- consider a range of different issues and analyze each
- use a balanced argument throughout
- support your argument with relevant and accurate evidence
- reach a relevant and supported judgment which answers the question.

Your essays should include an introduction that sets out your main points. Do not waste time copying out the question, but do define any key terms that are in the question. The strongest essays will show awareness of different possible approaches to the question. You will need to write an in-depth analysis of your main points in several paragraphs, providing detailed and accurate information to support them. Each paragraph should focus on one of your main points and be directly related to the question. Finally, you should write a concluding paragraph. All of these skills are developed throughout the book in the Study skills section at the end of each chapter.

If you need to choose multiple questions to answer:
- Circle the two questions you intend to answer.
- Identify the command terms, and key words and phrases so you remain focused on them.

3 About this book

Coverage of the course content

This book addresses the key areas listed in the Cambridge International syllabus. The content follows closely the layout and sequence of the Cambridge syllabus, with a chapter representing each topic. Each chapter starts with an introduction outlining the key questions that it addresses. Each key question is accompanied by content that you are expected to understand and use when addressing the key question. Throughout the chapters, you will find the following features to aid your study of the course content.

Key terms

Key terms are the important terms you need to know to gain an understanding of the period. These are highlighted in the text the first time they appear in the book and are defined in the margin. They also appear in the glossary at the end of the book.

Key figures and profiles

Key figures highlight important individuals and can be found in the margin. Some chapters contain profiles that offer more information about the importance and impact of the individual. This information can be very useful in understanding certain events and providing supporting evidence to your arguments.

Sources

Throughout the book, you will encounter both written and visual sources. Historical sources are important components in understanding more fully why specific decisions were taken and on what contemporary leaders based their actions. They also help to explain both causes and consequences of past developments. The sources are accompanied by questions to help you dig deeper into the history of Modern Europe, 1774–1924. To help with analysing the sources, think about the message of the sources, their purpose, and their usefulness for a particular line of enquiry. The questions that accompany the source will help you with this.

Extension boxes

Occasional extension boxes will include a variety of additional information that goes beyond the syllabus to help further your understanding of the topic.

Key debates

Within each key question of the syllabus, a key debate summarizes different historical views and opinions of events and individuals.

Activities

Activities and tasks throughout the book will help you develop conceptual understanding and consolidate knowledge.

Summary diagrams

At the end of each section is a summary diagram that gives a visual summary of the content of the section. It is intended as an aid for revision. Try copying the diagram into your own set of notes and, using information from the chapter, provide precise examples to develop each point. This will help build your knowledge of the issues that relate to the key question.

Chapter summaries

At the end of each chapter is a short summary of the content of that chapter. This is intended to help you consolidate your knowledge and understanding of the content.

Refresher questions

Questions at the end of each chapter will serve as a useful tool to test your knowledge of what you have read. These will serve as prompts and show you where you have gaps in your knowledge and understanding.

Study skills

At the end of each chapter, you will find guidance on how to approach both writing a successful essay and also how to evaluate sources. These pages feature the kinds of questions you may come across in assessment. There is also analysis of, and comment on, sample answers. These are not full responses to the questions. We have written them to help you see what part of good answer might look like.

End of the book

The book concludes with the following sections.

Glossary

All key terms in the book are defined in the glossary.

Further reading

This contains a list of books that may help you with further independent research. At this level of study, it is important to read around the subject and not just rely solely on the content of this textbook. The further reading section will help you with this.

Overview

This course is designed to develop an understanding of the key events of Modern Europe from 1774 to 1924 and the nature of the significant changes that shaped the continent and its people over this period.

This time period is sometimes described as Europe's "long nineteenth century" by historians. Historians have grouped together major developments as a specific set of changes, which are not confined to one century, but stretch across a whole era. This was a time of dramatic change from much of the past for many European people. This included political, social, religious, economic, cultural, and intellectual changes which affected everyone, sometimes in violent and destructive ways. This transformed Europe with new political cultures, new industries, and new ideas, which formed and fragmented nations.

At the beginning of this course, we look at the old ways of French society, known as the *Ancien Régime*, where people lived in strict social orders for centuries. During the Early Modern period, monarchies and autocratic societies were common. However, Modern Europe is characterised by revolutionary changes which led to the creation of new nations, new political systems, and widespread political movements among the people. These political movements challenged the way society had worked for centuries as people sought to find the best new systems. Rapid industrialisation redefined the relationship between worker and employer, increasing inequality.

These changes happened in different ways and at different speeds across Europe. As the nineteenth century went on, European nations became more united than ever before. Many things such as culture, industry, and scientific progress brought a common European feeling. Modern European nations had had many shared features, institutions, and structures. However, there were still deep divisions, resentments, and disagreements about ideas and territories, which would affect the whole continent in the twentieth century.

This course will cover the causes, sequence, and effects of these events as independent topics that provide an overall chronology to structure both knowledge and understanding of the development of Modern Europe.

France, 1774–1814

We will start by examining how France developed into a Modern European nation. Like many European countries in the eighteenth century, France was ruled by a king who held total power. A growing population, changes to how the Church worked in French society, social class divisions, and regional differences made it increasingly difficult to rule this way. Additionally, France's involvement in long and expensive wars made things harder for the government. This course starts in 1774 and describes the lives of different classes of people, including urban workers, craftsmen, peasants, the aristocracy, and a growing middle class of professionals. By looking at key events, we will identify the causes of significant political change in France.

France is an excellent case study to understand the pressures for change and the call for improvements to existing structures in eighteenth-century Europe. Enlightenment thinking, commercialisation, and scientific advances all challenged established ideas, institutions, and social structures. However, in the case of France, these reformist ideas became instrumental in revolutionary thinking because of the problems and policies pursued by the French government, which reached a crisis point by 1789.

The rapid pace of revolutionary events in France had vicious and violent consequences. In a very short time, the lack of consensus about how France should be governed led to extreme political instability, culminating in the "Reign of Terror". In an attempt to restore stability, a new government led by a committee called the Directory was set up. The Directors ruled France from 1796 to 1799. However, overwhelmed by problems of war, economic crisis, and political unrest, the government was overthrown by a coup led by a successful general, Napoleon Bonaparte. His adoption of the role of "First Consul" eventually led to his seizure of power as Emperor of France. Despite the promise of revolution, mass participation, and the development of revolutionary ideas proposing *'liberté, égalité, fraternité'*, by 1800 France was again ruled by an authoritarian elite.

In this course, the causes and consequences of these events will be examined, together with investigating the role of significant individuals and important groups. The similarities and differences between people and their ideas, and the significance of old loyalties and new thinking will be studied.

To help you understand how "Modern Europe" was formed, this course also covers the end of the Napoleonic Wars and up to German Unification in 1871. This links the first part about France to the rise of Germany, showing how Napoleon's French Empire influenced German territories. This included political, social, and legal changes. The French invasion also caused a strong reaction in Germany. Despite the region's diversity, the influence of French ideas helped Germany to form a sense of *Volksgeist* or "the spirit of the people", based on shared heritage and language. This developed into the first ideas of a "German nation" and nationalism.

These topics are also linked as there was a reaction to the revolutionary era in France, which was one of anxiety and concern. Many of the other European countries had been shocked and appalled by the revolutionary events in France and were keen to ensure political and social stability in their own countries. The old ruling families wanted to retain their power. There was intense suspicion of new "liberal" ideas of "liberty" and "equality," which could destabilize their own countries, politically and economically.

Liberalism and nationalism in Germany, 1815–71

Germany was not a single country in 1815. Instead, it was a confederation (group of states) which had evolved over time from the medieval and Early Modern period, when it was part of the Holy Roman Empire. This empire was made up of kingdoms, duchies, principalities, and city-states which had many differences but also shared some similarities, such as a common language. After the Battle of Leipzig and the defeat of Napoleon, there was a settlement called the Congress of Vienna. The objective of this Congress was to create new boundaries in Europe and address key issues affecting the constitutional order. The main idea was to create a balance of power in Europe to maintain peace. However, it was also a conservative effort to eliminate liberal and revolutionary ideas and to preserve the traditional monarchies. After the Congress of Vienna, 39 predominantly German-speaking states formed an association called the German Confederation.

Emerging ideas at this time included the idea of nationalism. Nationalists believed that the separate German states should unify, based on their shared language and culture. However, at first this was a minority view, as most ordinary people felt far more loyal to their own region, with specific dialects, traditions, and customs. Additionally, there was little religious or economic unity. There were also emerging ideas linked to those which had emerged in France, which argued for liberal principles for the people, including the freedom to criticize the government in the press, and to hold political meetings and festivals. More democratic ideas, based on sovereignty of the people, started to emerge.

These emerging ideas of liberalism, democracy, socialism, and nationalism led to the German revolutions of 1848–49, which aimed to transform the Confederation into a unified Germany – a federal state with a liberal constitution. Although they were initially successful, the revolutions failed because of internal divisions and the ability of the old rulers to retain the loyalty of their armies. The experience of 1848–49 also led conservatives such as Bismarck to seek the opportunity of Prussian supremacy and an end to the domination of Austria in the region. The ideas of Bismarck were underpinned by the belief that economic strength and military action were the key to Prussia's development. Bismarck's role will be covered in depth when studying this course, assessing his aims, objectives, ideas, and strategies.

The end of the Germany section of the course covers the hugely significant changes that led to the emergence of a united Germany by 1871 and the considerable concerns of its immediate neighbours. Strategic diplomacy, military victories, and economic strength all combined to transform the previously fragmented region into a major European power. This set the stage for Germany's significant role in subsequent European and world history.

The unification of Germany in 1871 had profound and far-reaching consequences, both within Germany and internationally. The emergence of a powerful and unified Germany significantly altered the balance of power in Europe and led to increased rivalries and colonial contention with France, which had been defeated in the Franco-Prussian War. This rivalry contributed to a complex web of alliances and tensions that eventually led to the First World War. However, the arrival of a strong and united Germany also put considerable pressure on the Russian Empire to the east. Germany's geographical proximity and economic superiority influenced Russia's economic strategies, most especially with trade in Eastern Europe. Politically, the rise of Germany as a nation-state inspired nationalist movements within the Russian Empire, particularly among minority ethnic groups. Russia's Tsarist regime was oppressive and resistant to reform but recognised the need for fresh alliances to protect Russian territory and the Tsarist autocratic system. This exterior threat, combined with the rise of Japan as an imperial power on its eastern borders, posed a challenge for the Russian authorities, who were already dealing with internal pressures and demands for reform.

Russia from autocracy to revolution, 1881–1924

Our final topic therefore focuses on developments within Russia as the state changed through a sequence of revolutions from a Tsarist autocracy to the establishment of a communist state. It will consider how and why revolutionary events developed in Russia and why the old regime was unable to prevent its own demise. A vast empire with uneven development, Russia in 1881 was a volatile state with many emerging challenges.

This course looks at Tsardom and the challenges to the autocratic state from 1881 to 1894. It covers how Tsar Alexander III and his key advisors responded to political, economic, and social issues, as well as the rise of new ideas that challenged Tsarism. It also examines how revolutionary thinking and new economic ideas affected the old structures of Tsarist autocracy, which was put under pressure to make changes. The tension between revolution and reform in 1905 is explored, along with the factors that increased pressure on Tsar Nicholas II. The course also covers why the Tsar abdicated in February 1917 and how a Provisional Government tried to reform Russia.

The next sections then look at the causes of further revolutionary change and the reasons why revolutionaries were able to seize power in 1917. Key events, significant individuals, and new concepts and ideologies which became agents of change, are investigated in a structured approach to understanding the reasons for the transformation of Russia by 1924.

1 France, 1774–1814

> **Introduction**
>
> This chapter looks at why revolution broke out in France in 1789. It considers the nature and problems of the French state before 1789 (the *Ancien Régime*) and how these were transformed by the events from 1789 to 1792, when the French monarchy was eventually overthrown after attempts to share power between the king and an elected assembly failed. It explains why there was so much political instability in the period 1790–95 and why the revolution became more extreme. The rise to power of Napoleon Bonaparte in 1799 is considered, as well as the changes that he brought to France, firstly as Consul and then as Emperor. There is also explanation of Napoleon's fall from power. You should consider the following questions throughout this chapter:
> - ▶ What were the causes and immediate consequences of the 1789 Revolution?
> - ▶ How and why did France become a republic by 1792?
> - ▶ How well was France governed in the period 1793–99?
> - ▶ What caused the rise and fall of Napoleon Bonaparte?

KEY DATES

1774		Louis XVI comes to the throne
1787		Assembly of Notables to discuss financial problems
1789	May	Estates General meets
1789	20 June	Tennis Court Oath
1789	14 July	Storming of the Bastille
1789		October Days
1791		Flight to Varennes by Louis XVI
1792		War with Austria and Prussia (start of War of the First Coalition)
1793		Execution of Louis XVI
1793		Terror
1794		Coup of Thermidor
1795		Directory
1798		Start of the War of the Second Coalition
1799		Coup of Brumaire; Napoleon takes power
1802		Concordat with Papacy
1804		Civil Code
1804		Napoleon becomes Emperor
1805		War of Third Coalition
1808		Peninsular War
1812		Napoleon invades Russia
1814		Napoleon abdicates
1815		Hundred Days
1821		Napoleon dies on St. Helena

1 What were the causes and immediate consequences of the 1789 Revolution?

The French Revolution had long-term and short-term causes. It was brought about by resentments in French society about inequality and privilege. These were reinforced by the writings of the **Enlightenment** and, more directly, by economic distress. In the short term, it was brought about by the monarchy's failure to solve a growing financial crisis and by Louis XVI's inability to manage the process of reform and rising political demands. The consequences of the events of 1789 were, in the short term, to bring about shared power by the king and an elected assembly, but in the longer term to establish a republic and the abolition of the monarchy. This brought war and the rise of a military leader who declared himself Emperor in 1804.

> **KEY TERM**
> **Enlightenment** This is the name given to the growth of scholarly and intellectual writing on many aspects of philosophy, science, the arts, economics, government, religion, and politics in the eighteenth century. These writings often questioned established religion, the monarchy, and social inequality, and were seen as a major cause of revolution.

LOUIS XVI

Louis XVI was the grandson of Louis XV. As his father had died in 1765, Louis came to the throne when his grandfather died in 1774. Personally kind, he was not dynamic or decisive. He was interested in many new ideas, particularly those connected to naval matters. However, he was unable to deal effectively with the growing financial problems, and he did not support ministers who wanted to make changes. He accepted advice to go to war against Britain in 1778, which made the situation worse. He eventually agreed to summon the Estates General, the equivalent of a parliament, which had not met since 1614, but then was unable to control it. Historians' views about Louis XVI are divided. Some argue that he was indecisive, stubborn, and unintelligent. Others believe he was a well-intentioned but unfortunate ruler, at a time of great change.

Most historians, however, do agree that because he shifted between support for change and a desire to use force to prevent it, he allowed events to get out of control. His position became increasingly dangerous after he was forced to live in the centre of Paris, not his palace at Versailles, by popular action in October 1789. He unwisely attempted to flee in June 1791 and reluctantly became a constitutional monarch. He unwisely supported a war policy in 1792 and was blamed for the French failures. Louis was overthrown as king in August 1792 and was executed in January 1793.

The *Ancien Régime* and pressure for change

The term '*Ancien Régime*' refers to the rule of the French monarchs before the revolution of 1789.

Absolute monarchy and the structure of government

The monarchy in 1774 was hereditary, and in theory it was "absolute." That meant that, apart from God, there was no authority above the king. The king therefore controlled everything. In the seventeenth century, the king's power had increased under "the Sun King," Louis XIV (1661–1715). One saying attributed to him was *"L'état, c'est moi"* – "I am the state." He appointed ministers; he issued edicts or laws; he decided on war and foreign policy. In practice he controlled the Church. There was no elected parliament, and there were no political parties. It was treason to oppose royal policy, and there was censorship of publications.

There were assemblies known as "*parlements*," but these were courts of law, whose members acted as judges. They had to officially record royal edicts to turn them into laws. Opposition might come if the judge thought that a new edict clashed with previous royal laws.

> **KEY TERM**
> *Ancien Régime* This was the term that was used in the revolutionary period in France from 1789 to describe the old type of political system. It was a term used to show disrespect for the old French monarchy.

However, this could be overridden by a special ceremony called a "*lit de justice,*" where the king appeared and declared that an edict was in fact legal. The highest of these courts was the *Parlement de Paris* – consisting of eminent lawyers and officials but not elected like a modern parliament. There were also provincial *parlements*. They played no part in actual government. There was a Council of State entirely chosen by the king. There was little in the way of a modern cabinet of ministers; mostly, each minister saw the king separately. The most important post was the Controller General of Finance.

Local government of the royal provinces was conducted by an official called an Intendant, appointed by the king. These professional administrators were powerful but did not have a large body of officials by modern standards. Taxes were not collected by state officials but by private individuals or groups. They bought the right to collect taxes on behalf of the king and were known as "Tax Farmers."

The last time that France had had any sort of elected assembly had been in 1614. After 1302, there had been a body called the Estates General. This was elected by France's three official classes – the clergy, the nobility, and the commoners – but this had fallen out of use with the growth of an absolute monarchy.

The king relied on the nobility to be officers in his army and to take leading posts in the Church – this was the main role of the hereditary aristocracy, the *noblesse d'épée*. The administration was undertaken by people given grants of nobility for service – the *noblesse de robe*.

There were considerable variations in how much influence royal government had. There were some provinces that had stronger local traditions and less royal control. In others, royal government was much stronger. Certain areas had privileges such as lower taxes, and the Church controlled some areas.

By modern standards, France was quite a divided country:
- There were no uniform laws. Every area had its own traditional laws.
- There were no uniform weights and measures.
- There were many areas which were so remote that officials rarely visited.
- French was not universally spoken or understood, and there were many local dialects and languages.

The unifying element was the monarchy, supported by the royal army and the Catholic Church.

When Louis XVI came to the French throne in 1774, he inherited problems. Some of these were long term and were to do with how France was governed and the inequalities of French society. Others, especially financial problems, were a result of costly wars fought in the reign of his grandfather, Louis XV.

French Society: the Estate system and the discontent of the Third Estate

Louis XVI inherited a country that was deeply divided and unequal. France was made up of different classes, called estates. Most of the French people were in the Third Estate. Of these, some 80 per cent were **peasants** and the rest urban workers, tradesmen, and a growing middle class. Above them were the First and Second Estates, who had privileges that the majority of French people did not have.

The First Estate was churchmen and nuns and comprised only 0.5 to 1 per cent of France's population. The official religion of France was Roman Catholicism. The Church owned 10 per cent of the land and was exempt from **direct taxes**. The Church controlled education. It also censored publications. Members of the Third Estate had to pay land taxes (tithes) and fees for services such as weddings and funerals to the Church. Within the Church, members of the nobility held nearly all important and richer posts. This contributed to a growing divide between the ordinary clergy and wealthy bishops.

The Second Estate was formed from the nobility, who comprised less than 1.5 per cent of the population. Both types of noble (the *noblesse d'épée* and *noblesse de robe*) did not have to pay certain direct taxes. Most of the leading officers in the armed forces, government

KEY TERMS

Noblesse d'épée This means "nobles of the sword" and refers to the swords used by medieval knights who earned their titles for military service to the king. These nobles were seen as more prestigious than the *noblesse de robe*.

Noblesse de robe This refers to the "robes" they wore as many of them were judges. These nobles obtained their titles for public service.

Peasants This refers to the majority of the French people. They were primarily farmers, often working small plots of land, or tenant farmers paying rent to landlords. Their standard of living was generally poor.

Direct taxes Taxes levied on personal income or property.

ministers, provincial governors, and important office holders such as the local administrators and diplomats were members of the aristocracy.

The nobles' status as lords of the manor enabled them to hold courts and receive payments from their tenants. These payments were known as **feudal dues** and were owed to them because of their noble status. This status had been changed slightly in the eighteenth century, and some of the middle classes were able to lease the rights from nobles. This meant they, as well as nobles, could charge dues, collect shares of the harvest, and charge tolls and fees for use of local bridges or even for grinding grain in mills to make flour for bread. However, while the middle classes could gain maximum revenue from these rights, they still were discontented by their lack of opportunity in running the state. Many peasants resented the feudal payments, especially in times of hardship.

Though socially privileged, the hereditary nobles were not necessarily rich or politically influential. Their role in decision-making had been reduced in the previous century and, while they enjoyed privileges and status, they were not key players either in local or central government. Some enjoyed a lavish lifestyle as honored courtiers with the royal family at Versailles, the great royal palace outside Paris, as well as in their local country mansions or "*châteaux*," but some were not much richer than their tenants.

The French economy grew in the eighteenth century, especially due to profits from the tobacco trade through enslavement in the French West Indies. As the seaport cities expanded, the wealthier merchants often became richer than many of the poorer nobles. The growth of Paris and provincial cities meant that the professional classes – lawyers, doctors, managers, writers, and some manufacturers – grew in wealth. The urban middle classes also grew in confidence and education. There was greater awareness of the issues of the day. There were more books, more newspapers, more discussions, and more awareness of the old-fashioned privileges of the nobles. Comparisons were made with Britain, where trade, industry, and finance were perceived as pathways to prestige and influence. There was increasing resentment about the tax privileges of the nobles and clergy. An increasingly educated and ambitious urban middle class resented not being able to gain higher positions in the state.

To many of the middle class, France seemed to be ruled in an outdated medieval way, and there was increasing interest in reform and the need for some sort of representation in an elected assembly. The growth in the French middle class from about 700,000 in 1700 to 2.3 million by 1780 meant that this class was more numerous and likely to resent the privileges of the first two Estates. There was greater literacy and a growth in demand for books and journals, many of which were critical of the *Ancien Régime*. The businessmen and merchants resented restrictions on trade such as internal customs and lack of uniform weights and measures. There were large numbers of lawyers who wanted political change and who also wanted a society which would give more opportunities for people of talent to prosper whether their background was privileged or not. Even among the clergy, poorer priests were resentful about the domination of the Church by aristocratic bishops and abbots. Paris was the most populous city, with 620,000 people by 1789. The next largest city was Lyon, with only 145,000. This meant that Paris was disproportionately large and influential. It had a large underclass of servants, casual labourers, peddlers, itinerant craftsmen, and 25,000 sex workers. Many people lived in overcrowded and often unhealthy conditions. Subject to hardship when bread prices rose, they sometimes resorted to popular protest. Like the more prosperous middle classes, they were reading more and had greater awareness of new ideas about the people having rights.

The American War of Independence

France's international standing had been hit badly by conflict in the eighteenth century. Several wars saw Britain expand its empire and France lose control of vital areas. In the Seven Years' War (1756–63), France and Britain had fought for control in Europe, in North America, and in India. Rather than setting up permanent settlements as the British had done, the French had largely focused on fur trading and building forts in Canada. France lost its American empire in the war, but in the process the British had laid the basis for the loss of its own colonies. To recoup the costs of the victory, Britain tried to tax the American colonies in a way not attempted before. Opposition grew among colonists who believed

> **KEY TERM**
>
> **Feudal dues** Payments made to lords by peasants based on traditional privileges. These varied greatly from region to region, but some common payments were *champart* (a part of the grain or produce), *corvée*, and *banalités* (fees for using the landlord's equipment, such as flour mills, bakers' ovens, or grape presses). Tenants were also subject to landlords' courts.

> **ACTIVITY**
>
> Make a list of social grievances that French people had in the reign of Louis XVI. Which factor or factors do you think were the most significant in being likely to bring about revolution? Explain your reasons.

in "No taxation without representation," and disputes grew, with fighting breaking out in 1775. This led to a full-scale armed rebellion and war between colonial forces under George Washington and the British army.

For France, the American War of Independence was a chance for revenge, but quite a dangerous one. For the monarchy to ally with rebellious subjects who were demanding parliamentary representation before paying taxes and who called for "liberty or death" was a dangerous policy. Eventually, in 1778, French troops were committed to America. French volunteers such as the liberal Marquis de la Fayette (see page 15) aided the colonists, and France played a major role in British defeat. The Americans fought for the sort of liberty that their French allies did not have. The key document, the Declaration of Independence, in 1776 stated "all men are created equal" and made it clear that they had natural rights to "life, liberty, and the pursuit of happiness." But in France, men were not equal and had no such rights.

As well as increasing France's already severe financial problems, the war therefore increased political discontent among those who wanted more of a say in politics at home. The war was also disappointing, as last-minute British naval victories restricted the hoped-for gains of rich West Indies slave colonies when peace was finally made in 1783.

The influence of the Enlightenment

The Enlightenment refers to a growth of interest in scientific knowledge and a discussion of all sorts of ideas in Europe and North America in the late seventeenth and eighteenth centuries. The interest in knowledge was reflected in the work of scholars such as **Denis Diderot**, who attempted to gather all knowledge into an encyclopedia. Greater knowledge led to treatises – which were written investigations which sought to explain major topics. There were works on change – on agriculture, on industry, on finance, education, on the pursuit of happiness, and on the nature of government. This expansion of intellectual activity was the work of an elite group of thinkers and scholars. However, it had wider effects, particularly in matters of religion and politics.

There were doubts cast on traditional religious beliefs and the power of the Church to censor inquiries that threatened Christian beliefs. There was also the general questioning of traditions, and this affected belief in absolute monarchy. The English political theorist John Locke was highly influential. He questioned whether the divine right of monarchs to rule should be respected when they threatened the natural rights of their subjects. This idea was seen in the American Declaration of Independence.

The most famous political influence in France was the work of Jean-Jacques Rousseau (a French-speaking Swiss writer, 1712–78) who questioned why, "Man is born free, but is everywhere in chains" in his book *The Social Contract*, which suggested that men and women obey laws as part of an unwritten contract with those in power, not as a matter of obedience to God-given authority.

The new ideas were studied not only by the middle class but also by some nobility. Even Queen Marie Antoinette read Rousseau. A major political writer in France was the Baron de Montesquieu (1689–1755), who argued that there should be a division between those who govern, those who discuss laws, and the judges, to ensure a balance of power to protect the subjects from excessive state power. In Paris, Enlightenment ideas spread to the ordinary people, especially independent craftsmen and shopkeepers.

KEY FIGURE

Denis Diderot (1713–84) was an influential writer from the Champagne region of France who attempted to bring together knowledge into an encyclopedia begun in 1750 and completed in 1772. This quest for knowledge was highly influential, and other Enlightenment writers followed suit; as more was known and could be accessed, more could be questioned, so the effect was to promote more criticism of governments and institutions, and to encourage more intellectual curiosity.

> What evidence from Source 1.1 shows opposition to the *Ancien Régime*? Match this to your knowledge of France before 1789.

SOURCE 1.1

An Enlightenment view of liberty. From Jean-Jacques Rousseau, *The Social Contract*, published in 1762

The tyrant assures his subjects he will give them civil peace and tranquillity. Granted; but what do they gain, if the wars his ambition brings down upon them, his insatiable greed, and the bad conduct of his ministers press on? What do they gain, if the very tranquillity they enjoy does not end the miseries? Tranquillity is found also in dungeons; but is that enough to make them desirable places to live in?

To renounce liberty is to renounce being a man.

> **KEY DEBATE**
>
> **HOW IMPORTANT WERE THE IDEAS OF THE ENLIGHTENMENT IN BRINGING ABOUT THE FRENCH REVOLUTION?**
>
> Many historians writing about this period see the ideals of the Enlightenment as a driving force. France was an increasingly literate and politically aware nation. Popular awareness of ideas about progress, reform, liberty, and political participation had been steadily growing. The idea that men had natural rights was a powerful one and it was these ideas that made the events of 1789 more than just a protest movement.
>
> Other historians put social and economic factors at the forefront. The massive economic discontent following a run of bad harvests and growing popular discontent have been seen as more important than the ideas of the Enlightenment. The growing class consciousness of the middle classes and the resentment of the old feudal social system have been judged by some historians as more fundamental reasons for revolutionary change.
>
> There are other views as well. Some put fear at the heart of the events of 1789, not a commitment to rational ideas, especially in key events like the storming of the Bastille, the peasant disturbances of the Summer and the October Days. Rather than a clash of ideas, others see political misjudgements as the reason why the revolution developed.

Long-term financial problems

Because of special tax privileges for certain people, taxes were not shared equally. The French monarchy faced financial problems because it lacked a uniform, nationwide, and effective means of collecting taxes. There was a history of selling positions of power and responsibility to raise money – not only positions in the legal system but also in the financial system. The French state could not collect enough taxes through tax farmers (see page 3) to meet expenses and had to rely on loans. In normal times, there was a financial shortfall, but two expensive wars fought by Louis XV – the **War of the Austrian Succession 1740–48** and the **Seven Years' War 1756–63** – had increased the debts. In 1748, France had a debt of 1 billion livres, and by 1763 this had risen to 1.8 billion. A lot of the taxes raised were spent on paying interest on a very large debt.

> **KEY TERMS**
>
> The **War of the Austrian Succession 1740–48** and the **Seven Years' War 1756–63**
> France had fought two prolonged wars in the eighteenth century. In both conflicts, France had limited success, considering the high costs of pursuing war. The wars increased the French national debt considerably.

Long-term economic problems

> **KEY TERM**
>
> **Bread riots** A common feature of French life was riots by poor, and often hungry, people to seize corn or take bread from bakers.

There were also long-term economic problems. Most French people were peasant farmers, and most lived in hardship. France before 1774 was used to **bread riots** and economic hardship in many rural communities. Poor harvests caused food shortages. Less food being available caused the price of food to increase. With more and more of their incomes being needed just to buy enough food, people had less money to spend on manufactured goods and luxuries. Of course, business owners also needed to buy food, and so the price of these goods also increased, which made them even less affordable. As nobody could afford to buy non-essential products, many people lost their jobs and businesses. In Lyon, a city in the south of France famed across Europe for its silk, almost half the city's workforce was unemployed by 1790 as inflation and the rising cost of living devastated the silk trade. Population growth had meant that urban populations had grown. This was particularly true of Paris, where there were very poor districts. As a result of the poor rural harvests, this had the effect of causing food shortages and higher prices. In the cities, this in turn meant that demand for manufactured goods decreased, as there was less money available for luxuries. As a result, there was widespread unemployment in cities. Customs duties on goods moving between provinces made food more expensive during bad years, and the customs posts were very unpopular.

> What is the attitude of the writer of Source 1.2 to the French nobility?

SOURCE 1.2

A churchman writes about the Third Estate in a pamphlet. From the Abbé Sieyès, *What Is the Third Estate?*, 1789

What is the Third Estate? Everything, but shackled and oppressed. What would it be without the privileged order? Everything, but free and flourishing. Nothing can succeed without it; privileged persons, far from being useful to the nation, enfeeble and injure it; the noble order does not enter at all into the social organisation; it is a burden upon the nation.

ACTIVITY

Identify the main problems facing Louis XVI in 1787. Put them in order of importance.

Attempts to deal with financial and economic problems up to 1787

The need to reform was pressing, but Louis failed to take the lead to make necessary changes, despite being well intentioned. He appointed capable ministers but did not support them, letting the situation worsen. He reluctantly agreed at last to a special assembly of notables to discuss the financial crisis in 1787, but this failed to agree to a plan, and so he accepted the summoning of the Estates General and even allowed a nationwide consultation to put forward grievances. This was a huge gamble and might have worked had he himself led the movement for change, but in fact it led to revolution and eventually his overthrow and execution.

Turgot and early attempts to reform

Faced with a deficit of 37 million livres, in 1774, Louis XVI appointed an economic expert as his key minister – the Controller General of Finances. Given that the deficit was, in modern terms, at least £6000 million, some drastic action was needed, and **Anne-Robert-Jacques Turgot** had plenty of ideas. He wanted to boost national wealth by freeing trade, reducing price controls, ending tax privileges, and improving communications. He lasted only two years in the role. His policies caused large-scale food riots: the "Flour War" of 1775. He was dismissed in 1776 when the queen and privileged aristocrats at court turned against him.

Necker and the Compte rendu

Turgot's successor, a Swiss banker called **Jacques Necker**, was also inventive. He aimed to cut back on the sale of offices and reduce the amount of tax money that went to tax farmers. To show transparency in government, he published the national accounts in the *Compte rendu* (report to the king) of 1781 – a bestseller, as French people wanted to know the secrets of finance. He had raised money for the American War through loans, and the publication of accounts was to keep investors' confidence. However, this was a step too far for his enemies at court. He too was dismissed.

KEY FIGURE

Anne-Robert-Jacques Turgot (1727–81) was the leading minister of Louis XVI in 1774–76 and proposed economic and financial reforms which, if followed, might have prevented the revolution. Unpopular with the people because of the rise in bread prices, and with his rivals at court, he was not backed by Louis XVI and fell from power.

KEY FIGURE

Jacques Necker (1732–1804) was a Swiss lawyer and banker who was France's finance minister three times. He was first put in charge of royal finances in 1777. To try to build confidence so that people would be prepared to lend money to the state, he published the *Compte rendu*, an optimistic account of the king's government's financial situation in 1781 – a remarkable step, as these matters were previously thought to be not a matter for public knowledge and discussion. This was thought too radical by many at court, and he resigned. He was recalled in 1788 and seen as a major reforming influence. His dismissal in 1789 caused a wave of public discontent (see page 13 on the Storming of the Bastille), and he was recalled. He was more a symbol of reform than a figure who actually achieved much, and he resigned in 1790.

KEY FIGURE

Charles de Calonne (1734–1802) was an experienced administrator whom Louis XVI appointed as finance minister in 1783. He wanted to make changes to reduce the debt but failed to gain the confidence of a special Assembly of Notables, and was dismissed in 1787. He lived in England during the revolution.

KEY TERM

Corvée This was an obligation to work on the public roads or the king's highways. It was unpopular, and as the nobles and clergy were exempt it caused a lot of resentment.

Calonne

Necker's eventual successor in 1783 was the experienced aristocratic administrator **Charles de Calonne**.

Calonne had three key ideas:
- to end tax privileges in the payment of the key land tax called the *taille*
- to increase prosperity by abolishing internal customs duties
- to end the unpopular **corvée** duty.

When this did not meet with the approval of the *parlement*, Calonne turned to another striking proposal. In 1787, he called a special assembly of notables, leading figures in the nation, aristocrats, and royal princes. This was a failure, and Calonne was dismissed in April 1787.

The financial and political crisis 1787–89

The issue of the deficit had become so important by 1787, because of the problems of maintaining confidence among lenders and investors, that the French state would not go into bankruptcy. It seemed vital to reform the royal finances to make sure that royal government could carry on. In reality, the French national debt was not overwhelming by modern standards and not even by the standards of other countries at the time. However, the management of it was very complex, and it was widely believed that there was a crisis, and this threatened the credit status of the monarchy. Some sort of tax reform was needed, but the problem was how to get it accepted by the privileged classes.

The Assembly of Notables and the failure of Calonne's reforms

Calonne resorted to calling an old-fashioned and defunct body called the Assembly of Notables. This aristocratic group had last been called in 1626. The Assembly of Notables was made up of clergy and nobles (the First and Second Estates). There were 144 members, only 10 of whom were not nobles. Calonne's idea was that if the most influential people were behind reform, then tax income would rise and, more importantly, France would regain the confidence of investors, and the Crown could once again borrow money. When it came to it, the notables would not accept reform, and the Assembly failed.

There was some opposition in principle to nobles losing privileges, but this was not the main reason. The way that Calonne planned the reforms was criticised, and many thought they were inadequate. The notables greatly resented his criticism that they were blocking reform because of their desire to keep their privileges. They claimed to protect themselves from over-powerful ministers and 'tyranny'. While not rejecting the reforms as such, the Assembly wanted to link them to greater political participation in government. The nobles and clergy were prepared to accept a reduction in their privileges, but not without the calling of the Estates General.

The risk of calling this Assembly did not pay off. Calonne had proposed some striking reforms, but when the Assembly would not agree, he was dismissed. His successor, **Etienne-Charles de Loménie de Brienne**, tried again.

KEY FIGURE

Etienne-Charles de Loménie de Brienne (1727–94) was a noble who, as Archbishop of Toulouse, was also an important churchman. He played a leading role in the Assembly of Notables and was appointed finance minister in 1787. Brienne was opposed by the *Parlement de Paris* when trying to pass financial reforms begun by Colonne. In July, he was forced to agree to the meeting of the Estates General but then resigned in August. He was made a cardinal in 1788. He died in prison during the Reign of Terror (see page 34).

What is the attitude of the cartoonist of Source 1.3 towards the summoning of the Assembly of Notables? Use details from the **provenance** as well as the source in your answer.

KEY TERMS

Provenance Provenance is a term which means the origin or source of a document or artifact. It is important to know a source's provenance so you can assess its authenticity and reliability by considering factors such as who created it, when and where it was created, and why it was created. Identifying and evaluating the provenance of a source will help you assess the value of the source in understanding historical events, by assessing its useful qualities and its limitations.

Protestants Followers of the religious reforms begun in the sixteenth century. There were wars between Catholics and Protestants in the sixteenth century. Protestants were granted toleration in 1598 but this was ended in 1685 when the Protestants, or Huguenots as they were called, were persecuted.

KEY TERM

Enclosure The enclosing of land by hedges or fences in order to divide up large open fields.

SOURCE 1.3

A cartoon *Buffet of the Court* published in France in 1787. Calonne: My dear Notables, I would like to know with which sauce you would like to be eaten? Notables: But we don't want to be eaten at all! Calonne: You're avoiding the question!

Brienne and the involvement of the *Parlement de Paris*

The usual way to pass edicts was for the king's decisions to be approved by the *Parlement de Paris*, so lawyers could officially record them. As the *parlement* was not elected, this was not a case of having changes approved by the nation's representatives as when the British parliament passed the government's financial budget. As Calonne had proposed, Brienne put forward a series of far-reaching reforms. He proposed to solve the financial problems by a new land tax paid for by all. He also proposed other changes – reform of the customs barriers, provincial assemblies, civil rights for **Protestants**, and the ending of torture. However, the *parlement* feared that the government would have too much power.

By 1788, the king had lost patience after supporting Brienne far more than he had supported the previous ministers. When the *parlement* continued to refuse to register the changes, he exiled its members, announced plans to end *parlement*'s rights to register edicts, or orders, and arrested leading members.

The members of the *parlement* became popular heroes, standing up to the royal ministers. There were demonstrations in favour of the exiled judges, including the famous "Day of Tiles" on June 7, 1788 at Grenoble, when crowds threw down roof tiles in protest. Louis relented, and the wealthy lawyers returned to Paris. The only solution seemed to be to get wider approval for change. Once again, the government looked to the past and decided to call an Estates General. This was to be the most significant move towards revolution.

Economic problems

The political crisis and the failure of reforms came at a time when France was experiencing a serious economic crisis, which led to social unrest. A series of bad harvests since 1785 and a fall in trade and employment created a great deal of urban discontent. There was less food, and it was too expensive for people to buy. There were 80,000 unemployed people in Paris by 1789, and large towns and cities saw food riots in the spring and early summer. Food prices peaked in July 1789 and coincided with the outbreak of revolution. In the countryside, peasants came under pressure as landowners tried to take over lands traditionally used by the villages as a whole. Landlords **enclosed** common land and forests that poorer farmers used for

ACTIVITY

Make a list of the key consequences of the policies followed by Louis XVI's ministers: Turgot, Necker, Calonne, and Brienne. Which of these policies had the greatest impact?

animal grazing and gathering wood, nuts, and berries. By 1788, there were increasing instances of peasants refusing to pay dues and taxes, and attacks on the manor houses (*châteaux*) of landlords.

Though economic discontent produced violence and unrest by poorer people in both towns and the countryside, it also created unrest among the middle classes. Between 1785 and 1787, increased trade barriers and stricter tax collection affected manufacturers and traders. New customs posts and a new wall enclosing Paris were set up. State price controls and trade guild restrictions frustrated businessmen. The unfairness of the tax system made matters worse and seemed to show that there was a major need for change.

The king's decision to call the Estates General

On 8 August 1788, the king declared that he would summon the Estates General. The importance of this decision cannot be overstated.

- It led to widespread discussion of the grievances of the whole nation. Traditionally, the calling of the Estates General was preceded by local meetings to draw up lists of grievances called *Cahiers de doléances* or "registers of grievances" (literally "writing books of things which caused pain or distress").
- For the first time in the century, there were elections for delegates to this grand meeting of the estates.
- It led to considerable expectations of reform and change.
- Brienne resigned, and Necker was reappointed as Finance Minister. He returned from Switzerland and was expected to take charge of a program of change discussed and agreed to by the whole nation.

Previous meetings of the Estates General had been dominated by the first two estates – the nobles and the clergy. Voting was traditionally by estate, not by head. Thus, the much more numerous Third Estate could be outvoted by the first two estates who represented no more than 2 per cent of the nation. However, there was an expectation that the whole nation should be consulted. Great hopes were placed on this body as a traditional way to consult the nation.

Because it was a historic body, the old ways were followed and these involved the estates separately drawing up lists of grievances. In the past, very little notice had been taken of these, and kings had been under no obligation to act on them; the grievances were bound in books and duly stored but not debated.

The Cahiers de doléances

All over France, there were meetings to draw up grievances or matters that those attending wished to raise. This signalled that something remarkable was happening. The nobility, clergy, and commoners met separately and showed a considerable awareness of national as well as local affairs. All sorts of grievances were raised, and meetings were held in the smallest of villages. See Sources 1.4–1.6 for some examples from the different discussions which show the range of concerns.

SOURCE 1.4

Some demands in the *Cahiers de doléances* from the clergy and nobility from Blois, in central France

The clergy of Blois

1. That France is a true monarchy, where a single man rules and is ruled by law alone.
2. That the general laws of the kingdom may be enacted only with the consent of the king and the nation. If the king proposes a law, the nation accepts or rejects it; if the nation demands a law, it is for the king to consent or to reject it; but in either case it is the king alone who upholds the law in his name and attends to its execution. ...
6. That the Estates General should not vote otherwise than by order.
8. That no tax may be laid without the consent of the nation.
9. That every citizen has, under the law, a sacred and inviolable right to personal liberty and to the possession of his goods.

The nobility of Blois

Happiness ought not to be confined to a small number of men; it belongs to all. It is not an exclusive privilege to be contested for. It is a common right.

In accordance with this principle, the nobility of the bailliage (district) of Blois believe itself in duty bound to lay at the feet of the nation all the pecuniary exemptions which it has enjoyed or might have enjoyed up to this time, and it offers to contribute to the public needs in proportion with other citizens, upon condition that all direct taxes be comprised in a single land tax money.

SOURCE 1.5

Some demands in the *Cahiers de doléances* from the Third Estate in Versailles, where Marie Antoinette lived

Art. 1. The power of making laws resides in the king and the nation.

Art. 2. The nation being too numerous for a personal exercise of this right, has confided its trust to representatives freely chosen from all classes of citizens. These representatives constitute the national assembly.

Art. 3. Frenchmen should regard as laws of the kingdom those alone which have been prepared by the national assembly and sanctioned by the king.

Civil and criminal laws shall be reformed.

Art. 20. The military throughout the kingdom shall be subject to the general law and to the civil authorities, in the same manner as other citizens.

Art. 21. No tax shall be legal unless accepted by the representatives of the people and sanctioned by the king.

Art. 22. Since all Frenchmen receive the same advantage from the government, and are equally interested in its maintenance, they ought to be placed upon the same footing in the matter of taxation.

SOURCE 1.6

Some demands from the Third Estate in Carcassonne in southern France in the *Cahier* drawn up in February 1789 at a special meeting

10 Voting in the new assembly should be by head, not by estate.

11 No class, organization, or individual citizen may lay claim to tax privileges.

12 The dues exacted from commoners holding lands should be abolished, and also regulations which exclude members of the Third Estate from certain positions, offices, and ranks which have hitherto been bestowed on nobles.

13 There should be no arbitrary orders for imprisonment ... any tax exemptions. ... All taxes should be assessed on the same system throughout the nation.

14 Freedom should be granted also to the press.

> Compare sources 1.4 and 1.6. Note the similarities and differences between the different estates. How do they differ, and why?

There was unrest caused by high bread prices, and the discussions led many to want change. Though there were different expectations, many people were pleased with the opportunity to present their grievances. The level of political discussion was very high: debating societies talked about reform in the language of the Enlightenment – especially "liberty." The *Cahiers de doléances* contain calls for tax reform, ending privileges, and making the Estates General a permanent body, as well as changes to feudal payments. Most lists did not indicate a desire for radical change. However, all agreed that reform was needed, and they welcomed the meeting of the Estates General.

The meeting of the Estates General and the National Assembly

When the Estates General met at Versailles on May 5, 1789, it consisted of 278 nobles from the Second Estate, 330 churchmen from the First Estate, and 604 representatives of the Third Estate (i.e., the rest of the population represented mostly by the middle class). The king started badly by ordering each estate to its own meeting hall. He saw this as a meeting of three separate estates, two of which could outvote the other, rather than one national body. The old-fashioned view of society was emphasised by the Third Estate being ordered to wear formal black clothes, in contrast to the colourful dress of the nobles. Many of them refused.

There was no clear leadership from the king and court on any issue. The First and Second Estates were divided among themselves about cooperation with the Third Estate, but they were united in an emerging sense that the Third Estate was intent on change that would have dangerous consequences for them. In the face of indecision from the king, and the active deadlock from the other estates, on June 17, 1789 the Third Estate declared that it was changing its name to the National Assembly. This, in effect, was an announcement that all the power was no longer with the monarchy, but instead that the people of France were represented by this assembly.

The Tennis Court Oath

When it appeared that they were locked out of their meeting room, the Third Estate met in a tennis court near the Palace of Versailles (see Source 1.7 below) on June 20 and declared they were a "national assembly," and swore an oath not to disperse until France had a constitution.

This was a key moment of the revolution and confirmed the change in the Estates General. Originally called by the king to advise him on terms that he decided, it had become a very different body by June 17. It had declared that *it* was the representative body of the nation. The oath taken on June 20 moved this idea forward by binding the members to form a new constitution which would formally end the absolute power of the king and give the people the right to elect representatives. This would mean that the government would be responsible to the nation and not just the king. This was truly revolutionary. The occasion was seen as so important and historic that the great artist Jacques-Louis David was commissioned to paint it in 1790 (see Source 1.7).

KEY TERM

Constitution A set of rules by which a country is governed.

What impression of the Tennis Court Oath is given by Source 1.7?

SOURCE 1.7

The Tennis Court Oath painting by Jacques-Louis David

ACTIVITY

Create a diagram showing the similarities and differences between the grievances of the three estates.

Louis's refusal to carry out reform

The king was not to be moved. On June 23 he held a meeting of the estates and told them to go away and consider and discuss proposals for reform separately. The Third Estate refused to obey the king. When 47 nobles joined them, Louis gave way and agreed that there should be one body and the three estates should join.

Thus, by June 1789, Louis was facing a situation that he had never intended. He had been forced to agree to one National Assembly but refused to give it any power and insisted that it continued as the Estates General had done: as an advisory body only. After Necker presented the assembly with some suggested changes to resolve the economic and financial problems, Louis dismissed him on July 11. The king then summoned troops to Paris. It seemed that Louis was preparing to use military force to restore his authority. This terrified many of the Third Estate deputies and many Parisians. However, it was the people of Paris who propelled revolution and became key actors on the political stage in a way that few had foreseen.

The outbreak of revolution

The revolution had begun, quite bloodlessly, before the event that France now celebrates as its beginning – the storming of the Bastille on July 14, 1789. However, there had already been much popular protest in Paris and regional centres when the *parlements* had closed. This was mainly a result of food shortages, especially after poor harvests in 1788. Paris had become a hotbed of political agitation. The authorities had virtually lost control of the capital. Spontaneous public meetings and the speeches of radical political agitators had created a mood of excitement. Therefore, the king's actions did not help, but the conditions for an outburst were already there.

The storming of the Bastille

Crowds attacked customs posts and, fearing military action to stop the Assembly, searched for weapons. They first took weapons from the Invalides military hospital and then moved to the Bastille to get gunpowder. Although the Bastille was mostly unused and held few prisoners, it symbolised royal power. The troops there fired on the crowds, but other soldiers joined the attacks against the authorities. The conflict ended with the killing of the fortress governor, the Marquis de Launay.

Crowds took to the streets, fearing royal troops might be used against them. In April 1789, there was unrest when a wallpaper manufacturer's home was attacked over wage cuts, known as the *Réveillon* riots, which were suppressed by the Paris police, the *Garde Française*. However, on July 14, members of the *Garde* joined the attack on the Bastille. Most civilians came from the southeast of Paris, an area with tall tenements and narrow streets, home to small craftsmen and traders. The key area was the Faubourg Saint Antoine, known for furniture makers and other craftsmen selling goods to rich areas across the Seine River. Many of the participants were literate and politically aware.

The Bastille was not a major part of royal power. The prison was largely disused, and its garrison was small. The weak response of the authorities to the actions of July 14 confirmed that the king would have to accept change and not rely on military force.

SOURCE 1.8

A Parisian newspaper reports the storming of the Bastille, July 1789

The conquerors, glorious and covered in honour, carry their arms and the spoils of the conquered, the flags of victory, the victory laurels offered them from every side, all this created a frightening and splendid spectacle. The people, anxious to avenge themselves, allowed neither de Launay nor the other officers to reach the place of trial; they seized them from the hands of their conquerors, and trampled them underfoot one after the other. De Launay was struck by a thousand blows, his head was cut off and hoisted on the end of a pike with blood streaming down all sides ... This glorious day must amaze our enemies, and finally usher in for us the triumph of justice and liberty. In the evening, there were celebrations.

Identify one similarity and one difference between Source 1.8 and Source 1.9. Note down specific details from each source to support your answers. Then, using your knowledge of the context, explain why you think the sources are similar or different.

KEY TERMS

National Guard An armed force of citizens formed in July 1789 to keep order.

Brigands People who attack and rob others, especially in mountains and forests.

SOURCE 1.9

The British ambassador reported to the government in London on July 30, 1789 on the events of July 14

The fate of the Governor M. de Launay is generally lamented, for he was an officer of great merit and always treated the prisoners committed to his charge with humanity: it may be observed that the mildness of the present reign in France is strongly characterised by the small number of persons who were discovered in confinement in the Bastille: yet these considerations were not sufficient to check the fury of the populace, animated by the success of the attack and heated with the spirit of vengeance.

To maintain order, the propertied classes of Paris (the electors of delegates to the Estates General) created a new city council and a National Guard – signs that the king's authority was being ignored and that the initiative had been lost by his government. The king accepted this on July 17.

The Great Fear and the August Decrees

The king had paid the price for his indecision. Events moved so quickly that he lost control.

Hearing that the king had given in to the nobles worried many peasants. Rumours spread that nobles had hired mercenaries and brigands to kill reformers and destroy crops. In response, armed peasants roamed the countryside to stop this, starting "the Great Fear". They raided grain stores, destroyed tax records, and burned *châteaux*. The attacks continued until August 6.

The news of the peasant attacks caused great concern in Paris. The peasants were not politically inspired and did not want to abolish the monarchy or even the nobility. They were concerned with dues and payments. The National Assembly, alarmed by the Great Fear, announced that it would make changes to restore public order. A debate on August 4 to deal with the crisis took an unexpected turn and what seemed like a big step forward. The August Decrees abolished feudalism. The dues paid to lords, the tithes or taxes paid to the Church, exemptions from paying taxes, and *parlements* were all abolished. Feudalism was declared at an end, and laws from August 5 to 11 confirmed this. However, although France had become much less feudal in theory, in practice not all payments were abolished. Payments, which were seen as part of a contract between landlords and tenants, remained. There was a great deal of disappointment in the countryside about the limited changes to payments, and rural unrest continued for some years.

The Declaration of the Rights of Man and of the Citizen

The end of feudalism was followed by the Declaration of the Rights of Man and of the Citizen, of August 26, 1789. All men were declared to be equal in rights. All citizens had natural rights. It stated that "sovereignty" lay with the nation – not the king. So, the right to make laws lay with the people, not the monarch. People were citizens, not royal subjects.

The declaration was influenced by the American Declaration of Independence, but like the colonists, the only people with rights were men, not women, and these rights did not extend to the hundreds of thousands of enslaved people who worked in the French West Indies. The idealism of the Declaration was undermined by a decree in October, which made a distinction between different people based on wealth (see page 39). Voting and participating in government were restricted to wealthier citizens, but all citizens were to enjoy the rights in the Declaration.

For all their limitations, the acts of August 1789 were very important in changing France and were the biggest consequence of the revolutionary events that had taken place since May 1789.

> Rewrite Source 1.10 in your own words so that the meaning is clear.

SOURCE 1.10

Extracts from the Declaration of the Rights of Man, August 26, 1789

1. Men are born and remain free and equal in rights.
2. The aim of all political association is the preservation of the natural and imprescriptible rights of man. These rights are liberty, property, security, and resistance to oppression.
3. The principle of all sovereignty resides essentially in the nation. No body nor individual may exercise any authority which does not proceed directly from the nation.
4. Liberty consists in the freedom to do everything which injures no one else.
5. Law can only prohibit such actions as are hurtful to society.
6. Law is the expression of the general will.

The king could do little except observe these major changes in French society and government. They were the unintended consequence of the decision to summon the Estates General and the king's misjudgements.

The "March of the Women"

By October 1789, Louis and his advisors were having second thoughts. The king resisted change. He resented his loss of status as representative of the nation and made some half-hearted moves to restore what he thought was the natural order of monarchy. He summoned troops from the Flanders Regiment, who were known to be loyal to him personally, to his palace at Versailles. At a reception for some of the officers, the revolutionary red, white, and blue cockade (emblem) was trampled underfoot.

With food prices high and with a great deal of hardship fuelling radical agitation in the poorer districts, another wave of public anger broke out. This "March of the Women" was led by the women of the Paris markets protesting about the price of bread. A great demonstration was held, and a march on the royal palace at Versailles took place. The National Guard and its commander, the **Marquis de la Fayette**, followed the crowds to Versailles, where they invaded the palace on October 5, 1789.

Up to this point, both the king and his ministers and the National Assembly had been meeting at Versailles. The events of October 5 forced both king and Assembly to move to the centre of Paris. It was hoped that if the king were living in the city centre, he would understand the need for better bread supplies and be more responsive to the people. The Assembly's move to the centre meant that they would later feel the influence of popular feeling.

The Assembly now tried to establish a new reformed France and to draw up a new constitution. Its new name – the **Constituent Assembly** – showed that it was working as an independent body, not as part of a royal government. In a remarkably short time, since May 1789, France had moved from being a traditional absolute monarchy based on a view that the king was chosen by God and backed by a privileged nobility and Church. By the end of 1789, France was experimenting with a constitutional monarchy with an elected assembly which had ended privileges, changed society, and opened the way for huge political change.

KEY TERM

Constituent Assembly An elected body whose task is to draw up a new constitution, or a set of rules under which a country is to be run.

KEY FIGURE

Marie-Joseph Gilbert du Motier, **Marquis de la Fayette** (1757–1834), was a high-ranking noble who was a professional soldier. Moved by the idea of liberty, he volunteered to help the American colonists in their war against Britain in 1777. He became a hero in America. In 1789, he was made commander of the new National Guard and helped to write the Declaration of the Rights of Man. He was not able to control the march on Versailles in October 1789 and was increasingly concerned about the radicalism of the revolution. He fled abroad in 1792.

ACTIVITY

Put the following events in a timeline. Summarise each event, and note the key changes brought about by each.
- The Storming of the Bastille
- The Tennis Court Oath
- The Declaration of the Rights of Man
- The October Days

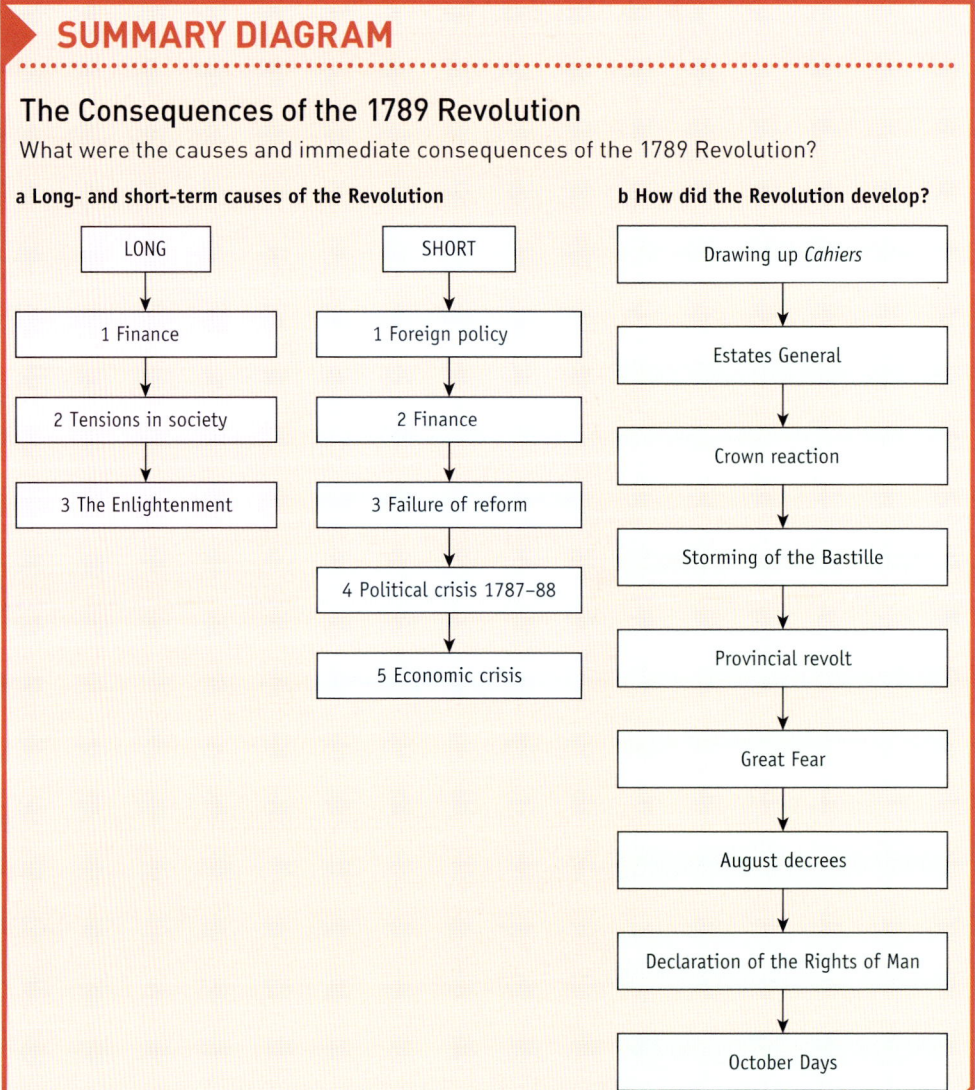

2 How and why did France become a republic by 1792?

After the events of 1789, the position of the king had been weakened. Members of the Third Estate wanted a new type of government created which protected the gains made. They wanted limitations on the king's power, the abolition of privileges for the nobles and clergy, and a fair system of taxation. However, there was no clear plan of how this would be achieved and how the monarchy, nobles, and clergy would accept this. The National Assembly, whose deputies were inexperienced in making laws and policies, had no obvious leaders. There was also the matter of the continuing economic problems and the high price of food.

It took until 1791 for a new constitution to be decided on in which power was shared between the king and the nation, represented by an elected parliament. Politics in France, especially in Paris, became more extreme, with some wanting even more revolutionary change. Abroad, the monarchs of Europe became fearful of revolutionary France, and there was the danger of invasion. At home, opinions were increasingly divided on the revolution's path. The king was discredited by a failed attempt to flee in June 1791, and when war finally broke out with neighbouring monarchs, and France stood in danger of being invaded, the monarchy fell in August 1792. France, like America, became a republic – a state without a monarch.

Revolutionary groups

Eighteenth-century France had no political parties in the modern sense. However, the discussions about the *Cahiers* and the relaxation of censorship and government control led to an expansion of political activity and the expression of a range of radical political ideas. Members of the National Assembly soon realised that, to gain influence in getting laws passed, they needed to form groups of like-minded members. They would meet outside the Assembly to discuss politics and often joined multiple clubs, changing allegiances as events unfolded. In 1790, clubs rapidly formed across France, with neighborhood networks developing in cities such as Bordeaux and Lyon. The main groups that emerged were: the Cordeliers, the Jacobins, the Feuillants, and the Girondins.

The Cordeliers, the Jacobins, and the Feuillants

In 1790, middle-class radicals founded the "Society of the Friends of the Rights of Man and of the Citizen", also known as the Cordeliers Club. Its members encouraged working-class membership. The leading speakers, **Georges-Jacques Danton** and **Camille Desmoulins**, wanted to extend the revolution to ensure that it represented the ordinary people.

> **KEY FIGURES**
>
> **Georges-Jacques Danton** (1759–94) was a radical lawyer who was an early leader in the Cordeliers Club. A powerful orator, he played a role in inciting support for the overthrow of Louis XVI. He was Minister of Justice in 1792 and played an important part in getting support for the war effort. He defended terror but fell out with Robespierre about its continued use. He and his fellow "Indulgents" were guillotined in April 1794.
>
> **Camille Desmoulins** (1760–94) was a radical lawyer who did much to incite the crowds in Paris in July 1789 prior to the storming of the Bastille. He wrote prolifically and published revolutionary newspapers, but he disagreed with Robespierre, his former friend, and paid for that with his life in 1794 when he was guillotined.

KEY TERM

Constitutional monarchy
A type of government where a royal ruler shares power with an elected assembly and is bound by a written constitution, or set of rules. The powers of the monarch have varied depending on the constitution, but this type of monarchy is different than an absolute monarchy, where the ruler has unlimited power.

The Jacobin Club started in 1789 when deputies from Brittany met in a former convent called St. Jacques. The club became powerful in Paris and connected with working people. It had many linked associations across France. Initially, it was more moderate than the Cordeliers, but it split in July 1791 (after the king's flight to Varennes – see page 25). Those who believed in a **constitutional monarchy** left to form a club called the Feuillants. They won the confidence of the king, who appointed their leading figures as ministers in

1791–92. However, they opposed the decision to go to war with Austria in 1792 (see page 26). This left the Jacobin club as a gathering of more radical members such as Maximilien Robespierre.

> What impression of the Jacobin Club is given by Source 1.11?

SOURCE 1.11

A woodcut showing a meeting of the Jacobin Club in 1789

The Girondins

The Girondins were named after the Gironde region, where many of its members came from. They were more moderate republicans who were prepared to accept a constitutional monarchy. The Girondins wanted to reduce the influence of Parisian workers and give greater attention to the ideas from other French regions. They were initially the allies and supporters of a journalist and intellectual, **Jacques-Pierre Brissot**, and included the influential political figures Jean-Marie Roland and his wife Marie-Jeanne (or Manon, as she was known). Their most notable policy was supporting the war with Austria (see page 26), and as this agreed with the aim of the king, they were appointed ministers in 1792. This led to the disastrous war against Austria.

> ### KEY FIGURE
>
> **Jacques-Pierre Brissot** (1754–93) was a journalist and intellectual who studied Enlightenment writers and supported the abolition of slavery. He set up a newspaper in 1789 which attracted radical support. He was a leading influence on the Girondin group in the Legislative Assembly and was heavily responsible for the war policy in 1792. His supporters were ministers but were overthrown in the coup of June 1792. Robespierre was a dangerous enemy, and Brissot was guillotined in June 1793.

Name	Nature	Some leading figures	Key aims
Cordeliers	Radical revolution	Danton, Desmoulins, Marat	Ending the monarchy; more power to the people
Jacobins	Initially moderate but became more radical	Robespierre, St. Just, Couthon	Ending the monarchy; opposing enemies of the revolution; encouraging a dedication to revolution as a rebirth of French life; more democracy
Feuillants	Moderate	Barnave, Lameth, Duport	A constitutional monarchy with limited voting for the people
Girondins	Revolutionaries but willing to accept constitutional monarchy	Jacques-Pierre Brissot, Jean Roland, Mme Roland	Supported war in 1792
Enragés	Extreme anti-monarchists and republicans	Hébert, Roux	Social revolution; ending of aristocracy; power to the people

More radical groups

Even more radical revolutionary ideas emerged in Paris. Those who believed in them were sometimes known as the *Enragés* (the angry ones), and they called for a popular democracy, the destruction of the old, privileged classes and the role of the king, and policies to share wealth among those experiencing poverty.

A revolutionary political culture developed, as Assembly deputies and citizens exchanged information and ideas. When royal censorship was abandoned in 1789, a vast number of printed newspapers were started and sold across the country, containing a mix of rumor, gossip, and debate. The most radical ideas, including advocating violence against nobles, were expressed by the revolutionary Jean-Paul Marat, who organised a newspaper called *The Friend of the People*.

SOURCE 1.12

Jean-Paul Marat writing in *The Friend of the People*, December 1790

Tell me, what confidence would we have in the word, in the protestations, in the oaths of a king who had summoned the nation only to engage it to fill the abyss dug by the wastefulness of his ministers, of the household princes, of his favourites, and of the other scoundrels of his court; of a king who tried to dissolve the National Assembly as soon as he found some opposition to his wishes; of a king who worked six weeks, and quite cold-bloodedly, at the execution of a terrible plan to put the capital to fire and sword, in order to punish its unfortunate inhabitants for the generous support that they seemed to promise the representatives of the nation against the attacks of despotism.

> What does Source 1.12 say about the king? What does this tell the reader about attitudes to the king? Note down specific details from the source to support your answer.

The growing influence of these groups and the fear of counter-revolution radicalized many people. What had begun as a moderate and bloodless revolution which called for a constitutional monarchy which would consult its subjects about key elements such as taxation had turned into a much more extreme movement by 1792.

> ## MAXIMILIEN ROBESPIERRE
>
> Born in Arras in 1758, Robespierre was the son of a lawyer. He trained in law in Paris and specialized in defending poorer people. Robespierre was elected to the Estates General in 1789. He developed radical ideas and was a member of the Jacobin club. Though opposed to war in 1792, he was a passionate believer in the revolution and strongly critical of the monarchy. He welcomed the overthrow of the Girondins and was a leading member of the Committee of Public Safety, supporting extreme measures of terror against perceived opponents. Highly influential with the Paris crowds, he became powerful and aimed to implement controversial changes such as the Cult of the Supreme Being in place of traditional religion. He lost support among the people and the Convention and was arrested, condemned, and executed in July 1794.

Counter-revolutionary groups

In July 1789, after failing to crush the first phases of the revolution, many nobles left France. They are known as the *émigrés*, and included the king's brothers, who established themselves in the lands of the German Archbishop of Trier, which bordered France. The *émigrés* urged other European monarchs to intervene to restore the power of Louis. They promoted resistance to the revolution in France.

Many others in France did not agree with these changes. There was particular resentment among many Catholics at the religious policies which ended the special position of the Catholic Church, took over its lands, and made priests officials of the state (see page 37). Opposition to the new ideas and to the control being exerted by the revolutionary assemblies in Paris gave rise to counter-revolutionary movements, which split France and led to civil war. These counter movements were strong in Brittany, where local forces known as Chouans opposed the revolution in favour of a restoration of the power of the Church and the king. In la Vendée in the west, there was resistance in 1793, and revolutionary armies fought bitter struggles against opposition. This frequently involved mass executions, such as those at Nantes in 1793 and also in Lyon, where special forces were sent from Paris to overthrow the royalist government that had been set up in the city.

> **ACTIVITY**
>
> Create a table or diagram of the different groups in France in 1791–92. Identify similarities and differences in their views and what changes they wanted to be made.

> What impression does Source 1.13 wish to give of this Chouan leader?

SOURCE 1.13

A portrait of a Chouan leader, 1840

Reasons for the counter-revolutionary groups' failure

The revolution was never strong in much of rural France, where many people distrusted the Paris-based leaders and remained attached to the Catholic Church and to the monarchy. Therefore, in some areas, counter-revolutionary forces grew in strength. However, they faced several challenges, which ultimately led to failure. A key reason for this was leadership. The king himself was never in a position to lead, and key members of the royal family were already in exile and therefore at a distance from events.

- Lack of organisation: Counter-revolutionary groups consisted of various factions with different goals and priorities. In western France, much of the opposition was due to religious reasons and was encouraged by the clergy. In southern France, the *émigrés* provoked the resistance. However, the groups were not coordinated and had local rather than national leaders.
- International isolation: Many counter-revolutionaries sought support from foreign monarchies, but this external aid was inconsistent. Additionally, although there were approximately 150,000 *émigrés*, only 5 per cent were actively engaged in the counter-revolution.
- Popular support: Revolutionary ideas had gained significant support among urban workers, making it difficult for counter-revolutionaries to receive widespread backing in the cities.
- Government suppression: Opponents of the revolution met with brutal repression by the revolutionary leaders. This was extremely effective in stopping counter-revolutionary action.

> **ACTIVITY**
> Write a brief explanation of the following terms:
> - counterrevolution
> - *émigrés*
> - Jacobin
> - Girondin.

> **KEY TERM**
> **Active citizens** French men over the age of 25. They contributed enough through taxes to be considered deserving of a role in governing the country and therefore had the right to vote for the deputies of the Assembly. Those who did not contribute in taxes, "passive citizens," did not have the right to elect deputies because a key role of the Assembly was to discuss taxation and how taxes would be spent on policies. Nevertheless, they were still citizens with rights, and not subjects who merely owed loyalty to a king.

Reforms: 1790–95

The Estates General renamed itself the National Assembly on June 17, 1789 and on July 9 became the National Constituent Assembly. While the king continued to appoint ministers, the Assembly passed legislation, which transformed and modernized France, and finally produced a written Constitution in September 1791. The right to vote was given to "**active citizens**:" all men over 25 who paid a certain level of tax (4 million people). Those who were ineligible were called "passive citizens" (3 million people). A newly elected assembly, called the Legislative Assembly (see page 26), lasted from September 1791 to 1792. The changes made after June 1789 were wide-ranging and important. Many historians see this period as the real start of the revolution.

Financial reforms, including *assignats* and taxation reform

A form of paper money was authorised by the Constituent Assembly (*assignats*).

This was a quick solution, creating funds to stimulate the economy through trade. However, this led to inflation (where the general level of prices for goods and services rose), leading to a decrease in purchasing power and depreciation of the currency as a whole. This meant that the value of the *assignats* decreased. This new currency was therefore unstable, which made the financial situation worse.

Instead of the traditional provinces, France was divided into 83 *départements* for elections and local government. These were divided into districts (547), cantons (4872) and communes (about 44,000), which were run by elected councils.

Justice

All previous courts were replaced by a uniform system. There was a Justice of the Peace in each canton, criminals were tried by jury, and torture and mutilation were abolished. Justice was free and equal for all. The old *parlements* were abolished, and the reforms of

August 1789 meant an end to the local courts run by lords of the manor. Work was begun on a new legal code which would apply to the whole of France, though this was not put into practice until 1804. The principle of a national legal system was established. Guilds lost their power to regulate trades.

Church reforms

There was a long tradition in France of royal power over the Church, so it was a logical step for the Assembly to take control of the Church. However, this was to be highly controversial. More than other changes, this led to opposition to the revolution. The Civil Constitution of the Clergy, passed on July 12, 1790, was a major change.

- Catholicism was no longer the official religion.
- Bishops' dioceses were reorganised to coincide with the 83 new *départements*.
- All other clerical posts apart from parish priests were removed.
- Appointment to any clerical post was by election.
- All Church property became the property of the state.
- Abuses such as churchmen holding more than one post were abolished.
- The clergy were to be paid by the state instead of collecting the tithe.
- Monasteries and convents which provided neither education nor charitable work were suppressed.
- Protestants were given full civil rights.

All churchmen had to take the Clerical Oath on November 27, 1790, swearing loyalty to the state and thus accepting this new policy. The Pope opposed the changes, and over half of the clergy refused to take this oath. These were known as non-jurors or refractory clergy. The king, as a loyal Catholic, was strongly opposed to the changes, as were many other people in France.

KEY TERMS

Civil Constitution of the Clergy The name given to the new official position of the Church in the revolution, which placed it under state control.

Diocese An area under the care of one bishop.

Refractory clergy "Refractory" means "resistant," with the idea of being disruptive and disobedient. In this case, the clergy did not accept their role as servants of the state and would not take the oath to the Constitution required of them. They were also called "non-juror" priests – i.e., they would not swear the oath. Later, they organized resistance against the revolution and were objects of hatred and vengeance for the radicals.

What is the message of Source 1.14? What additional knowledge could you use to consider whether this view of the Church was justified?

SOURCE 1.14

Cartoon showing the effects of the Civil Constitution of the Clergy, 1791. The text underneath reads: "Patience, Monsignor, your turn will come."

> **ACTIVITY**
>
> Copy and complete a chart like the one below to summarise the reforms taken by the National Assembly and National Constituent Assembly between 1789 and 1791. Do you think they can be seen as successful? Think about your criteria for success.
>
> | Reform | Evidence of success | Evidence of failure | Judgment on impact of measure |
> |---|---|---|---|
> | | | | |

Political instability

The revolutionary unity of the summer of 1789 did not last, with political instability increasing. This was due to various factors, including the growth of different political groups and opposition over issues such as the clergy taking the oath. There were different views about the pace of change and considerable division about religion. Growing numbers of the nobility and higher clergy opposed change and were determined to try to keep their privileges. Meanwhile, popular unrest across the country grew as a result of a poor harvest in 1790. Concern about popular radicalism grew as the increasingly radical press spread extreme ideas.

> **KEY DEBATE**
>
> **WAS THE CONSTITUTION OF 1791 DOOMED TO FAIL?**
>
> On one hand, there were critics of the monarchy and a build-up of bad feelings between Louis XVI and the people as a result of the attempted flight to Varennes. A constitutional monarchy was unusual in the Europe of the late eighteenth century and needed more political experience and goodwill to work. There was too much political radicalism in Paris and too much division, for example, over the Church reforms.
>
> On the other hand, it has been argued that a lot of peaceful reform had been achieved and that the new Constitution did make compromises, such as giving the king a veto. The suppression of the *Champs de Mars* demonstration did show that popular protest could be controlled. There was a feeling that the king's attempted flight should be forgotten, and there was a desire for stability. If the decision had not been taken to go to war, then the new Constitution might have had time to become established. Rather than inevitable weakness, it was the decision to wage war that led to the end of the monarchy.

Disagreement on the terms of the new Constitution

The National Constituent Assembly hoped the new Constitution would resolve many key grievances of the people. However, there was a lack of consensus on its terms, particularly who should be able to vote in elections. Key features of France's first written constitution had been discussed in the Constituent Assembly since July 1789 but were not put into place until September 1791:
- The king's title was not king of France but "king of the French".
- The king was given an annual grant of 25 million livres for his expenses.
- He was forbidden to raise troops against the Constitution or to leave the country.
- There was to be a constitutional monarchy with power shared.
- The king would choose the cabinet and ministers.
- The king had the right to veto (or refuse to accept) any measure for five years.
- The king must take an oath to the Constitution or be seen to have abdicated.
- A single elected Legislative Assembly would have rights to propose and pass laws, to raise taxes, and to determine the size and composition of armed forces. It was to organize national festivals to celebrate the new state.
- The Assembly would be chosen by active citizens (see page 21).

- Every two years, the active citizens would meet in local assemblies to select electors. The electors would have higher property qualifications. The total electorate would be 4 million and exclude passive citizens – including those not meeting the tax qualification, domestic servants, women, and actors.
- The electors would choose 745 representatives to the Legislative Assembly.
- No existing member of the National Constituent Assembly could be a member of the new Assembly.
- No ministers, officials, or judges could be a representative in the new Assembly.

The Preamble (Preface) to the Constitution stated clear principles that there were no hereditary titles, that there were no tax privileges, and that citizens had natural rights that the new government must respect. These included equal rights to hold office, and freedom of movement, assembly, speech, and writing. There were statements of intention for a new system of poor relief, public education, and a new code of law.

What was created reflected ideas of the separation of powers, and also natural rights and the sovereignty of the nation, rather than a divinely appointed monarchy.

All this seemed to go a long way to meeting the demands for change seen in the discussions of 1789, and with 4 million voters, France had much more political representation than most other countries in Europe. However, not all agreed. For the king and for the royalists who were in exile and plotting counter-revolution, this was dangerous. The power of hereditary monarchy had been severely weakened. For more radical revolutionaries, the fact that the king had a veto and still appointed ministers meant that there had been insufficient change and the nation was not powerful enough. For even more radical groups, the restriction on voting to active citizens was unfair. If all men were created equal, then all should vote. Also, the complex system of indirect voting was not democratic enough. For some – though an extremely small number – the exclusion of women went against natural human rights, and there were pioneer activists who campaigned for the political rights of women (see Source 1.15 below). This was frowned on by the male-dominated revolutionary groups. Nevertheless, a few thinkers such as the Marquis de Condorcet supported the feminist ideas of Olympe de Gouges and Théroigne de Méricourt. However, these won little general sympathy and were seen as part of the political extremism brought about by revolution.

What is the view of the writer of Source 1.15 about women's rights?

SOURCE 1.15

Olympe de Gouges, Declaration of the Rights of Women, September 1791

Mothers, daughters, sisters, female representatives of the nation ask to be constituted as a national assembly. Considering that ignorance, neglect, or contempt for the rights of woman are the sole causes of public misfortunes and governmental corruption, they have resolved to set forth in a solemn declaration the natural, inalienable, and sacred rights of woman: the sex that is superior in beauty as in courage, needed in maternal sufferings, recognizes and declares, in the presence and under the auspices of the Supreme Being, the following rights of woman and the citizens.

Woman is born free and remains equal to man in rights …

ACTIVITY

Compare the "constitutions" of France before 1789 and in 1791. Make two lists: one showing the changes and the other showing things that stayed the same.

The main issue was whether the Constitution was the end of change or whether further change was inevitable. Much depended on whether the king and the new Legislative Assembly could work together.

KEY FIGURE

Théroigne de Méricourt (1762–1817) was born in Liège. A trained opera singer, she became a courtesan in Paris. Enthused by the revolution, she spoke in the Cordeliers about women's rights. She became famous for having been arrested and imprisoned by the Austrians in 1792. She was known for advocating women's rights and played a notable role in the storming of the Tuileries Palace in August 1792. However, she faced party rivalry and was physically attacked by Jacobin women. This attack may have caused brain damage, and she spent the rest of her life in an asylum.

The Assemblies in France 1789–99

	Assembly	Government
May 1789 to June 17, 1789	Estates General	Advisory body called by Louis XVI
June 17 to July 9, 1789	National Assembly	Claimed to govern on behalf of the nation
July 9, 1789 to September 1791	National Constituent Assembly	Passed reforms and drew up the new Constitution
September 30, 1791 to September 1792	Legislative Assembly	Shared power with the king
September 1792–95	National Convention	Ruled revolutionary France
1795–99 Constitution of Year III	Council of 500 Council of Elders	Directory-governed, with two legislative chambers

The behaviour of the king and the flight to Varennes

Initially, Louis and many of those around him accepted the revolution and appeared willing to work towards a constitutional monarchy. However, the Civil Constitution of the Clergy troubled him. This was because of his strong religious beliefs and the ties between the Church and the Crown. The Assembly broke these ties by imposing new controls over the Church and confiscating its lands – actions that the Pope condemned. The loss of freedom by his enforced residence in Paris was also worrying him. When the royal family tried to leave Paris in April to spend Easter at Saint Cloud, crowds blocked them in. The National Guard ignored orders to clear their way. Louis saw that he was essentially a prisoner. Because of this, it was hard to see that the king could maintain his rights in any future formal constitution.

In June 1791, the royal family made plans to escape from France to join loyal troops in the Austrian Netherlands. From the fortress of Montmédy in Eastern France, Louis planned to negotiate with the Assembly, away from the restraints of Paris and its crowds. On June 20, 1791, the royal family left Paris in disguise and travelled east. They were recognized at Varennes and captured by supporters of the revolution. They returned to Paris under guard. The Parisian crowds watched in silence. Louis had left behind a proclamation denouncing the revolution. The results of this were as follows:
- His actions showed that Louis had not understood how popular the changes since 1789 were.
- The news of the escape provoked a wave of unrest in the countryside.
- The constitutional monarchy was in doubt as many lost trust in Louis's willingness to cooperate.
- 6000 noble army officers left the country to join the *émigré* nobles in Germany who were massing forces to rescue the king.
- Foreign powers were now concerned for the king's safety.
- Republicanism started to grow. The more radical political groups called for an end to the monarchy.

In the short term, the threats of being deposed and civil war led the king to accept the Constitution – which included a provision that if the king left the country, he would be seen to have abdicated. The suppression of unrest by the Assembly soon after showed that popular protest could be controlled and that more extreme radical views might not succeed.

The king and the Assembly agreed to work together. However, the incident was important in destroying the vital element of trust.

The demonstration at the *Champs de Mars*, July 17, 1791

A radical political group, the Cordeliers, organized a signing ceremony for a petition on a referendum on the fate of the monarchy at the *Champs de Mars*. Approximately 50,000 people attended. The Assembly called out the National Guard, led by la Fayette, to maintain order. The result was that the guards fired on the crowd. Up to 50 people were killed and the rest dispersed. This was seen by many as counter-revolutionary. In the aftermath, the

ACTIVITY

Look at three main causes of instability:
- the Civil Constitution of the Clergy
- the flight to Varennes
- the demonstration at the *Champs de Mars*.

Explain why each was significant, and then decide which was the most significant in causing instability.

ceremony's leaders, Brissot and Danton, fled, and the Cordeliers Club was shut down. These events showed that more extreme revolutionary leaders could organize popular action on a large scale. It also showed again that the Assembly, provided that the authorities were firm and had the support of enough armed force, could control popular action.

From constitutional monarchy to republic

As the king had accepted the new Constitution, the next step would be for a new Assembly to begin working with the king in France's new constitutional monarchy.

The Legislative Assembly

Elections took place, and on October 1, 1791, the 745 new deputies of the Legislative Assembly met for the first time. They were mostly wealthy, as expected from an election system that favoured the richer citizens. Few were nobles, many of whom had emigrated or retired to their country estates. A few deputies were clergy. Many distrusted the king after Varennes. A major problem was that no former member of the National Constituent Assembly could be elected, and the new deputies lacked experience. The queen thought they were "scoundrels and fools," but many were eminent and well-educated men. However, they faced the problems of growing radicalism, divisions in France, and threats from abroad. At first, the king appointed a moderate set of ministers – the Feuillants. However, there was growing opposition from a more radical party.

The declaration of war on Austria, April 1792

Meanwhile, when Louis's brothers and other nobles left France, they established themselves in Coblenz, over the border in modern-day Germany. At this time, Germany was over 1000 independent mini-countries under the nominal control of the Holy Roman Empire. The *émigrés* were sheltered by sympathetic German archbishops but did not get the support they needed for an invasion of France by the largest German powers, Austria and Prussia.

The European powers were not entirely unhappy to see France weakened by revolution. However, as the revolution became more radical, especially after Louis tried unsuccessfully to flee and it was clear he was a virtual prisoner in his own country, in July 1791, there was more concern. In August 1791, the king of Prussia, Frederick William, and the Emperor of Austria issued the Declaration of Pillnitz (see Source 1.16 below), threatening intervention in support of Louis. The Austrian Emperor Leopold was the brother of France's queen, Marie Antoinette, and was becoming concerned for her safety.

What can we learn from Source 1.16 about foreign opposition to the French revolution?

SOURCE 1.16

From the Declaration of Pillnitz, August 1791

His Majesty the Emperor and His Majesty the king of Prussia ... declare together that they regard the actual situation of His Majesty the king of France as a matter of communal interest for all sovereigns of Europe. They hope that that interest will be recognized by the powers whose assistance is called in ... to strengthen, in utmost liberty, the foundations of a monarchical government of the French. In that case, aforementioned Majesties are determined to act promptly and unanimously, with the forces necessary for realizing the proposed and communal goal. In expectation, they will give the suitable orders to their troops so that they will be ready to commence activity.

This led some in France to demand war against Austria. One of the leading supporters of this was the journalist Jacques-Pierre Brissot. He had many supporters, including a group of deputies from the Gironde region in the southwest (see page 18). They argued that a war would end the threat from the *émigrés* and deter foreign invasion. If French armies controlled the bordering territories from the Austrian Netherlands to the German Rhineland, it would make France easier to defend and protect from foreign invasion. The war would unite the nation behind the revolution and force the king to be a revolutionary leader.

The most extraordinary development was that the king supported the war. Both Louis and Marie Antoinette expected the coalition to beat France and restore their power. He dismissed his initial ministers – the moderate Feuillants – and replaced them with Girondins pro-war ministers in March 1792. Thus, war was declared on Austria on April 20, 1792 and subsequently on Prussia in June. It was to prove disastrous for both the king and the Girondins.

The course of the war in 1792

The start of the Revolutionary Wars went badly for France. Almost half the officers of the French army had become *émigrés*, and its soldiers were demoralised. They faced not only the well-trained Austrian forces in the Netherlands but also the powerful Prussian army. The French General Dillon was murdered by his own men soon after the fighting started. The French were soon retreating, with their generals urging peace talks. There was both fear and hardship among the key element of the Paris people – the so-called *sans-culottes*. These were politically aware, self-employed tradesmen and artisans who had become ardent and radical revolutionaries and supporters of those who wanted to abolish the monarchy. Economic problems were again causing discontent by 1792, with rising prices, shortages of food, and rising unemployment.

When the revolutionary armies were forced to retreat and Paris seemed threatened, there was mistrust of the king and growing suspicion that his Austrian queen was passing military secrets to the Austrians. There were calls for more revolutionary measures to defeat the enemy.

The king wavered. He would not support the Assembly's security measures. Two laws were passed which he vetoed. One law made not swearing the Clerical Oath a crime, labelling it as conspiracy against the state. Another law demanded the confiscation of property from any *émigrés*, including Louis's brothers, who refused to return to France. Louis XVI also dismissed leading Girondins from his government. He appeared to be obstructing the work of the Legislative Assembly. This increased his unpopularity. When he vetoed a proposal to call provincial troops in to defend the capital, this proved too much.

> **KEY TERMS**
>
> **Revolutionary Wars** The collective term for the War of the First Coalition (1792–97) and the War of the Second Coalition (1798–1802), where France fought against several European powers who opposed the revolution. The First Coalition included Austria, Great Britain, Prussia, the Dutch Republic, and Spain. The Second Coalition included Austria, Great Britain, Naples, the Ottoman Empire, Portugal, and Russia. France was successful, but this success came at a terrible cost, in money and lives. It also led to the rise of Napoleon Bonaparte.
>
> **Sans-culottes** This term literally means "those without breeches." Richer men wore breeches and stockings on their legs, but the poorer men wore trousers – so they were literally "without breeches." The *sans-culottes* were politically active and often not the very poorest of the people of Paris but small shopkeepers and artisans who resented the rich and were influenced by the radical ideas of clubs such as the Jacobins. They took a key role in many of the political disturbances of the revolution in Paris.

SOURCE 1.17

A French print of a *sans-culotte*

> Sources 1.17 and 1.18 show a French and an English view of the *sans-culottes*. Identify some differences between them using details from the sources. Why do these sources differ?

SOURCE 1.18

An English cartoon published on September 20, 1792 called *A family of* sans-culottes *refreshing after the fatigues of the day*

The overthrow of the monarchy, August 10, 1792

On June 20 in Paris, thousands of *sans-culottes* occupied the royal palace, the Tuileries. While not making any attempt to harm him, they forced Louis to wear a **red cap of liberty**. The end of the monarchy was in sight.

In July, following the decree of a state of emergency, provincial National Guards (*fédérés*) began to arrive in Paris, joining increased calls for the end of the monarchy. Meanwhile, in July, Prussia's army commander, the Duke of Brunswick, threatened in the Brunswick Manifesto to take reprisals if the royal family was harmed. This identified Louis with the enemy. It led to a dramatic increase in calls for a republic.

A more experienced Assembly might have taken action to calm Paris and to defend the Constitution. However, there were increasing fears of counter-revolution and a feeling that the revolution needed to be defended. On August 9, representatives from the Paris districts forced a major change. In a planned takeover led by key members of revolutionary clubs, including Danton, the Paris Commune was replaced by the Insurrectionary Commune, which called for the end of the monarchy. They were supported by the provincial troops who had come to Paris in July. The troops from Marseille had brought the war song which later became the national anthem (Source 1.19). It was a call for French people to defend the revolution.

> **KEY TERM**
>
> **Red cap of liberty** This was a soft conical hat based on the headgear of ancient eastern European people called the Phrygians. It came to symbolise revolutionary liberty and was often worn by the *sans-culottes*.

> Summarise in your own words the message of Source 1.19.

SOURCE 1.19

Lyrics of "*La Marseillaise*" a popular war song, originally sung by troops from Marseille during the French Revolution, which later became the French national anthem

> Let us go, children of the fatherland,
> Our day of glory has arrived.
> Against us the bloody flag of tyranny
> Is raised; the bloody
> Flag is raised.
> Do you hear in the countryside
> The roar of those savage soldiers?
> They come right into our arms
> To cut the throats of our sons, our comrades.
> To arms, citizens!
> Form your battalions,
> Let us march, let us march!
> That their impure blood
> Should water our fields.
> Sacred love of the fatherland,
> Guide and support our vengeful arms.
> Liberty, beloved liberty,
> Fight with your defenders; fight
> With your defenders.
> Under our flags, so that victory
> Will rush to your manly strains;
> That your dying enemies
> Should see your triumph and glory!
> To arms, citizens! etc.

Early on August 10, as thousands approached the Tuileries Palace, the king surrendered, and the royal family took refuge with the Legislative Assembly. The palace was attacked, and its defenders, the Swiss Guards, were killed in a massacre. The deputies were then forced to hand over Louis, who was imprisoned, and the monarchy was suspended. On August 11, the Legislative Assembly voted to suspend the king, replacing him with a

ACTIVITY

Find evidence for the view that the king was to blame for the ending of the monarchy. Find evidence that other factors were responsible. Which do you find more convincing, and why?

five-man executive council, and convened democratic elections for a new National Convention elected by universal male suffrage.

The September Massacres

The fortress of Verdun fell to Prussian forces on September 2. This increased fears of foreign invasion. Violent riots erupted in Paris, and anyone suspected of having royalist sympathies was attacked. The prisons were searched for suspected counter-revolutionaries, clergymen or nobles. In a killing spree that spanned over four days, more than 1300 prisoners were massacred. Many of the victims had no political views and included children accused of theft, killed just because they were in prison. These killings became known as the September Massacres.

By the end of 1792, the revolution had come a long way from the high hopes of 1789. The future for the king and his family was bleak.

> ### KEY DEBATE
> ### WAS LOUIS RESPONSIBLE FOR HIS OWN DOWNFALL?
>
> In 1789 there was little support for ending the monarchy and a great many declarations of loyalty in the *Cahiers*. By 1792, that support had broken down, and the monarchy was abolished. Explanations often stress that Louis was to blame for his own downfall and execution in January 1793. He had thrown away the chance to lead reforms and change in 1789 by mishandling the States General. He had failed to maintain control of events and failed to manage the constitutional monarchy. His incompetent attempted flight to Varennes resulted in a loss of confidence in him. By supporting war in 1792, possibly hoping that it would lead to a restoration of his power, he made a major error. Defeats in the war led to panic and suspicion, and a rise in the power of more extreme leaders.
>
> The alternative view is that he inherited financial and social problems which were beyond his control. His attempts to solve those problems raised expectations of change, which were difficult to meet. The growth in ideas for change and in grievances by an increasingly well-educated bourgeoisie, together with economic hardship brought about by bad harvests, created a revolutionary situation. Constitutional monarchy was not a common form of government at the time, and managing it was a difficult job. The strains of war and military setbacks created an atmosphere in which there was a genuine fear of foreign invasion. The militant proclamations of France's enemies helped to bring about the fall of the monarchy. This view suggests that Louis was more a victim of unusual circumstances than the cause of his own troubles.

The National Convention and abolition of the monarchy

The Legislative Assembly tried to carry on by appointing a more radical government, which aimed to abolish feudal payments and claim credit for ending the monarchy. But there was popular pressure for change. The electorate was widened to most men over the age of 21 and rose to 5 million. Domestic servants, women, and those living on charity were excluded. The primary assemblies chose electors on August 25, and the main elections were held in early September. The new assembly, now called the National Convention, was responsible for both government and lawmaking. However, it saw its main purpose as giving the country a new republican constitution.

On September 21, 1792, one of the first acts of the Convention was to formally abolish the monarchy from September 22. Louis was kept a prisoner in the Temple prison by the Commune of Paris. The new Convention voted to put him on trial. More radical members wanted to kill him without a trial. The trial began on December 26 and ended with a guilty vote. More moderate members wanted imprisonment and banishment, but the vote for execution was passed by 361 to 319 votes. Louis was guillotined on January 21, 1793.

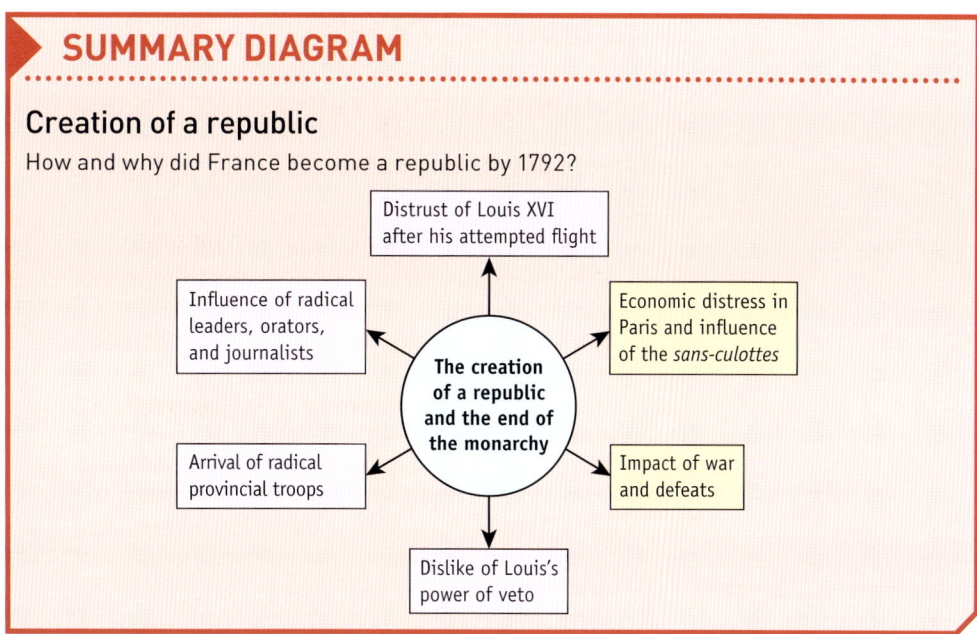

3 How well was France governed in the period 1793–99?

The king was tried and executed in January 1793, and France embarked on a more radical revolution. Its rulers faced considerable challenges. The nation was bitterly divided, and there was the threat of foreign invasion, which would crush the revolution. To defend the new state, its leaders took up severe measures. For the first time, war would be fought not just by soldiers and sailors but by the whole nation. Any opposition to this "nation in arms" would be crushed. Anyone suspected of being against the revolution or undermining the war effort would face death. The period between September 5, 1793 and July 27, 1794 was known as "the Terror." This was a term used by the leaders, who saw it as not only necessary but a way of purifying France. Executions by guillotine were carried out in Paris, and there were more deaths in the French provinces as a bitter civil war took place.

Against this background, the revolution adopted more radical ideas. Those who worried about the extent of the Terror were targeted by determined revolutionaries such as the Jacobin Robespierre. However, as the foreign threat decreased, concerns about the revolution's direction and Robespierre's power grew. He and his supporters had relied on the support of the *sans-culottes*, but this had been lost by July 1794, and his enemies overthrew him. The extreme Terror came to an end, and a new phase named after the month of Robespierre's fall, **Thermidor**, came about. A new constitution was introduced, giving power to a committee of Directors with two assemblies. This more conservative Directorate continued the war, but the influence of the Jacobins and the Paris crowds was ended. The civil war was brought to an end, but instability continued. There were a number of attempts to overthrow the Directors, and they became more and more reliant on military force. The most famous of the military leaders was the Corsican-born Napoleon Bonaparte. His victories in Italy 1796–97 and then in Egypt made him a national hero. When some of the Directors decided to use military force to strengthen their power, Napoleon Bonaparte obliged, and in 1799 there was a coup. The Directors were replaced by three consuls, but the new regime was dominated by Napoleon. The revolution became not the ideal constitutional state dreamed of by the men of 1789, nor the pure virtuous Republic of 1793, but instead a virtual military dictatorship.

KEY TERM

Thermidor The eleventh month of the French revolutionary calendar. Also, the name for the reaction against the Reign of Terror which began with the execution of Robespierre and his supporters.

Instability 1793–95

Problems facing France after the execution of Louis XVI

Effects of war on France by 1793

Many of the problems facing France were related to the war and its effects:
- There was a dangerous coalition of foreign enemies, and there was more determination after the shock of the king's death to crush the revolution. Already at war with Austria and Prussia, the new Republic also faced Britain from April 1793.
- This was not a war for territory but a war for sheer survival as France's enemies aimed at 'regime change'.
- There was a danger of revenge if foreign armies restored the monarchy and the *émigrés* returned.
- There was the need to mobilise the whole nation in order to meet the danger of invasion.
- France had lost many of its officers and needed to establish new revolutionary forces committed to fighting to preserve the new regime.
- Conscription of soldiers on a large scale was needed, but this often brought about opposition.
- There were powerful forces in the provinces opposed to the revolution, which led to civil war as well as a war being fought against other nations.

Influence of the sans-culottes

In 1792, the *sans-culottes* in Paris had tried to force change through violence, including invading the Tuileries Palace in August 1792 and taking part in the September massacres. They were a driving force behind the radical phase of the revolution and supported more extreme measures. After the execution of King Louis XVI, the *sans-culottes* continued to play a significant role in pushing for extreme measures, including the Reign of Terror, to protect the revolution.

In 1792, the sans-culottes in Paris had tried to force change through violence including invading the Tuileries Palace in August 1792, and taking part in the September massacres. They were a driving force behind the radical phase of the Revolution and supported more extreme measures. After the execution of King Louis XVI, the sans-culottes continued to play a significant role in pushing for extreme measures including the Reign of Terror, to protect the revolution.

Ongoing economic and religious divisions

Throughout 1793, economic hardship had created discontent, particularly in Paris, so the tensions which faced the old regime had not gone away. The disruption brought about by the revolution had caused unemployment in manufacturing, and prices of basic goods continued to rise. In addition, the religious changes continued to cause considerable opposition among Catholics, particularly in areas such as Brittany, where there was loyalty to the local aristocracy. Even within the ruling Convention, there were divisions and disagreements about the degree of force to be used to repress possible opposition to the revolution.

There was a danger that France, as a nation, would fall apart.

Disagreement within the Convention

Many of the previous deputies were re-elected to the Convention. Half of the deputies were lawyers. Most of the 749 members were not aligned to a particular group and were known as "the Plain." The meeting place contained ranked seating, sloping up from the bottom. The radical deputies – such as the Jacobins and the Cordeliers – sat high up on the left and so were called the Montagnards (mountain dwellers). The moderate deputies sat in the centre. The Girondins sat on the right-hand side of the raised seating.

The Girondins, despite their smaller number, were the dominant group in the Convention to start with. They had led France into war in 1792. They had support from the regions outside

> **ACTIVITY**
>
> Compile a list of key similarities and differences between the ideas of the Girondins and the Montagnards in 1793–94.

> **KEY FIGURE**
>
> **Jean-Paul Marat** was a physician, journalist, and revolutionary agitator. Born in Switzerland in 1743, he is best known for his role as editor of the radical newspaper *L'Ami du peuple* (The Friend of the People). Linked to a number of revolutionary groups, he denounced members of the more moderate faction, the Girondins. In revenge, he was assassinated in 1793. Celebrated as a martyr of the French Revolution, *The Death of Marat* (1793) an oil painting by Jacques-Louis David (see p. 35), is one of the most famous images of revolutionary France.

Paris and distrusted the popular revolutionary enthusiasm of the Parisian *sans-culottes*. They were moderate republicans but committed revolutionaries. They made up about 200 of the 749 members of the Convention and were able to win more support from the "the Plain" than the more numerous Montagnards.

The Montagnards were much more closely linked to the people and to the local government of Paris and spoke for the more radical *sans-culottes*. They wanted more democracy and equality, a greater war effort, and more persecution of enemies. They had clashed with the Girondins about the execution of the king and opposed the idea of putting the issue of his execution to a national vote. Bad feelings increased as journalists such as **Jean-Paul Marat** and Hébert attacked the Girondins as being traitors. When the Girondins set up a committee to prevent these attacks and arrested Marat, the Montagnards, with the help of the influential *sans-culottes,* got the support of the Paris Commune and the National Guard and in June 1793 forced the Girondins out.

The new constitution of 1793

In December 1792, a team of deputies from all groups in the Convention was asked to prepare a new republican constitution, to replace the constitutional monarchy of 1791. Its efforts were rejected in April 1793 by the Montagnards, led by Robespierre. After the fall of the Girondins on June 2 1793, a new committee of Montagnards revised the constitution in just eight days. It was accepted and then overwhelmingly approved in a public referendum. The Montagnard Constitution was very radical for its time.

- All men of 21 and over with one year residence who lived from their own labor or owned property, or who were married to a French woman, were classed as citizens.
- Primary assemblies of between 200 and 600 citizens were to vote for up to three electors, who chose deputies for the Legislative Assembly.
- There was one deputy for every 40,000 individuals.
- The Assembly was to meet for one year.
- The Assembly issued decrees (proposed laws), which were to be sent to the *départements* for approval.
- An executive council of 24 members be chosen from names put forward by the *départements* by the Assembly.
- The council would choose administrators and ambassadors.
- The council would be separate but could be called into the Assembly.
- Local administrators and justices were to be chosen by the assemblies of each commune.

> What do the extracts in Source 1.20 say about the hopes and ideals of those who made the 1793 Constitution of France?

SOURCE 1.20

Extracts from the 1793 Constitution

- The French nation is the friend and natural ally of free nations.
- It serves as a place of refuge for all who, on account of liberty, are banished from their native country.
- These it refuses to deliver up to tyrants.
- The constitution guarantees to all Frenchmen equality, liberty, security, property, the public debt, free exercise of religion, general instruction, public assistance, absolute liberty of the press, the right of petition, the right to hold popular assemblies, and the enjoyment of all the rights of man.
- The French republic respects loyalty, courage, age, filial love, misfortune. It places the constitution under the guaranty of all virtues.
- The Declaration of the Rights of Man and the constitution shall be engraven on tables, to be placed in the midst of the legislative body, and in public places.

However, the Constitution of 1793 was never put into practice. Given the dangers of war, the Convention put all its resources and attention toward the war effort. In October 1793, the Convention suspended constitutional rule in favour of revolutionary government, until the war ended.

The Committee of Public Safety

A 12-man Committee of Public Safety (CPS) had been created on April 6, 1793 to coordinate the war effort. It was initially dominated by Danton. However, it came to be led by more extreme revolutionaries, Robespierre, **Georges Couthon**, and **Louis de St Just**. **Lazare Carnot**, responsible for war strategy and personnel, was behind the decree of August 23 which ordered the *levée en masse* (**conscription**). The CPS also dispatched special **representatives on mission** to the armies to improve morale and supervise the generals. In 1793–94, 84 generals were guillotined or shot and 352 were dismissed on suspicion of treachery or defeatism.

> What impression of the CPS is given by Source 1.21?

SOURCE 1.21

An engraving from c.1793, showing a man holding his certificate of good citizenship before the Committee of Public Safety

COMITÉ DE L'AN DEUXIEME

In addition, the Committee of General Security was set up, consisting of 12 deputies. Their function was to oversee state security, including police, and prosecute foreign agents and counterfeiters of *assignats*. Both committees extended the power of central government to new levels. As the threat of invasion and defeat grew, the Convention and its Committees resorted to increased terror. Robespierre had become highly influential because of his popularity with the **Paris sections** and in the Commune, his dominance of the Jacobin club, and also his ability to sway the Convention. He became the best-known member of the Committee of Public Safety in July 1793 and played a crucial role in the revolutionary government until his overthrow in July 1794.

KEY TERMS

Conscription Enforced military service required by the state.

Representatives on mission These were deputies sent to ensure that armies and their leaders were loyal to the ideas of the revolution.

Paris sections The city of Paris was divided into electoral districts known as sections. These were run by their own officials and committees.

Total war War that involves using all the resources of a country and includes not just armies but the entire population.

KEY FIGURES

Lazare Carnot (1753–1823) was a mathematician and military leader who organised the French revolutionary army after 1793. He did much to introduce the idea of **total war**.

Georges Couthon (1735–94) was a lawyer from the Auvergne who became a leading Jacobin. He led the destruction of much of Lyon in 1793 and helped draft the repressive Law of 22 Prairial Year II (also known as the law of the Great Terror). He was guillotined with Robespierre in 1794.

Louis de St. Just (1767–94), son of an army officer from central France, and a failed law student, he became a leading and radical Jacobin and friend of Robespierre. He oversaw the revolutionary army and advocated for social reforms. He was guillotined with Robespierre.

What can we learn from Source 1.22 about the impact of war on the people of France? Consider any limitations you think this evidence has.

SOURCE 1.22

Decree of the Convention, August 1793, instituting national conscription

From this moment until that in which the enemy shall have been driven from the soil of the Republic, all Frenchmen are in permanent requisition for the service of the armies. The young men shall go to battle; the married men shall forge arms and transport provisions; the women shall make tents and clothing and shall serve in the hospitals; the children shall turn old linen into lint; the aged shall betake themselves to the public places in order to arouse the courage of the warriors and preach the hatred of kings and the unity of the Republic.

It is, accordingly, authorised to form all the establishments, factories, workshops, and mills which shall be deemed necessary for the carrying on of these works, as well as to put in requisition, within the entire extent of the Republic, the artists and working men who can contribute to their success.

Robespierre and the Reign of Terror

Robespierre had become a major revolutionary figure by 1793. This was because of his own qualities but was also due to the rapidly changing circumstances. He was a great orator, and people admired his simple, austere way of life. He appealed to the radical *sans-culottes* of Paris and was seen as a pure revolutionary dedicated to "the People" and defending the new order. His ruthlessness led him to abandon his opposition to the death penalty and to accept violence as necessary for the revolution.

The coming of the Terror

The National Convention deputies faced threats of external war and internal revolt as well as increasing demands from the *sans-culottes*. They established the Revolutionary Tribunal in March 1793 to try suspects of counter-revolutionary activities. This seemed to give a sort of official blessing to the type of violence exercised by the Paris mobs. In addition to this, a law was passed requiring each commune or section of a town or city to set up a **watch committee**.

They then faced a fourth, personal attack. On July 13, 1793, the radical journalist Marat was stabbed in his bath. Marat was a highly influential radical. His murder made it seem that counter-revolution was a danger. It had a profound effect in increasing support for extreme measures.

KEY TERM

Watch committees
Surveillance committees whose role was to watch for people suspected of plotting or carrying out anti-revolutionary activities. They played a major role in the Terror.

SOURCE 1.23

An engraving from 1793 showing the death of Marat

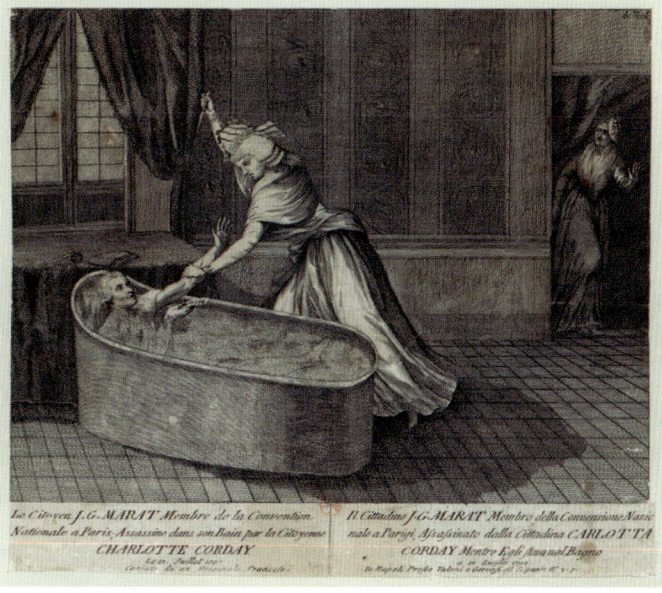

Identify some differences between Source 1.23 and Source 1.24. Note down specific details from each source to support your answers. Then, using your contextual knowledge, explain why you think the sources are different.

SOURCE 1.24

The painting showing the death of Marat by the famous artist Jacques-Louis David

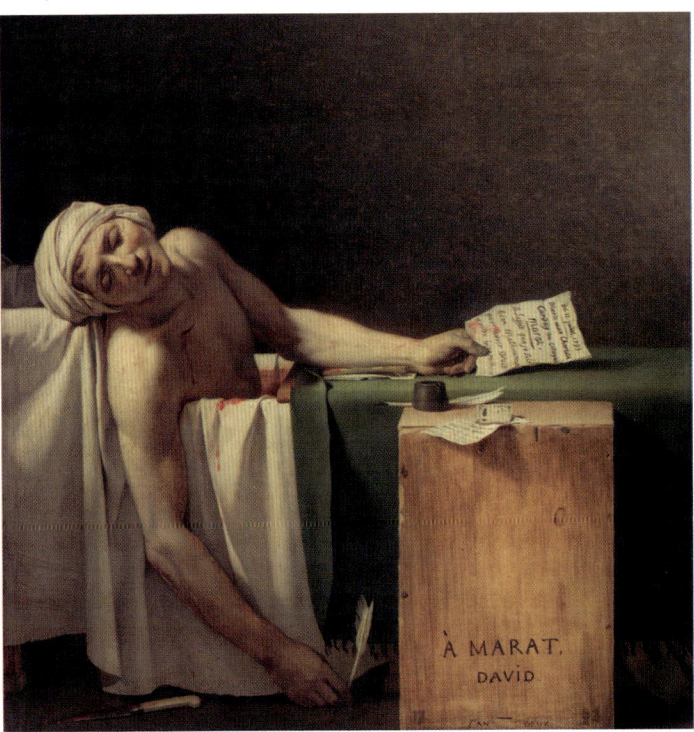

The need to enforce unity and defend the revolution were key reasons for the **Reign of Terror**. Each new step of increasing violence was seen as necessary for security. Another factor was ensuring the purity of the Republic and the revolution by purging corrupt and backward-looking elements. Robespierre expressed his view of the Terror in 1794:

> Terror is nothing more than speedy, severe, and inflexible justice; it is thus an emanation of virtue; it is less a principle in itself than a consequence of the general principle of democracy.

KEY TERM

Reign of Terror The period in 1793 and 1794 when people were arrested and executed throughout France for being enemies of the revolution. In Paris, there were 2585 condemnations to death between April 1793 and July 1794, though 2306 people were acquitted. The national total for the same period was 16,639. The pace accelerated so much in 1794 that the period between April and August 1794 is known as the Great Terror. The wide interpretation of counter-revolution meant that not just obvious enemies died but also non-juror priests and those accused of hoarding food or economic offences.

Political terror

On September 17, 1793, the National Convention, under pressure from the Paris crowds and demands from the sections, passed the Law of Suspects. This widened the definition of who was against the revolution to include royalists, federalists, relations of *émigrés*, and anyone without a certificate of loyalty from their local watch committee. The watch committees arrested suspects and sent details of the charges to the Committee of General Security. Prison numbers rose, and the Paris Revolutionary Tribunal was divided into four sections, two sitting at any one time, to speed up the trial process. In 1794, the speed of the process was increased again when no defence was allowed. The political enemies of Robespierre and the Montagnards were among those tried and executed.

KEY TERM

Hébertists A group who supported the journalist Jacques Hébert and his newspaper *Père Duchesne*. They wanted an increase in the Terror.

- The first political group to face trial and execution were the Girondins in October 1793.
- The queen, Marie Antoinette, was executed on October 16, 1793.
- "Enemies" such as the **Hébertists** who criticised Robespierre and the revolutionary government for not being radical enough were tried and executed in March 1794.
- Former comrades and colleagues who had expressed doubts about the Terror were purged and executed in April 1794. They were categorised as "Indulgents" and included Danton and Desmoulins.
- In May 1794 the general pace of execution of all sorts of people accused of counter-revolution increased, especially after the law of 22 Prairial Year II (June 10, 1794) reduced defendants' rights. In June and July 1794, there were 1584 deaths in Paris alone.
- The final political acts of terror in Paris were the execution of Robespierre and his supporters in July 1794 (see page 38).

Provincial executions

Several provinces had been in revolt, including la Vendée and Brittany. They had opposed the king's execution and resented the dominance of Paris and what they saw as the "mob." The worst atrocities of the Terror occurred in the suppression of these provincial revolts. The greatest number of victims of this wider terror were not aristocrats or politicians but ordinary people. Major factors were the ruthlessness of key representatives on mission and the revenge for atrocities committed against republicans by the insurgents.

In la Vendée, over 8700 people were executed. Many were guillotined or shot by firing squads; others were deliberately drowned in the River Loire. Such brutality ensured that guerrilla attacks and reprisals continued into 1794. By the end of the revolt, as many as 200,000 people had died.

In the south, an example was made of Lyon. The Jacobin Couthon executed 113 rebels in six weeks. Even this was seen as not decisive enough by the CPS. Couthon was replaced in November by **Collot d'Herbois** and **Joseph Fouché**. Their revolutionary commission sentenced 1673 people to death. To speed up the process, and to shock the local population, in December 1793, prisoners were placed in front of cannons and killed.

KEY FIGURES

Collot d'Herbois (1749–96) was an actor and playwright who was a Jacobin and became an increasingly militant member of the Paris Commune and the National Convention, opposing the Girondins. He was responsible for the bloody actions against counter-revolution in Lyon. He later turned against Robespierre but was sent to the penal colony in French Guiana by his enemies in 1795 and died there in 1796.

Joseph Fouché (1758–1820) was a Convention deputy sent to Lyon against opponents. He organised mass shootings. He turned against Robespierre in 1794 and helped to bring about his fall. In 1799, he became Minister of Police under Napoleon and continued in this post as an instrument of repression and surveillance. He was created Duke of Otranto.

ACTIVITY

Make a list of reasons for the Terror 1793–94. Decide which you would put as the most important and why.

KEY TERM

Cult of the Supreme Being Extremists wanted to replace Christianity with a Cult of Reason, but Robespierre wanted to continue to respect God but to link this with belief in republican virtues: to detest tyranny, to punish tyrants and traitors, and to rescue the unfortunate, to respect the weak, and to defend the oppressed. There were special rites and festivals to honor both God and these moral duties. The Cult was made official in June 1794 but was unpopular with both Christians and atheist radicals. It was seen as an eccentric idea of Robespierre's and helped ensure his downfall.

Religious terror

The "religious terror" had spread across France by early 1794. Religious symbols were destroyed, and pressure was put on clergy to give up their posts and marry. This had been driven by the *sans-culottes* in Paris, the revolutionary armies, and some representatives on mission such as Fouché, rather than the National Convention. Revolutionary hatred of the Catholic Church led to the removal of thousands of priests and the closure of churches. However, this was a sign of local terrorists getting out of control. Robespierre disliked the attacks and wanted to form a new revolutionary religion called the **Cult of the Supreme Being**, which merely acknowledged the power of a creator God.

> **KEY DEBATE**
>
> **WHAT BROUGHT ABOUT THE TERROR?**
>
> One explanation is that if the revolutionary government were to survive, it had little choice but to mobilise the whole nation. That meant taking complete control by conscripting men, taking resources, and ensuring total loyalty. Many felt that they needed to be completely ruthless for their survival, that counter-revolution had to be crushed in the provinces, and that any opposition or failure to maintain changes had to be punished. The Terror was primarily a means of overcoming opposition. It was also a means of preventing potential enemies from undermining the state. When the external threats lessened, then the Terror was brought to an end.
>
> The alternative explanation sees violence as ingrained in the revolution from the start and being part of the whole outlook of the revolutionary leaders. It was not so much the necessity of war but part of an attitude. This put political power and fulfilment of ideals before individual freedom or life itself. Men such as Robespierre had become captured by their own violent revolutionary language, so even their former friends and allies were condemned if they did not share the vision. For some, this extreme mindset explains the scale of killings and the lack of discrimination, so that even minor offences such as hoarding, overcharging, or producing substandard goods for troops were seen as disloyalty to the revolutionary cause. A purging of all elements not a hundred per cent committed to a pure revolution in the name of the people led to Terror.

The fall of Robespierre

By July 1794, the military situation had improved and there was no longer a serious threat of provincial rebellion. The need for terror was diminishing, and it was becoming unpopular. Also, since the law of Prairial and the increased influence of radical members of the CPS, the pace of executions in Paris had reached an unprecedented level. Even members of the CPS were having doubts, as were many in the Convention.

Robespierre had lost support and influence.
- He had been ill and had withdrawn from the CPS and the National Convention.
- There were longstanding quarrels with the supporters of de-Christianisation and the terrorists among the representatives on mission, notably Fouché.
- Robespierre had become a figure of ridicule over his recent role as high priest of the Cult of the Supreme Being.
- He had lost *sans-culotte* support because of his attacks on the Hébertists and threatened wage reductions.
- He had given other revolutionaries reason to fear that he might accuse them of conspiracy, given the rapid acceleration of executions in June and July 1794.

On July 26, 1794, in a long speech, Robespierre said there was a "conspiracy against public liberty" which involved deputies, the Committee of General Security, and even members of the CPS. He promised to name them. Moderates and terrorists alike were afraid they would be next, so they combined against Robespierre and accused him of dictatorship.

In what became known as *Thermidor* (see page 31), Robespierre and his close associates on the CPS, Couthon and Saint Just, were arrested on July 27. Later that day, they escaped and went to the Paris Commune to try to rally their supporters against those of the National Convention. They failed and were rearrested. Because Robespierre and his supporters had become armed rebels, after simply being identified, they were guillotined that afternoon. The greatest number of political victims of the Terror in a single day consisted of the supporters of Robespierre in the Convention, the Commune, and the Revolutionary Tribunal. The Terror ended after this bloodbath.

What impression of Robespierre's downfall is given in Source 1.25?

SOURCE 1.25

The morning of 10 Thermidor Year II by Lucien-Étienne Mélingue in 1877, depicting Robespierre, wounded during his arrest, lying on a table prior to his execution

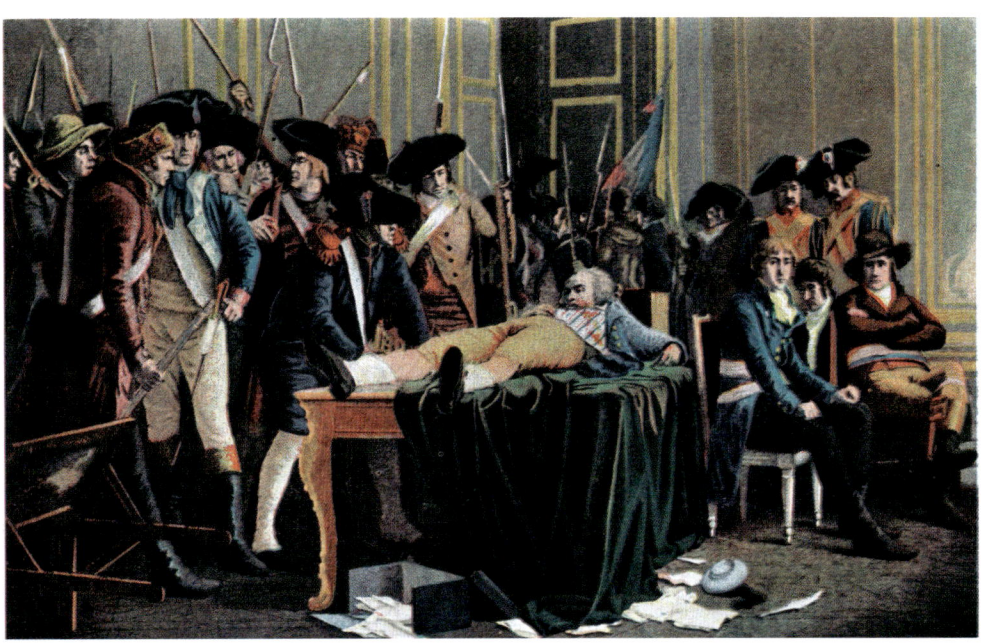

ACTIVITY

Copy and complete this table listing the reasons for the fall of Robespierre.

Reason for the fall of Robespierre	Explanation	Importance 1–5 (5 being the most important)	Why you have given this rating

EXTENSION

The Revolutionary Calendar

As part of the radical break from the past that the Convention wanted, in October 1793, a new calendar was announced. The years were renumbered from the start of the revolution, so Year I began on what had been September 22, 1792. The new months were named after their characteristics – October 22–November 20, for example, became Brumaire, the foggy month. The new calendar therefore began on 1 Vendémiaire Year I.

Economic problems

The bad harvests and high prices, together with longer-term economic problems in many areas of the countryside, had contributed to the events of 1789. The constitutional monarchy which had emerged was helped by better harvests in 1790. However, in 1791, once again harvests were bad. There were food riots in Paris in January and February 1792, and the rate of unemployment rose. This was partly because of the effects of the revolution. The departure of many aristocrats and richer people in French society meant that the demand for luxury goods fell. Those involved in many trades which supplied items such as lace, silk clothes, expensive shoes, and all sorts of consumer goods found their incomes were reduced, and many workshops closed. The revolt by enslaved people in the French West Indian colony of Saint-Domingue disrupted imports of some key items such as coffee and sugar and disrupted the profitable West Indies trade.

Inflation and paper money

Economic conditions were made worse by the issuing of paper money by the government. The new notes were called *assignats* and they were, in effect, transferrable IOUs (notes saying "I owe you") based on the wealth that the state had gained from taking over Church lands (see page 25). However, their value was unstable, and this resulted in rising prices. French people were reluctant to use this paper money. This caused a shortage of currency, which inhibited trade.

The economic problems continued into 1793. The value of the *assignats* fell by 50 per cent, and grain supplies were at dangerously low levels. The new Convention tried to impose controls in response to popular demands for actions against hoarders. However, price controls led to less grain being brought to market. This caused illegal trading or black market activities to flourish, raising prices even more and creating more social discontent. The more extreme elements in the Convention called for death for hoarders and new taxes on the rich.

The civil war which had broken out in the provinces by 1793 disrupted food supplies even more. The needs of war against European enemies used up resources and raised prices. In September 1793, the government passed the Law of the General Maximum. This controlled prices but also wages. The government did not put the interests of the urban workers before the need for stable prices. They prevented higher wages and took action against strikes by tradesmen such as plasterers, bakers, butchers, and printers. In March 1794, there were renewed attempts by the government to control wages.

> What is the purpose of Source 1.26? Note down ideas from your knowledge of events which might be useful to explain its purpose.

SOURCE 1.26

Jacques Roux, a radical member of the Paris local government (Commune) petitions the Convention, in June 1793. He refers to currency speculation involving the paper money (*assignats*)

Have you outlawed speculation? No. Have you decreed the death penalty for hoarding? No. Have you controlled trade (to ensure plentiful and cheap food)? Have you visited the poorer floors of the houses of Paris? You would have been moved to tears by the tears and sighs of an immense population without food and clothing.

The White Terror 1794–95

The Thermidorian Reaction is the term given to the period between July 1794 and November 1795 when the policy of Terror was ended and the more radical laws, such as the Law of the General Maximum (which set price controls) and the Law of Suspects, were abolished. The power of the CPS was reduced, and Robespierre's supporters became victims themselves. By November 1795, a more conservative constitution was set up. New figures emerged but none was as influential as Robespierre had been. The Jacobin club was closed down and outlawed in November 1794. This change encouraged a wave of violence against the radicals called the "White Terror," especially in provincial areas that had suffered from the Terror, such as Lyon and la Vendée. Groups such as the Companies of Jesus (in Lyon) and Companies of the Sun (in the South) attacked Jacobins to take revenge. Massacres and street murders led to over 2000 deaths. In la Vendée, the news of the execution of Robespierre inspired renewed violence and guerrilla warfare.

This wave of violence was called the "White Terror" because of the white colour of the cockades (ribbons) worn by royalists on their hats. However, despite this association with royalism, there was no movement to restore the monarchy. The Revolutionary Tribunal remained, but it was now used against those who led the Terror. Some, such as Collot d'Herbois, were deported to the French colony of Guiana, which was considered to be a fate worse than a death sentence. The Thermidorians welcomed back Girondins and more moderate revolutionaries and went back to earlier ideas, ending restrictions on trade and price controls and restoring religious freedom. The more unusual practices such as Robespierre's Cult of the Supreme Being were ended. Though some of the Thermidorian leaders had once supported Terror, they aimed, after Robespierre's fall, to bring greater stability.

> What can we learn from Source 1.27 about the nature of the "White Terror?"

SOURCE 1.27

A former member of the Convention, Louis-Marie Fréron, describes the "White Terror" in Marseilles

There was not one commune where, following Marseille's example, daggers were not plunged with joy into republican hearts. Everywhere, a kind of rivalry stirred up by the Furies, a contest for a prize to outdo all the rest in massacres. Neither age nor sex was spared. Women, children, and old men were ruthlessly hacked to pieces in the name of humanity, by cannibals who fought over the fragments. The *département* of the Vaucluse endured the same atrocities. That of the Basses-Alpes, whose people are naturally peaceful, hardworking, and law-abiding, did not escape the contagion.

> What does Source 1.28 suggest about the changes brought about by the Thermidorian Reaction?

SOURCE 1.28

A painting of 1795 showing two young men in Paris after the Thermidorian Reaction

The Parisian risings, 1795

The Thermidorians abolished price controls in 1794. This led to a fall in the value of the *assignat* and high inflation. At the same time, a harsh winter led to food shortages.

KEY TERMS

Germinal The seventh month in the French revolutionary calendar.

Prairial The ninth month in the French revolutionary calendar.

Vendémiaire The first month in the French revolutionary calendar.

The shortages led to a huge demonstration in Paris on 1 Germinal Year III (April 1, 1795). The National Guard stayed loyal to the Convention, and the demonstrators were dispersed. In the aftermath, some former supporters of the Terror were exiled to the "dry guillotine" of French Guiana, a French colony where many died of tropical fevers and other diseases.

The unrest of 20–22 Prairial Year III (June 8–10, 1795) was serious as some demonstrators were armed and some National Guards joined them. Loyal army units were able to regain control. This was the first deployment of the army in Paris since 1789. Some of the demonstration leaders were arrested, tried, and executed, and others were imprisoned. Thousands were disarmed, and the power of the *sans-culottes* was finally broken.

These risings demonstrated that change was needed. The radical Constitution of June 1793 was set aside, and instead the Directory was established, with a new and much more conservative constitution, on August 22, 1795 (see page 42). However, unrest continued. On October 5, 1795, a royalist demonstration in Paris, provoked by a law to ensure the new Councils supported the republic, led to an attempted coup known as the 13 Vendémiaire. A large crowd of demonstrators was dispersed by the artillery of loyal forces commanded by the young Napoleon Bonaparte (see page 45) who fired a cannon at the crowds.

The Directory 1795–99 Legislative Assembly

The Thermidorians produced a new constitution in 1795. France was to be ruled by a new governing committee of five, called the Directory.

The Constitution of the Directory (Year III)

The new constitution was designed to prevent a return to a monarchy and to avoid a dictatorship such as that of the CPS or control by the common people, the *sans-culottes*.

The National Convention was replaced by two councils:

Council of Five Hundred	Council of Elders (*Conseil des Anciens*)
All members had to be over 30 years old.	All 250 members had to be over 40 years old.
Initiated legislation.	Approved or rejected legislation.

Annual elections for each council ensured that the membership of one-third of each group changed every year.

ACTIVITY

Create a diagram showing the changes between the Convention (1793–95) and the Directory (1795–99).

There was an indirect system of elections. All males over 21 who paid direct taxes (approximately 5.5 million men) could vote for a special elite group called electors. These electors, rich men (approximately 30,000) who paid high taxes, voted for Council members.

The CPS (executive) was replaced by the Directory of Five:
- They were chosen by the Elders from a list drawn up by the Five Hundred.
- They held office for five years.
- One was chosen by lot to retire each year.

The aims of the Directory

The main aim of the Directory was to keep the achievements of the revolution, which had successfully modernized France and secured the rights of property holders while ending the instability of the period of the Terror. The aim was to limit experiments such as the Cult of the Supreme Being and to end the political infighting and indiscriminate terror. France needed financial and economic stability as well as internal unity. It also needed external security, and for the wars to be conducted successfully in order to keep the key territorial gains made. Above all, the Directory wanted the influence of the Parisian *sans-culottes* to be reduced and traditional authority and stability restored.

KEY TERM

Neo-Jacobins The main impetus of radical revolution had been slowed by the fall of Robespierre and the suppression of the more extreme groups. However, the ideas of the Jacobins had not died, and there was a radical opposition to the Directors which saw the regime as betraying the core principles of the revolution. These groups were not a united party and had been known as the neo- (or new) Jacobins. They were later suppressed severely after a failed attempt to assassinate Napoleon.

KEY FIGURE

François-Noel ('Gracchus') Babeuf (1760–97) was a radical journalist and agitator whose journal, the *Tribune of the People* urged democracy, rights for women, and an end to private property. He led a Conspiracy of Equals to take over the Directory in 1796 and was guillotined in 1797.

The problems facing the Directory

The constitution had several weaknesses: yearly elections led to instability, and there was no mechanism to resolve disputes between the Directors and the two Councils. This could, and did, lead to stalemate and inaction.

By 1795, the new Directory government faced many remaining problems in France. Though the threat from internal revolt had lessened, there was still unrest. The war with Austria continued. France had defended and even extended its borders, but the war was costly and difficult to bring to an end. The power of the *sans-culottes* was reduced, but restless crowds in Paris were still a potential problem. The "White Terror" had shown that royalist sentiment remained strong and that the divisions caused by the revolution, the Terror, the assaults on the Church, and civil war had not gone away. The emergence of successful military leaders could potentially have led to a military dictatorship.

The divisions of the revolution had not ended with the establishment of the Directory in 1795. France remained deeply divided.
- Some favoured a return to the monarchy.
- The so-called **neo-Jacobins** thought that Robespierre and the Jacobins had been right in their devotion to the ideals of the revolution.
- Conservative republicans wanted a return to the more moderate situation of 1791–92.

Successes and failures of the Directory

The Directory had successes and failures in dealing with France's problems.

Political successes and failures

The Directory was initially successful in suppressing opposition. This is shown by the prevention of the attempted coup of 13 Vendémiaire and in dealing with the Babeuf plot. The radical republican **François-Noel Babeuf** had planned to overthrow the Directory government. He wanted greater social and economic equality, which might have gained support, especially at a time of economic problems. However, he was betrayed, arrested, and executed in March 1796.

As unrest continued, the Directors became increasingly reliant on force and preventative action. A royalist plot to overthrow the government was discovered in January 1797. In September 1797, the royalists did well in the elections, and there was a danger of a return of the monarchy. In the coup of Fructidor (the twelfth revolutionary month, which lasted from mid-August to mid-September), the government seized power with the support of the French military. The coup targeted royalist and conservative elements in the government, resulting in the purge of over 130 royalists from the legislative body and the deportation or imprisonment of several monarchists. In May 1798, the "coup" of Floreal annulled the election of 127 deputies to ensure that the Directors removed any threat of a revival of the radical revolution by the re-emergence of Jacobins. Thus, they interfered with the election of possible enemies to both the right and the left. By now, internal power struggles and the exclusion of potential opponents in the Councils was commonplace.

However, by 1799 there were fears that there could be a return to the dangerous years of 1793–94. In order to maintain the war effort, the Directory had to resort to many of the features of the Jacobin state of 1793. The most unpopular was the mass conscription act of September 1798 (Jourdan's law). There was also considerable reliance on censorship and arbitrary arrest. The Law of Hostages of 1799 allowed areas resisting the government to be declared "disturbed." Local authorities could then arrest relatives of nobles, *émigrés*, and rebels, imprison them, and take their property. This law was never applied, but there were fears of a return to Terror. Regulations, such as a law that gave the authorities the right to refuse entry to Paris to anyone not wearing a revolutionary tricolour cockade in their hat, were reminiscent of the Robespierre period.

Financial successes and failures

The Directory had some significant economic issues to address, including the ever-increasing national debt, ongoing widespread poverty, and unemployment. Their key financial strategy in 1796 was an attempt to stabilise the economy by introducing a new currency – the *mandat*. However, this was a disaster. The new currency failed, due to heavy counterfeiting and lack of public confidence. *Mandats* were considered worthless by 1797.

However, the Directory did have some achievements, especially in finance. The Directory responded with attempts to collect tax more efficiently, and there was some reform of the tax system and debt reduction. Dominque-Vincent Ramel-Nogaret (1760–1829) was the Minister of Finance in 1796–99. He instituted a new land registry and set up tax offices to streamline the tax collection process. Nogaret issued government bonds which were redeemable for national lands in the "Bankruptcy of Two Thirds." This removed much of the debt that the revolution had inherited from the monarchy. However, the country still faced severe economic difficulties as a result of the disruption of traditional economic structures.

Military successes and failures

Thanks to successful generals, the Directors had military successes in the Revolutionary Wars. These successes included defeating Holland, Prussia, and Spain. Holland became a satellite state, northern Germany was neutralized, and Spain was forced to change sides and fight with France against the British. However, the most impressive victory was the conquest of northern Italy by Napoleon. This effectively ended the War of the First Coalition with the Treaty of Campo Formio, signed in October 1797. This created a French-controlled Cisalpine republic (meaning the southern side of the Alps). French power was dominant over Italy, and the rich conquests offered considerable financial resources. An expedition to Egypt in 1798, however, ended in failure, as the French forces could not overcome the superior British Navy.

Inspired by British success, the Second Coalition, including Britain, Austria, Russia, the Ottoman Empire, Naples, and Portugal, was formed in 1799. As the Revolutionary Wars continued, the French armies were pushed back into France from Germany and Italy. This meant the Directory could not continue to be funded by plunder. The threat of invasion made the Directory unpopular. France was war weary.

Political change

By summer 1799, there were divisions among the Directors and talk of a "*margouillis national*" (a national mess). The appointment of the veteran politician **Emmanuel Sieyès** as a Director was a key turning point. He plotted against the neo-Jacobin Directors and deputies in the so-called Coup of Prairial in June 1799 and had them removed, replacing them with more conservative figures.

Sieyès and his supporters now aimed to change the Constitution. This needed "a sword," a successful military leader who could ensure that his loyal troops suppressed any opposition that might occur. The aim was to strengthen the power of more conservative elements by using a successful general to provide military force.

The Directory had effectively ended the counter-revolution within France, had achieved military successes, had reformed finances, and had defeated much opposition. However, it had become dependent on military force and purges of members of the ruling body. It had not brought the stability and unity that France needed. Most importantly, it had left the way open for an ambitious military dictator to gain power.

> **KEY FIGURE**
>
> **Emmanuel Sieyès** (1748–1836) was a clergyman and political thinker. His pamphlet *What is the Third Estate?* was hugely influential in bringing about the National Assembly in 1789. He helped to devise the new *départements* and escaped being killed in the Terror. He urged reform of the Directory and became a Director in 1799. He masterminded the coup that brought Napoleon to power. However, his plans for a new constitution were changed by the First Consul, and he lost his influence.

ACTIVITY

List the successes/weaknesses and failures of the Directory 1795–99. Use your list to plan a mini-essay on whether the Directory was a success, a failure, or somewhere in between. Make sure you reach a clear and well-supported judgment.

ACTIVITY

Explain the issues in the summary diagram, and put the reasons for instability in order of importance, explaining your decisions.

SUMMARY DIAGRAM

Government of France

How well was France governed in the period 1793–99?

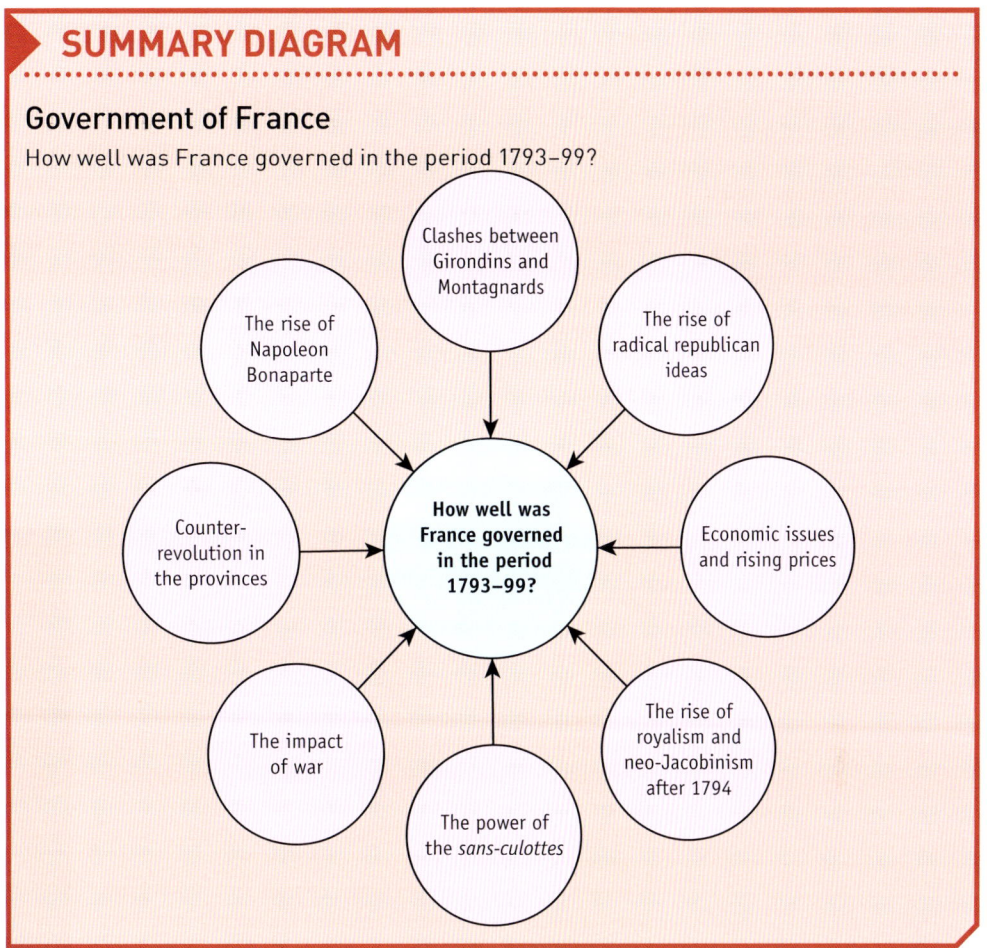

KEY TERM

Consul for Life
Napoleon Bonaparte had been made First Consul after the coup of 1799. In 1802, he declared himself the ruler of France, or Consul for Life. The term "consul" derives from a title used in the Republic of Ancient Rome.

4 What caused the rise and fall of Napoleon Bonaparte?

There was disagreement within the Directory government by 1799. Some members, led by Sieyès and Pierre Ducos, aimed at a purge of the two councils with the assistance of a military general. Through a deal with Napoleon, Emmanuel-Joseph Sieyès and his conspirators brought about the end of the Directory in November 1799. However, the plotters had underestimated Napoleon, who wanted power for himself and seized the opportunity to be named First Consul. In 1802, he became Consul for Life and effectively the sole ruler of France, before making himself Emperor in 1804. Bonaparte made significant domestic reforms; however, his military conquests dominated his rule and would eventually lead to his downfall in 1814.

▶ NAPOLEON BONAPARTE

Napoleon Bonaparte was born in Corsica in 1769. His family members were minor aristocrats, and his father was a lawyer. Napoleon was sent to France to study as a result of the family's collaboration with the French, who had recently taken over the island. He trained as a professional soldier, graduating from the military academy in Paris in 1785. He then became a lieutenant of artillery – the least fashionable and aristocratic part of the army – before being promoted to captain. Serious and withdrawn, he read widely and was deeply interested in the French Revolution. After military successes in 1796–98, he led a coup, which overthrew the Directory, and was made First Consul and then in 1802 Consul for Life in a new government. He made himself Emperor in 1804. He was brilliantly successful in campaigns against Austria, Prussia, and Russia in 1805–07 but his military success faded in wars in Spain and then Russia (1812). Though he was still capable of brilliant leadership, in 1813–14 opposition was too strong, and he abdicated in 1814. Returning to France in 1815, he was defeated at the Battle of Waterloo and died in exile in 1821.

Military historians continue to debate his reputation. However, the victorious outcome in Italy and the successes on the battlefield in Egypt were evident to a French public which had lacked heroic leadership. Napoleon used his political skill to maximise his achievements and build his own legend. Even after his fall in 1815, in lonely exile on a remote island called St. Helena, he rewrote history, adding heroic speeches to his troops in 1796 that he had not actually made at the time.

Napoleon is also well known for being one half of a famous couple. Josephine de Beauharnais was the widow of a plantation owner in the French West Indies. She married Napoleon when he was an ambitious young officer. He was deeply in love with her, and she was crowned Empress in December 1804. They had no children, and he divorced her in order to marry again, to have heirs who would succeed him.

Josephine de Beauharnais

Napoleon Bonaparte's military reputation and political ambitions

Napoleon Bonaparte's early reputation was gained at the siege of Toulon in 1793, a major naval base taken by the British. His use of artillery and his daring approach in gaining high ground showed a great understanding of tactics, and strong personal leadership. In Italy, he led a spectacular and fast-moving campaign, first targeting Austria's Italian ally, Piedmont, and then the Austrian forces themselves. His reputation was based on charismatic personal leadership, which boosted the morale of his troops. He also organized his forces to move rapidly and used artillery effectively.

Napoleon was appointed commander of the Army of the Interior after saving the Directors from being overthrown in 1795. He was therefore well known in political circles, and he had political connections – he married Josephine de Beauharnais, who had had a relationship with the Director **Paul, Vicomte de Barras**. Napoleon demonstrated his political ambitions by becoming an effective ruler in Milan and negotiating the important Treaty of Campo Formio in 1797, which gave France control over northern Italy's wealthy provinces. His expedition to Egypt to establish a French empire in the eastern Mediterranean, to cut off British trade routes to India, captured the imagination of many in France. The campaign as a whole was not a success but did not dent his personal reputation. Admiral Nelson led British naval attacks on Napoleon's ships at Aboukir Bay on the Nile in 1798, stranding Napoleon's armies, which led to their eventual defeat.

Napoleon enhanced and promoted his reputation within France. He issued heroic bulletins describing his victories and carefully kept the public informed of his successes. He was seen as a true general of the revolution, leading his men from the front, sharing their hardships, and showing personal bravery. He enjoyed building his legend. He was said to have embraced plague victims in Jaffa, personally fired a cannon at the bridge at Lodi against the Austrian forces, made inspiring speeches, and knew his men personally. He even had an affectionate nickname, "The Little Corporal." He returned to France in 1799, a highly popular figure with clear political and military ambitions. He was an obvious choice to help strengthen the powers of the conservative Directors.

> **KEY FIGURE**
>
> **Paul, Vicomte de Barras** (1755–1829) was a professional soldier who became a leading politician and helped to overthrow Robespierre in 1794. He was a member of the government in 1795 and helped Napoleon's career. Napoleon married de Barras's former mistress, Josephine. He was persuaded to support the coup of 1799 but was sidelined after that.

> What can we learn from Source 1.29 about Napoleon's success in Italy in 1796–97?

SOURCE 1.29

Napoleon's speech to his troops, March 1796

Soldiers, you are naked, ill fed! The Government owes you much; it can give you nothing. Your patience, the courage you display in the midst of these rocks, are admirable; but they procure you no glory, no fame is reflected upon you. I seek to lead you into the most fertile plains in the world. Rich provinces, great cities will be in your power. There you will find honour, glory, and riches. Soldiers of Italy, would you be lacking in courage or constancy?

> What is the attitude of the author of Source 1.30 to Napoleon? Why do you think the author might hold this view?

SOURCE 1.30

Napoleon's senior military surgeon gives an account of his actions towards plague victims, 1798

His presence among plague victims brought great consolations; he made the doctors treat several patients in front of him. They were piercing the swellings to relieve pain. He touched those who were most distressed to prove to them that they had an ordinary illness. He helped lift, or rather carry, the hideous corpse of a soldier whose tattered uniform was befouled by the bursting of abscessed wounds.

What impression of Napoleon's role in suppressing the uprising of Vendémiaire is given in Source 1.31?

SOURCE 1.31

A painting showing Napoleon leading the defeat of the royalist uprising of Vendémiaire, 1795

The coup of 1799

By 1799 there was talk of a "*margouillis national*," which means a "national mess" in French. There was a range of problems:
- The problems of inflation (rising prices) had been replaced by the problems of deflation (falling prices) and economic downturn.
- Military successes were less frequent, and there was less money coming into France from plunder of conquered territories.
- There was growing opposition, especially the increasing threat from a revival of Jacobinism and popular unrest. However, there were also opponents who were royalists and supported an end to the revolution.
- The Directory was divided, and some of its members were plotting a military coup to strengthen the government and put down opposition. The regime relied heavily on force to maintain itself, and there was the ongoing threat from European powers which had formed the Second Coalition against France in 1798.

The Directory had ceased to attract much support. It was therefore the problems and weaknesses of the Directory that brought about its end in the Coup of Brumaire in November 1799.

The chief plotters to overthrow the government were Emmanuel Sieyès and Pierre Ducos. They enlisted the support of their fellow Director Paul Barras. They had support in both councils but needed the threat of military action that was to be provided by Napoleon. A crisis was engineered when the Directors resigned. The meetings of the two councils were moved from central Paris to the outskirts at St. Cloud to prevent any popular demonstrations. There, Napoleon and loyal troops were gathered.

However, what was expected to be a short and successful takeover turned out to be a botched and farcical event.

The Council of Five Hundred (see page 42) put up more resistance than expected to the establishment of a new government. When they protested, Napoleon entered the Chamber but was met by furious opposition and shouts of "Outside the law." This was dangerous. If the troops had failed to support him, then Napoleon could have been arrested as a plotter.

At a crucial time, he wavered, but the day was saved by his brother Lucien, who claimed that Napoleon's life was being threatened. The troops rushed into the meeting room, and the deputies rushed out.

> Who was the author of Source 1.32? What was the purpose of writing this source?

SOURCE 1.32

Napoleon's version of events in the Coup of Brumaire in a proclamation on 10 November 1799

The councils being assembled at St. Cloud. Several members of the Council of Five Hundred, armed with daggers and firearms, circulated around them nothing but menaces of death. I then repaired to the Council of Five Hundred without arms, and my head uncovered, such as I had been received and applauded by the elders. Twenty assassins threw themselves upon me, and sought my breast. The grenadiers of the legislative body, whom I had left at the door of the hall, came up and placed themselves between me and my assassins. At this time, the cry of "Outlaw!" was raised against the defender of the law. They pressed around the president [Napoleon's brother Lucien Bonaparte], threatened him to his face. I gave orders to rescue him from their power, and six grenadiers of the legislative body brought him out of the hall. Immediately after, the grenadiers of the legislative body entered into the hall, and caused it to be evacuated.

The new constitution, 1799

Sieyès had already prepared a new constitution increasing the power of the government. The Directors were replaced by three Consuls initially ruling for 10 years. However, this was not strictly a dictatorship, as there was an elected legislature. In this extremely complex arrangement, the lower house had two bodies. The first was the Tribunate of 100 members aged 25 and above. The second was the Legislature, consisting of 300 members over 30 years old. The upper house was the Senate, consisting of 60 members over 40 years old. The actual government was dominated by Napoleon as First Consul – the other two had little influence. Napoleon appointed the Senate, who in turn appointed the members of the Tribunate and Legislature. The democratic element came from the male population (some 6 million) choosing a Communal List (600,000) who in turn chose a Department List (60,000) who chose the National List (6000) from whom the Senate chose the Tribunate and the Legislature. The First Consul and his Council of State proposed any new laws. These were approved by the Senate. They were discussed by the Tribunate and voted on by the Legislature. Napoleon justified the changes in a speech in November 1799 by stressing the decline between 1797 and 1799.

> What can we learn from Source 1.33 about why Napoleon was able to take power in 1799?

SOURCE 1.33

A speech by Napoleon in 1799

I left you peace, I find war. I left you conquests, I find enemies at our borders. I left you the millions (of francs) from Italy. I find misery and extortionate laws! Where are the brave hundred thousand soldiers, my companions of glory, now?

The coup had succeeded in strengthening the government, which could not be removed for 10 years and was sure of any of its measures being passed. In 1802, Napoleon was made Consul for Life, ending any chance of a change of government. In 1804, he declared himself Emperor (see page 51).

The coup removed instability because the army's support and weakened assemblies made future attempted coups unlikely.

The new regime retained some democratic elements; however, it was far from the most democratic of the constitutions of the French Revolution. Initially, all adult males voted for the first of the lists of people who would eventually make up the Legislature, though the elected assemblies had far less power than previous ones. The new constitution requested all men vote in a "plebiscite" or referendum. However, the government made it difficult for accurate outcomes to be recorded by distorting voting figures and making it difficult to vote "no."

> **ACTIVITY**
> 1 "Napoleon came to power because he was an outstanding leader."
> 2 "Napoleon came to power only because of the weaknesses of the Directory. His own abilities have been exaggerated."
>
> In pairs, find evidence to support view 1 and other evidence to support view 2. Discuss which view you agree with more and why.

Napoleon's initiatives as First Consul and establishing authoritarian control

Napoleon's immediate domestic aims:
- Secure and maintain his personal authority as ruler of France.
- Prevent opposition from internal opponents.
- Provide effective government with social and economic stability.
- Break the power and influence of the *sans-culottes* and therefore end radicalism.
- Restore national unity.
- Ensure that the French state could support the defence of France and its conquests since 1793 against foreign powers.

The new constitution did not limit the government's power effectively. Therefore, Napoleon could take several measures to achieve these goals:
- He took advantage of the First Consul's power to appoint ministers and bring in new laws.
- He remained in command of the armed forces and took control of foreign policy.
- He issued an amnesty to *émigrés* to try to increase unity.
- He took control of the police and increased their power.
- Censorship increased.

Napoleon extended his power in 1802 to become Consul for Life. This was presented to the people for approval in the tradition of the revolution, but in fact the results were rigged and only token opposition was shown.

Setting up new ministries and the Council of State

New ministries were created, including:
- Finance
- Civil and Criminal Legislation
- War
- Marine and Interior.

These ministries all reported to Napoleon. Auditors were created with the responsibility to support the administration of the council and oversee local administration. Alongside this, on December 13, 1799, Napoleon created the *Conseil d'État* (Council of State), which is still an important institution in modern-day France. It was responsible for drafting proposals for laws and played a part in advising the First Consul, and later Emperor, Napoleon, who would at times preside over the council. There were between 30 and 40 state councillors in Paris. They did a great deal of work during the Consulate and the Empire, participating actively in the management of administrative reforms. Napoleon was in charge of selecting and dismissing the state councillors.

The new system allowed Napoleon to finance extensive military campaigns and increase the efficiency of government. There were major changes in finance, law, and control of local government through prefects. This sort of modernised administration, which helped to unify France, had been called for since before the revolution. However, there was also an increase in police power, and the system depended heavily on rule by a dictatorial general.

Reform of the police force and the judiciary

The regime relied on a high level of surveillance, censorship, and punishment of dissent to stay in power. Joseph Fouché was an efficient minister of police. He reformed national and local policing to enforce Napoleon's authority. Daily reports were sent to Napoleon on matters of security. The jurisdiction of the police was wide and included monitoring opinion, ensuring that food prices were not too high to avoid discontent, policing economic measures, chasing deserters, and maintaining a system of spying and surveillance. There were special tribunals for crimes against the state.

- From 1810, there were state prisons for political offences.
- There were roundups of suspects.
- The police forces were increased significantly; for example, the *Corps de gendarmes* went from 10,000 to 15,000 in the first year of the Consulate.

The legal system was not allowed to offer any protection against the power of the regime. At both local and national level, central government appointed, and could remove, judges.

There is a debate about whether a **police state** was created. In Rouen, for example, there were few political prisoners, and prefects were often too overwhelmed by their other responsibilities to hunt down suspected critics.

> **KEY TERM**
>
> **Police state** A country where the activities of people are very strictly controlled by the government with the help of a police force, often working secretly against supposed enemies. The level of power and control is very great.

Propaganda and censorship

To counter opposition, the regime depended on a lot of images and propaganda. Much of this was inherited from previous leaders, who were adept at using all sorts of propaganda messages to gain support. Images of Napoleon as a great leader were published and paintings made in his honour. There were symbols such as the bee (see page 52) which related him to previous monarchs. The control of the media was important for Napoleon, and he is quoted as saying, "Four hostile newspapers are more to be feared than a thousand bayonets." The huge growth of newspapers and journals had been a major feature of the revolution, but the Napoleonic regime reduced newspapers considerably. Sixty newspapers were closed in 1800 alone, and the remaining ones were subject to strict censorship. The government produced its own version of events in an official paper called *Le Moniteur*. Both as Consul and as Emperor, Napoleon took a close personal interest in ensuring that there was control of the arts and literature. Publishers had to gain official approval before printing plays, novels, and pamphlets. A developed system of official censorship was put in place affecting all printed material, with punishments for those not submitting to the official code of practice.

SOURCE 1.34

An English visitor to Napoleon's France. Anne Plumptree, *Narrative of Three Years Residence in France 1802–1805*, published in 1810

I felt as free in France as in England. I went wherever I wanted and was always treated with politeness and hospitality, just like during peacetime. The government was only harsh towards troublemakers. I saw progress in public works, industry, commerce, and the arts, and did not find the people unhappy or the government hated. I observed that speech was as free in France as in England. People freely expressed their opinions and sentiments on Bonaparte and his government, whether favourable or unfavourable, without any fear, even in public settings.

SOURCE 1.35

A famous critic of Napoleon's tyranny, Germaine de Staël (commonly known as Madame de Staël), whom Napoleon exiled, writes critically of the Empire after its fall. (*Considerations on the Principal Events of the French Revolution*)

It is generally after long civil troubles that tyranny is established, because it offers the hope of shelter to all the exhausted and fearful people. This was true of Bonaparte. His scheme for arriving at the domination of France rested upon three principal elements – to satisfy men's interests at the expense of their freedom, to dominate public opinion by lies, and to give the nation war instead of liberty.

> What different messages about Napoleonic France are given in Sources 1.34 and 1.35? Use the provenance to explain why you think they are so different.

> **ACTIVITY**
>
> In relation to the power and control of the government, what was different in Napoleonic France compared to the *Ancien Régime*? Were there any similarities in the ways that the different governments kept control?

Control of elections

Local government was controlled by the change in the way that France's 83 *départements* were ruled. Prefects were appointed with wide responsibilities, to allow Napoleon to maintain control of the different regions.

The constitution allowed for little control over the actions of Napoleon. The Tribunate discussed laws but could not vote for them. The Legislative Body voted but could not discuss. The Senate was appointed by Napoleon. He also controlled major towns as he appointed mayors and nominated members of town councils.

Napoleon justified the changes in a speech in November 1799 by stressing the decline of France between 1797 and 1799.

> **ACTIVITY**
>
> Fill in the table about the consequences for France of Napoleon coming to power in 1799. Make a judgment about the importance of each by marking it 1–5, with 5 being most important.
>
> | Consequence | Explanation | Judgment 1–5 |
> |---|---|---|
> | | | |
> | | | |
> | | | |
> | | | |
> | | | |
> | | | |
> | | | |

Emperor Napoleon

The Consulate has been seen as a monarchy in all but name. Napoleon enjoyed more power than Louis XVI had done as constitutional monarch after the changes from 1789. He had put into practice reforms which had proved impossible for Louis and his ministers from 1774. He had given France greater internal stability than the *Ancien Régime*, virtually ending the riots and disturbances which had often accompanied bad harvests even under strong kings. However, this stability depended heavily on the energy and personality of the Consul and not on a system. In the event of Napoleon's assassination or death in battle, France could easily be plunged once again into instability and civil war.

In 1804, the whole nature of the regime was changed by the decision of the Consul for Life to go a step further towards personal power and declare himself Emperor. There were two elements which may have led to the Empire of 1804. The first was undoubtedly Napoleon's ambition and desire to promote his family. He had a strong belief in his destiny to rule and a great desire that his family and his children, when he had any, should be rewarded. Also, he wanted any future son to inherit the crown so that the underlying system could continue with the support of a new aristocracy led by the Bonaparte family.

> What impression of the Emperor is given in Source 1.36? Note down specific details from the source to support your answer.

SOURCE 1.36

Napoleon on His Imperial Throne by Jean-August-Dominique Ingres, painted in 1806

Another reason for creating the Empire came from the notables. The Council of State and the Tribunate and Senate were in favour of a monarchy. There had been plots against the Consul, particularly those masterminded by the Breton opposition leader Georges Cadoudal. The fear of royalist plots was great enough for Napoleon to order the kidnap and execution of the exiled Bourbon prince, the Duc d'Enghien, from Germany in 1804, one of his most controversial and shocking acts. The army leaders, too, were in support, and Napoleon had received a great many petitions to take the next step and make himself hereditary ruler. The Empire saw a change in style. A new aristocracy appeared, with special robes and symbols. Napoleon's brothers were given grand titles. Heavy symbolism appeared. Napoleon wanted people to see him as part of the French royal tradition. He decided to use the emblem of a bee as his personal motif. This had been a favored symbol of the ancient Merovingian kings of France, especially Childeric (436–481). Charlemagne (747–814) was also featured in paintings and tributes. Court ceremonials became grander.

Napoleon thought that Emperors were at a higher level than mere kings, so members of his family could be elevated to kingship. His brother Louis became king of Holland. His brother Joseph became first king of Naples and then king of Spain. His brother Jerome became king of Westphalia in Germany. Even one of Napoleon's generals, Murat, became king of Naples. The Empire was supported by rewards which went beyond Napoleon's family. The Legion of Honor and grants of land were given to 25,000 people. The Napoleonic elites – officers, administrators, wealthy supporters – were given posts and honors. The elites were known as "the masses of granite" on which the Empire was built. The Empire also saw impressive public buildings and public works. But Napoleon himself was careful to retain the image of the simple soldier. On campaigns which took him out of France for a long period – 1805–07, 1809, and 1812–13 – he dressed plainly and was seen to share in the hardships of his men, even if his arrangements were actually quite lavish.

ACTIVITY

Look at these statements:

"Napoleon made himself Emperor just for reasons of personal ambition."

"Napoleon made himself Emperor for the good of France."

Make a list of evidence from your knowledge to support each statement.

> In Source 1.37, what does Napoleon cite as the reason he continued his military campaigns? From your knowledge, create a list of other key reasons.

SOURCE 1.37

Napoleon reflects on his situation as Emperor (1809)

My empire will be destroyed if I cease being fearsome – if my son is not a great military commander – if he is not able to do what I do – then he will fall off the throne. Among established kings, a war's only purpose is to take a province or capture a city. But with me, it's always a question of my existence as a monarch.

To secure his dynasty, Napoleon divorced Josephine and married the Austrian princess Marie-Louise of Parma in 1810. They had a son and heir, the Duke of Reichstadt, a year later. In reality, the chances of creating a dynasty were slim. Napoleon the Emperor faced constant opposition from Britain and spent years fighting other European monarchs. In the end, the survival of the Empire was based on his ability to defeat his enemies on the battlefield rather than any real legitimacy.

Napoleon could have used the brief periods of peace in 1802–03 and 1807–08 to reset his relations with European powers and concentrate on ruling France and its Empire. However, he was driven to further military conflict; his state was set up for war, and Napoleon could not establish stable and peaceful relations with other powers. By 1807, Napoleon's conquests and dominance in Europe made it unlikely that the other European powers would permanently accept such a powerful leader with such ambition and confidence.

Napoleon's domestic reforms

Although military conquests dominated Napoleon's rule, he also made significant domestic reforms.

Legal reform, the Code Napoleon

The revolutionary idea of efficient and uniform administration, replacing the old privileges and regional differences from before 1789, also led to significant legal reforms. For many years, had been widespread discussions of introducing one uniform legal code for the whole of France. Napoleon applied himself to the problem. He encouraged the drawing up of a Civil Code of law in 1804 and later commercial and criminal codes by 1807. Thus, laws were made uniform throughout France.

- Property could be bequeathed more freely and did not all have to pass to the eldest son.
- The ending of feudal rights that the revolution had brought about was confirmed in law.
- Privileges such as those of the Church were ended.

- The property rights of those who had gained land from the Church or from the nobility during the revolution were confirmed.

These elements, together with the very fact that there was one national, uniform legal code, could be seen as beneficial for many property owners and met a lot of the demands expressed in the *Cahiers de doléances* of 1789. However, other reforms were harsher.
- The Code permitted the reintroduction of enslavement in French overseas colonies to protect the rights of slaveholders who had lost their "human property" during the revolution. This reimposed enslavement and attempted to reconquer the liberated population by the invasion of Saint-Domingue.
- The authority of husbands and fathers was reinforced. Married women could not own property in their own right. Wives who survived their husbands did not automatically inherit their property. Husbands were favoured in disputes about custody rights of children; divorce requirements were stricter for women than men. Women could gain divorce only if their husband had been unfaithful and if the other woman was actually brought into the family home, but any infidelity on a woman's part was grounds for divorce.
- Fathers' rights to control their children were reinforced, and employers' rights over their workers were also recognised.

In this way, male authority was strengthened in society – over wives, children, workers, and enslaved people. The main support for the regime came from property owners as they were the main beneficiaries of the reforms.

Educational reform

Another key revolutionary idea had been equality and opening opportunities to talented people regardless of class. The ideal would be to have an educational system open to everyone. This could not be achieved, but Napoleon was very interested in educational reform to produce the administrators and officers France needed. In 1802, the Consul founded 45 state academies, or *lycées*, which provided scholarships for 6400 boys. Beneficiaries were mainly the sons of officers and officials. The aim was to offer technical education of a high standard. After 1805, there were more state secondary schools established. The 300 new schools were tightly organized, with a common national curriculum and strict regulations as to timetables and the content of lessons. Napoleon's education system did not promote creativity or free thinking. It focused on developing skills useful to the nation and promoting national unity and obedience.

Financial and economic policy

The period of peace between 1801 and 1804 allowed Napoleon to initiate other important measures as Consul.

Taxation and bread prices

There were improvements in tax collection which built on the work of the Directory. Tax records for land were improved, and the collection of both direct and indirect taxes became stricter and less corrupt.

A major cause of unrest before 1799 was inflation and the rising price of bread. Anxious to avoid popular disturbances, Napoleon imposed price controls, and the regime did its best to stabilize prices of essentials such as bread. Napoleon also imposed regulations to maintain the quality of the "Revolutionary loaf," which had been weakened during the revolution by the use of cheaper ingredients.

Bank of France

An important financial measure was the creation of a Bank of France in 1800. Britain and the Low Countries (modern-day Belgium and the Netherlands) had established national banks in the seventeenth century. This allowed secure issuing of paper money and made lending to the state more secure. In order to bring greater financial stability to help trade and to make borrowing easier, the Consul introduced a new currency, the *franc de germinal*, based on gold and silver coins whose content of precious metal was closely controlled. This finally ended the danger of inflated paper currency.

Religious reform: the *Concordat* with the Catholic Church

Religious change was an important element of the Consulate. Religious disputes had divided France since 1790 and many priests had rejected the state Church established by the revolution and had refused to swear an oath of loyalty. Religion had motivated much of the opposition to the revolution in the provinces, and it was vital for national unity that Catholics were reconciled to the state.

Napoleon began negotiations with Pope Pius VII in 1800, and an agreement called the *Concordat* was reached in 1801 and published in 1802.
- Roman Catholicism was recognised as the religion of the majority of French people.
- The Roman Catholic Church formally recognised Napoleon as the legitimate ruler of France.
- The Church was free to organize public worship.
- The Church remained under state control, with its clergy paid by the state and leading appointments made by the First Consul.
- Church lands which had changed hands during the revolution were to be kept by the new owners.

The Church was thus in a special position. As the Church had suffered a lot from anticlerical actions during the revolution, it was reassuring for it to be given something of its old status back. Nonetheless, Napoleon retained a lot of control. Churchmen were appointed by the state and had to preach that people should be loyal to Napoleon and the state. The state retained its control over registering births, deaths, and marriages, which it had taken in 1790. The need to be loyal to Napoleon was often preached by clergy appointed by the regime. However, after the *Concordat*, most French Catholics felt that they could support both France and the Catholic Church.

ACTIVITY

Make a table. In the first column list the major reforms:
- Legal reforms
- Education reforms
- Financial reforms
- The *Concordat*

In the second column, explain briefly what each achieved.

In the third column "grade" each reform out of 6 – with 6 meaning "most significant for the people of France" and 1 meaning "least significant for the people of France" of the Consulate's reforms. In the fourth column, explain your "grade."

Look at your "top mark reform" – perhaps it is legal reform. Now, plan an essay about that reform, for example:

"Assess the view that the Code Napoleon was the most important of the reforms of the Consulate."

ACTIVITY

How did the policies and reforms of Napoleon's government impact different people in France? Create a table of how they affected different people's lives, for example, women, men, churchmen, poor people.

Reasons for Napoleon's fall from power

By 1807, Napoleon had gained an astonishing amount of power both at home and abroad. He had defeated the three major European powers and had discussed with the Russian tsar a division of the world between them. Only Britain remained undefeated, and British land forces were not large enough to defeat Napoleon. At home, an authoritarian state and effective censorship and propaganda maintained his authority. This was helped by the sense of national pride for France's military victories and conquests, dominating both Italy and Germany. Yet this power was to last only another seven years, as Napoleon abdicated in 1814.

The effects of Napoleon's failure to defeat Britain

British sea power was dominant after the defeat of the French navy at the battle of Trafalgar in 1805. Britain's trading wealth and empire provided the huge sums of money to pay Austria and Prussia to fight Napoleon on land. Britain managed to support the people of Spain and Portugal in a long struggle against French domination (1808–14). Britain's relentless hostility led Napoleon into a disastrous policy of economic warfare – the Continental System – which backfired against him.

The failure of the Continental System

The British fleet was able to blockade French ports. This led to a decline in the trade of cities such as Bordeaux and Nantes. The Continental System was designed by Napoleon as an economic attack on Britain in retaliation for the British naval blockade, but it had a wider purpose. Britain was the only major industrial power in Europe and depended on finding markets for the products it manufactured. It also had a flourishing trade in re-exports of goods imported from the British colonies. Its lucrative trade had enabled it to pay subsidies to other European powers to fight the French since 1793. Hitting British trade would be likely to bring about unemployment in British factories and to encourage radical unrest among workers, weakening the war effort. In Napoleon's Berlin Decrees of November 1806, France, Italy, Spain, Switzerland, Holland, and the Confederation of the Rhine were forbidden to trade with Britain, which was declared to be in a state of blockade. European ports from the Baltic Sea in the north to the Mediterranean Sea in the south were shut against British trading ships.

> **KEY TERMS**
>
> **Naval blockade** A form of naval warfare in which the ships of a nation prevent vessels from leaving and entering ports of their enemies to injure their trade.
>
> **Confederation of the Rhine** A union of all German states except for Austria and Prussia, created by Napoleon in 1806 (see Figure 1.1).

Historians' views differ about how badly Britain was affected. Some argue that there was very little effect on Britain because of new markets developing in North and South America, while others suggest that in 1811, Britain's trade with the continent fell by as much as 50 per cent, causing hardship and unrest. However, Britain continued to resist France, and Napoleon had not brought Britain to the point of negotiating peace.

The Continental System was undoubtedly a failure for France. The loss of British trade created discontent throughout Europe. British goods were needed so badly that smuggling became rife and led to subsequent police actions. All this made Napoleonic rule unpopular. The blockade failed to defeat Britain, and it led to pressure on Napoleon to control the whole European coastline. This led him to war in Portugal and then Spain. However, its biggest consequence was as a contributing factor in the invasion of Russia in 1812, to ensure the system was being enforced.

Though the British navy could fight France at sea and cut off its ports, Britain had only a small army, so it was difficult for Britain to fight directly with Napoleon's armies. Britain relied on using its economic power to give money to allies. However, the French invasion of Spain allowed Britain to use its armies to support Spanish resistance against the French.

Outcome of the Peninsular War 1808–14

Napoleon ordered the invasion of Spain in 1808 and put his brother Joseph on the Spanish throne. He did not personally command the French forces in the long war that followed, which became known as the Peninsular War. The invasion was so costly in men and resources that it also became known as "the Spanish ulcer." French forces found themselves facing determined resistance from the Spanish people, who resented rule by the French, but also stubborn opposition from British forces led by Sir Arthur Wellesley, who became Duke of Wellington. Atrocities by both French armies and Spanish guerrilla forces made French occupation costly and dangerous. The British built defences around Lisbon and retreated to them when the French forces were too strong. Britain was well supplied by its navy. There were some heavy battles which were costly for France and achieved little. French forces were driven out of Spain in 1813, and Wellington's troops crossed into France and besieged the large French city of Toulouse. The war weakened Napoleon's campaigns elsewhere, as 300,000 troops were held in Spain in a war they could not win. Moreover, the Peninsular War challenged the whole idea that French armies could not be defeated.

What impression of the nature of the war is given in Source 1.38?

SOURCE 1.38

One of famous Spanish artist Goya's scenes from the war entitled *The Disasters of War*

EXTENSION

Napoleon and enslaved people

Pre-revolutionary France had several colonies in the Caribbean, which had large numbers of enslaved people. The most important was Saint-Domingue (present-day Haiti). There was a revolt on the island led by Toussaint Louverture in 1791. This led to the revolutionary government abolishing enslavement in all colonies in 1793–94. Saint-Domingue became independent, but Napoleon was determined to get it back and made an attempt to regain the island and reconquer the liberated population. Toussaint was sent to die in an Alpine fortress. Napoleon re-enslaved people across all French colonies.

Growth of nationalism in the empire

France's military success meant that much of Europe was under French control by 1812.

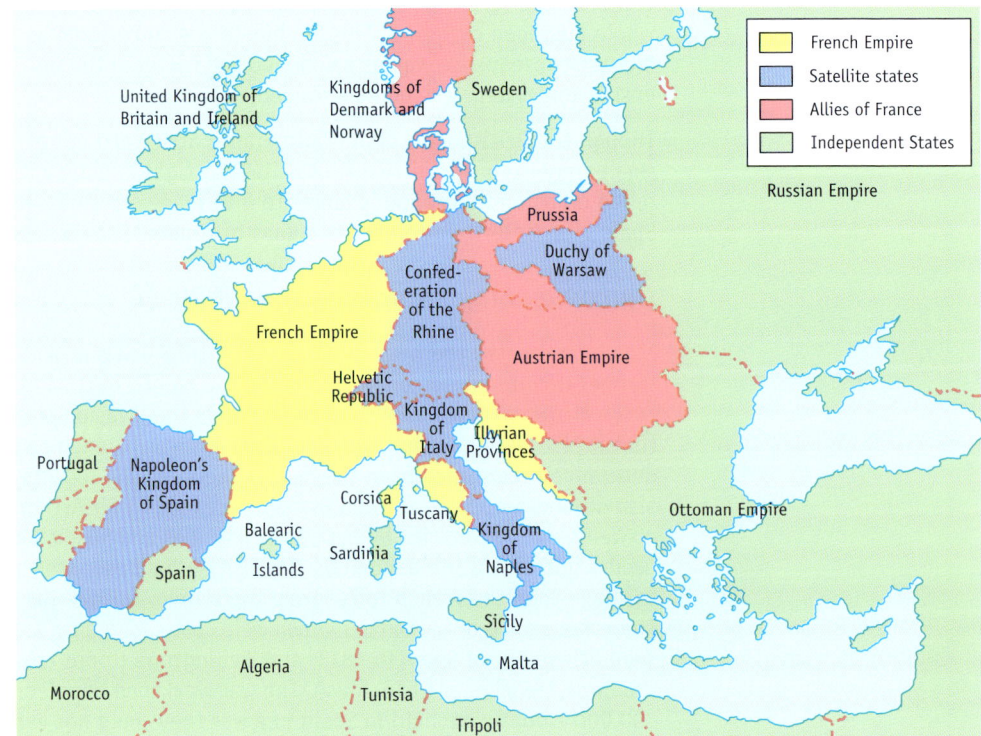

Figure 1.1 Areas controlled by France in 1812

The extent of the empire by 1812

The "Grand Empire" reached its greatest extent by 1811. It consisted of:
- France up to its "natural frontiers" – the Alps, Pyrenees, and River Rhine, including Belgium
- annexed territories – Piedmont (1802), Swiss Confederation (1803), Ligurian Republic (1805), and the Grand Duchy of Tuscany (1809)
- satellite states – kingdoms of Italy (1805), Naples (1806), Holland (1806), Westphalia (1807), Spain (1808), the Confederation of the Rhine (1806), and the Duchy of Warsaw (1807).

After their defeats in 1806 and 1807, Austria and Prussia were forced into alliance with the Empire. The annexed territories were treated as part of France, with the same rights and obligations as any other region. Like the other regions, they provided tax income and soldiers but received the benefits of the Empire, such as the legal and administrative changes made by Napoleon in France.

The rise of nationalism

The creation of a more united Germany and Italy under French domination did, to some extent, encourage new national feeling. The Grand Duchy of Warsaw recreated a Polish state that had been destroyed by Russia, Austria, and Prussia dismantling the kingdom of Poland in the 1790s. The resistance to French rule sparked a sense of regional and national pride – for example, in Calabria. Calabria, in southern Italy, revolted against the French in 1806, leading to a long guerrilla war. Spain and Portugal experienced persistent and successful resistance against French rule from 1808 to 1813, during the Peninsular War (see page 57), and the Tyrol went into revolt in 1809 under Andreas Hofer. There was a considerable amount of passive resistance and local disturbances. Opposition did not take the form of nationalist risings but rather dislike of foreign occupation and exploitation. Napoleon later claimed that he had called new nations into being, but nationalism was less a support for new nations than a desire to end French taxation and conscription.

Declining popularity at home, conscription, and the deteriorating economy

By 1814, Napoleon's popularity at home was declining. The very heavy losses of men and the strains of the terms of conscription were leading to more opposition. Conscription was evaded on a large scale, and desertion rates were high. In Spain, the rate of desertion was so high the British were able to recruit ten infantry battalions made up of troops who had fled the French armies. The heavy losses of troops also had a wider impact on society and future population growth. The benefits of conquering new lands were decreasing. French control was weakening, taxes were high, and economic problems were growing due to lost trade and the British naval blockade of French ports. Economically, industries associated with the war effort – iron and textiles – developed, as did trade with the rest of Europe. Inland areas on continental trading routes, such as Alsace on the River Rhine, prospered, while other areas, such as the maritime ports, suffered from the British blockade. By 1814, more domestic opposition was becoming apparent when members of the Legislative Body (*Corps législatif*) demanded peace and were dismissed.

> **EXTENSION**
>
> **Terms of conscription**
>
> Conscription for all men aged 18 to 25 was introduced in 1793. The Directory maintained this in the Jourdan Laws of 1798 saying, "Every Frenchman is a soldier and must defend the country." There were some exemptions – for example, if a doctor deemed someone medically unfit. Conscription was done by lottery, but those selected could pay someone else to go instead. This meant that most of the nobility and middles classes were able to avoid it.

Outcome of the failure of the campaign against Russia, 1812

France had defeated Russian troops in a war in 1805–07. Napoleon had signed a peace treaty with the Russian tsar in which they agreed to work together to dominate Europe. By 1812, relations between Napolean and the tsar were poor.
- Russia had not helped France in a war against Austria in 1809.
- Russia's ruling class was hostile to Napoleon.
- Russia continued to trade with Britain – the tsar refused to enforce the Continental System.

For these reasons, as well as the decline in the army's morale due to the Peninsular War and wavering support for the regime in France, Napoleon decided to invade and defeat Russia before the tsar turned against him and allied with Britain. He hoped for a short and successful campaign:
- Russia had a smaller population than France and its Empire.
- The French army was superior.
- Other European countries had been unhappy with the Russian tsar's alliance with Napoleon in 1807, so Napoleon was counting on their support.

However, Napoleon's campaign in Russia was weakened because so many of his best troops were still fighting in Spain in 1812.

Napoleon assembled an astonishing 655,000 men to take on Russia's 240,000. The central invading force was 450,000. The rest were held back in support. This was one of the largest European armies ever. It was made up of conscripts and volunteers from all over Europe, not just France.

In the end, after a costly victory at Borodino in September 1812, the invading forces entered Moscow – to find that most of the inhabitants had gone back to their villages, leaving a city that was usually home to 275,000 with only 6000 people.

> ### EXTENSION
>
> **War against Austria in 1809**
>
> Austria had fought a war against Napoleon in 1805 and had been badly defeated. The Treaty of Schönbrunn led to a marriage alliance between Austria with France.

> ### EXTENSION
>
> **The Battle of Borodino (September 7, 1812)**
>
> The Russian forces occupied a strong defensive position to protect Moscow from the French invasion. Napoleon attacked the city on September 7, 1812. He hoped to win by attacking the less well-defended part of the Russian line. This failed. Napoleon relied on attacking the Russians head-on. There was none of his usual skill or use of surprise. Napoleon failed to destroy the bulk of the tsar's forces, which were able to withdraw.

What explanation is suggested by Source 1.39 for France's defeat in Russia in 1812?

SOURCE 1.39

Baron Lejeune, a commander in the French army, recalls the Battle of Borodino

General Kutusoff, however, using a fortified defensive position, immediately pointed 100 pieces of cannon upon us, while a large group of elite Russian grenadiers who had been hidden from view, advanced to attack us. Smoke from the guns was whirled up in dense masses, enveloping and almost suffocating men and horses. Our victory was dearly bought.

What can we learn about the experience of French troops in the Russian campaign of 1812 from Source 1.40?

SOURCE 1.40

From the memoirs of the French soldier Sergeant Bourgogne

While we were in Krasnoë and the immediate neighbourhood, the Russians, 90,000 strong, surrounded us – to right, to left, in front, and behind, nothing but Russians – thinking, no doubt, they could soon finish us off. But the Emperor wished to show them it was not quite so easy a thing as they imagined; for although we were most wretched, and dying of cold and hunger, we still possessed two things – courage and honor.

The Russian villagers fled to the woods, leaving little for the invaders to live on. The French armies ran out of food. The organization needed for such a mammoth advance was simply not there. Before September, 100,000 French troops had been lost to illness. The heavy fighting at Borodino lost 60,000 more troops. The plan had not been to wage a long winter campaign, and Napoleon's armies did not have the supply chains to support this. All of Napoleon's previous campaigns had depended on living off the land, but the destruction of crops by the retreating Russians made this impossible. When Napoleon finally got to Moscow, he did not find the supplies he needed. With limited medical facilities and with extreme weather conditions, Napoleon's forces became increasingly weak.

By October 19 Napoleon, though he had taken Moscow, was no nearer to victory. The city had been abandoned, plundered, and then destroyed by fire. Essentially, Napoleon had been trapped by Russian commanders, who used Russia's vast distances to lure the French away from their supply lines. The destruction and pillaging by the French had alienated the population, and many thought Napoleon was the **Antichrist**.

Many peasants joined with the army in attacking the French, so the Russian forces outnumbered Napoleon's troops. By October, his central invading force of 450,000 had been reduced to 100,000, and they were further depleted by a long retreat. Only 25,000 returned to their base in Poland. However, the Russian losses amounted to some 300,000, and the economic loss was considerable – Smolensk and Moscow were destroyed, as were many villages and smaller towns.

> **KEY TERM**
>
> **Antichrist** Following a reference in the Bible, in St. John's gospel, many Christians believe that just as God sent his son to Earth as Jesus, so the Devil would send his son to bring destruction, not salvation. There was a belief that he would take the shape of a tyrannical ruler, and some believed this was Napoleon.

> **KEY DEBATE**
>
> **WAS THE RUSSIAN CAMPAIGN THE MAIN REASON FOR THE FALL OF NAPOLEON?**
>
> Napoleon compared the Russian campaign to a storm that shakes a tree but leaves it more firmly fixed in the soil. He later blamed Spain for his fall. Historians are divided on the issues of whether the Russian campaign in 1812 was the turning point which led to his downfall. Many historians agree that the Russian campaign can be considered the turning point because of the sheer scale of the losses – not only of men but of horses and war materials. It damaged the view that Napoleon could never be defeated and encouraged other European nations (Austria and Prussia in particular) to join Britain and Russia and led to Russia attacking France in Germany.
>
> On the other hand, the campaign did not actually end the war, and Napoleon was still able to raise large forces in 1813 and 1814. The coalitions against him were not fully united, and there were concerns about Russian forces in western Europe. It might have been possible for Napoleon to stay in power had he accepted peace terms after failures in Germany, despite the losses in Russia.

Impact of the defeat at Leipzig, 1813

Victories in Spain and Russia encouraged greater determination by Napoleon's enemies. Even with the defeats suffered in 1813, the allies did not give up. Finally, they defeated France at the Battle of Leipzig on October 16–18. In the Battle of Leipzig, the united allied forces were aware of Napoleon's tactics and were able to take effective measures against them. There was no rapid and decisive victory; instead a series of battles wore down Napoleon's troops. The allies also had greater numbers – 300,000 against 190,000 men. Napoleon's army, many of whom were not French, were also very tired and hungry. The three-day battle ended with heavy losses and forced Napoleon's army to start retreating in order to defend France. They were then hit by disease.

Allies capture Paris

The Congress of Châtillon was a peace conference held from February 5 to March 5, 1814. The main participants were the Coalition allies (Britain, Russia, Prussia, and Austria) and France, represented by Napoleon. The allies offered a peace treaty based on France returning to its so-called 'natural frontiers' – allowing Napoleon to keep Belgium and the Rhineland. He refused these terms.

Napoleon decided to fight on with 60,000 men against an allied force of 200,000. He attacked forces advancing on Paris and did have some success; however, the enemy got increasingly close to the capital city. The casualties of the battles made some of Napoleon's enemies ready to negotiate with him. However, the British foreign minister, Lord Castlereagh, encouraged them to keep fighting to defeat Napoleon for good. The advances continued. The Châtillon peace conference was broken off on March 19. The allies reaffirmed their determination to act together at the Treaty of Chaumont. Napoleon's final attacks failed.

Napoleon left 17,000 men commanded by Marshal **August de Marmont** to defend Paris. He then took his main army to attack the Coalition forces in eastern France, aiming to disrupt their communications and supply lines. He aimed to divide enemy forces and defeat them separately, but the allies ignored this and pressed on to Paris. They entered the city after defeating a final French counterattack on March 31, 1814.

> **KEY FIGURE**
>
> **August de Marmont** (1774–1852) was of a noble family. He served with Napoleon in Italy and Egypt and again in the war of the Third Coalition. He was made governor of Ragusa in Illyria and fought in the 1809 war against Austria, but not with distinction. He fought as a Marshal in Germany in 1813–14 and led a retreat back to France. He abandoned Napoleon and allowed his forces in Paris to surrender in 1814. Loyal to Louis XVIII in 1815, he failed to save the Bourbon monarchy during the rebellion of 1830 and went into exile with the former king Charles X.

Napoleon's supporters deserted him. Most people welcomed the allied forces. Even ministers who had been loyal to him, such as foreign minister Talleyrand and police chief Fouché, turned against him. Most of the marshals urged his abdication. On April 3, 1814 the Senate declared Napoleon deposed and on April 6 invited Louis XVI's brother to be king, with the title Louis XVIII. The allies took control of Empress Marie Louise and her son. Marmont refused to obey Napoleon's orders for further action, and on April 14 Napoleon abdicated. On April 20, he said farewell to his Imperial Guard and was then taken to Elba, a small Mediterranean island, accompanied by 1000 soldiers.

> *How convincing is Napoleon's explanation of his abdication in Source 1.41?*

SOURCE 1.41

A speech from 20 April 1814 by Napoleon Bonaparte, after his failed invasion of Russia and defeat by the allies

Soldiers of my Old Guard: I bid you farewell. For twenty years I have constantly accompanied you on the road to honour and glory. In these latter times, as in the days of our prosperity, you have invariably been models of courage and fidelity. With men such as you, our cause could not be lost; but the war would have been interminable; it would have been civil war, and that would have entailed deeper misfortunes on France.

I have sacrificed all of my interests to those of the country.

I go, but you, my friends, will continue to serve France. Her happiness was my only thought. It will still be the object of my wishes. Do not regret my fate; if I have consented to survive, it is to serve your glory. I intend to write the history of the great achievements we have performed together. Adieu, my friends. Would I could press you all to my heart.

What led to the abdication of 1814?

In some ways, Napoleon's weaknesses and mistakes led to his abdication. However, the abdication was also due to the strengths of Napoleon's enemies.
- The major defeat at Leipzig was very important.
- Napoleon refused to negotiate to try to keep his throne because he continued to believe that he would always win.
- He could not persuade the generals and his own people to make a last stand in defending Paris.

- His forces had lost huge numbers of experienced soldiers. Many of the conscripts were inexperienced youths – the so-called "Marie Louises," summoned to the forces by the Empress Marie Louise when she was regent.
- The military power of the allies backed by British subsidies and sea power were too powerful by 1814.
- The allies decided not to negotiate and were determined to force Napoleon from power.
- The allies had a numerical advantage. Also, they had gained an understanding of Napoleonic tactics after fighting for so long.
- They did not let themselves be isolated. The Treaty of Chaumont was signed on March 19, 1814. Britain, Russia, Prussia, and Austria agreed to maintain the struggle against Napoleon and to work together for 20 years to maintain peace after his final defeat.

ACTIVITY

Below are five factors that affected Napoleon's downfall. Award each factor a grade out of 6; the higher the grade, the greater its importance. Explain why you have given each point its grade.
- The strengths of Britain, Russia, and their allies
- The Peninsular War
- The Russian campaign
- Domestic and economic problems in France
- Nationalism in European countries

▶ SUMMARY DIAGRAM

The rise and fall of Napoleon

What caused the rise and fall of Napoleon Bonaparte?

Rise	Fall
Military reputation in Italy	Long-term failure in Spain and Portugal
Political connections	Strains on Empire of taxation and conscription
Self-publicizing achievements	Long-term British hostility
Weaknesses of Directory	Losses in Russia 1812
Conspiracy of Directors to change Constitution	Coalition of European powers against him
	Victories of allies in Germany in 1813
	Failure to come to terms with allies
	Invasion of France
	Loss of domestic support

CHAPTER SUMMARY

The revolution which broke out in France in 1789 was a result of long-term issues in the French monarchy and French society. The nobility and higher clergy were exempt from most taxes and enjoyed a privileged position when it came to gaining positions of power and responsibility. The bulk of the population were tenant farmers who had to pay a range of feudal payments to noble landlords, while the nobles and churchmen enjoyed tax privileges. The middle classes, growing in wealth and confidence, saw their progress blocked by privileged aristocrats and resented the unequal taxation. Inspired by the ideas of the Enlightenment, they saw little chance of the political reforms they were reading about. The monarchy suffered from severe financial problems, brought on by war, which brought it to the verge of bankruptcy. From 1787, there were bad harvests and high prices. There were increasing demands for reforms. Louis XVI agreed to summon a meeting of the Estates General. As a result of this, divisions became even wider. The Estates General became the National Assembly. The royal government's authority was weakened by unrest in Paris and in the countryside.

Hopes for change were dashed by profound disagreements over voting procedures. Louis tried putting restraints on the Assembly and appeared to threaten to use force. This led to widespread panic. Crowds seeking weapons stormed the Bastille fortress in Paris in the summer of 1789, unrest spread through the French countryside, and, in a wave of enthusiasm for change, the Assembly promised to end feudalism. In October, hungry crowds forced the royal family and the Assembly to move from Versailles to Paris, and the process of drawing up a new constitution was begun. Rapid changes were made, such as ending aristocratic titles, reorganizing local government, and bringing the Church under civil control.

During this time, new political ideas and discussions emerged as various political clubs and groups formed. These clubs, including the Jacobins and Girondins, played a crucial role in shaping political discourse and policy. Some of these were radical enough to demand an end to the monarchy. There were threats of foreign intervention and counter-revolution in France. This came in 1792 after the new constitution of 1791 failed to work and the king rashly encouraged war against Austria and Prussia. In September, a republic was declared. The king was executed in January 1793.

Both internal civil war and external war led to a period of revolutionary terror in 1793–94 until there was a reaction against radical change and the introduction of a more conservative constitution. The regime known as the Directory depended on military success, and the rising general Napoleon Bonaparte became a famous figure. In 1799, discontented politicians plotted a coup and enlisted Napoleon in the plot. Napoleon ruled France as Consul, then Consul for Life, then Emperor in 1804. As Consul, Napoleon oversaw some very important changes to France in law, education, government, finance, and religion. The decision to proclaim himself Emperor gave his regime more stability and a sense of permanence. However, Napoleon's power really relied on military successes and prestige. Wars were fought with enormous success in 1805–07. By then, Napoleon dominated Europe. However, failures in Spain and then a disastrous expedition to Russia in 1812 saw the regime start to unravel. Though Napoleon raised very large armies to replace the half a million men lost in Russia, he could not achieve victory on a large scale again. He was forced to abdicate in 1814.

REFRESHER QUESTIONS

1. What were the financial problems facing the French monarchy by 1789?
2. What economic hardships faced the people of France in 1788?
3. What was the Tennis Court Oath?
4. How did Louis XVI mishandle the Estates General in 1789?
5. What happened in the Terror?
6. Why did the Directory fall?
7. How did the reforms of the Consulate change France?
8. Why did Napoleon decide to become Emperor?
9. Why was Napoleon less successful in battle after 1807?
10. What led to Napoleon's abdication in 1814?

Study skills

Source questions

Understanding and interpreting sources

Assessment questions frequently test your understanding and interpretation of sources. Sources can be either written or visual. It is vital that you take time reading each question and studying all the sources carefully.

Comparing sources

Questions on comparing sources will ask you to make a judgement about how far two sources agree and disagree regarding evidence about, or attitudes towards, a historical person, event or issue. You will need to identify points of similarity and difference by analysing the sources and provide evidence from the sources to back this up – for example, "Sources A and B agree that the king approved of Calonne's plan for the economy, as in source A it says, 'The king talked in highest praise, and in Source B it is noted that the king 'approved of his plans.'" You will then need to explain why the sources are similar or different, using your own contextual knowledge.

- First, read the question carefully. Identify the subject of the question – who or what is the question asking you to consider? Does the question want you to consider *attitudes towards*, *evidence about*, or *responses to* events?
- Be careful to compare the correct sources for this question. Tip: write the two source letters down clearly at the start of your plan, and double-check them with the question before you start writing your response.
- Then, read each source carefully. Take notice of the overall message of the source to understand the argument or point of view of the author. This means that the source should be viewed as a whole rather than divided into individual sentences which, taken alone, might convey different ideas from that of the whole source.
- Next, consider the provenance. This means the nature (what type of source it is), origin (who wrote or produced the source), and purpose of each source. This will help you suggest reasons for similarities and differences. You will need to use your contextual knowledge to make this judgement.
- Write down notes as you read the sources.

Writing your response

- Plan out your answer. Identify at least two points of similarity and difference and the evidence to support each one, in brief, on your plan. This will make writing your response more straightforward.
- You do not need to provide a summary of the sources or a summary of the historical context.
- Do not write out large sections of the source in your response. This will take up too much of your time. Select the most important parts of the source, and write them out clearly. Do not use an ellipsis to evidence a whole sentence, for example, 'How ... assembly' as this does not identify the specific evidence needed. A sufficient selection from the source might need to be only three or four words long. Be precise and concise.
- Structure your response. Start with the similarities and follow with the differences.
- You will then need to develop your comparison. Are there more differences than similarities or more similarities than differences? Why? What explains this? Your response should consider the nature, origin, and purpose of both sources and relevant contextual knowledge of events to explain why the points of similarity and difference exist.

> **ACTIVITY**
> Read the sources and the question that follows carefully.

SOURCE A

Turgot, the finance minister, memorandum to the king, August 1774

There must be no increase in taxation because of the poor condition of the people.

There must be no more loans because each loan reduced royal revenue because of the interest payments.

There is only one way, and it is to make our expenses lower than our debts, low enough for us to save money to pay off old debts. Without this, the first cannon shot (if we were to go to war) would force the state into bankruptcy and dangerously weaken the Crown.

SOURCE B

A French nobleman, who was a member of the Assembly of Notables, writing in his memoirs in 1797

The most striking of the country's troubles was the chaos in the finances, the result of years of extravagance made worse by the expense of the American War of Independence, which had cost the state over 1200 million livres.

Calonne had a bold and wide-ranging plan, which the king promised to support. This would have changed the whole system of financial administration. The worst problems were the unfair distribution of taxation, the cost of collecting taxes, and the abuse of privilege by the richest section of taxpayers.

SOURCE C

A French nobleman objects in the debate in the Assembly of Notables, 1787

The King does not have the authority to bring in a new tax payable by all. Only the Estates General could give the necessary consent for such a tax.

A permanent tax should not be payable by everyone. Farmers have the resources of the crafts, labor, and trade, which noblemen and clergymen do not have. It would not be fair that while the nobleman fights and the priest celebrates divine services, they should not have the privilege of not paying a permanent tax.

SOURCE D

An English traveller in France records the views expressed by guests at a dinner party he attended in 1787, written in 1792

There was a great confusion in the finances, with a deficit that was difficult to provide for without calling an Estates General. There were no talented ministers to provide any solution to the financial crisis.

There was a king on the throne without the resources of mind that could govern in such a moment.

The court was depraved and thought only of pleasure.

A great unrest existed among all ranks of men, eager for change.

A strong current of liberty had increased since the American Revolution.

Read sources B and D.

Compare these two sources as evidence about the problems of the French monarchy. [15 marks]

ACTIVITY

Read sources B and D again. Both can be used as evidence regarding the problems of the French monarchy but they have similarities and differences between them. Try to find two similarities and two differences.

Difference explained	Support from the text

Similarity explained	Support from the text

It is a good idea to break down all the problems which are present in Source B before starting your answer:
- chaos in finance
- extravagance
- cost of American war
- unfair distribution of taxation
- cost of collecting taxes
- abuse of privilege.

Then see if Source D contains any of the points. Points mentioned in one source but not in the other are not considered a difference. You should concentrate on points that are mentioned in both sources.

Immediately, there is agreement about finance – not "chaos" but "great confusion," which is very similar. Therefore, both agree that there were big financial problems, and the evidence is in the wording "chaos" and "great confusion."

So far so good, but the next direct point of comparison does not come until the end, as the American war is also seen as a problem – though for a different reason. However, for both this is an issue, so both sources agree. There is possibly a third general agreement that the privileged classes are a problem, but that is a bit less obvious. In Source B, they are abusing privilege, and in Source D the court is depraved – for this, you have to understand that the courtiers were privileged.

When it comes to differences, neither source is saying that there were no problems, but Source D goes beyond finance. The most direct difference is that Source D has no time for any of the ministers and says that "there were no talented ministers," but Source B is less critical and praises Calonne's "bold and wide-ranging plan." Of course, you have to know that Calonne was a minister. Source D mentions the need to call the Estates General, which Source B does not, as this refers to 1786, when this was not yet the issue; that was a year later, when the writer of Source D was in Paris. Source D refers to the demands for liberty and the great unrest, which Source B does not, perhaps because a French courtier was not mixing with the same sort of people that an English traveller was.

Often, evidence only partly corresponds, and it is important to look at similarities and differences.

Considering how far sources support a view

These questions are looking for a considered judgment about the extent to which *all* the sources support and/or challenge a particular view which is stated in the question. You will need to judge "how far" they do so. Some sources might be *nuanced* and both support and challenge. You must make careful use of all of the sources and evaluate them to come to a judgment about which side of the argument is stronger – do the sources mostly support or challenge the view in the question?

Make sure you read the question very carefully before you start to plan your response.

Writing your response

A typical question will take the form of a statement, and a question to ask how far the sources agree or support the view. For example:

Read all of the sources. "The financial crisis was the most important issue facing France in 1789." How far do these sources support this view? [25 marks]

In this type of question, you need to consider all four of the sources provided. You will have already looked at two of these in depth when looking at the question on page 66.

- Create a brief plan listing sources A–D. Make brief notes as you analyze them. How does the source connect with the view given in the question? Does it agree or disagree? Where is the evidence in the source? Which sources strongly support or challenge the view and which are more restrained?
- In some cases, the source will be *nuanced*. This means that the source could be used to both support and challenge the view in the question. This could be implicit or explicit in the text or image, and you may need to use your contextual knowledge to recognize the nuance in the source. This might come from your knowledge of key individuals or important events which may have affected the reason for the view in the source.
- You will need to consider how useful the evidence contained within the sources is to your answer with relation to the view stated in the question. This involves thinking carefully about who wrote it, why it was written, and what type of source material it is. For example, a source could be an extract from a diplomatic letter written to a foreign power by their ambassador. If so, what might make this a useful and reliable source of information, and what might make it less useful? Was it written at the same time as key events took place, or afterwards? Could this affect how objectively the information in the source is being phrased? Why would this affect its usefulness? Why might official documents be different from private letters? Make sure you include comments on the specific source, not just generic comments on the type of source it is.
- You may be asked to consider a visual source such as a cartoon or a poster. It is important to be able to see its meaning in relation to the issue in the question and consider its nature, origin, and purpose together with contextual knowledge. You will need to consider why it was produced and by whom. Consider the image and what is emphasized – what is the focal point of the image? How is the subject portrayed? Is the portrayal sympathetic or satirical? Are there any associations to the images through clothing, emblems, flags, or equipment (religious, military, or social)?
- You will also need to use your knowledge of events to judge whether the source is stronger or weaker evidence. Does it agree factually with the other sources? Does that match your own knowledge? What important details do you know about the context of events which inform your opinion about whether the source is likely to agree or disagree with a particular view?

The activity below will help you practice identifying key points from sources and evidencing this with information from the source.

ACTIVITY

Look in detail at the question at the top of this page, and identify its focus. Then, look at sources A, B, C and D. Make a copy of the table below. You will see that one part has been done for you. Now fill the rest in for sources B–D.

Source	What is this source saying about the key issue?	What evidence from the source shows this?
A	Indicates serious financial problems and bad conditions. Does not say problems will cause a revolution but says they are serious and would be made worse by war. Real threat to the Crown because of the financial situation.	"poor condition of the people" danger of "bankruptcy" "dangerously weaken the Crown"
B		
C		
D		

On the basis of what each source shows about the importance of finance, group the sources. Which sources say that finance is the key issue, and which suggest that it is not just finance but other issues? Is there a source which is *nuanced* and supports and challenges the view in the question?

Essay questions

Understanding the task and planning an answer

When preparing and writing essays, it is important to understand from the outset what the essay question is asking you to do.

How to plan and write your response to a causal essay question

In essay questions that ask you to explain the *causes of an event*, you will need to show your understanding of the reasons why something happened or why someone acted in the way they did. You should focus on the key issue of causation, analyzing a range of factors to show how they are connected, and reach a supported conclusion about why something happened.
- These questions will focus on *causation*. This means that you will need to identify a range of causes.
- You need to show detailed knowledge and understanding of the reasons why a specific event occurred or why someone adopted a particular course of action.
- This will be the combined effect of several factors, both long- and short-term.
- You will need to show how these factors are connected.
- Be analytical – identify causes, and assess them against each other. Do not write a narrative of events.
- Produce a reasoned conclusion for your explanation.

How to plan and write your response to an analytical essay question

Analytical essay questions require the consideration of a historical issue and its significance, weighing the relative importance of factors or assessing the failure or success of policies or institutions. You will need to make a judgement to specifically answer the question "to what extent" or "how far."
- You need to address the question rather than the topic – ensure you identify the main focus of the question.
- Structure your answer, maintaining a balanced approach to each factor.
- Ensure that your arguments are appropriately supported with detailed contextual knowledge.
- You will then need to consider the relative importance of these different factors and come to a judgment.

Planning an answer

Once you have understood the demands of the question, the next step is planning your answer. The plan should outline your line of argument. This means that you will need to think about what you are going to argue before you start writing. This should help you maintain a consistent line of argument throughout your answer. It also means that your plan will be a list of reasons about the issue or issues in the question, which will ensure an analytical response. Simply having a list of dates would encourage you to write a narrative or descriptive answer – instead, you will need to be analytical. However, you will need to use your contextual knowledge to evidence your arguments.

"The most important reason for the French Revolution (to 1789) was the spread of the ideas of the Enlightenment." How far do you agree? [20 marks]

Consider the question above. Your plan should be structured around issues such as these:
- Why was the Enlightenment important?
- What other reasons are there for the French Revolution (to 1789)?
- Why are these reasons important?
- Are they more or less important than the Enlightenment?
- What is your overall view, having looked at the key factor and the other causes?

A plan for this essay might take the following form:

1. The Enlightenment. What key ideas influenced the revolution, e.g., Rousseau and the Social Contract; Voltaire and scepticism about religion? Montesquieu and the idea of a balance of power. Make the view that it was the most important factor clear by linking these ideas to events, e.g., "the Declaration of the Rights of Man"; the calls for a National Assembly to reflect the sovereignty of the nation; the Tennis Court Oath.

2. Other factors: privilege and financial problems which led to the calling of the Estates General. Possible links to Enlightenment ideas.

3. The desire of the middle classes for greater opportunity – Sieyès. More informed and politically aware urban population again linked to spread of ideas.

4. Economic grievances: bad harvests, urban unemployment, peasant discontent – less linked to ideas.

5. Political mistakes of king and government in handling 1789 crisis. Perhaps disappointed those who were led by study of new ideas to expect change.

6. Conclusion: This will weigh up the relative importance of Enlightenment ideas and bring together interim conclusions in previous paragraphs. Perhaps arguing that, though few might have read the Enlightenment philosophers, the key ideas were very powerful among the educated middle class of the Third Estates in the Estates General, and other grievances were linked to them OR argue that the ideas had been common for years before the revolution, but when bad harvests and a financial and political crisis led the king to call the Estates General, it brought a revolution that included some of the ideas.

Planning answers to these questions will help you put together a structured answer and avoid the common mistake of listing reasons with each paragraph essentially saying "Another reason for the French Revolution was …"

Planning an answer will help you focus on the actual question and not simply write about the topic. Under the pressure of time in an assessment, it is easy to forget the importance of planning and just to start writing; this will usually result in an essay that does not have a clear line of argument, or changes its line of argument halfway through, making it less convincing.

2 Liberalism and nationalism in Germany, 1815–71

> **Introduction**
>
> Before 1789, 'Germany' was not a country but a collection of 360 independent states. After 1815, this had reduced to 39 separate states but the chance of there being a unified Germany seemed remote. Austria dominated central Europe and surrounding powers were unlikely to accept a new Germany. Attempts at unity in 1848 had failed. However, by 1871 the whole situation had changed with the creation of a German Empire. This had been achieved by Prussian military and economic growth and by the adept diplomacy of its leading statesman, Otto von Bismarck. This chapter deals with the causes and consequences of the revolutions of 1848 and the events and developments that led to the creation of the German Empire in 1871, through the following questions:
>
> ▶ What were the causes of the revolutions of 1848–49?
> ▶ What happened during the 1848–49 revolutions and what were their consequences?
> ▶ Why was Bismarck appointed Minister President and what were his aims in the period up to 1866?
> ▶ How and why was the unification of Germany achieved by 1871?

▶ KEY DATES

1806	Napoleon dissolves Holy Roman Empire
1813	War of Liberation
1815	Treaty of Vienna German Confederation formed
1819	Carlsbad Decrees
1832	Hambach Festival
1834	*Zollverein* formed
1848–49	Revolutions in Germany
1850	Humiliation of Olmütz
1862	Bismarck becomes Minister President of Prussia
1863	Alvensleben Convention
1864	War between Denmark, Austria, and Prussia
1865	Convention of Gastein
1866	Austro-Prussian War
1867	North German Confederat Luxembourg Crisis
1869	Hohenzollern Candidature
1870	Franco-Prussian War
1871	Creation of the German Empire

1 What were the causes of the revolutions of 1848?

In 1848 and 1849, nearly all of Europe, except for Russia and Britain, experienced major revolutions. Key elements included middle-class discontent about the lack of effective parliaments. In German-speaking regions, there were also hopes for a new German nation which would bring together those who shared the German language and culture. The revolutions were also driven by economic discontent and popular unrest.

Germany by 1815

Before 1789, Germany was not a unified country but a collection of independent states. German was spoken in many areas of central Europe, but aside from language, there was little to bring these different states together. And even then, there were distinct regional variations. There were 360 different states, some large and some small. There were also some self-governing free cities run by elected councils. These councils were dominated by richer citizens, and ordinary people had little participation in government. None of the states was a republic. Apart from some smaller areas ruled by leading churchmen, princes ruled most larger states. There was an overall authority over most of what became Germany called the Holy Roman Empire. This was traditionally headed by the Emperor of Austria, who also ruled considerable non-German-speaking territories – for example, Hungary, the modern-day areas of the Czech Republic and Slovakia, and part of modern-day Poland. The larger states, apart from Austria, were Saxony, Prussia, and Bavaria. Their traditions were very different. Prussia, as was the case with much of northern Germany, was Protestant. Bavaria, as with much of southern and parts of eastern Germany, was Catholic. Some states had developed armies and governmental organizations, and strong economies; others were little more than cities or small rural areas with miniature administrations.

The coming of the French Revolution and the rise of Napoleon Bonaparte as ruler of France transformed this region of Europe. Prussia and Austria, the largest military states, were unable to prevent conquest by France. This conquest began during the Revolutionary Wars (1792–1802) and was continued by the wars waged by Napoleon, who became Emperor of France in 1804. His armies dominated central Europe, and he was able to abolish the Holy Roman Empire in 1806. He ruled some German states directly and some by setting up puppet rulers. This unified Germany to a considerable extent and led to some modernization. Under Napoleon, German states adopted modern laws and government systems as had been introduced by the revolution in France. Prussia had to modernize after its defeat by Napoleon in 1806. Though it remained independent, it was dominated by France until 1812. Napoleon did not want to overthrow an established monarchy such as Prussia and did not have the resources to occupy it in the same way that he did the smaller states of western Germany. Austria was defeated by France in 1805 and again in 1809 and lost its dominance over Germany.

> **KEY TERM**
>
> **Holy Roman Empire** This is the name given to the lands of central Europe which owed allegiance to an overall emperor. It was a medieval union of princes and cities which had its origins in the coronation of Charlemagne in 800. In practice, the lands were independent, with little central government. Since the fifteenth century, the Holy Roman Emperor had been the ruler of Austria, the Habsburg royal family. The Empire was formally dissolved by Napoleon Bonaparte in 1806.

Figure 2.1 Under Napoleon, most German states were part of the Confederation of the Rhine

However, Napoleon's ambition caused his own downfall. He was unable to defeat Britain, he could not control Spain, and he unwisely invaded Russia in 1812. In this campaign, he endured considerable losses and in a series of battles in 1813–14 was driven out of central Europe and by the Coalition forces of the United Kingdom, Austria, Prussia, Russia, Spain, Sweden, Portugal, and various German and Italian states. He was forced to abdicate in 1814.

> **KEY DEBATE**
>
> ### HOW IMPORTANT WAS NAPOLEON IN CREATING A UNITED GERMANY?
>
> Napoleon prided himself on bringing unity to Germany, which he imposed in the Confederation of the Rhine. Supporters of this view would point out that the ending of the old Holy Roman Empire established the idea of a unified Germany. After Napoleon's fall, there was no return to the old Germany, and the Congress of Vienna had a profound impact on Germany, which would eventually lead to union. The hostility towards Napoleon encouraged German national feeling, and the Napoleonic era saw an upsurge of nationalist ideas.
>
> Some historians would challenge this view. The new Germany of 1815 was very divided. Austria dominated, but the Habsburgs were not exclusively German rulers and had lands in the East and Italy. Metternich, the German chancellor, distrusted nationalism and did his best to suppress it. The German middle class under Napoleon was too small to support nationalism, and it was not until later, with economic and social change, that nationalism really grew. These historians believe it is a mistake to attribute too much influence to the Napoleonic era and its consequences.

The Congress of Vienna and the formation of the Confederation

The victorious nations – Austria, Russia, Prussia, and Britain – were anxious not to see further influence of revolutionary ideas and to keep France contained. This meant ensuring that Germany was more stable and less open to attack. The peace conference known as the Congress of Vienna redrew the map of Europe. It was attended by the rulers of Austria, Prussia, and Russia. Its main diplomats were Metternich (the Austrian foreign minister), Castlereagh (Britain's foreign secretary) and Talleyrand (the French foreign minister). The delegates first met in September 1814, five months after Napoleon's abdication. The Congress finished in June 1815, shortly before the final defeat of Napoleon. It aimed to prevent further revolution in Europe and to ensure that another Napoleonic figure could not invade Europe.

The decisions of the Congress led to the power of monarchs in the German states being restored and the strengthening of Germany as a whole, by having only 39 states in place of the 360 which existed in 1789. Austria, Prussia, Saxony, Bavaria, and Württemberg were the largest. There were also smaller states and four independent cities. Austria had previously dominated leadership of the Holy Roman Empire. It continued to dominate because it was the leading military power and it covered such a large area, including lands in eastern Europe and northern Italy.

The power of Prussia was increased by giving it lands on the Rhine, the Rhineland, Westphalia, and the Ruhr region to act as a barrier to France. The Rhineland areas turned out to be rich in coal and ore and were later extremely important for industrial development. Three-fifths of Saxony also went to Prussia, as did some land from the former state of Poland.

The Congress decided that all states were loosely associated through the formation of the Confederation, or "*Bund*". This had no overall government as such, but there were meetings of all the German states at an assembly (*Diet*) at Frankfurt am Main. In order for the monarchs to be able to enjoy their new power in peace, a system of regular meetings was set up – the Congress system – though this was not long-lasting and had broken down by 1822.

> **KEY TERM**
>
> *Diet* The name given to the assemblies of parliaments of the German states.

The strengths and weaknesses of the Confederation

By replacing the very divided Germany that existed in 1789 with stronger and larger states in a confederation, the Congress reduced the chance of future foreign invasions such as those that had occurred under Napoleon. There was also opportunity for greater economic cooperation (see page 85). The 39 states were able to maintain their own identity and were not placed under the direct rule of Austria. Though there was little democracy, there were state constitutions, and there was an overall assembly for the whole Confederation.

However, there were many weaknesses which led to problems later on:
- The Confederation did not give the German states overall unity as a distinct nation, as the union was only a loose one. This disappointed German nationalists. Moreover, Austria had large areas of land which were outside the Confederation.
- The Confederation may have reduced the chance of foreign invasion, but any future threats would be reliant on the military power of the larger states.
- The dominance of Austria meant that its leaders, especially Metternich, were able to impose controls on freedom of political expression in all the German states. This built up resentment, as Metternich's system of control was unpopular, and finally led to revolution in 1848.

Figure 2.2 Germany in 1815

> ## PRINCE CLEMENS VON METTERNICH
>
> Prince Clemens von Metternich (1773–1859) was the son of a minor noble in the Rhineland. Like his father, he became a diplomat, rising to be the Austrian ambassador to Napoleon's France in 1806. He became Foreign Minister in 1809 in the wake of Austria's defeat by Napoleon. He favoured keeping the peace with France but did join the British-led coalition against Napoleon in 1813 when negotiations for a general peace failed. He worked to keep the coalition together and played a leading role in the Vienna negotiations after the war, which resulted in Austria acquiring northern Italy and gaining significant influence over Germany. He took a leading role in European diplomacy after 1815 and supported harsh measures to suppress unrest in both Austria and other parts of Europe, opposing new ideas. He did not foresee the revolutions in Austria which forced him from power in 1848, and he lived in exile in Britain until his death in 1859.
>
>

ACTIVITY

Read the section starting on page 73, and compare and contrast Germany in 1789 and Germany in 1815. List what changed and what remained the same.

The impact of Metternich's system on the states of Germany

The Holy Roman Empire had been dominated by Austria. The leadership of Austria continued in the Confederation after 1815, but the control Austria imposed on other German states was much greater. The major revolutions which broke out in the states of Germany in 1848–49 were partly caused by a desire to overthrow the restrictions on German political and intellectual life, imposed by Austria and its chancellor or chief minister, Prince Clemens von Metternich.

In what became known as the "Metternich system," Metternich aimed to suppress liberalism and nationalism, which he saw as threats to Austria and European monarchies. Nationalist ideas were problematic for Austria, with its large multinational empire dominating Germany. Liberalism wanted to give more people a voice in government, opposing the idea that monarchs ruled by divine right and were accountable only to God.

The states of the *Bund* had mostly adopted constitutions and had elected *Diets*, but the power of these assemblies was very limited, and only in the southern German state of Baden was there a very liberal constitution. It was easy for Metternich to ensure that the assemblies could not challenge the power of the rulers, and he later forced censorship and political repression on them.

As Austria was the leading military power and the largest state in the Confederation, Metternich had considerable influence over its members. The rulers of Austria, Russia, and Prussia had agreed, in what came to be known as the Holy Alliance, to resist any change in Europe and maintain the dominance of the monarchs, the ruling aristocracy, and the Church. There was to be no spread of nationalism and no introduction of parliaments, voting, or free discussion. The subjects were to obey and respect their traditional masters.

However, Metternich faced forces in Germany which had been influenced by the new ideas from the French Revolution of liberty and equality. He also faced a new interest in a different kind of nationalism – of a single German state which would take in German speakers and reflect German ideas and culture. Some of these nationalist ideas went beyond just wanting all German speakers to be together in one state. Many thought that Germans had traits that marked them out from other peoples (see Source 2.1). Metternich had little sympathy for this sort of emotional nationalism. He saw himself as part of an international culture dominated by educated and enlightened nobles who knew best what their rulers and their subjects needed. He looked back to the ordered world of the eighteenth century. Many, especially younger people in the German states, wanted to look forward to a new world of greater national unity and independence.

> In Source 2.1, identify the key elements of German nationalism according to the author. Select specific phrases to support your ideas.

SOURCE 2.1

An extract from a poem, 'The German fatherland' by Ernst Moritz Arndt, written in 1806

Where is the German's fatherland?
Then name, oh, name the mighty land!
Wherever is heard the German tongue,
And German hymns to God are sung!
This, German, is thy fatherland.

This is the German's fatherland,
Where faith is in the plighted hand,
Where truth lives in each eye of blue,
And every heart is staunch and true.
This is the land, the honest land,
The honest German's fatherland.

This is the land, the one true land,
O God, to aid be thou at hand!
And fire each heart, and nerve each arm,
To shield our German homes from harm,
To shield the land, the one true land,
One Deutschland and one fatherland.

> What was the key element in German nationalism according to the author of Source 2.2?

SOURCE 2.2

An extract from a book, *Addresses to the German Nation*, written in 1807 by German philosopher Johann Gottlieb Fichte

Those who speak the same language are joined to each other by a multitude of invisible bonds by nature herself; they understand each other and have the power of continuing to make themselves understood more and more clearly; they belong together and are by nature one and an inseparable whole. It is not because men dwell between certain mountains and rivers that they are a people, but, on the contrary, men dwell together – and, if their luck has so arranged it, are protected by rivers and mountains – because they were a people already by a law of nature which is much higher.

Thus was the German nation placed – sufficiently united within itself by a common language and a common way of thinking, and sharply severed from the other peoples – in the middle of Europe.

> **ACTIVITY**
>
> Write a brief explanation of the following terms:
> - nationalism
> - liberalism.

The Carlsbad Decrees

Metternich resorted to repression to maintain his "system." Abroad, he supported joint action by the great European powers – Russia, Britain, Austria, and France – against any change to the Vienna settlement. Within Germany, there were harsh laws against free expression. In 1819, the pro-monarchist playwright Kotzebue was assassinated by a student. Metternich called representatives of the larger German states together at Carlsbad and pushed through repressive decrees. These laws increased control over education and censorship.

Special inspectors were placed in universities to ensure that liberal and national activity was suppressed and a watch kept on lecturers and students. Teachers and professors were to be removed if they were seen to be promoting liberal or national ideas. Student nationalist groups were made illegal. Students seen as disruptive were to be expelled and forbidden from joining other universities.

A press law forbade any journal or newspaper to be published without government approval. Editors who permitted "subversive writing" would be banned from publishing any material for five years. A special investigating committee would look into suspected plots or conspiracies intended to challenge authority. In 1820, the *Bund* agreed to limit the topics that elected assemblies in individual states could discuss and also to confirm that armed force might be used in the case of individual states supporting revolution.

The impact of the Decrees

The censorship in Germany was widespread and extended from newspapers and pamphlets to works of history and literature. Schiller's famous play *William Tell*, written in 1804, was censored after 1819 because it showed the Swiss hero defying Austrian authority. Even Baden, which had a liberal constitution, dared not allow freedom of expression. The universities removed radical professors and students. The king of Prussia had wanted to be more liberal but was forced by Austrian pressure and his fellow princes to enforce the repressive laws. Police opened mail, searched homes, and used spies and informers.

> What can we learn from Source 2.3 about Metternich's control of Germany?

SOURCE 2.3

Press Law of the Carlsbad Decrees, 1819

Publications that appear in the form of daily papers or as [periodical] issues, may not be conveyed to print in any German Confederal State without the foreknowledge and prior approval of the state authorities. If publications give any Confederal state cause for legal complaint, this complaint should be settled against the author or publisher of the publication.

All published writings appearing in Germany must be furnished with the name of the publisher and, insofar as they belong to the class of newspapers or periodicals, also with the name of the editor. Published writings for which this rule is not observed may not be circulated in any Confederal state and must, if such takes place in a secret fashion, be confiscated immediately upon their appearance, and the disseminators of the same must receive an appropriate fine or prison sentence.

> What can we learn from Source 2.4 about why Metternich wanted to impose censorship and political control on Germany?

SOURCE 2.4

Clemens von Metternich, *Political Confession of Faith***, 1820**

Union between the monarchs is the basis of the policy which must now be followed to save society from total ruin ...

The first principle to be followed by the monarchs, united as they are by the coincidence of their desires and opinions, should be that of maintaining the stability of political institutions against the disorganized excitement which has taken possession of men's minds ...

Let [the Governments] in these troubled times be more than usually cautious in attempting reform and change, to the end that good itself may not turn against them – which is the case whenever a Government measure seems to be inspired by fear.

Let them be just, but strong; kind, but strict.

Let them maintain religious principles in all their purity, and not allow the faith to be attacked and morality interpreted according to the social contract or the visions of foolish sectarians.

Let them suppress Secret Societies, that disease of society.

The impact of Metternich's system

Metternich attempted to hold back change by using the influence of the most powerful of the members of the *Bund* to force the German states to apply censorship and police action against nationalists and liberals. However, this proved futile in the end because his system did not offer anything very positive to the people of Germany.
- The memories of Napoleonic rule remained strong and offered an alternative of a more unified and more liberal Germany.
- Early-nineteenth-century censorship could not stop the spread of ideas, even if they had to be read cautiously and secretly.
- The development of the German economy in the period to 1848 brought about change that the Metternich system could not easily control. Railways and factories brought greater urban growth and a changing workforce which undermined the traditional world of the eighteenth century that Metternich wished to maintain.
- The development of German culture in this period – painting, poetry, literature, and especially music – that censorship did not control had the unforeseen result of encouraging a sense of German identity and nationalism.
- Austria was associated through Metternich with repression, and hostility to national hopes and aspirations. This undermined the *Bund* and ultimately led to the emergence of a Prussian-led Germany in 1871.

> ## ACTIVITY
>
> Reread the section on Metternich. Find material which justifies each of the following statements:
> - "Metternich was a responsible conservative who succeeded for a long period in bringing stability to Germany."
> - "Metternich imposed an outdated system on Germany which ignored its best interests and was doomed to fail."
>
> How justified do you think both of these statements are?

The influence of liberal ideas
The aims of the liberals

The French and American Revolutions had spread political ideas which opposed traditional royal authority. There was a wider belief that there were natural rights and that people should be citizens, who should have a voice in the way that countries were run, rather than being subjects bound to obey unelected rulers. These ideas were not necessarily democratic in a modern sense, as few liberals wished to extend full rights to those without property, women, or people of different ethnicities. Early-nineteenth-century liberals believed that there should be elected assemblies to which governments should be accountable, and that states should not be allowed to ignore the rights of their citizens. These rights included freedom of expression and opinion, freedom to trade, and freedom from arrest without charge and from punishment without a lawful trial. The desire for liberalism had been seen in revolutions in Spain and Italy in 1820, in France in 1830, and in the movement for parliamentary reform in Britain, which led to the reform of parliament in 1832. German liberals did not all have the same aims, but there were some unifying features:
- a belief in progress, and opposition to the power of rulers and traditionalist aristocrats and clerics
- a belief in representative parliaments which would represent the interests of the people
- a belief that there were natural rights for citizens against censorship, arbitrary imprisonment, and oppression by rulers
- a belief in freedom of individuals to prosper and be independent
- a belief in freedom of trade and ending restrictions on commerce.

> What does Source 2.5 show about Metternich's attitudes toward nationalism?

SOURCE 2.5

A letter from Metternich to the Emperor, 1841, which gives an unfavourable view of opposition in Germany

In all four countries, France, Germany, Italy, and Spain, the agitating classes are principally composed of wealthy men, trying to gain personal advantage for themselves. They are paid officials, men of letters [writers], lawyers, and those involved in education. Their aim is to improve their position in society.

The emergence of the middle class

In the half-century after 1815, the population of German-speaking Europe grew by 60 per cent, from 33 to 52 million. The fastest growth was in areas where there was technological and economic change. This change did not transform Germany into an industrial society, but manufacturing and internal trade did grow. The road network went from 15,000 km in 1820 to 53,000 km in 1850. Canals expanded, the first railway was opened in 1835, and by 1848 there were 2000 km of track. Steam power also grew. There were 400 steam engines in 1834 and 1200 in 1850. Populations grew rapidly in the cities, and this in turn encouraged more intensive arable farming, with a 40 per cent increase in cash crops from 1815 to 1850. The easing of traditional trade barriers within Germany meant greater trading and more wealth.

These changes led to a growing middle class. The country remained overwhelmingly rural, with 72 per cent of people working on the land even by 1848. However, there were significant developments in key areas. The professions – for example, lawyers, doctors, teachers, lecturers, surveyors – expanded rapidly in the late eighteenth and nineteenth centuries. There was growth in business activity and in manufacturers, traders, and shippers, as well as in the businesses associated with economic activity, such as bailiffs, farm managers, insurers, and bankers. There was also considerable growth in culture and education – the numbers involved in professional music, theatre, art, literature, and publishing grew. There were 16,000 students enrolled in higher education in Prussia in 1820, and this increased to 30,000 by the end of the 1830s and 100,000 by 1850.

There was also the development of the state bureaucracies. Though the nobles dominated the higher ranks, the administrations of the states were open to educated middle-class Germans.

The importance of this growth was that the ideas of liberalism and nationalism spread. The most receptive audience for ideas about political, social, and economic change were the middle-class urban dwellers with the education to absorb new thinking. They were also open to change because of discontents.

The German middle class was often frustrated at the lack of opportunity in states whose higher offices were dominated by the traditional nobility. They resented the control over freedom of speech. The worst combination was the existence of constitutions and *Diets* which allowed limited control by elected representatives over governments and their policies, and restricted discussion. The censorship imposed by Metternich was particularly unpopular with well-educated, middle-class Germans. The economic growth was not enough to provide sufficient jobs for graduates, and opportunities in state service were limited by noble privilege. Thus, there was growing discontent, especially by the 1840s.

Metternich failed to see how widespread discussion of change had become. Despite all his efforts, discussion of liberal ideas went on among students, in chambers of commerce, in state assemblies, and in debating societies. Many liberals were respectable businessmen, manufacturers, merchants, and craftsmen.

The extent of support for liberalism in Prussia

Liberal ideas could not be easily discussed in Prussia before 1848 because of the state's fear of revolution and the impact of repressive measures. Student groups were more nationalist than liberal, but their demands "honor, freedom, and fatherland" did include calls for a constitutional monarchy with an assembly. Liberal discussion groups did meet – for example, the 'Circle' movement of local informal discussions. These were potentially illegal

> **ACTIVITY**
>
> Reread the section above and list, in order of importance, the effects that the growth of the middle class had on Germany in 1815–1848.
>
> Compare your list with others in the class to see if you agree on the main consequences of this development.

and had to be careful and secret, though they did include some liberal army officers and prominent local figures. All sorts of associations such as *Gymnastic* and sports societies did discuss politics. However, all organisations were closely watched and controlled, Chambers of Commerce often discussed liberal economic ideas and went beyond their function to discuss politics but again had to be careful not to be prosecuted. The influence of liberal ideas was stronger in urban centres such as Berlin and particularly in the Rhine, where there was a liberal newspaper. In the Prussian heartland, the very strong military tradition and the powerful Prussian state restricted the growth of liberalism, and in rural areas there was much less interest in political change. The revolutions of 1848–49 were predominantly urban, and a desire for a greater Germany was not always linked to a desire for liberal political and economic change.

The growth of nationalist ideas

Before 1789, there was little support for a united Germany, and loyalties to individual states or regions were strong. German speakers were widely spread through central Europe. There were religious differences between north, south, and east Germany. Many educated Germans thought French was the language of civilization. There were many dialects and ethnic groups in the Holy Roman Empire and the Germanic world. What changed was the influence of the occupation of Germany by the French during the Revolutionary and Napoleonic period. This brought greater unity of law and administration to large areas of Germany. This in turn led to a period of reform and modernization in Prussia. There was resistance to French occupation which inspired later generations of nationalists. Student volunteers were formed into a resistance group by the Prussian officer **Adolf von Lützow**. They took the name *Frei Korps* and were also known as "the Black Troopers." With their black uniforms and death's head insignia, they acted as fighters in the struggle against the French in the so-called "War of Liberation" in 1813.

However, they were never numerically significant in the war against the French, and there was no mass nationalist rising. Many Germans fought as part of Napoleon's armies rather than against them, and the Battle of Leipzig was fought mainly by regular Prussian troops. The student soldiers, however, became an inspiration for nationalist student movements which arose after 1814.

Nationalism, in the sense of a belief in a united Germany, was not a mass movement, but there were strong intellectual influences on the educated middle class. German philosophers such as Herder, Fichte, and Hegel wrote about the unique character of the German *Volk*. Hegel was a great admirer of the Prussian state. Others argued for a new German state. These included the poet Ernst Arndt, who wrote of a "fatherland." The most enthusiastic support for these ideas came in students' unions (see page 82). Festivals were organized to celebrate important Germans – for example, at Wartburg in 1817, which promoted the sixteenth-century religious reformer Martin Luther as a German national hero. It was here that the ruler of Saxony had protected Luther from being arrested and tried for his challenge to the Catholic Church.

There was widespread interest in what was a golden age of German music, literature, and art. The greater the interest in German culture, the greater the desire for freer discussion and an end to the domination of Metternich. Though not all nationalists were liberals, there was a clear overlap.

National feeling was also increased by the development of a strong German culture in the arts. The arts had thrived in eighteenth-century Germany but as part of a wider European culture. However, literature and poetry in the first half of the nineteenth century showed the beauty of the German language, especially when set to music by composers such as Schubert and Schumann. German opera and symphonic music became world-renowned. Weber and Wagner explored Germanic legends and folklore. The development of Berlin showed the expertise of German architects, and the paintings of artists such as Caspar David Friedrich had a distinctly German theme of romantic forests, ruined chapels, and wintry landscapes. The Brothers Grimm explored folk tales and fairy stories.

> **KEY FIGURE**
>
> **Adolf von Lützow**
> (1782–1834) was a professional soldier from a military family. He fought against the French in 1806 and became an ardent opponent of Napoleon and a Prussian nationalist. He fought as a volunteer against the French in 1809 and was wounded. He was allowed to form a force of guerrilla fighters known as the *Frei Korps* or the Black Troopers. His troops were badly defeated in 1813 and disbanded in 1814. He continued to serve in the Prussian army.

> This painting in Source 2.6 has been seen as representing troubled times. How would you use knowledge of Germany in 1818 to support this view?

SOURCE 2.6

Wanderer above the Sea of Fog, 1818, by Caspar David Friedrich

The impact of the 1830 revolutions on German states

The July Revolution in Paris and the Polish Uprising against Russia in 1830 had the effect of stimulating desire for change in parts of Germany. Demonstrations and disturbances occurred in many places as people protested against economic conditions and political repression. In Brunswick, Saxony, Hanover, and the Electorate of Hesse, the ruling dynasties were compelled to make concessions on constitutions and civil rights. However, the 1830 Revolutions, though having an impact on Italy, France, Poland, Belgium, and Switzerland, had limited effects on Germany. In the key state of Prussia, actual resistance was limited but the news of the revolution stimulated discontent. As Metternich said, "When France sneezes, Europe catches a cold."

There was, however, the first major mass political demonstration in Germany. The Press and Fatherland Association organized a national rally to demand the creation of a democratic German nation-state. More than 20,000 people gathered at Hambach Castle on May 27, 1832. Many carried flags in black, red, and gold – the colours of the *Burschenschaft*, the name for the liberal students' associations, which started to be used as a symbol of German unity.

The events in Europe and parts of Germany could be seen as eventually leading to the wider revolutions of 1848–49, but in Germany the powers of the rulers were strong enough to suppress resistance.

Support for nationalist ideas in the universities

The most enthusiastic support for nationalist ideas came in students' unions called *Burschenschaften* after 1815. German universities had been changed by reforming professors, and there was a sense of scholarship having a duty to change and reform society, not just to impart knowledge. The initial impulse for a new idealistic nationalism came at the University of Jena in Thuringia. Students were part of a generation growing up in the liberation of Germany from French rule. It was seen as noble and heroic to sacrifice your life for freedom. Most of the students were from educated middle-class families. They rejected hopes from their elders for stability, and they pushed for change and the ideas of a new nation and for liberalism. "Honor, freedom, and fatherland" was one of their key mottoes. Older student fraternities had been very class-conscious, but the post-1815 groups were more open. Radical students, according to the Heidelburg Union of students, strove to "maintain and strengthen national custom and power, spiritual and physical justice, honor, and equality of rights among all members as long as they uphold learning, law, morality, and fatherland." The movement urged physical strength and athletic exercises but also included undercurrents of antisemitism and hostility to foreign influences.

> ### EXTENSION
>
> **Antisemitism in German nationalism**
>
> Emancipation of Jewish people was associated with the influence of the French Revolution. Demands by Jewish groups for full rights at the Congress of Vienna were resented by conservatives. In 1819, a large amount of rioting and attacks against Jews took place, often with the support of student groups. In August, the Jewish population of Würzburg was driven out, and violence spread through Bavaria and reached Rhineland cities and Bremen, Hamburg, and Lübeck. The Jewish writer Heinrich Heine in 1840 warned that German nationalism would eventually cause a massive disruption to Europe which would be greater than the French Revolution.

Student societies became subject to more control in the 1820s, which drove some of them to become secret societies. However, more students were inspired to action by the 1830 revolutions across Europe. Student radicals eagerly followed the call of the *Vaterlandsverein* (National Association), an organisation of adult activists, to Frankfurt in April 1833 and attempted to seize the capital of the *Bund* as a starting point for a universal uprising. Some 50 radical students, led by several adult intellectuals and artisans, stormed the police headquarters on the evening of April 3, 1833. The Frankfurt *Wachensturm* (storm of awakening) came to nothing. Nevertheless, it was the first armed threat in Germany against the Metternich system and an important precursor of the 1848 revolt. Student nationalism remained an important element in German life in the period up to 1848.

> Look at sources 2.7 and 2.8. Compare the attitudes in these sources about the condition of Germany.

SOURCE 2.7

A student, Arminius Riemann, at the Wartburg Festival of 1817 speaking bitterly of disappointed hopes after the defeat of Napoleon by German troops in 1813

Four long years have passed by since the Battle of Leipzig defeated Napoleon. The German people then built up lovely hopes. They have all been frustrated! Everything has turned out to be disappointing. Much that is great and splendid could have happened but has not taken place. Many fine and noble feelings have been treated with mockery and contempt. Only one prince has honoured his word [to grant a constitution], and in his free land we are celebrating the festival of the Battle.

SOURCE 2.8

A speech delivered during the Hambach Festival in 1832 by a lawyer, Philipp Siebenpfeiffer, who had helped to organize the event

Fatherland – freedom – yes! A free German fatherland – that is the meaning of today's festival. These are the words that have echoed like thunder throughout all the German territories, rattling the bones of all traitors to the German national issue, yet encouraging all true patriots. May Germany rise again from the debris under which time's force and the nobles' treachery have buried it.

And the day will dawn when Germans from the Alps and the North Sea, from the Rhine, the Danube, and the Elbe rivers, will embrace as brothers; when all the suffocating regulations and tolls, all the symbols of division, obstruction, and oppression will vanish. This is the spirit of today's festival, the spirit of the renaissance of our fatherland.

> What impression of the Frankfurt *Wachensturm* (storm of awakening) is given by Source 2.9?

SOURCE 2.9

Painting showing the Frankfurt *Wachensturm* of 1833

> **ACTIVITY**
>
> Many liberals were also supporters of German nationalism in this period. How similar were the views of nationalism and liberalism in German states up to 1848?

Reactions to the growth of nationalist ideas

Metternich equated national pride and nationalist feeling with opposition to his system. He therefore responded to the growth of nationalism following news of the 1830 Revolution in France with measures to restrict freedom of speech. This had the opposite effect from what Metternich had intended: instead of supressing nationalism, the Six and Ten Articles led to its increase.

The Six Articles and Ten Articles, 1832

Metternich put pressure on Prussia and the larger states to agree to the Six Articles, which applied to the whole Confederation from 1832. These limited the rights of the *Diets* or assemblies in constitutional states and reinforced the authority of the rulers. The Six Articles made the Confederation's laws dominant over individual state laws, ensuring federal law took precedence. This move further restricted individual states from passing liberal measures or limiting rulers' power. The Ten Articles of July 5, 1832, as well as reaffirming control of the press, prohibited unauthorized political organisations, meetings, appeals, and festivals.

> What does Source 2.10 show about the level of control imposed by Metternich in the 1830s?

SOURCE 2.10

From the Ten Articles

Art. 3. Extraordinary popular assemblies and popular festivals, namely those whose time and place were previously neither customary nor permitted, may not take place, no matter under what name and to what purpose, in any Confederal state without prior approval of the competent authority. Those who give occasion to such assemblies or festivals by appointment or announcement are subject to an appropriate punishment. Even at permitted popular assemblies and popular festivals, it should not be tolerated that public speeches with political content are held; those who are guilty of this are to be forcefully punished, and whoever abuses any popular assembly in order to propose addresses or resolutions and have them approved by signature or oral consent is to have more severe punishment imposed on them.

Art. 4. The public carrying of insignias on ribbons, rosettes, or the like, whether it be by natives or foreigners, in colors other than those of the country to whom the carrier belongs as a subject – the unauthorized putting up of banners and flags, the erection of liberty trees and similar rebellious symbols – is to be strictly punished.

However, the resources available to the authorities were not those of modern dictatorial states. Radical thought was driven underground but not destroyed. Monarchs sometimes resisted conservatives – for example, the king of Prussia refused the demands of conservative ministers to suppress all craftsmen's and workers' organizations. It was not possible to prevent national feeling or to suppress all liberal ideas. The revolutionary spirit could not be eradicated, and in 1848 a wave of revolutions in Germany and the Austrian Empire forced Metternich to flee to Britain and ended his "system."

Reasons for the growth of nationalism in the 1840s

The growth of nationalism in the 1840s was due to economic and cultural factors:
- The *Zollverein* had increased economic links between the German states (see below).
- The growth of urban centres in the 1840s caused an increase in the middle class. It was this section of society which was most interested in nationalism.
- The growth of railways increasingly linked the German states together. It brought Germans more in touch with each other (see page 86).
- Greater literacy, education, and circulation of newspapers and books helped develop a common language and spread of ideas.
- The growth of music, art, and literature gave a sense of a specific German culture. Artists such as Philipp Otto Runge explored folklore and myths about ancient Germany. German opera became less dependent on Italian models. German songs, including art songs by composers such as Schumann and folk songs, helped spark interest in the German language and promote unity. Songs such as "*Die Wacht am den Rhein*" (the Guard of the Rhine) and "*Deutschland über alles*" (Germany over all) became well known.
- Mass tourism in the German states took off in this period as passenger steamboat services became popular on the Rhine. Karl Baedeker created a set of travel guides which included detailed maps, timetables, and star ratings. These became hugely popular with the middle classes, promoted a sense of pride in the natural and built environments of the German states. These cultural developments were likely to be far more important in promoting a sense of pride in German-ness than patriotic societies and political groups.

Due to these factors, by 1848 there had been a significant growth in awareness of German identity, but there was no consensus about a future German state. The problem lay in defining a possible new "Germany". Would it include Austria, the most important state in the Confederation of 1815, even though its emperor ruled over a host of eastern European nationalities? Those who believed so thought in terms of a *Grossdeutschland* (greater Germany). Or would a new Germany consist only of the "purely" German states? There was a problem, too, with this *Kleindeutschland* (small Germany). Prussia had taken lands from Poland at the end of the eighteenth century and also included Slavonic people such as the **Sorbs** or **Wends**. Thus, a 'small Germany' would still encompass lands of very different traditions and religious beliefs. It would be difficult to establish the boundaries of any new Germany, and such a state would not easily be accepted by the surrounding powers, especially France.

Even by 1848, the idea of moving from a general interest and admiration for all things German to actually creating a new Germany seemed like a distant possibility. Most German speakers retained their loyalty to their individual states, and the overwhelmingly large rural population had a limited interest in nationalism in any form.

> **KEY TERM**
>
> **Sorbs** or **Wends** By the mid-nineteenth century, there were about 165,000 of these Slavonic people with their own languages, customs, and cultures living in the border areas between modern-day Germany and Poland.

> **ACTIVITY**
>
> Reread the section on nationalism. Find evidence to support the views below:
> - German nationalism was most significant in the arts and should not be exaggerated as a movement for change.
> - German nationalism was a powerful and important movement by 1848.
>
> Which do you think is more convincing, and why?

The economic and political impact of the Prussian Customs Union on Germany – Zollverein

The economic disunity caused by numerous customs barriers between the German states in 1815 reinforced their political disunity. Taking goods from one part of Prussia to another at the start of the nineteenth century could involve paying 63 different customs duties. Germany had huge numbers of customs posts, and economic progress was severely hindered by a lack of internal free trade. As part of a general modernization, Prussia removed its internal customs barriers in 1818. Because its territories were separated and other states lay between the Rhine and its main eastern lands, it negotiated agreements with the intermediate states to remove barriers in 1819. This led to other Germanic states forming commercial unions. A general agreement was made between the Prussian union and the other unions in 1834 and was known as the *Zollverein* (customs association or union). This was a significant event.

- Austria was excluded, so its leading role in the German confederation was weakened. It would not have been possible to include the vast amount of non-German lands in the Austrian Empire in the customs union. Most other German states were linked in an economic agreement but Austria was not.
- Prussia led the creation of the customs union, hinting at its potential to lead greater German unity.
- Freer trade led to greater prosperity, particularly in Prussia, where industries, trade, and road and rail networks expanded.
- The ending of customs restrictions encouraged the growth of railways, which acted as a unifying factor between the German states.
- Greater prosperity encouraged both urban growth and the growth of the German middle class.

> **KEY TERM**
>
> *Zollverein* German, meaning "customs" (*Zoll*) "union", or "association" (*Verein*). A group of countries which have agreed to trade without paying tariffs when goods are moved from one area to another.

SOURCE 2.11

What can we learn from Source 2.11 about the impact of the Zollverein on Germany?

An English observer in the 1840s writes about the *Zollverein*

The *Zollverein*, by directing capital to internal in preference to external trade, has had a great influence in improving the roads, the canals, the means of travelling, and the transport of post – in a word, giving additional impulse to inland communications of every sort. On every side, beneficial changes are taking place. Railways are being constructed in many parts of the German territory – steamboats are crowding the German ports – everything is being transported with greater cheapness and rapidity. Saxony has profited most, being more advanced in manufacturing than most of the German states. To her, it has opened up a market of 26 million consumers.

The *Zollverein* did not produce political unity in itself. Within Germany, there remained suspicion of Prussia, especially in the Catholic south, which saw the largest state in this economic union as militaristic, with a different Protestant religion. However, it did establish greater economic unity, and there was a body set up to regulate customs, called the Customs Parliament, which included most of Germany and not Austria, and so undermined the Austrian-led Confederation.

The impact of railway development

The growth of the German economy in the nineteenth century was closely linked to the expansion of the railway network. In 1835, there were 6.5 km of track in Bavaria alone, but from 1839 most major cities were linked by rail. By 1840, there were 500 km of track, and by 1850 this had grown to 5800 km, nearly doubling again to 11,300 km by 1860. Some German governments built state railway systems. In Prussia and Saxony, the lines were built by private companies with some state support. Some governments distrusted railway development because they thought they would undermine traditional authority.

Rail connections between different states had the effect of boosting economic cooperation and unity. There was a far greater ability for goods, services, and workers to travel throughout the German-speaking lands. The economic impact of railways as a stimulus to growth helped Prussia develop because it promoted greater urbanization and helped the growth of a larger middle class. Railways also enabled news and information to spread more quickly and made many isolated areas feel more connected and less remote. It linked Prussia's eastern and western lands. The economic and social impact of railways also had major political implications. They helped develop a sense of nationalism and a greater sense of a national culture.

However, the impact of railways should not be overstated. By 1848, many rural areas were not linked by rail. Local loyalties, dialects, and customs were still strong, and most people retained a clear sense of identity with their state. Also, railways could be used to increase the speed with which governments could move armies to repress uprisings.

Problems facing the German states in the 1840s

There were long-term trends which threatened to bring discontent in Germany:
- resentment against the censorship and controls of the Metternich system
- a growing middle class, increasingly well educated and influenced by ideas of liberalism and nationalism
- moves towards greater economic unity, which encouraged more desire for more political unity
- more national awareness in terms of the arts and culture, which encouraged more people to think in terms of German unity.

However, given the limited number of urban dwellers and the predominance of rural life and the power of the states to enforce the Metternich system, these trends alone would not have been likely to result in political revolution. What changed the situation in the 1840s was the growth of economic and social problems resulting from population growth.

Economic and social problems in the 1840s

Germany's population grew from around 22 million in 1815 to 33 million in 1848. This put pressure on agriculture, and there was more demand for farm produce. This was increasingly difficult due to lack of labor as people left rural areas for better-paid work in towns and cities. Meanwhile, more available labor in urban areas created opportunities for larger factories and extended workshops. However, this changed the nature of employment. In place of the close relationship between small employers and traditional craftsworkers working together and where employers felt a duty to look after the welfare of their workers, there was more distance between employers and their workforce. Greater trading opportunities increased the desire for profits and, in common with other industrializing countries, Germany experienced problems with working conditions. Hours were often long, and cheaper female and child labor was exploited. Though not massively industrialized Germany did see changes to its workforce. The greater availability of labor had a depressing effect on wages.

In addition, rising populations meant that there was a rise in prices. Especially after 1845, there was quite rapid inflation. Living standards suffered, and discontent grew. In some slum areas of Berlin in the 1840s, 2500 men, women, and children lived in 400 rooms in great tenement blocks. Unemployed men could be classified as beggars and put to work on treadmills in special workhouses.

The impact of industrialisation on skilled workers

The rise in technology and larger workplaces also hit traditional crafts. Much of industry before 1815 had been conducted on a small scale in the home. Textiles had been particularly important, and the handloom weavers were the backbone of the industry. With more use of power looms and larger units, the domestic weavers suffered a decline.

Life was difficult, not only for many workers, but also for peasants. There had been many who had left the land in the 1840s, either for cities or to emigrate to the USA. Rent was high, and many aristocratic landlords were ruthless in exploiting their workers or taking over common land to make profits from the growing internal trade.

The impact of urbanization

Alongside population growth, Germany saw the most rapid growth in urbanization in its history in this period. The proportion of people living in towns went from around 10 per cent – a figure which had been unchanged since 1500 – to 17 per cent by 1850. However, it was still much lower than in other countries, such as France at 19 per cent, and substantially lower than Britain's 39 per cent. In 1848, most of Germany was still rural, and urban growth was greater in some areas than others. Areas with heavy industry such as Westphalia in Prussia or parts of Saxony, as well as those with increasing administration such as Berlin, saw high levels of urbanisation. In other areas, urbanisation was much more limited.

Urbanisation tended to emphasize divisions, but it also had effects which encouraged political change. Urban centres had a higher proportion of educated middle-class Germans, more attracted than country dwellers to the new ideas of nationalism and liberalism. Cities were also cultural centres, and the growth of the arts was a unifying element as German music and literature helped bring people together.

As in other parts of Europe, the towns and cities could not cope with the influx of people from the countryside. Rent went up, and newcomers had to share overcrowded, older buildings. The infrastructure also struggled. Water supplies were often poor, and sewage was not removed. All this resulted in poor health and disease, especially in poorer areas.

> What can we learn from Source 2.12 about why there was revolution in Berlin in 1848?

SOURCE 2.12

This journalist wrote about living conditions among the poorest workers in Berlin. From Heinrich Bettzeich, *The physiology of Berlin*, 1846.

They had nothing. Not a bed nor a table, without firewood, clothes, shoes, or stockings, no work, no money, no potatoes, no prospects, no consolation, no charity. Hope only of the workhouse or a miserable death in the poor house – only rags and straw and dirt and vermin and hunger, hunger howling in their guts.

The growth of socialism

The problems of the 1840s were the background for a new interest in political ideas beyond liberalism and nationalism. Some radical thinkers saw the system as focusing on making money for business owners while making conditions worse for workers. The most famous was **Karl Marx**, who condemned the exploitation of the **proletariat** by the new capitalist class. Marx argued that new production methods alienated workers from what they produced, exploiting them in a capitalist system.

The dependence on markets also meant that more were liable to periods of unemployment and hardship. The emerging doctrine of **socialism** attacked the whole business system, arguing that profit was the result of exploitation and denying workers the just price for their labor. The only remedy was to overthrow the entire system and give political power to the workers.

> **KEY TERMS**
>
> **Proletariat** Karl Marx gave this term to the industrial working class that had emerged from the industrial revolution and the growth of large-scale factories.
>
> **Socialism** The political belief that the state should own major means of production and operate them for the benefit of workers, rather than landowners or business investors who profit by exploiting workers.

> **KEY FIGURE**
>
> **Karl Marx** (1818–83) was born in Trier in western Germany. Marx studied law in Bonn and Berlin but was more interested in philosophy. In 1843, he moved to Paris, where he became increasingly radical politically. Expelled from France, Marx went to Brussels, where he wrote *The Communist Manifesto* with Friedrich Engels. In 1849, Marx moved to London, where he wrote *Das Kapital*. His ideas were particularly influential in Germany, though the first "successful" communist revolution was in Russia, a country Marx thought too economically backward to have any chance of a communist regime.

The economic crisis of 1846–47

An immediate crisis was caused by poor corn harvests in 1846 and 1847 and also by a potato blight which affected Germany and other parts of Europe, especially Ireland.

Potatoes were both a source of income and a staple food for rural people. The famine produced by these failures caused widespread starvation and unrest. Corn prices rose by 50 per cent, and this meant that workers in cities paid a much higher proportion of their wages simply to survive. On top of this came a trade recession in Europe generally, which meant wage reductions and job losses.

The situation by 1848

A toxic mix had emerged by 1848 of rural and urban hardship. Political ideas such as socialism and democracy fed on this discontent in the same way that middle-class grievances led to the greater interest in ideas of constitutional government and nationalism.

These economic and social problems were not unique to Germany. Much of Europe experienced:
- a rising industrial workforce facing the threat of unemployment, low wages, and poor living conditions in expanding cities
- an agricultural population under pressure from rising population and not having enough workers or land
- a rising middle class resentful of aristocratic domination and inadequate social opportunities – either to gain employment in state government or in business
- memories of the French Revolution and ideals of liberal representative government for the middle classes, the overthrow of royal and aristocratic power, and more democracy for the ordinary people.

The outbreak of revolution in France in 1848 was the cause of widespread revolution in Europe. In Germany, these different discontents reached a critical point and resulted in a major challenge to the settlement of 1815.

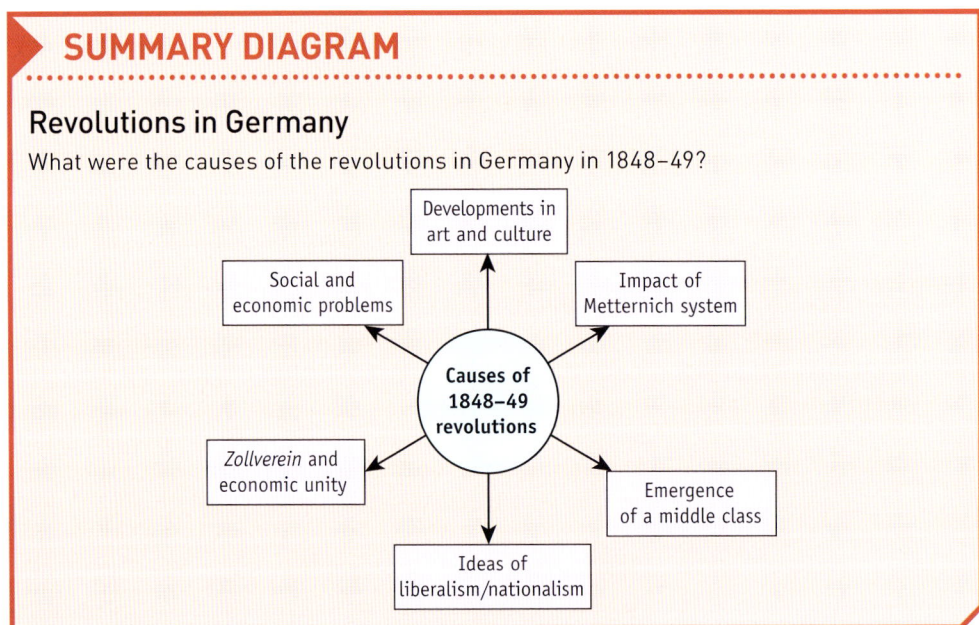

> **SUMMARY DIAGRAM**
>
> **Revolutions in Germany**
> What were the causes of the revolutions in Germany in 1848–49?
>
> Causes of 1848–49 revolutions:
> - Social and economic problems
> - Developments in art and culture
> - Impact of Metternich system
> - Emergence of a middle class
> - Ideas of liberalism/nationalism
> - Zollverein and economic unity

> **ACTIVITY**
>
> Draw up a table showing different causes of the 1848 revolutions in Germany in one column; in a second column, briefly explain the importance of each cause; in the third column, "grade" the importance of the factor on a scale of 1 to 6, with 6 being the most important. In the final column explain your "grade."

2 What happened during the 1848 revolutions, and what were their consequences?

The revolutions of 1848 were serious but did not succeed in their aims of establishing a new Germany. They were sparked by events in Europe and were also caused by economic problems, political discontent, and the growth of an educated middle class in Germany. Initially successful, the revolutions failed because of internal divisions and the ability of the old rulers to retain the loyalty of their armies. However, in the longer term the revolutions had major consequences. The old order was not completely restored, and there were new constitutions; most importantly, the hopes for a new nation were raised, and Austria was shown to be weak. The experience of 1848–49 also led conservatives such as Bismarck to see that Germany would not be united by middle-class liberals but that Austrian domination could be ended if Prussia was strong.

The spread of revolution in the German states, 1848–50

The news of the overthrow of the French monarchy in a revolution of 1848 led to unrest in Germany. The first states affected were those of the south, where there was more of a liberal tradition. This included Bavaria, where the king was unpopular and there had already been unrest. A series of local revolts then broke out across Germany, reflecting different discontents. Peasant unrest was widespread, with attacks on landowners and tax officials. There were some revolts inspired by socialist ideals and a desire for a republic. In many states, there were calls for more powers to be given to the assemblies. In Austria, there were disturbances which led to the fall of Metternich, after which he fled to Britain in March. In Prussia, in the so-called "March Days," where widespread demonstrations led to violence. The Prussian King Friedrich Wilhelm IV gave way under pressure and accepted many demands (see page 92).

Unrest forced similar concessions in other German states. The unrest took on a new dimension with the meeting of delegates from various German states in late March to arrange for a new National Constitutional Assembly at Frankfurt. The initiative came not from Prussia but from the minister of the small state of Hesse-Darmstadt, the liberal **Heinrich von Gagern**. These hopes were not realized. Divisions soon appeared among the revolutionaries, and a conservative reaction developed. The middle classes began to fear popular unrest. In Austria, the power of the emperor was restored by loyal troops. When the revolutionary, impulse subsided, the Prussian king was able to regain control, and troops restored royal authority in October. The tsar of Russia, who had not been faced with revolution, gave his support to the restoration of Habsburg control in eastern Europe. Austria was strong enough to prevent a new German union, and by 1850 the old German Confederation was restored and many of the liberals were exiled or imprisoned. Popular unrest had been repressed. Revolutionaries such as Marx had been driven out of Germany. The authority of landlords, factory owners, the police, the army, and traditional rulers had been reinstated.

> **KEY FIGURE**
>
> **Heinrich von Gagern** (1799–1880) was a Bavarian aristocrat who first became a soldier and fought against Napoleon at Waterloo. He then trained as a lawyer and became a strong supporter of liberal and nationalist ideas. He was well known for his political views and in 1848 became chief minister of Hesse and then president of the new German parliament. He worked for a new union which would exclude Austria. Unable to achieve his aims, he withdrew into private life.

KING FRIEDRICH WILHELM IV

Friedrich Wilhelm IV (1795–1861) was the son of King Friedrich Wilhelm III. Prussia had been invaded and defeated by France in 1806 and the royal family was forced to flee from Berlin. In 1813, he took part in the military campaigns against the French. He was a poor solider and more interested in the arts and in religion. He saw monarchs as chosen by God but also thought they should behave moderately. He became king in 1840 and was a patron of music and architecture. His reign saw the growth of Berlin, and he promoted new buildings and also worked to improve the Prussian economy. He relaxed censorship and established an amnesty for political prisoners. His early life made him resist political change, but in 1848, he embraced it and raised hopes that he would become [otherwise, sounds as though the hopes are his own] the king of all Germany. However, his belief in the divine right of kings led him to refuse a crown offered "from the gutter," that is, with the support of ordinary people rather than the aristocratic elite. He accepted a new constitution and restored monarchical authority after the defeat of revolution in 1848–49. He suffered from a stroke which left him incapacitated in 1857 and died in 1861.

The fall of Metternich

The crucial event in bringing about revolution was the sudden collapse of Metternich's control. When revolution broke out in Austria, it weakened princely power in Germany. Smaller states lacked resources to control their populations, and when the Prussian monarch made concessions, others followed suit.

> What point is the cartoonist in Source 2.13 making about Metternich's failure? What details in the source can you identify and explain with your knowledge?

SOURCE 2.13

A cartoon of Metternich's flight from Vienna, 1848

Metternich had already faced rivalry at court from his political opponent, the finance minister Kolovat, and from the Archduke John, the son of the Austrian emperor, Leopold I. There was mounting social and economic discontent in Austria, particularly in the poorer parts of Vienna. What triggered popular demonstrations was news of revolution in Paris against King Louis Philippe. Student demonstrations on March 10, which Metternich had not foreseen, led to troops firing on the crowds and killing five people. This spread the unrest, and there were fears of a French-style revolution. During a ceasefire, another leading member of the Austrian royal family who had been hostile to Metternich, the Archduke Ludwig, made it clear that Metternich had lost support and that his safety could not be guaranteed. Without armed forces, with revolutionary unrest in Hungary and Italy, and with the danger of Vienna getting out of control, Metternich departed to exile in Britain. His system had become too rigid, and his attempts to control growing nationalist and liberal demands could not be continued without more violence than the Austrian royal family and government could accept.

> **Fear of revolution**
>
> The overthrow of the French King Louis Philippe had been the first sign of widespread European revolutions in 1848. Ruling families and nobles feared that monarchies would fall because demonstrations in Paris had already caused the collapse of the French monarchy. There were also fears that the great French Revolution, which began in 1789 and had resulted in the execution of King Louis XVI in 1793, would be repeated in the European monarchies.

Revolution in Prussia

Prussia experienced the problems common to all German states in the period leading up to the 1848 revolutions: catastrophic crop failures, bread riots, and a serious business recession. In early 1847, King Friedrich Wilhelm IV, responding to the growing crisis, summoned delegates from the eight provincial local assemblies to consider Prussia's financial problems. For the first time, there was a national assembly, called "the United *Diets*" but the king did not make it a permanent parliament and little came of the meeting. Prussian liberals called for a new parliament and liberal rights. The news of revolution in France, the fall of Metternich, and the concessions made in response to popular unrest in other parts of Germany led to demands for further reform in Prussia.

The March Days

> **KEY TERMS**
>
> *Junker* The term for a Prussian-landed aristocrat, often seen by the use of the word "*von*", meaning "of", in names.
>
> *Kamarilla* The king's courtiers or favourites, the inner circle.

The king made some concessions, but the army lost control in Berlin and fired at a crowd at the royal palace on March 18. This led to barricades being erected and violence in which hundreds of civilians and 24 troops died. This shocked the king, who withdrew troops from Berlin and made a remarkable series of changes, not only in liberalizing Prussia but also in taking a lead in a possible unification of Germany. The unrest was focused on urban and industrial centres. The Prussian nobles, or *Junkers*, who held traditional power in the countryside, did not approve of change. Though there were some liberal army officers and civil servants, the conservative elements were stronger. The Prussian king had delayed responding to demands for change, and this had led to violence and the danger of an extreme revolution, which many of his fellow German rulers had tried to avoid. However, now Prussia took the lead in making changes that Metternich had worked so long to avoid.

Role of Friedrich Wilhelm IV of Prussia

The king now became the key figure. He promised that a constituent assembly would draw up a new constitution for Prussia and offered concessions in terms of political freedom and ending censorship. He also stated that he would take the lead in unifying Germany, adopting the red-black-gold national colors and stating, "Henceforth, Prussia is merged with Germany." He appointed Ludolph Camphausen, a liberal leader, banker, and businessman from the Rhineland, as his chief minister and included some liberals in his government. These measures ended the violence and unrest and raised hopes of a Prussian-led liberal nation.

However, most of the king's *Kamarilla* (council of advisers) were conservatives. They became concerned when the Constituent Assembly met in May and voted to be able to control the royal government in the manner of British parliaments. The demands of the revolutionaries

KEY TERM

Three-tier system Each district was divided into three classes of voters according to the amount of tax paid. This voting system made sure that the wealthies two-thirds (class 1 and 2 voters) appointed the majority of the members of the *Landtag*.
This gave the wealthiest an in-built advantage and guaranteed the continuing dominance of the *Junkers*. This undemocratic system persisted in Prussian elections until 1918.

in Prussia also became more democratic and radical. This was due to the emergence of more radical political groups and leaders such as David Hansemann, a rich and influential businessman originally from Hamburg who was a major figure in railway building.

Across Europe, revolutions subsided as rulers strengthened their control. The Prussian king responded similarly by appointing a military general as prime minister. General Count Brandenburg ordered the Prussian assembly to meet away from Berlin, and when they refused, he declared martial law and dispersed troops.

To avoid a repeat of the events of March, the king announced a new constitution based on plans drawn up by the Constituent Assembly but with wide emergency powers for the king. The new constitution established an elected lower house of parliament, called the *Landtag*. Members were elected through a three-class franchise system, where voting power was based on the amount of taxes paid. There was also an upper house of parliament called the *Herrenhaus*. The upper house was appointed by the king. Many middle-class Prussians were happy to have the stability of a monarch but with an elected parliament which was based on a system that gave the wealthier classes more votes. This **three-tier system** made Prussia into a conservative **constitutional monarchy** which lasted until 1918. The king was also unsure about a united Germany, not being willing to lose control of purely Prussian military forces and foreign policy. He demonstrated this in March 1849 by taking the decision to reject an offer of being German Emperor. He supported counter-revolution and accepted Austrian pressure to abandon a new German union of Erfurt in 1850. He disappointed the hopes of many but did institute some changes in Prussia.

What impression of Friedrich Wilhelm is given by Source 2.14? Note down specific details from the source to support your answer.

SOURCE 2.14

A drawing from 1848 showing Friedrich Wilhelm IV in a parade in Berlin in March. He is shown following German flags in the colours of the revolution.

KEY TERM

Constitutional monarchy A government where a royal ruler shares power with an elected assembly and is bound by a written constitution or rules. Unlike an absolute monarchy, where the ruler has unlimited power, the monarch's authority in this system varies based on the constitution.

The initial responses of the German states to the 1848 revolutions

The speed of events in February and March 1848 was a key reason for the sudden collapse of resistance by the states to the forces of change. Faced with pressure from elected assemblies and from many middle class and respectable officials and professionals, the rulers abandoned hopes of crushing the revolts by armed force. They knew that it would not be possible to rely totally on military power without a very considerable loss of life. They were also aware of the fate of the French King Louis XVI, who was executed by his own people in 1793 during the French Revolution.

There was more of a liberal tradition in the smaller states of South Germany, and these were the first to make concessions. On February 27, 1848, a meeting of citizens in Baden demanded a **bill of rights** and even greater powers for the assembly, already one of the most liberal in Germany. Similar meetings were called in Württemberg, Hesse-Darmstadt, Nassau, and other German states. Strong, popular support for these movements forced rulers to give in to many of the so-called March Demands. In Bavaria, royal troops suppressed demands for change. However, both the conservatives and liberals opposed **King Ludwig I** because of his unpopular mistress, Lola Montez, and he abdicated. Previous developments such as the granting of liberal constitutions in the south and the particular unpopularity of the king of Bavaria helped to explain the initial response in this region.

In the north, the disturbances also produced change. Not all German rulers were despotic in outlook. The king of Saxony, **Frederick August II**, accepted change peacefully in 1848. The Saxon government resigned in March 1848 after demands for change. The liberal Karl Braun introduced the abolition of censorship; reform of the **franchise**; reform of the judiciary; the public recognition of clubs, societies, associations; and having the army swear an oath on the Constitution. Not until May 1849 were there violent clashes in the capital, Dresden.

In Prussia, King Friedrich Wilhem IV made initial concessions (see page 92). The immediate changes that he accepted were the creation of a middle-class Civic Guard to maintain order, the calling of a new assembly to draw up a new constitution which would reduce the power of the monarchy and allow for more representative government, and an acceptance of German nationalism.

> **KEY TERMS**
>
> **Bill of rights** A legislative guarantee to citizens of a country that their liberties will be respected and that they will not be subject to arbitrary rule.
>
> **Franchise** The right to vote in elections.

> **KEY FIGURES**
>
> **Ludwig I of Bavaria** (1786–1868) was king of Bavaria between 1825 and 1848. A patron of the arts and passionate about Greek culture, he was a prolific builder. Initially liberal, he became more conservative after 1830. He alienated conservatives with his relationship with the actress Lola Montez (Eliza Gilbert) and also faced popular unrest in 1844 and 1848, when he abdicated.
>
> **Frederick August II of Saxony** (1797–1854) was a progressive young prince. He was regent from 1830, with his father introducing reforms to Saxony. He became king in 1836 and continued a reforming policy. He appointed liberal ministers in 1848 but dismissed them in 1849. Angry crowds forced him to flee until he was restored to power by Prussian and Saxon troops. He was killed when he fell in front of a horse in 1854.

What impressions of the initial disturbances in March 1848 are given by Source 2.15?

SOURCE 2.15

The revolutionary Karl Schurz was a student in Bonn in 1848. He joined the revolution but fled in 1849 to the USA, where he later became a senator. His *Reminiscences* (1907) were published after his death.

Great news came from Vienna! The fall of Prince Metternich! The students organized themselves as the armed guard of liberty. In the great cities of Prussia, there was a mighty commotion. Not only Cologne, Coblenz, and Trier, but also Breslau, Königsberg, and Frankfurt-am-der-Oder, sent deputations to Berlin to entreat with the king. In the Prussian capital, the masses surged upon the streets, and everybody looked for events of great import.

While such tidings rushed in upon us from all sides like a roaring hurricane, we in the little university town of Bonn were also busy preparing addresses to the sovereign, to circulate them for signature, and to send them to Berlin. On the 18th of March we too had our mass demonstration. A great multitude gathered for a solemn procession through the streets of the town. The most respectable citizens, not a few professors, and a great number of students and people of all grades marched in close ranks, enthusiasm without bounds broke forth. People clapped their hands; they shouted; they embraced one another; they shed tears. In a moment the city was covered with black, red, and gold flags, and not only the *Burschenschaft*, but almost everybody wore a black-red-gold cockade on his hat.

Compare the attitudes to revolution shown in Sources 2.15 and 2.16. Note down one similarity and one difference between them.

SOURCE 2.16

In this Berlin cartoon of March 1848, the Prussian King Friedrich Wilhelm IV is shown, supported by the army, shutting out demands from his middle-class subjects for a new constitution.

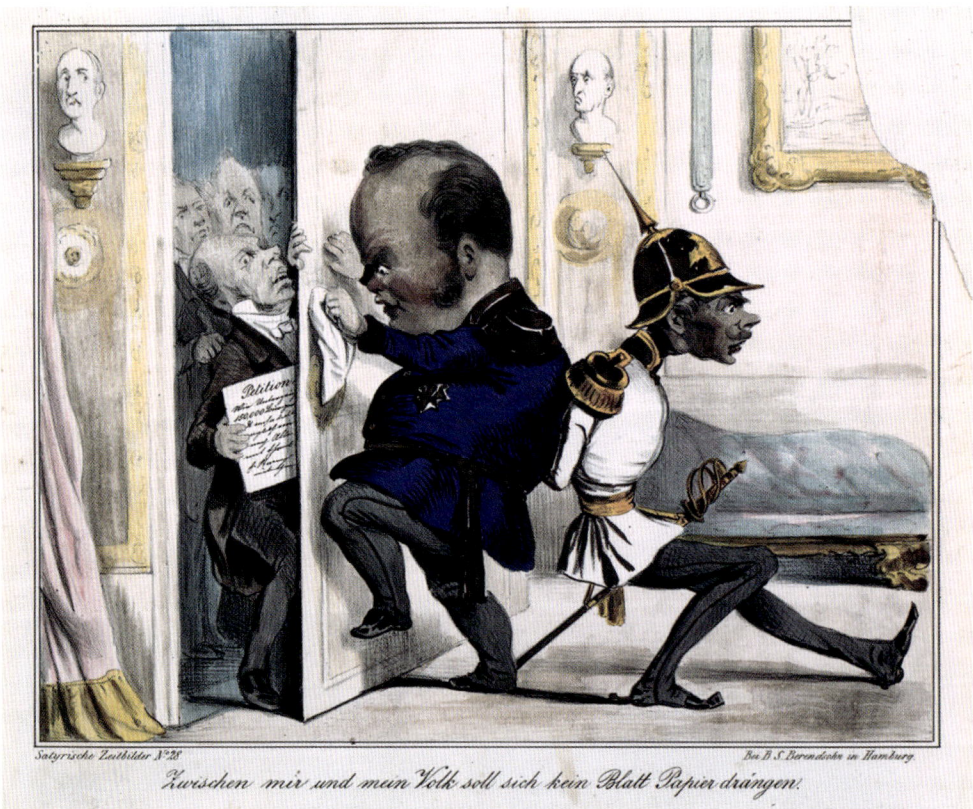

KEY TERM

Constituent Assembly
An elected body whose task is to draw up a new constitution, or a set of rules under which a country is to be run.

The Frankfurt Parliament

The idea of a **Constituent Assembly**, or *Vorparlament*, for the whole of Germany was a radical idea but stood little chance of success.

What can we learn from Source 2.17 about the nature of the Frankfurt Parliament?

SOURCE 2.17

The Frankfurt Parliament, painted in 1848

Formation and actions of the parliament

On March 8, 1848, the assembly of the old German Confederation announced that there would be elections for a new assembly to draw up a constitution for a united Germany. It met on May 18 in St. Paul's Church in Frankfurt. The majority of members were wealthy professionals, such as businessmen, teachers, and lawyers. It was described as the "professors' parliament." There were also some members of the nobility and wealthy landowners. One member of parliament was a peasant. There was huge enthusiasm for a new nation but also differences between those who wanted a "greater Germany" (*Grossdeutschland*), including Austria, and those who favoured a "small Germany" (*Kleindeutschland*), excluding Austria and its non-German empire. There were also differences between conservatives, anxious to retain the old social order, and the more radical liberals and democrats.

Nevertheless, the assembly continued its work and completed a constitution. The proposed constitution excluded all non-German lands from the proposed German empire and provided for a hereditary emperor, a democratic legislative body, a governmental ministry, and a supreme court. There was also an Act concerning the "Basic Rights of the German People" (which was adopted on December 21, 1848). This established:
- the equality of everyone before the law
- the abolition of all class privileges
- personal and political liberties, such as freedom of the press, freedom of expression, freedom of association, freedom to practise a trade or profession, and freedom of movement, and the abolition of the death penalty.

The parliament was reliant on Prussia for armed force. In April 1848, Prussia sent forces into Holstein after the parliament at Frankfurt asked for help when the German-speaking provinces of Schleswig and Holsten rejected Danish rule. In early May, Prussian forces moved into the Danish province of Jutland. The Russian tsar had let it be known that he disapproved of these actions by Prussia. Friedrich Wilhelm IV made peace, and Denmark retained Schleswig and Holstein. This showed the limited power of the new national body and its reliance on Prussia.

In March 1849, the parliament agreed on a German constitution with an emperor governing alongside two houses of parliament – one elected and one filled with German princes. The crown was offered to Frederick Wilhelm IV, in the hope that he would lead a national revolution. He was chosen because only Prussia had the military strength to resist Austria if it decided to oppose the arrangement. However, Frederick Wilhelm IV declined, believing the parliament lacked legal authority, and announced that he would accept the throne only if the other German princes offered it. Ultimately, the new constitution was not accepted. The German princes had recovered their confidence during the delay while the parliament discussed their options. After Frederick Wilhelm IV refused the crown, the other German princes withdrew their constitutions and started to suppress liberals and overturn concessions. The overall authority over Germany went back to the Confederation created in 1815, dominated by Austria.

SOURCE 2.18

Extract from the opening speech of Heinrich von Gagern when elected as President (or Speaker) of the National Assembly

We wish to create a constitution for Germany, for the whole empire. The call and the authority for this creation lie in the sovereignty of the nation ... Germany will be one ... Unity she wishes, unity she will have.

Reasons for the collapse of the Frankfurt Parliament

One explanation for the collapse of the Frankfurt Parliament is the unrepresentative nature of the membership of the assembly. Educated, middle-class professionals dominated, with limited representation from both manufacturing and trading interests and from both land owners and peasants – despite the fact that over 70 per cent of Germans were not bourgeois urban dwellers. Far from offering decisive action, the assembly members spent a lot of time on detailed legalistic discussions. It was not until October that a draft constitution for Germany was produced and a bill of rights proposed. By this time, the revolution had lost impetus and had become divided.

Divisions

A second reason is that there was no fundamental agreement on what the new German state would be. Some advocated a greater Germany including Austria and some of its empire but not Hungary. The Catholic south had more in common with Austria than the Protestant north. The other solution was a smaller Germany excluding Austria, but that would mean the dominance of Prussia. Prussia's lands made up two-thirds of a reduced Germany, and it was not universally trusted or admired in Germany. By October, it was accepted that the *Kleindeutsch* (small) solution would be adopted, but again by that time a reaction against change had set in.

Limited appeal

A third explanation is that the assembly offered little for the majority of Germans, especially the peasants, and that the revolution lacked popular support. The middle-class delegates supported property rights. There was little support in the parliament for state intervention to protect workers or for protective tariffs to keep out cheap foreign farm imports, although peasants and landowners wanted these measures. One reform that did occur was the ending of feudalism. This was the practice, used in parts of Germany, whereby the peasants owed personal services to lords in return for working their lands. Though this was ended, the landowners received generous compensation and still dominated the countryside, especially in eastern Germany.

Overreliance on Prussia and its army

A fourth possible explanation is based on the overreliance of the assembly on Prussian military power in a dispute with Denmark. The Danish king had wanted to incorporate the provinces of Schleswig and Holstein into Denmark. The German Confederation opposed this but had to rely on the Prussian army.

The assembly had been part of a wave of enthusiasm for change in March and April 1848. Through the summer of 1848, there had been increasing divisions within the German states between the middle-class moderates and those who wanted to make more decisive social and political changes. The loss of impetus allowed conservative elements to become stronger and to advocate ending the revolutions by force. The monarchs had not lost the loyalty of their armed forces, which remained strong. When the time was right, the forces of monarchism began to regain control.

> What does Source 2.19 show about German nationalist feelings? Look at the specific features in the painting: the double-headed eagle, the broken chains, the sword, and the branches. Use your knowledge to relate this to the foundation of the Frankfurt Parliament.

SOURCE 2.19

Germania by the artist Philipp Veit in 1848 shows the national colors being held by the symbol of a united Germany.

The impact of the 1848 revolutions

In the short term, the revolutions failed to achieve the aims of liberal and national change. In October, there was a reaction in Prussia, with an armed takeover of power as troops occupied the capital. The new assembly in Prussia was dissolved. In Saxony, the dismissal of the reform cabinet in 1849 led to violent clashes in Dresden between radical revolutionaries and the armed forces of Saxony and Prussia, ultimately ending the revolution. The Habsburg monarchy reasserted its control, not only of the Germanic lands in Austria, but also over Hungary, Poland, and its Slav territories by the use of military force supported by the tsar of Russia. These actions were mirrored in many of the other German states, and the revolutionaries of 1848 were not determined or united enough to resist these changes.

Prussian military power was not adequate to deal with a challenge from Austria over the dominance of Germany. Conservative pressure, too, led Friedrich Wilhelm IV to put the interests of the Prussian monarchy before the difficulties and expense of being a new German emperor.

However, new ideas had spread, and Prussia had a new constitution, which survived the conservative reaction. Nationalism continued to grow, and even conservatives now had ambitions for Prussia, rather than Austria, which had seemed too weak to dominate Germany. For one ambitious aristocrat from eastern Prussia, Otto von Bismarck, the lesson of 1848 was clear. Change was not going to come about from weak and divided liberals endlessly discussing rights and liberty, but by the military and economic strength of Prussia and its monarchy. Nationalism needed to be separated from liberalism to bring about a united Germany, which in Bismarck's view would be an expanded Prussia.

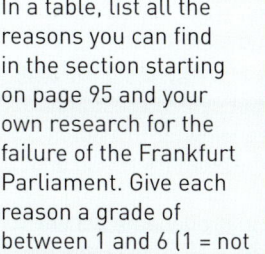

ACTIVITY

In a table, list all the reasons you can find in the section starting on page 95 and your own research for the failure of the Frankfurt Parliament. Give each reason a grade of between 1 and 6 (1 = not very important, 6 = very important). Create an essay plan for an essay on why the Frankfurt Parliament failed.

What does Source 2.20 show about German nationalist feelings?

SOURCE 2.20

Johann Gustav Droysen, a liberal supporter of unification, in a speech to the Frankfurt Parliament, 1848

We cannot conceal the fact that the whole German question is a simple alternative between Prussia and Austria. In these states, German life has its positive and negative poles – in the former, all the interests which are national and reformative, in the latter, all that are dynastic and destructive. The German question is not a constitutional question, but a question of power; and the Prussian monarchy is now wholly German, while that of Austria cannot be. We need a powerful ruling house. Austria's power meant lack of power for us, whereas Prussia desired German unity in order to supply the deficiencies of her own power. Already, Prussia is Germany in embryo. She will "merge" with Germany.

Study Source 2.21. What reasons does Frederick Wilhelm IV put forward to explain his refusal of the Imperial Crown?

SOURCE 2.21

Friedrich Wilhelm IV, King of Prussia, Proclamation of 1849

I am not able to return a favorable reply to the offer of a crown on the part of the German National Assembly [meeting in Frankfurt], because the Assembly has not the right, without the consent of the German governments, to bestow the crown which they tendered me, and moreover because they offered the crown upon condition that I would accept a constitution which could not be reconciled with the rights of the German states.

OTTO VON BISMARCK

Otto von Bismarck (1815–98) was born in Prussia into a *Junker* landowning family. Bismarck attended Göttingen University and became a member of the administration of the Prussian state. He was hostile to liberalism and a firm supporter of royal government. He was elected a member of his local assembly and was well known for his outspoken views. He was elected to the Frankfurt Parliament but scorned the liberals. Suggested as a member of the Prussian royal government, he was seen as too extreme by the king ("red reactionary, steeped in blood, only useful when the bayonet rules").

He came to the view that Germany should be united under the rule of the Prussian monarch but that parliaments and liberal rights would never make this happen. Instead, military power, industrial might, and skilful diplomacy had to lead the way. Though socially and politically conservative, he was opposed to the dominance of Austria. His first major appointment was as Prussian ambassador to the German Confederation, where he opposed Austrian plans to join the *Zollverein*. He became highly interested in diplomacy and served as ambassador in St. Petersburg (1859) and later in Paris (May 1862). He was a strong believer in *Realpolitik* (see page 109) – that not idealism but self-interest and power drove politics and international relations. He was appointed Minister President in Prussia in 1862 and remained in power until 1890. His wars with Denmark (1864) and Austria (1866) led to an expanded Prussia and a North German Confederation (1867). War with France (1870–71) completed unification when South Germany became part of a new German Empire. Bismarck faced ongoing hostility from France after 1871 and did his best to protect Germany by forming alliances with Austria, Italy, and Russia. In the 1880s, Bismarck changed his position about attempting to claim territory as colonies, and this became part of Germany's foreign policy. At home, he clashed with Catholics and a growing socialist movement. He failed to work with Wilhelm I's successors and was dismissed after a dispute in 1890. He died in 1898.

Reasons for the reassertion of Austrian control

The key to events in Germany lay with developments in the Austrian Empire. The overthrow of Metternich had resulted in the monarchy making concessions. Famously, the emperor had said, "Tell the people I agree to everything." With revolution in Italy and Hungary, and unrest in the German and Slav lands, the scale of unrest was too much and too sudden to be met with force. A radical constitution was accepted and a Constituent Assembly called. Unrest was so acute that the emperor was forced to leave Vienna in May 1848.

The recovery of Austria

However, even by the summer there were indications of recovery. Risings in Italy were put down, and Austria defeated nationalist forces under the king of Piedmont at the battle of Custoza. In Hungary, Austrian forces, aided by Russian troops, used overwhelming force to defeat an independence movement, with a final victory at Vilgos in August 1849.

A break with the weakness of the past was made when Emperor Ferdinand abdicated and was replaced by the young Prince Franz Josef, who remained emperor for the rest of the century. Conservative forces, especially the army, had restored Habsburg power. A crucial element had been the support of Russia, whose Tsar Nicholas I was a firm believer in **absolute monarchy**.

The strength of the conservatives: a return to Austrian domination

By the summer of 1849, there had been a return of more conservative regimes and a defeat of more radical elements in Germany. Austria provided the forces to support this conservative backlash and was strong enough to be able to resume its domination of Germany.
- It had strong and victorious armies, which had defeated nationalism in the Czech lands, Poland, Hungary, and Italy.
- It had the military support of Russia and its powerful army and absolute ruler.
- It faced a divided Germany whose main attempt at the creation of a rival German state had failed.
- Its only possible rival was Prussia, but the Prussian armed forces were not strong enough to resist Austrian pressure.
- Prussian conservatives would not have supported any conflict with Austria, and the Prussian king was not a dominant or decisive figure.

In Prussia, the new constitution was very favourable to the conservative landed classes. The lower house of parliament was elected by a three-tier system which gave landowners and the richer middle classes much more influence than less affluent people. A third of the representatives were elected by only the wealthiest and most powerful 5 per cent. In any case, the parliament had limited power. The royal government was not responsible to parliament, and there was an upper house of nobles whose consent was also necessary for any laws.

Divisions between the revolutionaries

The strengthening of conservatism helped Austria return to domination, but a key factor was division among the revolutionaries. The Constituent Assembly which met in June in Vienna was divided and ineffective, and there was little agreement between German speakers and other nationalities such as the Czechs. Imperial forces crushed an attempt to create an independent Czech state in June. The breakaway by Hungary found little support among the German revolutionaries. Radical unrest in Vienna was finally crushed by the Austrian army in October 1848. The moderates were divided from the radicals by a new constitution offered in March 1849. In Prussia and Germany as a whole, moderates had been divided from more radical opposition groups. Rural areas were divided from urban areas and the workers and their political supporters from the property-owning middle classes.

> **KEY TERM**
>
> **Absolute monarchy**
> Rule by a monarch with complete freedom to pursue any policy without accountability to an elected assembly or the people. Absolute monarchs often claimed divine right, believing they were chosen by God and responsible only to God.

> **ACTIVITY**
>
> Create a table of similarities and differences between the aims and position of Prussia and Austria as you read through this section, pages 101–5.

Changing relations between Austria and Prussia after 1848

Before 1848, the Prussian state and its conservative supporters had accepted Austrian influence and the Metternich system. However, a rift appeared after 1848.

The humiliation of Olmütz

An advisor to Friedrich Wilhelm IV, **General Joseph von Radowitz**, aimed to link the hopes of the German middle classes more to the Prussian state by a union with Saxony and Hanover. This would be different from the proposed *Kleindeutsch* policy of the Frankfurt Parliament in that the states were dominated by political conservatives and monarchists. It would share the conservative three-tier franchise of Prussia rather than the more democratic constitution of the Frankfurt Parliament. As it was the best hope for national unity, some 150 former Frankfurt deputies agreed to it at a meeting at Gotha. Under pressure from Prussia and its armies, some 28 states joined the Erfurt Union by the end of August 1849. During the period of negotiations, Austria had been preoccupied with suppressing the movement for Hungarian independence. The new chief minister of Austria, Prince Felix Schwarzenburg, was determined to uphold the power of the Habsburg monarchy and opposed the Union. The Austrian government put pressure on Saxony and Hanover to leave the Union and supported conservative opposition in Prussia. The Austrians put forward an alternative to the Erfurt Union, in which Austria, Prussia, and the larger states would govern together. As a result, Saxony and Hanover withdrew from the Erfurt Union.

Relations between Prussia and Austria worsened to the point of a likely war. Russia backed Austria in opposing the Union. Conservative groups in Prussia influenced the king toward abandoning the Union. Prussia yielded to Austrian pressure at the Olmütz conference on November 29, when it also finally abandoned the Union. The hopes of the Frankfurt nationalists for a Prussian-led independent Germany were ended. There was little that Prussia could do to oppose Austria, given the more powerful Austrian forces and Austria's support from Russia. The climbdown became known as the "humiliation of Olmütz" and was seen as a mark of shame for Prussia.

> **KEY FIGURE**
>
> **Joseph von Radowitz** (1797–1853) was a Catholic aristocrat from western Germany who had fought for Napoleon. He became a senior officer in the Prussian army after 1815 and was used as a diplomat. He became de facto Foreign Minister in 1848. He took a leading part in developing the Erfurt Union and urged war against Austria for opposing it. He resigned when this did not happen.

> **KEY DEBATE**
>
> ### IS IT RIGHT TO SEE THE REVOLUTIONS OF 1848 AS FAILURES?
>
> One historian described 1848 as "the turning point which did not turn," and analyses often focus on the reasons for "failure." Instead of a united Germany, which idealists had hoped for, and a new national parliament, the revolutionaries were too divided to achieve a new liberal state. The revolutionaries were divided for a number of reasons. Firstly, they had different goals. The middle class aimed for liberal reforms, while the working class sought radical changes to improve its living and working conditions. There was no centralised leadership, leading to fragmented strategies. The revolutionaries also had varying ideologies, with some advocating nationalism, liberalism, or socialism, while others preferred more conservative approaches. Ultimately, divisions about a "small Germany" and a "greater Germany" were too big. The middle classes became worried about radical working-class agitation. The power of Austria was restored by its loyal armed forces. The king of Prussia did not step up to take leadership. The old conservative regimes returned, and Austria asserted its power over Prussia. Bismarck summed up failure in 1862 when he said that unification would never be possible by parliament, only by "blood and iron." The liberal leaders disappeared from history.
>
> On the other hand, though aims were obviously not achieved, it may be unhelpful to see 1848 as just a failure. The revolutionaries had achieved a national parliament and hope for a united Germany. Liberalism was not destroyed, and the liberals gained more influence after a change of king in Prussia in 1858 and a new Progressive party in Prussia. Elsewhere in Germany, there were strong liberal groups and an ongoing hope for unity, inspired by the creation of a united Italy. Though conservative regimes returned, there were still constitutions, even in Prussia, with freedom of discussion, elections, and assemblies. Austria had been weakened by the disturbances of 1848–49. The aim for greater unity in Prussia came to be taken up by powerful conservative political and military figures, while the economic union – the *Zollverein* – and continued growth of industry and railways brought Germany together more. In this view, the events of 1848 did not turn the clock back, or destroy liberalism or the chances for unification.

> **ACTIVITY**
>
> Using material from this chapter and any other reading you have done, find evidence for each of these viewpoints about the consequences of the failure of the 1848 revolution:
> - "In 1850, the chances for greater German unity were small."
> - "In 1850, there were still sound reasons for nationalists to be hopeful that German unity would occur."
>
> Which view do you support, and why?

Economic issues

Between 1850 and the eventual establishment of a Prussian-dominated German Empire in 1871, there were a number of important developments that changed the economy and society in Germany. The tensions of the 1840s gave way to what has been seen as "the quiet years." This is true politically, as the upheavals of 1848 and 1849 were not repeated. However, there was a period of rapid economic change.

Economic growth

German industry and trade benefited from a general European prosperity in the 1850, as well as from having the internal free trade of the *Zollverein*. Internal trade in Germany (excluding Austria, which was not a member of the *Zollverein*) doubled between 1850 and 1857. Railways doubled in the 1850s from 5800 km to 11,300 km.

Almost all economic statistics in the period show rapid growth. Steam engine capacity went from 260,000 to 850,000 units of horsepower. Pig iron production increased from 229,000 to 529,000 tons. Cotton production increased from 900,000 to 2.2 million spindles.

The key driving force behind industrial growth was textiles. The shift from small-scale workshop production to mass production based on steam power was seen not only in larger states such as Austria and Prussia, but also in the south, in Baden, Württemberg, and Bavaria. This in turn generated demand for increased coal production, which saw a rapid expansion. Technical change encouraged the growth of pig iron smelted by coke. Using coke instead of charcoal increased the scale of production and the quality of the iron.

In addition, there was growth in the German financial sector, with banks willing to lend money and support enterprises. There was also an increase in paper money – there was 50 times more paper money in circulation by 1860 than there had been in the 1840s. This helped consumer industries and facilitated trade.

Economic growth encouraged national unity. Easier transport, the movement of workers, and the greater interchange of products between different regions all broke down the barriers between different regions which had been such a feature of eighteenth-century Germany.

Economic change also had a considerable effect on German society. There was the growth of a distinct class of industrial workers that Karl Marx called the proletariat. This had doubled between 1848 and the 1860s to a million. Whole towns or urban districts had become "working-class" areas. They had interests in common which crossed state boundaries. Workers in textile factors in Bavaria had common concerns with those in Prussia. However, this should not be overstated – the majority of Germany remained rural. On the other hand, German society was rapidly changing.

Economic development and growth in Prussia

Although all German states experienced economic growth, Prussia's growth was the most significant.

The ending of restriction from traditional trade guilds in Prussia meant the growth of free enterprise. It was easier to set up factories, and by 1860 there were 2000 industrial enterprises employing more than 50 workers each. There was a virtual revolution on the land

> **ACTIVITY**
>
> Write a brief explanation of the following terms:
> - *Zollverein*
> - *Kleindeutsch*
> - *Grossdeutsch*.

as feudal obligations and serfdom were finally ended, with 640,000 Prussian peasants being free from control and able to farm independently. This not only increased food supply, but it also gave industry a much-extended internal market.

The demand for more machinery and technical improvements encouraged growth in engineering. Precision tools developed, which meant there could be mass production of interchangeable parts. With this growth came the development of greater engineering knowledge and education, and a growth in skilled workers. Thus, by the 1860s Prussia had developed its economy because it had key elements needed for economic growth, namely:
- a supply of labour because of ongoing population growth
- free internal trade
- improving transport – railways, better roads, and steamships, as well as canals and navigable rivers
- governments sympathetic to free enterprise
- technical skills
- raw materials
- a stronger internal market with a free peasantry.

Disagreements over the *Zollverein*

The German customs union had done much to bring prosperity to Prussia and the states of Germany but had not included Austria. Once the Austrian government had restored order in its empire, it proposed that Austria should be included. This made economic sense as the large empire offered big market opportunities. Austria wanted the whole of the Habsburg Empire to be included, but this proved to be unacceptable to the current membership. However, Austria had humiliated Prussia over the union of Erfurt, and the inclusion of Austria in what was a Prussian-dominated economic union would have meant the danger of even more loss of influence. Many German states favored Austrian inclusion to balance Prussian power, as there were concerns about Prussian economic dominance in Germany through growth of the *Zollverein*. However, existing members were not happy with the proposed tariffs to protect Austrian industry. In 1853, Austria signed a trade agreement with the *Zollverein* which included a review about membership in 1860. This agreement helped Austrian economic growth. Austria never joined the *Zollverein*.

Many saw that economic developments might eventually produce a united Germany. By 1860, this was seen as most likely to be *Kleindeutsch* because it would emerge from the *Zollverein,* which continued to exclude Austria. However, some states, such as the Hanseatic towns, Hamburg and Bremen, continued to resist joining the *Zollverein* to maintain their independence and protect their economic interests.

The *Zollverein* helped to build Prussian economic power and influence, but it was by no means certain that it would develop into anything more than an economic union. There were considerable cultural and religious differences between Prussia, a largely Protestant state in its eastern homeland with a strong military tradition, and the largely Catholic states of the south, which did not share Prussia's military culture.

Economic and financial problems facing Austria

Austria was outside the *Zollverein* and still experienced economic growth. The idea that Prussia grew while Austria totally stagnated is not true. Austrian textile production more than doubled in the 1850s. Its rail network expanded from 1620 km to 5400 km. Its imports doubled, and its exports tripled. Steam power tripled and iron production doubled. All this occurred when Austria was outside the *Zollverein*. However, in general, the Austrian economy lagged behind that of Prussia. This was because of the great difference in development in the different regions of the empire. Much agriculture, which made up 70 per cent of Austria's economy was communal and for local markets only. There were areas of greater development – for example, in Lombardy in northern Italy – but overall growth was uneven. Similarly, some industries grew in areas such as Vienna and Bohemia and Moravia, particularly in coal, metals, and textiles. However, overall, Austria did not utilise its resources as effectively as Prussia did. There were also financial problems from the mid-1850s which meant that Austria was unable to sustain its spending on its armed forces.

ACTIVITY

Create a list of key economic changes in Prussia. Identify the key enabler for change (e.g., population growth, raw materials). Then, make a comparison list with economic change in Austria. What are the main reasons for the differences?

> What is the message of Source 2.22? What additional knowledge could you use to consider whether this view was justified?

SOURCE 2.22

A liberal newspaper in 1857 writing about the links between economic and political unity

There is an intimate connection, in Germany, between the national economic development and the need for national political development. The commerce and transportation of a country demand one code of law, one national legislation, one defence policy to protect trade. These needs have been satisfied in other countries, but not within Germany. A common code of law, common legislation for the whole of the country, remains a pious wish, unlikely to happen, and our traders are defenceless abroad.

Political issues

There was no certainty that economic development would bring about unification. When it came to a showdown between Austria and Prussia in 1866, most of Prussia's economic partners sided with Austria. Political concerns about Prussian domination were more important. However, the interest in nationalism grew, as did the hopes for a new liberal German state.

The growth of liberalism

The formation of the National Society in 1859 was important in bringing together various associations pressing for a united Germany. Its membership grew rapidly and half of its members were Prussian. This, and the huge growth of various specialist all-German associations of engineers, lawyers, graduates of the *Gymnasium*, musicians, businessmen, workers and political groups, indicated that regional divisions were breaking down and nationalism was growing.

Alongside this was the growth of liberalism. There were liberal groups and parties in many states and an increasing interest in some key liberal ideas in the 1850s, especially in free trade. With a growing population and economic growth, there were calls for an end to government controls and protective tariffs. With the end of censorship, the Prussian constitution of 1850 allowed for elections and political discussion. A growing middle class discussed liberal political and economic ideas. In 1858, the new ruler of Prussia, Wilhelm I (see page 107), offered a "new era" by appointing more progressive ministers. The formation of a Progressive Party in 1861, which won 104 out of 352 seats in the Prussian lower house of parliament, was the culmination of the development of liberal support. This was strong in areas in the west, which Prussia had gained in 1815. These areas were more urban and industrial and also had more links with western Europe. Big urban centres in the east such as Berlin also saw more liberal support grow.

The 1848 revolution was a setback, but not the end of the struggle for a united and liberal Germany. With a strong interest in national culture, more liberal politicians in office, more membership of nationalist associations, and greater economic prosperity and cooperation, there was every expectation that German unity might become a reality.

Prussia's international position

The major challenge in forming a new German nation was Prussia's international standing. The emergence of a new power in central Europe under Prussia's leadership would be opposed by its neighbours. The balance of power would be destabilised, and if the new state were liberal, then conservative powers would feel threatened. Russia had intervened in 1848 to stop the incorporation of Schleswig-Holstein. Austria would not stand by and see its influence in Germany ended. France would not accept a major new state on its border. Prussia was not strong enough in military terms to meet intervention by other powers, as had been shown when Austria threatened war over the Erfurt Union. However, there were changes which improved the situation. The first was the Crimean War (1854–56), when Russia was isolated and fought alone against Britain and France without support from Austria. The second significant event was Austria's defeat by France in the Italian War of Independence in 1859, resulting in the loss of the valuable province of Lombardy in northern Italy and a considerable decline in international prestige.

ACTIVITY

Were economic or political factors more important in explaining the changing relations between Austria and Prussia in 1848–59? List the factors and give each a "grade" out of 6. Explain the reasons for your grades.

Bismarck's role up to 1859 and his attitude towards Austria

Bismarck had little sympathy for liberalism or nationalism. His background as a Prussian aristocrat or *Junker* made him concerned only with the interests of Prussia and its monarchy. Yet he took the cause of German nationalism further than any of the idealistic nationalists of 1848. He made highly effective use of changing circumstances and also of Prussian economic and military power and was one of the greatest diplomats in European history. His role in 1848 was as a bitter opponent of liberalism and a supporter of traditional monarchy. He was an enthusiastic member of the conservative group in the Prussian parliament and welcomed the restoration of royal power.

In 1851, the Prussian king made Bismarck the Prussian envoy to the German Confederation, which met in Frankfurt. Bismarck's devotion to Prussia was stronger than his conservatism, and he clashed with Austria's representatives. He shifted his stance from being a conservative opponent of German unity to actively seeking to reduce Austrian influence over the German states and to enhance Prussian power and control. He had been affected by Prussia's humiliation in 1850 (see page 101). He thought that conservative forces in Prussia should take the lead in a more united and powerful Germany. He also thought that German liberals would support unity above political liberalism. In order to undermine Austria's control, Bismarck came to support friendship with Russia, Austria's traditional rival in eastern Europe, and also France, even though conservatives distrusted France and its ruler, Napoleon III.

SOURCE 2.23

What is the writer of Source 2.23's view of Austria?

Otto von Bismarck, letter to the Prussian Prime Minister von Manteuffel, 1856

Because of the policy of Vienna [the Congress of Vienna, 1815], Germany is clearly too small for us both [Prussia and Austria]; as long as an honourable arrangement concerning the influence of each in Germany cannot be concluded and carried out, we will both plough the same disputed acre, and Austria will remain the only state to whom we can permanently lose or from whom we can permanently gain ... I wish only to express my conviction that, in the not too distant future, we shall have to fight for our existence against Austria and that it is not within our power to avoid that, since the course of events in Germany has no other solution.

Bismarck was unhappy about Prussia's lack of influence in European affairs and disliked internal changes in Prussia. In 1857, a more liberal era came into being in Prussia as Friedrich Wilhelm IV was ill and his brother Wilhelm became regent and then emperor in 1858. Bismarck was sent off to Russia as ambassador in 1859. From there, he could not influence Prussian policy with Austria.

In 1859, Austria was involved in a war which became the Italian War of Independence, where France and Napoleon III supported more Italian unity by aiding the Italian state of Piedmont to gain the Austrian-controlled province of Lombardy. Austria was defeated in large-scale battles and Bismarck was eager to take advantage to weaken Austrian control of Germany. However, the Prussian policy was to prevent France from taking further advantage by putting troops into the Rhineland to warn France not to take further Austrian territory in Venetia. Even with a weakened Austria, there seemed little chance of ending Austrian domination or achieving German unification, as Prussia's army needed modernisation and other European powers did not want to see changes in central Europe.

ACTIVITY

Find evidence in this section for the view that "by 1859, German Unification had little prospect of succeeding" and the view that "the prospects for German Unification by 1859 had become much better." Which do you think is more convincing, and why?

EXTENSION

The war of Italian unification 1859

The Italian state of Piedmont in northern Italy had been growing in economic strength and political influence in the 1850s under Premier Cavour. He sought to expand territory in the north and secured support from Napoleon III for a war against Austria, which controlled northern Italy, including Lombardy, Venetia, Milan, and Venice. Austria was defeated by French and Piedmontese forces in heavy fighting in 1859, and Piedmont took Lombardy, but Venetia remained under Austrian control until 1866.

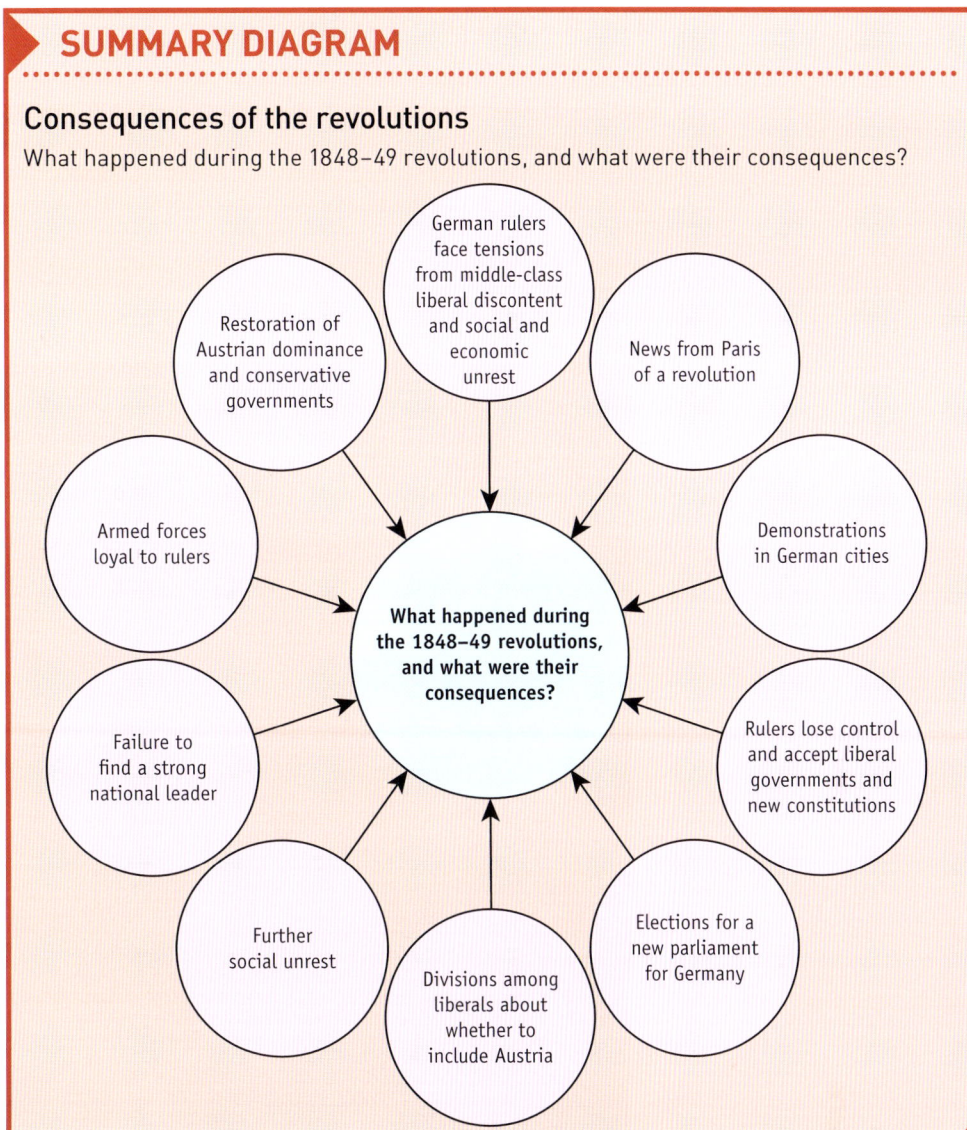

3 Why was Bismarck appointed as Minister President of Prussia, and what were his aims in the period up to 1866?

This section deals with the impact that Bismarck had on the development of Prussia, which resulted in it overthrowing Austrian domination of Germany and becoming the dominant power by controlling the north. The hopes of the 1848 revolutionaries were that German states would be more united by national feeling and political means. For Bismarck, greater unity would be brought about by the power of Prussia's economy and army and by clever international diplomacy.

The constitutional crisis

Bismarck came to power because of a political crisis in Prussia. It was vital for the Prussian government to reform the armed forces if it were to end the domination of Austria. However, army reforms were opposed by the liberal majority in the Prussian parliament. This brought about a constitutional crisis. In this dangerous situation, King Wilhelm I was persuaded to appoint Bismarck as prime minister based on his reputation of strength of purpose and character. In 1862, Bismarck took office with results that were to shape the future of Germany.

The accession of Wilhelm I

In 1858, illness made it impossible for Friedrich Wilhelm to continue to rule Prussia. His brother Wilhelm became regent, and subsequently king in 1861. This began a so-called "new era" with new reforming policies. The elections of 1858 had produced a liberal majority in the Prussian parliament, and the regent aimed at domestic reform. However, one reform which did not please the liberals was the reform of the army.

WILHELM I

Wilhelm von Hohenzollern (1797–1888) was the second son of King Friedrich Wilhelm III. He fought in the wars against Napoleon and took part in the final defeat of the French emperor at Waterloo in 1815. A skilled professional soldier, he helped crush the 1848 revolution in Berlin. In 1857, his brother, King Friedrich Wilhelm IV, had a stroke, and Wilhelm took over as regent, becoming king in 1861 on his brother's death. He feared another revolution in 1862 but supported Bismarck, who served him as Prussian Minister President and then, after the creation of the German Empire in 1871, as Chancellor. Their relationship was often difficult despite Bismarck's belief in the monarchy.

1797	Born
1814	Began serving in the army
1848-49	Helped repress the revolutions by commanding the army
1858	Became regent following his elder brother Friedrich Wilhelm's illness
1861	Became king on the death of Friedrich Wilhelm
1867	Became the president of the North German Confederation
1871	Became emperor of new united Germany
1888	Died after a short illness

KEY FIGURE

Albrecht von Roon (1803–79) was a deeply conservative supporter of the Prussian monarchy and a friend of Bismarck's since the 1830s. He was an expert in military geography and planning. Appointed Minister for War in 1859, he aimed, with like-minded senior officers, to reform the Prussian army – a task which needed the support of a strong civilian leader.

Proposals for army reforms and the reaction of the liberals

When Austria had gone to war against France in Italy in 1859, the Prussian army was mobilized. This was to put the army into a state of readiness if Prussia were to take advantage of Austria's preoccupation with war against France. However, the mobilization had shown weaknesses in organization and war readiness. **Albrecht von Roon** was appointed Minister of War the same year. His task was to reform Prussia's army. He proposed creating a larger force by adding 23,000 men. This would mean creating 49 new regiments and also developing a more professional force. Prussia had relied heavily on a substantial part-time reserve force called the *Landwehr* or citizen soldiers. Von Roon wanted to separate this from a larger, fully professional full-time force.

His proposals were met with a great deal of resistance in Prussia's parliament – the *Landtag*. Liberal deputies regarded a professional army with suspicion after its role in suppressing the revolutions of 1848–49. They objected to the costs and also to the downgrading of the citizen soldiers of the *Landwehr*, whom they saw as a safeguard against any future attempt to use the army to impose absolute rule. They used their votes to block expenditure to pay for the army reforms. In May 1862, the opponents of reform gained a majority in the *Landtag*.

This was a crucial time. If Prussia were to be able to challenge Austrian domination, it needed an improved army. It could not be a great power without a professional and well-equipped military force. The economic changes had given it the potential for influence, but as the humiliation of Olmütz showed, without military reforms it would remain under Austrian domination. The clash between parliament and the king's government was a serious one. If the *Landtag* could block spending, then it could dominate policy. But if the king overrode parliament and ignored the constitution, then it could mean a recurrence of revolution and a reliance on brute military force.

The formation of the German Progressive Party

Germany's first political party, the DFP – the Germany Progress (or Progressive) Party – emerged at the time of the regency of Wilhelm I. After 1848, there was a loosely organized group of liberal members in the *Landtag* which opposed the conservative government of Prussia and its supporting deputies. Some of the liberals allied with the nationalist association, the *Nationalverein*, to form a distinct party in 1858. This linked those who wanted more parliamentary government, with a government responsible to the representatives of the people and more freedom of expression, with a drive to unite the German people in one nation. Its leaders were highly articulate intellectuals such as Rudolf Virchow and Theodore Mommsen. Its program did not include full democracy. Only property-owning men could be elected representatives, tasked with "looking after" the interests of poorer people. Additionally, it emphasized the rule of law, protecting individual rights from state censorship, and control over political discussion. The leaders aimed for a united Germany, led by a liberal Prussia which would exclude Austria, which they saw as backward and reactionary. They had support from trading and manufacturing interests and also from professional classes. They were bitterly opposed by the Prussian landowners, especially Bismarck, who scorned their views as idealistic. This liberal group dominated the Prussian lower house of parliament from 1861 and led the rejection of the budget of 1862, thus blocking the army reforms. They were horrified when their most bitter enemy, Otto von Bismarck, was appointed Prime Minister (Minister President) in 1862, and many expected a repeat of the 1848 revolution and even a civil war.

ACTIVITY

Bismarck was and still remains a controversial figure. By additional reading, extend your knowledge about why he is so controversial. Identify why some historians have seen him as a brilliant nation builder and why others have seen him as cynical and an enemy to liberal progress. What is your view?

Bismarck's appointment and how he resolved the crisis

This clash between the government and parliament was a critical point for the constitution. It was a dangerous time and needed strong leadership. Von Roon summoned Bismarck from Paris with the famous telegram "*Dépêchez-vous. Periculum in mora*" ("Hurry up" in French; "Danger in delay" in Latin). Wilhelm I appointed Bismarck as Minister President in September 1862. This was due to Bismarck's reputation among conservatives and the advice of von Roon, who believed Bismarck had the determination and strong character to push through the essential military reforms.

Bismarck was an extreme character, but this was seen as a make-or-break situation. Give in, and Prussia would become a weak power dominated by liberals who wanted a new nation state but without the military force necessary to achieve it. Standing up to parliament meant risking the end of the monarchy and a bloody struggle between conservatives and liberals.

> What is Bismarck's attitude to how Prussia should enable German unity in Source 2.24?

SOURCE 2.24

Bismarck put the issue clearly to the budget committee of the Prussian parliament (*Landtag*) on September 19, 1862.

Prussia must build up and preserve her strength for the advantageous moment which had already come and gone many times. Under the Treaty of Vienna, Prussia's borders were not ensuring the healthy existence of the state. The great questions of the day were not settled by speeches and parliamentary majorities – that was the mistake of 1848 – but by blood and iron.

This was a key statement. Prussia had lost the opportunity to lead a new conservative union in 1850 (see page 101). It lost the opportunity to take advantage of Austria's war against France in 1859. It could not go on with its territories separated from each other by other states. The revolutions of 1848 had shown the limitations of discussion with no action. Economic strength and military action were the key to Prussia's development. There was nothing here about German nationalism, and there was a scorn for "speeches and parliamentary majorities" which indicated precious little respect for constitutional politics. Instead, there was brutal realism – what is known as **realpolitik**. What lay behind this was a cold calculation. After observing the events of 1848 and 1849, Bismarck did not think that the parliamentary opposition or the middle-class liberals would take their opposition beyond speeches, meetings, articles, and general displeasure.

His view is summed up in an exchange with Wilhelm I which appears in Bismarck's memoirs. The king is supposed to have said, "They will cut off your head – and mine afterwards!" Bismarck is supposed to have replied, "And so ...? We will all die sooner or later. Can we perish more honorably than I fighting for your majesty's cause and your majesty fighting for his God-given rights?" For Bismarck, the cause was Prussia, not Germany; for the monarchy, not for the constitution.

> **KEY TERM**
>
> **Realpolitik** Politics which considers not ideals or aspirations but takes a hard look at national interests.

> What is Bismarck's attitude to parliament and the constitution in Source 2.25?

SOURCE 2.25

From Bismarck's memoirs published in 1899 and written during his retirement

Never, not even at Frankfurt, did I doubt that the key to German politics was to be found in princes and dynasties, not in politicians, whether in parliament and the press, or on the barricades. The opinion of the cultivated public as uttered in parliament and the press might promote and sustain the determination of the dynasties. The Prussian dynasty needed to see that the rule of the future German Empire would eventually fall to it, with an increase of consideration and power.

Bismarck's solution to the problem of lacking funding for army reform was to devise what he called the "gap theory." The constitution was said not to have envisaged a breakdown of government, so rather than having a "gap", which prevented the normal running of the state, the government could collect taxes without parliament's consent. This was a piece of rather desperate constitutional theory to disguise what amounted to bypassing parliament and resorting to a dictatorship. Bismarck was not an elected leader: he relied totally on royal power. The constitution was being ignored and the very basis of any sort of parliamentary regime undermined. Though there seemed to be little alternative, Bismarck did not have the full support of Wilhelm I or his queen, who hated him. It was not a situation which could go on indefinitely; without some successes, it was unlikely that Bismarck's term in office would last.

> What is the view of the cartoonist of Source 2.26? How would you use knowledge of Bismarck's relations with parliament to assess whether this view was justified?

SOURCE 2.26

A cartoon of Bismarck published in a satirical Prussian magazine, *Kladderadatsch*, in 1866

SOURCE 2.27

Bismarck explains his view to the *Landtag*, January 27, 1863

The constitution upholds the balance of the three legislative powers [i.e. the king's government headed by Bismarck, the upper house, and the lower house] with respect to the budget. None of these powers can force the others to give way. The Constitution therefore points the way to compromise. If compromise is thwarted in that one of the three powers wishes to enforce its own views in a doctrinaire way, compromise will be impossible and conflict will take place. The life of a state cannot stand still, so conflicts become a question of power. Whoever has the power goes ahead with his views, for the life of a state cannot remain still even for a moment.

> How does Source 2.27 show that Bismarck believed more in realpolitik than in constitutions? Compare this with Source 2.28 below.

SOURCE 2.28

Bismarck, shown with part of a traditional Prussian spiked military helmet on his head, is holding the Constitution of Prussia and saying, "I can't rule with this." From the satirical magazine *Kladderadatsch*, 1863.

The protests of the liberals were ignored. Bismarck fought hard to strengthen the wavering support of the king. The army reforms went ahead. In the end, this was a turning point. It confirmed Bismarck in power so that the first critical moves towards unification could be taken in 1863 and 1864. It allowed for the development of the army, which, in the end, was the vital element in the unification by defeating Austria in 1866 and the subsequent defeat of France in 1870. It confirmed that there was a new, if brutal, realism at work in Prussian leadership which was to ensure victory even if at a cost. It also confirmed that liberal and parliamentary development in Prussia was to take second place to the needs of the army and that Prussian growth was to be dominated by conservative monarchism.

The Congress of Princes, August 1863 and relations with Austria

The domestic dispute confirmed Bismarck's authority in Prussia and permitted him the freedom to pursue vital elements of foreign policy. Crucially, Bismarck insisted that Wilhelm I did not attend the Congress of Princes, a conference proposed by Austria in 1863 to reform the German Confederation. Much against his inclination, the king agreed. This meant that the Congress (and Austria) was totally undermined.

Bismarck's intention was to exclude Austria from German affairs and strengthen Prusa's dominance. His long-term aim was to end the Austrian-dominated Confederation, not to reform it. Therefore, he intentionally undermined the Congress, which was totally ineffectual without the involvement of Wilhelm I.

The second major initiative to promote Prussian influence and undermine Austrian power was Bismarck's decision to cooperate with Russia in suppressing unrest in Poland. Both Prussia and Russia had taken Polish lands when the Polish state collapsed and was divided among its neighbours at the end of the eighteenth century. In 1863, the Poles under Russian control went into revolt. In the Alvensleben Convention, Prussia agreed to joint action to suppress Polish resistance, though this proved unpopular and Bismarck had to backtrack and agree to be neutral and not to aid Russia. Nevertheless, it established good relations with Russia, something which was to be of vital importance in the diplomacy of the 1860s and the move towards ending Austrian domination.

> ### ACTIVITY
>
> Using information in this chapter, including sources, and any additional reading, find evidence for each of these views:
> - "Bismarck had few set ideas about how to unify Germany but just improvised and responded to events."
> - "Bismarck had a clear vision for increasing Prussia's power over a united Germany."
>
> Which do you think is more convincing, and why?

War with Denmark, 1864

In 1893, a dispute arose which offered a great chance for Bismarck to move closer to his goal of ending Austrian control of Germany.

Causes of the war

Since 1460, the kings of Denmark had ruled two border provinces not as part of Denmark but as dukes of Schleswig (an area of mixed German and Danish speakers) and Holstein (an area of predominantly German speakers). German nationalists had wanted both duchies to be part of the German Confederation in 1815, and Danish nationalists had wanted Schleswig to be part of Denmark. In 1848, the Danish king tried to take over Schleswig. The German speakers resisted and called on the Frankfurt Parliament, Austria, and Prussia for help. Prussian troops were defeated, but Britain and Russia stepped in to insist that Denmark did not make Schleswig part of Denmark itself.

In 1863, the king of Denmark died, leaving no direct heir. His throne was inherited by Christian of Glucksberg – but his claim to Schleswig and Holstein was disputed. German nationalists thought that Frederick of Augustenburg had the rightful claim. But the Danish king who ascended to the throne in November 1863 annexed the duchies. The feeling in the *Bund* was to take action to install Frederick as duke and keep the duchies part of the Confederation.

Reasons for Bismarck's involvement

Bismarck needed to demonstrate a success to undermine liberal opposition to his policies in Prussia. He also wanted to find an issue which would weaken Austria and possibly provide an excuse for a showdown. Bismarck did not want to see any victory by the *Bund*, which he wished to destroy, not strengthen. He wanted any action to be taken by Prussia. This would assert its military power and gain prestige both in Prussia and among the supporters of German nationalism in other states. He persuaded Austria to take joint military action against Denmark.

The outcome of the war

In January 1864, Austria and Prussia invaded Schleswig and Holstein. The fighting was intense, with Denmark offering dogged resistance. However, the resources of Prussia and Austria were too great. The invasion spread into Denmark itself. A peace conference failed, and fighting resumed in June, with the final battle taking place in northern Jutland at Lundby. Austria and Prussia occupied the two duchies and the smaller Duchy of Lauenberg. Unlike in 1848, there was no foreign intervention. The Treaty of Vienna was signed between Denmark, Prussia, and Austria on August 1, 1864, with the Danish king giving all his rights in Schleswig and Holstein to Austria and Prussia, who also took control of Lauenberg and small border areas of Denmark.

Figure 2.3 The location of the duchies of Schleswig and Holstein and major battles from the war with Denmark

There was no agreement on Schleswig and Holstein, however. Bismarck wanted to annex them to Prussia. Austria wanted to install the Duke of Augustenburg to keep them in the *Bund* as self-governing states.

What can we learn from Source 2.29 about the reasons for Prussian victory in the war with Denmark?

SOURCE 2.29

A scene from the 1864 war with Denmark at Dybbøl. The heavy artillery of the Danish defences proved a difficult hurdle for Prussian forces.

The Convention of Gastein

In 1865 the two countries finally agreed by the Convention of Gastein to divide the duchies. Holstein would be run by Austria, and Schleswig by Prussia. However, Prussia and Austria would have joint sovereignty over both duchies. The Duchy of Lauenberg, an additional disputed territory, was given over outright to Prussia. It was not likely that this would be a final settlement. The agreement soon broke down, and the joint control was the immediate cause of a war between Austria and Prussia in 1866.

The importance of the dispute and the military action which followed can be summarized as follows:
- The authority of the *Bund* was undermined. Instead of joint German action, the issue was decided by an agreement between Prussia and Austria alone. The *Bund's* favoured candidate was not installed. The Austrians had allowed their influence over the *Bund* to be weakened. When they rejected the Convention in 1866, it caused a war.
- Prussia gained Schleswig in practice, if not in terms of law. This strengthened Prussia.
- Prussian forces showed themselves brave and successful against the Danes, and Prussian patriotism was stirred by the war and the victory in April 1864 at Dybbøl in Denmark. (The ease of Prussian victory is often overstated; the Danes had formidable defensive positions at Dybbøl, where the main battle took place, and some powerful artillery and warships. The fighting was bitter, and there were severe casualties on both sides.) The success of Prussian forces increased the prestige of Prussia and undermined Austria.
- The great powers of Europe stood aside and allowed Prussia and Austria to gain lands – the lesson was drawn by Bismarck that intervention in future conflicts was not likely. It would be unlikely that Austria would find allies.
- The war provided justification for further military expansion and showed the potential of the use of force. It justified Bismarck's claim that unification would be won by "blood and iron."

Increased tension between Austria and Prussia

Bismarck persuaded Austria to join an invasion of Denmark which went beyond the duchies. In the end, Prussia gained more, and it was Prussian rather than Austrian military forces which were seen as more responsible for the defeat of Denmark and taking revenge for events in 1848. Austria's position as the leading power in the German Confederation was undermined by the division of the duchies. The joint administration was likely to lead to tensions, which Bismarck could use to provoke a conflict with Austria. Running a Protestant German state far from Vienna was difficult for Austria, and it had gained little from the war, whereas Prussia had seemed to be the leading supporter of German nationalism and had improved its military reputation, as well as gaining land. By taking the rights of the rulers of Denmark in Schleswig and Holstein and not making them independent elements in the German Confederation, Bismarck had weakened the Confederation and Austria, which was its dominant influence. The Confederation had played no part in the war, nor was it involved in the final settlement.

What can we learn from Source 2.30 about the reasons for Prussia's war with Austria in 1866?

SOURCE 2.30

Bismarck writes to the Prussian ambassador in Paris after the Danish War in 1864

You believe that there is some hidden virtue in German public opinion, parliaments, newspapers, and the like which might support or help us in a policy of creating a German union. I consider that a radical error. Our strength cannot proceed from a press or parliamentary policy but only from our position as a great military power. I consider at the moment our correct policy at present is to have Austria with us. But whether the moment of separation comes and on whose initiative it will come, we shall see. I am by no means averse to war – quite the reverse.

Preparation for war with Austria

The war with Austria was the major turning point of Bismarck's leadership. Since the 1850s, he had understood that the military defeat of Austria was the key to Prussian expansion and dominance of Germany. The administration of Schleswig and Holstein could provide the excuse for war, but other factors led him to hope that Prussia could be successful.

- Economic and industrial expansion had given Prussia a strategic rail network which could be used for transporting troops quickly, and a superior weapon – the needle gun. This was a breech-loading rifle, which meant it could be reloaded faster, and it fired more rapidly and accurately than the Austrian weapons. It was developed as a result of German engineering skills and manufactured in factories using standardized parts and modern techniques.
- The army reforms had begun to create a more professional Prussian force, and there was an effective military leader, Helmut von Moltke, who understood the principle of assembling and concentrating forces quickly and decisively. The experience of modern war in the Danish conflict was also useful.
- Bismarck had worked hard to improve relations with Russia by cooperation over a revolt in Poland. At the same time, Austria's traditional links to Russia had been weakened because it had not supported its former ally during the **Crimean War**, which Russia fought against Britain and France in 1854–56.
- Austria itself had been weakened by war in Italy in 1859, when its forces had been defeated by France, and it had lost control of most of its valuable Italian lands in 1861.
- Industrially, Austria was less developed than Prussia, but rather than general economic weakness being a factor, it was the limited railway links to Austria's border with German states that was a key factor.

However, the bulk of the German states supported Austria. Bismarck had ignored their wishes in 1864 over Denmark, and Prussian military expansion was distrusted.

Secret alliance with Italy

Bismarck had secured an alliance with Italy in April 1865. This agreement committed Italy to supporting Prussia in a war against Austria. Italy aimed to regain the province of Venetia, which had remained under Austrian control since 1861. The new Italian state which emerged in 1861 included only part of the Italian-speaking lands. Rome remained outside the kingdom, ruled by the Pope and defended by France. Venice and the province of Venetia stayed under Austrian control. Italy wanted to regain Venetia, and Bismarck took advantage of this. In a potential war between Prussia and Austria, it would be crucial for Austria to be distracted by fighting in Italy.

ACTIVITY

Create a list of consequences of the war with Denmark. Create criteria to make a judgment about how important these consequences were. Use the impact of events over time in your judgment.

KEY TERM

The **Crimean War** (1854–56) was a war between Britain, France, and the Ottoman Empire on one side and Russia on the other. France and Britain were eager to prevent Russian expansion into the Ottoman Empire. The war was fought in the Crimean Peninsula. Austria did not support Russia, despite the help it had received in 1849. A series of battles led to a British and French victory which excluded Russian warships from the Black Sea and destroyed the Russian naval base at Sevstopol.

Meeting with Napoleon III at Biarritz, October 1865

Since Napoleon's defeat in 1815, French power had revived. Napoleon's nephew, Charles-Louis Napoleon (Napoleon III), had come to power as president of the republic proclaimed in 1848 and made himself emperor in 1852. In the event of a war between Austria and Prussia, the attitude of France was crucial. Napoleon III had a very powerful army, and if he decided to intervene, this would alter the military balance. Bismarck had hoped for an alliance with France, but Napoleon III was not ready for this. Instead, there was no firm agreement but an understanding that if Prussia went to war with Austria, France would not intervene. This cleared the way for a war, though there was no certainty that Prussia would win on its own. Napoleon probably thought that there would be a long struggle which would allow Italy to take Venetia from Austria – something that he supported. It would also mean that both Prussia and Austria would be weakened, which would increase France's relative power. He was to be greatly mistaken as the war led to a powerful new Prussian state on France's border.

> What is the attitude of the cartoonist in Source 2.31 towards the Biarritz meeting between Bismarck and Napoleon III?

SOURCE 2.31

German satirical cartoon of the "diplomatic breakfast" in Biarritz, October 1865. Napoleon III says: "Do take the oysters but give me the wine in exchange." Bismarck replies: "A thousand apologies but the wine goes with the oysters." It refers to an unequal advantage for Bismarck in his discussions with Napoleon. The lady in the background may be Katarina Orloff, who had a relationship with Bismarck. They met in Biarritz.

> ## NAPOLEON III
>
> Charles-Louis Napoleon Bonaparte, born in 1808, was the son of Napoleon's brother, the king of Holland. Educated in Germany, he spent his youth in Italy, where he became a passionate supporter of nationalism. He was forbidden to live in France after 1831 and led a number of uprisings against the French king, Louis Philippe. In 1848, he returned and was elected president of the new republic in 1848. He took full power in December 1851 and became emperor in 1852. He pursued vigorous policies of economic expansion, railway building, and the rebuilding of Paris. Abroad, he fought the Crimean War and the war of Italian unification.
>
>
>
> He built up the French army and aimed to be the key statesman of Europe. By 1870, he was moving towards a more liberal empire with a new constitution. He overestimated French military strength in 1870 and was defeated by the Prussian army and captured at the Battle of Sedan in September 1870, which ended his rule. He died in exile in Britain in 1873.

The reasons for the outbreak of war between Prussia and Austria

Two events turned the growing hostility between Prussia and Austria into war.

Bismarck's proposal to the federal Diet for a new constitution

Bismarck had alienated Austria by two actions. The first was his refusal to accept Austrian membership of the *Zollverein* when the agreement was due for renewal, and the second was the proposal on April 9, 1866 of a revised federal constitution with a new assembly elected by all adult males (universal male suffrage). This was an unlikely proposal from a conservative statesman who had overridden opposition in his own Prussian parliament. Austria reacted negatively. This attitude turned opinion in Prussia against Austria and helped to stir up bad feelings.

Austria's violation of the Convention (Treaty) of Gastein

Bismarck encouraged unrest in Holstein against Austrian rule and demanded control of military forces in Holstein and Schleswig. He also proposed plans for the Kiel Canal to link the Baltic and North Seas. With France's assurance that they would not support Prussia, Austria broke the Convention of Gastein and raised the Schleswig and Holstein issue in the German Confederation. This led Wilhelm I to believe that Austria was trying to control all of Germany, prompting Bismarck to send troops into Holstein, starting the war.

Compare the views of the reasons for war in Source 2.32 and Source 2.33. What similarities and differences are there? Identify specific evidence from each source to back up your answer.

SOURCE 2.32

Field Marshal Helmut von Moltke writing about the causes of war with Austria in 1866

The war of 1866 [between Prussia and Austria] was entered on not because the existence of Prussia was threatened, nor was it caused by public opinion and the voice of the people; it was a struggle, long foreseen and calmly prepared for, recognized as a necessity by the Cabinet, not for territorial aggrandisement, for an extension of our domain, or for material advantage, but for an ideal end – the establishment of power. Not a foot of land was exacted from Austria, but she had to renounce all part in the hegemony of Germany ... Austria had exhausted her strength in conquests south of the Alps, and left the western German provinces unprotected, instead of following the road pointed out by the Danube. Its center of gravity lay out of Germany; Prussia's lay within it. Prussia felt itself called upon and strong enough to assume the leadership of the German races.

KEY FIGURE

Helmut von Moltke (1800–91) was brought up in Denmark, where his Prussian father served with the Danish army. He joined the Prussian army and became a skilled military trainer. He served in the Ottoman Empire as a military advisor and fought in Egypt. He became a member of the Prussian general staff and took a particular interest in railways. Moltke studied military theory and rose to be chief of staff and eventually field marshal, leading the campaigns in Denmark, Austria, and France.

The outcome of the Seven Weeks' War

The war that Bismarck provoked in 1866 was not a foregone conclusion. It was a considerable risk. Austria was not a weak power. A long war might well have brought foreign intervention. It would also have led to much opposition at home. Wilhelm I was unhappy at waging war against a fellow Germanic monarch and was conscious that the majority of the rest of Germany was against Prussia. Everything depended on a rapid victory. Largely because of Austrian military incompetence and the rapid movement of Prussian forces into Bohemia, this was what Prussia achieved. The war lasted only seven weeks, and there was a decisive battle at Sadowa (or *Königgrätz*) on July 22, 1866. The Prussians, even though their forces were smaller overall, had managed to get 221,000 troops to the front to fight 206,000 Austrians. The outcome determined the fate of Germany.

SOURCE 2.33

Letter from British Foreign Minister, Lord Clarendon, to Lord Augustus Loftus. Loftus was appointed British ambassador at the court of Prussia in 1865.

> Austria will face war rather than the humiliation which Prussia seeks to inflict upon her; and in adopting that course I think she is perfectly right. A disastrous war is better than voluntary disgrace. But in the name of all that is rational, decent, and humane, what can be the justification of war on the part of Prussia ...? To destroy the present equilibrium of power would be a misfortune for the rest of Europe, and as such would be resented—in fact, the more the question is considered, the more certain it seems that Prussia will array against her the public opinion of Europe, as an aggressive and unreasonable Power; and we have no wish for that.

The war saw the end of Austrian domination of Germany. The Austrian Empire reorientated itself eastwards and took on Hungary as an equal partner in 1867, creating the Austro-Hungarian Empire. Together, the Austrians and the Hungarian Magyars dominated the eastern European nations of the Empire and accepted the loss of power in both Italy and Germany.

The Treaty of Prague

The peace treaty which Austria signed with Prussia in August 1866 was deliberately lenient. There were no victory parades, no annexations of Austrian land. Venetia in Italy was given to Italy, despite Austrian military successes against the Italians. The German Confederation was dissolved, but Austria otherwise remained intact. Bismarck did not want to add any Catholic or non-German territories, and he wanted to keep the option of future diplomatic relations with Austria.

> What can we learn from Source 2.34 about Bismarck's diplomatic ability?

SOURCE 2.34

Bismarck's advice to Wilhelm I prior to the war with Austria, 1866

We have to avoid wounding Austria too severely; we have to avoid leaving behind in her unnecessary bitterness or desire for revenge. We ought to keep the prospect of becoming friends again. If Austria were severely injured, she would become the ally of France. Acquiring Austrian lands such as Austrian Silesia or Bohemia would not strengthen the Prussian state. Vienna cannot be ruled by Berlin as a mere dependency.

Austria's allies in Germany suffered more than Austria itself. Prussia annexed Schleswig and Holstein, Hesse-Cassel, Hanover, Nassau, and Frankfurt. Four million Germans became Prussian subjects. Frankfurt was forced to pay a large fine to Prussia. The king of Hanover was expelled and his fortune confiscated. The expanded Prussia became the largest and most dominant state in a new confederation – the North German Confederation.

The southern states did not lose territory, nor did they pay compensation for opposing Prussia, but they were drawn into an alliance with Prussia. If Prussia were attacked, then the forces of southern Germany would be placed under Prussian control, and the south would lose its independence.

The formation of the North German Confederation

The greatest outcome of the war was the creation of the North German Confederation, the *Kleindeutsch* state that the revolutionaries of 1848 had so desired, though it had been created in a way that they had certainly not wanted. This state was given a new constitution which was extended to the whole of Germany in 1871.

The new German Confederation was a federal state. Each of the states kept its separate governments, except for those which had been annexed. They had their own laws, rulers, and assemblies. They raised local taxes and provided local services such as education.

> **KEY TERM**
>
> **Suffrage** The right to vote. "Universal suffrage" is the right of all adults to vote; "universal male suffrage" limits this right to adult men.

The overall authority for the North German Confederation was the Prussian king, who was the permanent president of the Confederation and his government – in other words, the overall authority was Bismarck. The new government controlled key areas of defence, trade, and foreign policy across all states. Laws affecting the whole confederation were to be made in the new parliament. The upper house, or *Bundesrat*, consisted of representatives from each state. These were sent (not elected) according to size. Prussia, the largest state, sent 17 out of 43 representatives. Saxony sent four, and most other states simply sent one. The lower house – the *Reichstag* – was elected by universal male **suffrage**.

This seemed progressive, but it was intentionally a different model of government than that supported by middle-class liberals. In any case, the *Reichstag* had limited powers. The lower house had control of the federal budget, 90 per cent of which was devoted to military spending. This was too vital an aspect for Bismarck to let out of his control, so there was to be no vote on this until 1872. Any measure passed by the *Reichstag* needed the approval of the upper house and the President of the Confederation, so the rights and responsibilities of the elected part of the constitution were very limited.

KEY DEBATE

BISMARCK: MASTER PLANNER OR IMPROVISER?

There has been much historical debate about whether Bismarck was a master planner who envisaged the direction that a new Germany would take, or whether he was merely an improviser who had some general objectives but no very clear idea how to put them into practice. Older historical studies tended to see Bismarck very much as a master planner. They argued that only the most elaborate military and diplomatic preparations could have ensured the success of German unification. The preparations were part of a plan, as expressed by Bismarck, long before his famous memoirs in which he said he put into operation a well-thought-out strategy to unite Germany.

Other interpretations see Bismarck with a general aim of increasing the power of the Prussian monarchy but taking advantage of circumstances rather than having anything like a specific plan.

For some historians, even though he did not have a detailed plan, he had "a strategy of alternatives" and his skill was choosing the right one and setting up a situation which allowed him to choose. Some see him as "a political genius," others as a skilful manipulator of circumstance.

Liberals change their attitude towards Bismarck

A domestic outcome of the war with Austria was a shift in public opinion from opposing liberal ideas to supporting Bismarck's virtual dictatorship. In the elections to the Prussian *Landtag* (lower house) in 1866, conservative and pro-Bismarck supporters increased their vote, while the liberal deputies were reduced from 253 to 148. The enthusiasm for Prussia's rapid victory and the creation of a new Germany was so great that a new party – the National Liberals – was created which supported Bismarck's policy. Together with the main conservative party – the Free Conservatives – Bismarck had a working parliamentary majority.

The Indemnity Bill, 1866

KEY TERM

Indemnity Bill The word "indemnity" means that Bismarck was freed from all responsibility or blame for having ignored the constitution. In effect, the liberals were saying that military and political success justified illegality – a dangerous precedent to set.

Significantly, the disputes over the military budget were put to one side by an **Indemnity Bill** in which parliament gave retrospective legality to Bismarck's undermining of the constitution since 1862. In retrospect, it was the end of any hope for a liberal Germany and the victory of "blood and iron." The bill saw a split between nationalism and liberalism. In 1848, the supporters of national unity had assumed that a new German state would be a liberal, parliamentary one. However, after 1866, the enthusiasm for a new national state overcame hopes for a more liberal state. The liberals accepted Bismarck's contempt for parliament, his establishment of a powerful army without consent, and his provocation of war just because he was successful in expanding Prussia.

ACTIVITY

Bismarck was a master of realpolitik

Create a table listing evidence from the period 1862–1866 to support this statement, and evidence to challenge it.

Support

Example: Alliance with Italy – Bismarck secured a strategic alliance with Italy in 1865, ensuring Austria would be distracted by a potential Italian attack on Venetia.

Challenge

Example: International Concerns – Bismarck's aggressive policies and military actions created concerns among European powers about potential destabilization.

> **ACTIVITY**
> Complete a table showing the similarities and difference between liberalism and nationalism in 1866 compared with in 1859.

> **SUMMARY DIAGRAM**
>
> ### Minister President Bismarck
>
> Why was Bismarck appointed Minister President in 1862, and what were his aims in the period to 1866?
>
> | Why was Bismarck appointed Minister President? | Aims 1862–66 |
> | --- | --- |
> | Reputation as a strong supporter of monarchy | Build up Prussian army |
> | Links with von Roon and Prussian aristocratic leaders | Get Russian support for more Prussian power |
> | Urgent need to push on with military reforms | Undermine Austrian influence and domination |
> | Experienced diplomat | |

4 How and why was the unification of Germany achieved by 1871?

The change from 1848–50 to 1867 was remarkable. In place of a weak and divided national movement, unable to dislodge Austria from its position of dominance over an ineffective German Confederation, a new Germany had emerged, backed by a strong Prussian army and a well-developed and expanding industrial economy. Bismarck's considerable insight and strategic acumen had ultimately paid off, leading to Prussia's increased power and influence in the new *Kleindeutsch* state. However, German unification as such was far from complete. Any more union with South Germany would bring opposition from France. There was also the danger of a war of revenge by Austria, despite the lenient Treaty of Prague. At home, industrial development had brought problems of urban slums and social discontent. The huge change in the balance of power in central Europe meant that it was of vital importance to pursue careful diplomacy with the other European powers. Growing nationalist feeling in Germany had been aroused by the successes of 1864 and 1866, but it was not in Prussia's interests to go further. Like many successful statesmen, Bismarck in 1867 had to face the implications and potential dangers that his victories had brought. The result was even greater unification by 1871.

Pressure from nationalists to complete the unification process

The defeat of Austria had brought about a *Kleindeutsch* state dominated by Prussia, which had joined its territories. The northern states had some control over their affairs under the federal constitution, but Prussia, with its strong military and economy, dominated the new Confederation. However, the main southern states remained outside the new Germany, as did Austria. So not all German speakers were part of the new Germany, and the new Confederation did include some non-Germans. Thus, nationalists, though obviously pleased by the unification achieved by 1867, were conscious that their ambitions for all Germanic people to be in one state had not been achieved and that the southern states might, in the future, align themselves with fellow Catholics in Austria or France rather than with the largely Protestant Germans of Bismarck's Prussian-dominated Confederation. There was considerable support for the National Liberals in both the old Prussia and the territories taken by Prussia. This was fuelled by anti-Catholic feeling, as the Pope condemned nationalism. It was also increased by hostility towards France as Napoleon III's wishes to gain Luxembourg were revealed. To make the new Germany secure would entail control of the South German states. The desire to be part of a Prussianized Germany was not strong in those states. There were increasing expressions of pride in the new Germany, its culture, and its military and economic progress – and nationalism, with its fear of French influence, did play a part in the greater unification.

Problems with the southern states, including lack of political unity

Bavaria, Württemberg, Baden, and the smaller states of Upper Hesse and Hesse Darmstadt had supported Austria in 1866. Even though they had not been taken over in the way that Hanover and Saxony had been, their freedom of action had been restricted by secret military alliances with the North German Confederation. There was also pressure to align the training and organization of their armies with those of Prussia. There was considerable resentment about this when the alliances were made public in 1867.

The *Zollparlament*

In 1868, Bismarck decided on a new expansion of the *Zollverein* – a *Zollparlament*. There were elections to a special parliament for members of the *Zollverein*. This was greeted enthusiastically by the National Liberals. The members of the *Reichstag* of the Confederation were automatically members of the new *Zollparlament*, but there were elections in the south. This might have been a way to unite Germany. However, the southern states elected regionalist representatives who were opposed to integration with Prussia. This showed the lack of enthusiasm among voters for being included in the North German Confederation, with its Protestant majority and Prussian leadership. Religious and political divides showed a lack of unity in Germany as a whole. It seemed unlikely that joint economic interests or a natural progression of German culture would bring about unity. Yet many believed that without including the southern states in a united Germany, the new German state was very vulnerable. France came to be seen as the major threat.

> What can we learn from Source 2.35 about German national enthusiasm? Consider the tone, emphasis, and imagery in the source.

SOURCE 2.35

Lyrics for a song from 1870 "The watch on the Rhine," which was widely sung in Germany

They stand, a hundred thousand strong,
Quick to avenge their country's wrong;
With filial love their bosoms swell,
They'll guard the sacred landmark well!
Chorus: Dear Fatherland, no danger thine;
Firm stand thy sons to watch the Rhine!

The dead of a heroic race
From heaven look down and meet this gaze;
He swears with dauntless heart, "O Rhine,
Be German as this breast of mine!"
Chorus: Dear Fatherland, no danger thine;
Firm stand thy sons to watch the Rhine!

While flows one drop of German blood,
Or sword remains to guard thy flood,
While rifle rests in patriot hand,
No foe shall tread thy sacred strand!
Chorus: Dear Fatherland, no danger thine;
Firm stand thy sons to watch the Rhine!

Napoleon III's ambitions

France was the key to Bismarck's diplomacy. France had a powerful army and had defeated Austria in the war of Italian unification in 1859. Napoleon III saw himself as a key figure in European diplomacy and saw Germany as an area of special interest. He and Bismarck had met in 1865 at Biarritz (see page 115), and Bismarck gained French neutrality in the event of a war with Austria.

Napoleon, however, lost his role in holding the balance of power between Austria and Prussia with the very quick Prussian victory in 1866. He hoped for some sort of compensation for the expansion of Prussia to ensure that the expansion did not extend to South Germany, which he wanted to keep as a possible area of influence. However, in place of a divided Germany, which might have been influenced by France, there was a new German state – the North German Confederation, this time dominated by Prussia.

The Luxembourg Crisis 1867

Napoleon had lost a lot of his bargaining power, and Bismarck was not going to offer much in the way of compensation. This was made very clear in the Luxembourg Crisis.

Causes of the crisis and why Bismarck encouraged it

Luxembourg was a small state on the border of France, Belgium, and Prussia. In 1815, it was agreed that it would be linked to the kingdom of the Netherlands, and its significant fortifications would be manned by a garrison of Prussian troops, which would act as a barrier against France. In 1867, a financial crisis in the Netherlands led to the French offering to buy Luxembourg, a move that Napoleon III hoped and perhaps expected that Bismarck would support. Bismarck was initially happy that France could be satisfied by this and encouraged the purchase.

However, German opinion was so opposed that even Bismarck could not merely agree to that. Having won liberal support by victory over Austria, Bismarck could not afford to have another confrontation, especially as Wilhelm I was also opposed to allowing France to expand in a territory on Germany's border. The generals were ready for war if France went ahead, but Bismarck was reluctant.

Outcome and effects on relations with France

Instead of going to war, Bismarck called an international conference in London. Bismarck agreed to withdraw Prussian forces, and it was decided that Luxembourg should be independent. This was actually favorable to France, but Napoleon and French public opinion saw it as a betrayal. France did not gain compensation for allowing Prussia to defeat Austria. Relations between France and the North German Confederation had worsened significantly. The crisis had brought the prospect of a war closer.

It seemed to Napoleon that Bismarck had gone back on his agreement at Biarritz, but there had been no formal treaty. Napoleon III was a ruler who depended on prestige and diplomatic victories, so this was a humiliation. For Bismarck, it was major cause of concern. The South German states were vulnerable to France. A resentful France might ally with these states and even with Austria against Prussia. The only hope for security would be to bring South Germany into the Confederation and to end any military threat from France. However, the French army was seen as the most powerful in Europe. Bringing in largely Catholic states to the Confederation would be likely to cause divisions. Also, the South German states were more liberal than Prussia. A larger Germany would also cause anxiety for its neighbors, Russia and Prussia, and even for Britain.

There was no easy solution to this problem, and it is not certain that Bismarck was committed to expansion. He had little interest in nationalism as such and had made it clear that the time was not "ripe" for further growth.

The Hohenzollern Candidature

Bismarck had consolidated the Prussian-dominated North German Confederation and added to Prussian territories. A weakened Austria was in no position to oppose this growth of Prussia. Britain had accepted the changes, including the acquisition by Prussia of Hanover, with its links to the English Crown. Russia had stayed out of the developments of the 1860s. However, France was resentful. The Catholic states of South Germany might be influenced by France. It was not impossible that France would ally with a fellow Catholic state, Austria, and there was a danger that Russia might change its mind because of the changed situation in central Europe and the emergence of a strong and more united Germany. Success had not brought security.

Bismarck may or may not have planned a war against France, but it was an option, and he was willing to take advantage of circumstances which arose in 1868 to give him the opportunity for a military solution. The Hohenzollern Candidature offered Bismarck the chance to progress with this option.

In 1868, the Spanish Queen Isabella was overthrown in a revolution. Rather than establishing a republic, the new government looked for a foreign royal family to provide a ruler. One candidate was Prince Leopold von Hohenzollern-Sigmaringen, the nephew of Wilhelm I of Prussia. He was married to a Portuguese princess, so had some links to Iberia.

If a Prussian prince became king of Spain, France would feel surrounded by Prussia – so this was a dangerous development.

Spanish crown accepted by Prince Leopold

Neither Wilhelm nor Leopold was enthusiastic, but Bismarck pressed them to accept. It was not unusual for princes to accept the throne of foreign countries. There was a strong possibility that opposition would build up and that international opinion would be unfavorable. It is not surprising that Leopold was unwilling and agreed only as a matter of duty to what Bismarck argued was in the interest of Prussia.

Why did Bismarck encourage the candidature?

There are a number of potential explanations for Bismarck's encouragement of the plan. Possibly, he planned to provoke France into war. He might have hoped that it would provoke a hostile French reaction and anti-German feeling which would drive South Germany away from France. He may have wanted to provoke a situation which might be of benefit to Prussia – perhaps confirming to Austria and Prussia that the French were unreasonable.

SOURCE 2.36

Bismarck writing to the Prussian ambassador to Bavaria, February 26, 1869

Violent events would bring about further German unity. To assume the mission of bringing about a violent catastrophe is another matter. Arbitrary interference in the course of history has never achieved anything except to shake down unripe fruit. That German unity is not yet a ripe fruit is obvious. We can put the clocks forward, but time does not move any faster.

> Consider Source 2.36 as a source of evidence about Bismarck's view of future unification. Who was the intended audience for this source? What impact might this have had on the attitude shown in the source?

These developments might have driven Bismarck into considering a war with France:
- By March 1870, French military growth was a matter of concern. Napoleon was equipping his forces with modern rifles and field guns; he had built up a reserve of a million men and was negotiating with Austria. This led Bismarck to consider a war before French military power became too strong.
- South Germany was showing distinct signs of hostility towards Prussia. There was no guarantee that the enforced military alliance with Prussia would be honored or that South Germany might not prefer an alliance with France and Austria. If this continued, then a war with France would be difficult, and Bismarck needed to take action before the southern states became too aligned with France and Austria.
- The growth of national feeling in Prussia and its military development meant that there would be little point in waiting for a future war. There were detailed war plans, transportation was available for getting troops to the French frontier, and the Prussian forces had new rifled heavy artillery developed by the Krupp armament firm. This new technology improved accuracy and range, which gave Prussian forces a significant advantage in firepower.

The French reaction

However, other elements drove Prussia into war. In France, a new foreign minister, the Comte de Gramont, was appointed, who was much more hostile to Prussia. An error by a clerk in Spain gave him opportunity to protest. The Spanish parliament (*Cortes*) had been dismissed before it had endorsed the candidature of Prince Leopold. Had the *Cortes* agreed, then it would have been difficult to withdraw. As it was, this gave the chance for France to protest and for Prussia to rethink. The candidature was withdrawn on July 12, 1870. That might have resolved the crisis if it had not been for a meeting between Wilhelm I and the French ambassador Benedetti on July 13, 1870 at the German spa town of Ems.

The Ems telegram

The Ems meeting was not aggressive. Benedetti passed on a request that never again would a Hohenzollern candidate be supported as king of Spain. Wilhelm I politely refused. The king reported the conversation to a leading diplomat who notified Bismarck via telegram. Seeing his opportunity, Bismarck edited the telegram to make it seem as if France had arrogantly demanded something from Germany which Germany refused to accept.

In both France and Germany, public opinion ran high, and the war which had been brewing since the acceptance of the candidature in March 1870 now became inevitable. A tide of German nationalism ensured that the South German states would respect their military obligations to Prussia. A tide of French nationalism pushed Napoleon III into war.

> How do the two versions in Sources 2.37 and 2.38 differ in the impression given of the encounter between Wilhelm I and the French ambassador Benedetti?

SOURCE 2.37

The original Ems telegram and Bismarck's edited version

Telegram from Privy Councillor Abeken to the German Chancellor Count Bismarck Ems, July 13, 1870.

His Majesty the King writes to me: "M. Benedetti intercepted me on the Promenade in order to demand of me most insistently that I should authorize him to telegraph immediately to Paris that I shall obligate myself for all future time never again to give my approval to the candidacy of the Hohenzollerns should it be renewed. I refused to agree to this, the last time somewhat severely, informing him that one dare not and cannot assume such obligations à tout jamais. Naturally, I informed him that I had received no news [about the withdrawal of the candidacy] as yet, and since he had been informed earlier than I by way of Paris and Madrid, he could easily understand why my government was once again out of the matter." Since then His Majesty has received a dispatch from the Prince [Charles Anthony]. As His Majesty has informed Count Benedetti that he was expecting news from the Prince, His Majesty himself, in view of the above-mentioned demand and in consonance with the advice of Count Eulenburg [a leading diplomat] and myself, decided not to receive the French envoy again but to inform him through an adjutant that His Majesty had now received from the Prince confirmation of the news which Benedetti had already received from Paris, and that he had nothing further to say to the Ambassador. His Majesty leaves it to the judgment of Your Excellency whether or not to communicate at once the new demand by Benedetti and its rejection to our ambassadors and to the press.

SOURCE 2.38

Bismarck's edited version of the telegram

Official Press Release, edited by German Chancellor Count Bismarck

After the reports of the renunciation by the hereditary Prince of Hohenzollern had been officially transmitted by the Royal Government of Spain to the Imperial Government of France, the French Ambassador presented to His Majesty the King at Ems the demand to authorize him to telegraph to Paris that His Majesty the King would obligate himself for all future time never again to give his approval to the candidacy of the Hohenzollerns should it be renewed. His Majesty the King thereupon refused to receive the French envoy again and informed him through an adjutant that His Majesty had nothing further to say to the Ambassador.

Declaration of war by France

France had been successful in ending the threat of a German monarch on the Spanish throne. The Prussian royal family did not wish to pursue it. The South German states did not support any growth of the influence of the Prussian house of Hohenzollern. Bismarck had thought of resigning. However, the French foreign minister, Gramont, went too far in demanding an assurance that the candidature would never be revived, asking for an apology and threatening war. Napoleon III depended on being a strong ruler at the head of a great power. In the face of what seemed to be a humiliating snub from Wilhelm I, and facing the threat from a major power emerging in central Europe, he decided on a showdown. Bismarck had engineered a French declaration of war.

Summary

It was a major achievement for Bismarck to enter the wars against Denmark and Austria without foreign intervention and to keep France out of German affairs. However, it came at a price. Napoleon III could not be expected to accept the major change in central Europe without any compensation for, or consultation with, France because his whole regime depended on his prestige and the restoration of France as a leading European power. Bismarck might have bought Napoleon off by allowing him to purchase Luxembourg, but he was prevented by the forces of nationalism in Germany, which he had himself unleashed. It became difficult for him after 1867 because no option was "the right one." After 1867, he was unable to establish good relations with France. He could not allow the situation to drift because of the danger that France would unite with Austria and South Germany against him. However, war was a dangerous option. Even if Prussia and the German Confederation won, France would remain an enemy and could not be contained forever.

The Franco-Prussian War, 1870–71

The war with France completed unification, as the military alliance between Prussia and the South German states meant that they joined as Prussia's allies, and this led to them being a formal part of a new German empire after the defeat of France.

Why Bismarck was in a strong position

If a showdown with France had to come, then Bismarck was in a strong position by 1870 in terms of domestic support, military strength, and lack of international support for France.

Lack of international support for France

Bismarck could count on the isolation of France. Austria might have allied with France to gain revenge for its defeat in 1866, but the lenient terms of the peace treaty had helped to reduce resentment. Austria looked eastward, away from Italy and Germany, after 1866, and, by forming the dual monarchy of Austria–Hungary in a major change in 1867, saw the future more in terms of its leadership of an eastern European empire. In any case, Austria was not in a military or economic position for another major war and had nothing to gain. Russia had little to gain from supporting either France or Prussia. Tsar Alexander II was pursuing internal change and did not wish to embark on a war.

Europe expected a long struggle between France and Prussia and was waiting to see how the war progressed. The tsar favoured the more conservative and traditional monarchy of Prussia, and Bismarck had worked hard to make sure there were good relations with Russia. Britain was more concerned about the effects of a French victory and any threat to the vital area of the Low Countries (Belgium and the Netherlands). It was a long-standing fear in Britain that a strong power such as France would control these countries, which might be used as a base to threaten Britain. There were more cultural ties between Britain and Germany, so British neutrality was likely. Italy had recently been fighting Austria to regain Venetia, so was busy absorbing new lands into a kingdom of Italy, which had considerable internal problems. Its aim was the removal of French troops from Rome and the gaining of the city for the new Italy, so it would not be likely to take any action to support Napoleon III.

Weakness of the French army

In military terms, the French army was well equipped with modern rifles and was fighting on home ground. However, it lacked the battle experience of the Prussian forces, and its organization was inferior. It was also numerically smaller, with 260,000 operational troops against the German 462,000. The French army was slower to mobilise its large reserve forces, and French forces arrived at the frontline on the border between France and Prussia without the full complement of troops and equipment, as advanced guards were sent on prematurely, and had to wait for reinforcements. German forces were sent in at full strength.

> **ACTIVITY**
>
> Compare the aims of the different players in the Luxembourg Crisis and the Hohenzollern Candidature. Include Napoleon III, Bismarck, Wilhelm I, and Leopold.

The French muzzle-loading artillery was inferior to the German weapons, and French leadership was poor. The French strategy of falling back on fortifications played into German hands. French tactics showed a lack of organization and grasp of the terrain. The French generals lacked the professional skills of Helmut von Moltke and his general staff.

The strength of the Prussian army under Moltke

The army reforms, which Bismarck had supported during parliamentary reform, had put Prussia in a strong position. German troops had gained battle experience in Denmark and in the war against Austria. In addition to the effective needle gun, which helped the speed and accuracy of the infantry, there had been a considerable expansion of Prussian heavy artillery developed by the Krupps factories in the Ruhr region. These breech-loading cannons were more accurate and destructive than any heavy artillery. As well as weapons, the Prussian forces were supported by an increase in railways. The Prussian general staff were masters of logistics – the technique of moving men and resources to the front line rapidly. This had proved to be of great value in 1866, and it allowed German forces in 1870 to be assembled far more quickly than those of France.

The command structure of the Prussian army was effective, with responsibility given to smaller units to ensure flexibility, with good intelligence work and careful planning to ensure movement of supplies. The forces of the allies of Prussia had been trained in Prussian techniques as a result of the military alliances with the south and the incorporation of the armed forces of other states in the North German Confederation. Moltke's leadership qualities were those of a master planner rather than an inspirational and charismatic commander, but they were suited to modern warfare, where concentration of force and efficient use of transport were war winners. Inspiration was supplied by nationalist fervor among the German forces in defending the homeland and demonstrating superiority over a France which had humiliated the previous generation by the victories of Napoleon. However, the outcome of a war against what was thought to be the greatest European military power was not taken for granted.

Impact of the German victory at Sedan

The German forces under Moltke moved rapidly to the border with France. Within days of the start of the war on July 28, 1870, 300,000 troops had been assembled. However, the initial attacks were costly, and there was no immediate, decisive battle as there had been against weaker Austrian forces at Sadowa in 1866. The battles of Worth and Spicheren, on August 5 and 6, were costly. The French commander, Bazaine, decided to fall back on the French fortifications at Metz. There were two more encounters as Prussian forces attacked them. These took place at Gravelotte on August 18 and at St. Privat-la-Montagne. The French forces did not follow up the initial repulse of the German attacks and again fell back on Metz. A relief force under Marshal MacMahon was sent to break the siege.

French forces retreated to the border fortress of Sedan, where German strengths could be used effectively against them. Firstly, Moltke moved 150,000 troops quickly to assault the fortification, and secondly, the superior German heavy artillery was suited to a siege. The bombardment and capture of Sedan on September 1, 1870 was not only a major victory in the sense of inflicting greater casualties on France (17,000 to the German 9000), but it also had the spectacular result that Napoleon III, who had been with his forces, was captured. This meant that France was trying to fight a war and organize a change of regime at the same time.

France continued the war as a republic. Marshal Bazaine held out at Metz while German troops besieged the fortress, but large German forces laid siege to Paris, where a government of national defense had been formed. Again, siege warfare was well-suited to German strategic strengths.

What impression of the French military is given by Source 2.39?

SOURCE 2.39

A British war correspondent reporting on French irregular troops in August 1870

Between Laon and Rheims, I passed through Chalons and Epernay, at which places I saw, for the first time, the francs-tireurs, or free-shooters. The corps was, in the most comprehensive possible meaning of the word, irregular. The men who composed it were not only irregular in everything they did, but appeared to glory in their irregularity. They seemed to have very few officers, and the few they had were seldom, if ever, to be seen on duty with the men. The latter had evidently souls above obedience, for they did very much what they liked, and in the manner they liked. They evidently hated the regular army, and the latter returned the compliment with interest.

Armistice agreed, January 28, 1871

France was far from giving up. They fought a **guerrilla war** in north France with irregular units attacking German forces, leading to reprisals. Irregular troops and units were French groups fighting as civilians without uniforms. They were treated harshly by German troops, who often executed prisoners, adding to the bitterness of the war. Another substantial battle was fought at St. Quentin in January 1871. There was bitter fighting in the Vosges region. However, French troops could not break the siege of Paris or inflict a decisive blow.

The French government had withdrawn to the south and decided, under the leadership of veteran politician **Adolphe Thiers**, to seek peace terms. On January 28, the Armistice of Versailles was signed, suspending fighting and starting negotiations to end the war. The end of the regime of Napoleon III meant that the war had lost its original purpose, and it was clear that fighting the superior German forces would lead to heavy losses and possibly a revolution, which conservatives such as Thiers feared.

KEY TERM

Guerrilla war A war fought not by regular armies on battlefields but by irregular, often improvised, groups attacking enemy forces and communications.

KEY FIGURE

Adolphe Thiers (1797–1877) was a lawyer, journalist, and historian from Marseille. He served King Louis Philippe as foreign minister and prime minister until the 1848 revolution ended his reign. He was a leading European figure and was chosen by the French parliament in Bordeaux to be national leader in February 1871. He negotiated a peace treaty with Prussia and suppressed the revolutionary Commune in Paris. He led France until 1873.

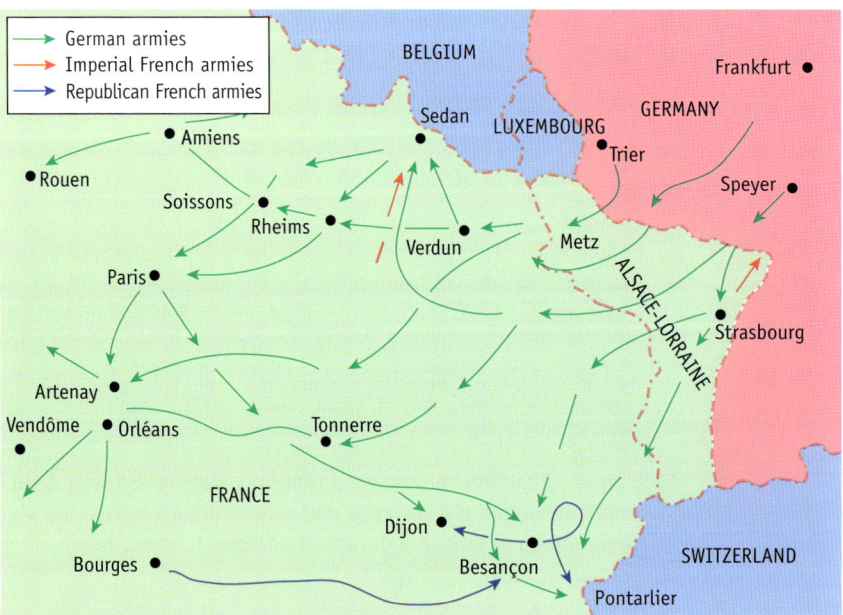

Figure 2.4 The Franco-Prussian War, 1870–71

Treaty of Frankfurt, 1871

The Treaty of Frankfurt saw Germany gain the provinces of Alsace and Lorraine, acquiring the city of Strasbourg and the fortress of Metz. France also agreed to pay a fine (indemnity) of 5 billion francs.

The taking of the two border provinces, which did have some German speakers but were nevertheless well-established parts of France, was reluctantly accepted by Bismarck as a concession to German national feeling and to Wilhelm I. The type of lenient peace that he had insisted on with Austria was not possible given the excitement and the losses incurred. There had to be some visible gains.

The final settlement was delayed by a revolution in Paris. The government there was overthrown by a radical commune which wanted to continue the war and take revenge on the governing classes. Eminent hostages, including the Archbishop of Paris, were shot. These events brought back memories of the Terror in the French Revolution and took place as Prussian forces surrounded the capital, watching as French government forces attacked Paris and took revenge. A final humiliation for France was that the new German Empire, unifying the South German states with the North German Confederation, was proclaimed in the Palace of Versailles – the great home of the former French kings.

KEY DEBATE

WHO WAS MORE RESPONSIBLE FOR THE FRANCO-PRUSSIAN WAR?

It is possible to see Bismarck as the key to the war. He knew that Napoleon III depended heavily on international prestige and saw himself as a key figure in European politics. It was inevitable that he would feel marginalized by the Prussian victory of 1866 and the reordering of power in central Europe, but Bismarck antagonized France over Luxembourg. There was no security for the North German Confederation without either a determined attempt to be on good terms with France or a conflict. The issue of the Spanish candidature showed that Bismarck had decided on conflict before France's military strength increased and the South German states moved closer to France. Bismarck also had to act before a possible friendship between Austria and France might encircle the new German state he had created. His deliberate alteration of the Ems telegram was the final push towards war.

This view of intentional conflict can be challenged. Bismarck needed a period of peace and stability to consolidate his new North German Confederation. France had formidable military strength, and there was no certainty of a successful outcome in a short war. A victory would cause huge resentment and lead to the need for long-term preparations against a future war of revenge. It would also unleash a wave of popular nationalism, which Bismarck despised. It is unlikely that Bismarck planned a war to bring the southern states into a new Prussian-dominated empire. There was little to be gained by adding millions of Catholic subjects to a largely Protestant state, and the more liberal nature of southern Germany as opposed to Prussia would be unwelcome. What drove the war, in this view, was the increasing instability of French policy and the unwillingness of Napoleon III to accept loss of influence in Germany and in European affairs. Bismarck was not an enthusiast of war. In 1866, he told a dinner guest who asked about a future war with France, "Anyone who has ever looked into the glazed eyes of a soldier dying on the battlefield will think hard before starting a war."

His support for the candidacy of a Hohenzollern prince was possibly reckless, but it was the French reaction which was the key element in bringing about war. Napoleon III was conscious of the need for a distraction from internal problems, eager to please French nationalism, confident in his army, and ready to pursue a dangerous policy of provocation.

ACTIVITY

Look back on the attempt to unify Germany by the Frankfurt Parliament in 1848 (see page 84). Compare this with the establishment of the German Empire in 1871. Identify similarities and differences between their aims, constitutions, and forms. Create a comparative table to highlight the key points.

KEY TERM

Kaiser German word for "emperor."

The creation of the German Empire in 1871

The French Empire had been defeated and had fallen. Now, the Prussian king was raised from the status of President of the North German Confederation to that of emperor. Prussia had become an empire. It lacked the different nationalities of the Russian, Austro-Hungarian, and British empires and did not have overseas possessions. Instead, this was an empire of princes, ruling over mostly German speakers with small minorities of Danish, Polish, and French people.

Concessions to the southern states

The southern states were now joined to the North German Confederation with the addition of the two conquered provinces of Alsace and Lorraine, ruled under Prussia. The federal structure of the North German Confederation and its key characteristics became the basis of the empire's constitution. The individual states (*Länder*) remained self-governing in most internal matters. Bavaria even kept its own army. They decided on the election of representatives to their local assemblies. The overall imperial government was appointed by the emperor – a hereditary role given to the kings of Prussia – which controlled foreign and defense matters and could introduce legislation for the whole of Germany. However, the southern states were responsible for local affairs and kept their hereditary rulers. They also sent representatives to the new *Bundesrat* (see page 130). The regiments of the armies of the southern states kept their identity, though they were incorporated into the German army. The royal rulers pledged loyalty to the new German emperor in a similar way to their ancestors who pledged loyalty to the Holy Roman Emperors, so a total break with the past was avoided. However, Prussia was definitely dominant.

Wilhelm proclaimed *Kaiser*

The German *Kaiser* commanded the allegiance of the royal houses of other German states, and the ceremony proclaiming the empire was dominated by royalty. It was not proclaimed in Germany but instead in occupied France, at the royal palace built by Louis XIV at Versailles. The civilian governments, the state assemblies, and the people were not involved. Bismarck gave himself an impressive military uniform (to which he was not entitled) for the occasion. The contrast between 1871 and 1848 could not have been stronger. Bismarck was keen to make sure there was no similarity to the situation in 1848 where Friedrich Wilhelm IV was offered the "crown from the gutter" by commoners and parliamentarians. Bismarck ensured that the princes of Germany were the ones who offered the crown to the king of Prussia in a special ceremony. The new empire and its constitution (see page 130) came about from Bismarck and Prussian military victory. The German princes had little option but to approve and proclaim their loyalty to the new emperor.

> What does Source 2.40 say about the nature of the German Empire? Note down specific details from the source to support your answer.

SOURCE 2.40

A painting of the proclamation of Wilhelm I as German Emperor, in the Hall of Mirrors at Versailles, January 1871

Figure 2.5 The German Empire in 1871

Constitution of the new Reich

For the empire, there was an elected lower house of parliament called the *Reichstag*, which met in Berlin. It could vote on imperial legislation and could control the imperial budget. However, most of the budget was military-related, and the voting for it was held every seven years, which was justified by the long-term nature of military planning. Adult males over 25 could vote, giving Germany one of the widest franchises in Europe.

The government was run by the Imperial Chancellor – Bismarck until 1890. Bismarck and his ministers were not elected and not responsible directly to the *Reichstag*, only to the emperor.

There was also a federal assembly called the *Bundesrat* consisting of representatives from all the states. In both the *Reichstag* and the *Bundesrat*, Prussia dominated as the largest state, comprising two-thirds of the new empire.

The domination of Prussia, Bismarck, and the emperor and the central role of the army led to the view that the new empire was essentially an absolutist monarchy with a facade of parliamentary rule. It was argued that this ended any hope of a liberal Germany. There are elements of truth in this, given the domination of Prussia and the limited role of the imperial parliament. However, it is not the whole picture.

- Bismarck kept a constitution and did not simply adopt a Russian-style absolute monarchy.
- There were parliaments in many of the individual states, which allowed for wider voting than in Prussia itself, which retained the three-tier franchise until 1918.
- Liberals were a strong force in the new Germany. Bismarck worked with them in the 1870s to bring about economic changes such as free trade and uniform weights and measures, which were part of the liberal agenda.
- Germany remained a state governed by laws, even though those laws could be repressive and were later turned against groups whom Bismarck saw as hostile, such as socialists and Catholics.
- Bismarck was not a member of the *Reichstag* and did not depend on it, but he did explain his policies to the parliament and worked to ensure that he had parliamentary support.

The constitution seemed to have liberal and even democratic elements, but as Prussia made up two-thirds of the new Germany, it dominated the *Reichstag* and *Bundestag*. Bismarck dominated the government, and because the new parliament could vote on the military budget only every seven years, it had little control over the army. Foreign policy remained firmly in Prussian control. The constitution has been described as a cover-up of control by the Prussian monarch and his powerful minister, Bismarck. However, states did keep some control of their own affairs, as federal and political parties were allowed to do so; perhaps this was unfair. Bismarck dominated the new nation, and though he despised parliament, he worked with it. The new Germany, as he predicted, had been created by "blood and iron." The militarism and nationalism which characterized it were ultimately to bring about war, dictatorship, and division.

> **ACTIVITY**
>
> Create a diagram showing the process of change in constitutions from 1815 to 1871. How much continuity was there?

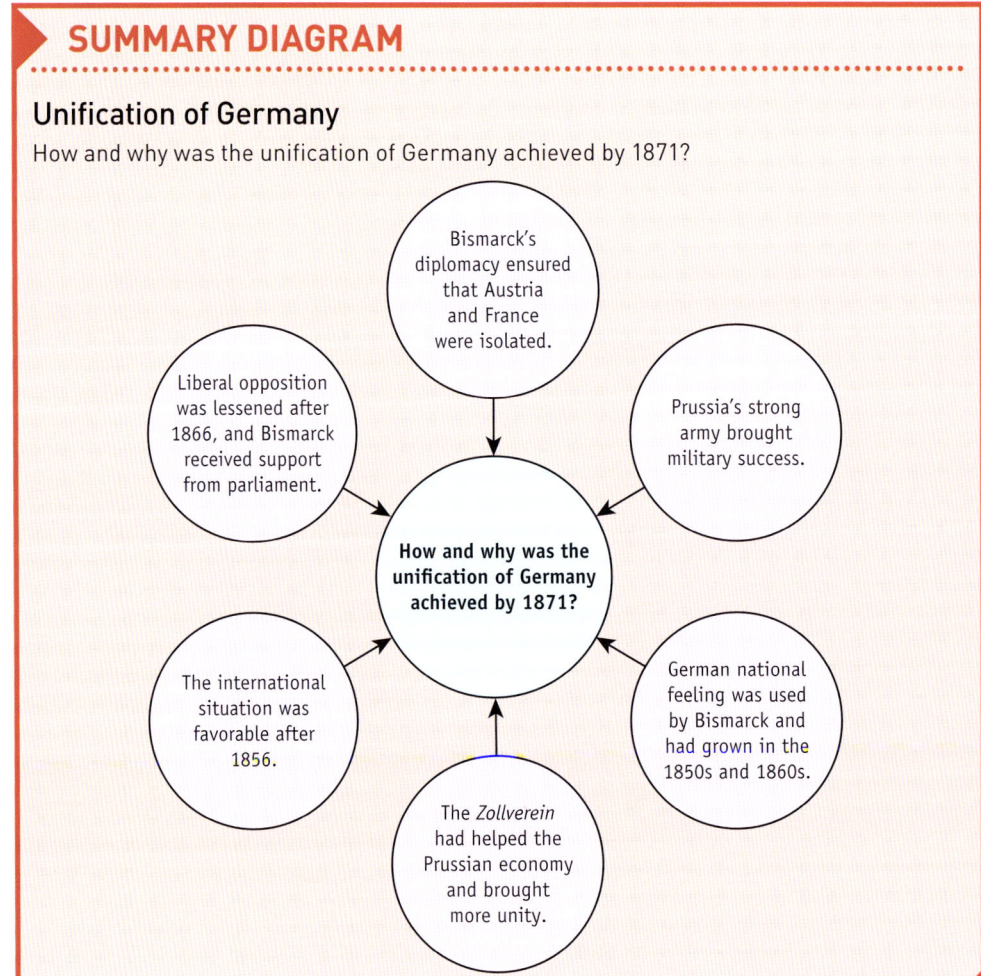

SUMMARY DIAGRAM

Unification of Germany
How and why was the unification of Germany achieved by 1871?

- Bismarck's diplomacy ensured that Austria and France were isolated.
- Prussia's strong army brought military success.
- German national feeling was used by Bismarck and had grown in the 1850s and 1860s.
- The *Zollverein* had helped the Prussian economy and brought more unity.
- The international situation was favorable after 1856.
- Liberal opposition was lessened after 1866, and Bismarck received support from parliament.

ACTIVITY

What was the most important factor in bringing about German unification?

Take each of the key reasons in the summary diagram and, on separate cards, explain its importance. Put the cards in order of importance. Compare your order with others in the class and discuss why there are similarities and differences.

After this, plan an essay: How important was Bismarck's diplomacy in bringing about German unification?

CHAPTER SUMMARY

The chapter has outlined the situation in Germany after 1815, when there were nationalist hopes and a desire, especially among students and some of the middle class, for a united and liberal Germany. These hopes ran up against the determination of Austria and its leader, Metternich, to keep Austria in overall control of a confederation of monarchies and to resist change. However, by 1848 it was no longer possible to maintain this system. The growth of the German economy and the development of a larger and more nationalistic middle class, together with economic grievances among workers and peasants, led to revolutions. A new German parliament assembled, and the early stages of the revolutions of 1848 saw changes in many German states. However, these did not last, and military forces suppressed revolutions and restored the authority of Austria and its monarchical allies. The humiliation of Olmütz showed how difficult it was going to be for even a conservative German union to be formed without Austria's permission. What developed, though, was greater nationalism and the economic power of Germany in general and Prussia in particular. However, this alone would not bring greater union. The arrival of Bismarck to power in Prussia marked a new era. He pushed through vital military reforms and by his diplomacy ensured that Austria was isolated and also that there was a reason for war. The joint war against Denmark in 1864 was a mistake on Austria's part. It strengthened Prussia's military reputation and gave Bismarck an excuse to go to war against Austria in 1866. Prussia won the war and brought about a big change in Germany with a new North German Confederation. However, with French hostility and the exclusion of South Germany, there was a dangerous situation, which was resolved only another war. Again, Prussia was successful, and again war led to greater German unity with the creation of the German Empire in 1871.

REFRESHER QUESTIONS

1. What were the signs of growing nationalism in Germany in 1815–48?
2. How did Metternich try to control Germany?
3. Why was there social and economic discontent by 1848?
4. What was the humiliation of Olmütz?
5. What were the indications of economic growth in Germany by 1871?
6. How was the North German Confederation brought about?
7. Why did Prussia and France go to war in 1870?
8. How did Bismarck ensure that no major foreign power intervened in his wars of 1866 and 1870?
9. Give any three reasons why unification was more successful in 1871 than in 1848–49.
10. How liberal was the 1871 Constitution?

Study skills

Source questions

Evaluating sources considering provenance

Once you are sure what the source is saying about the issue in the question (not just what the source is saying generally), you need to think what questions you need to ask yourself about its provenance (that is, who wrote it, when it was written, where it was written, and why). You will be presented with a variety of sources in assessments. These may include written extracts such as speeches or memoirs, or visual sources such as cartoons, posters, and photographs. These need to be analyzed carefully to decide if each is a stronger or weaker source as evidence in response to the question.

The danger is assuming that all diaries are reliable because the person involved in the historical events wrote them, or all newspaper articles are unreliable because the journalists want to sell papers, or all records of conversation are useless because the person might not remember the exact words. Try not to generalize about evidence by "type" – your response needs to be tailored to each source rather than being a stock response to the type of source. All sources need to be viewed with a critical eye, and not accepted at face value.

After looking to see what the source is, ask yourself some key questions. The nature of the source, its origin, and purpose will provide a good basis for your analysis:

- Why was it written? For example, if it is a speech, why was it delivered? What was the author's motive? How has that impacted what has been said/written?
- Who is the intended audience? A diary or a letter will have a different audience than a public report or a newspaper. Not all letters will be "private."
- When was it written? Something written in the middle of a historical development, when it is not clear what will happen, is very different than something written later, when the outcome is known. Equally, memoirs may be written well after the events occurred but still be strong evidence because of the person who has authored them.
- Is the source written by someone directly involved in events? Do you know some contextual information about this person? Remember that eyewitnesses might not be reliable or may withhold details for different reasons. You will need to use your own contextual knowledge to assess how accurate the details are from your knowledge of events.
- How typical is it? The source will give opinions by the author, but those ideas might not be typical of opinions at the time.
- What is the weight or value of this source as evidence in response to the question? What opinions are held? Does it strongly support one side over another?

Let us consider one source, Source A, in relation to the question:

"The main aim of the 1866 war was to secure Prussia's dominant power in the German Confederation." How far do these sources support this view? [25 marks]

Is this a stronger or weaker source of evidence in response to the question?

Answer the following questions to analyze the source.
- Who wrote the source and what was his connection to the war?
- When was it written? Was this a long time after the war?
- Why was it written?
- The source comes from a memoir. Who do you think would be the intended audience?
- What are the main points in the source which relate to the key focus in the question, which is securing Prussia's dominant power?
- What are the tone and emphasis of the source? Does it use "loaded language" which shows a particular view?
- How likely is it to be a reliable source of information? What might make it unreliable?
- What is the context? What do you know from your contextual knowledge about what was happening when this source was written? How might this effect Moltke's views? Use your knowledge of the dissolution of the German Confederation to interpret the source.
- Do you recognize the name of the creator of the source? If so, what would you expect their opinion to be? Does the content of the source match your expectation?

SOURCE A

Field Marshal Helmut von Moltke recalling the war of 1866 in his memoirs, published in 1893

The war of 1866 [between Prussia and Austria] was entered on not because the existence of Prussia was threatened, nor was it caused by public opinion and the voice of the people; it was a struggle, long foreseen and calmly prepared for, recognized as a necessity by the Cabinet, not for territorial aggrandisement, for an extension of our domain, or for material advantage, but for an ideal end – the establishment of power. Not a foot of land was exacted from Austria, but she had to renounce all part in the hegemony of Germany … Austria had exhausted her strength in conquests south of the Alps, and left the western German provinces unprotected, instead of following the road pointed out by the Danube. Its centre of gravity lay out of Germany; Prussia's lay within it. Prussia felt itself called upon and strong enough to assume the leadership of the German races.

Analyzing visual sources

You may be presented with a visual source to evaluate. This should be analyzed and evaluated in the same way as a written source, but you will need to make inferences based on the way the image presents information.

Visual sources include cartoons, photographs, and paintings. When writing about visual sources, you have to consider the context and provenance of the source. One way to do this is to consider various questions about the source such as the ones in the activity below.

ACTIVITY

Look at source 2.40 on page 129. Analyse this source, looking at both content and provenance.

Construct an answer to the following focus question using source 2.40.

"Bismarck was instrumental in the creation of a German nation-state." How far does the source support this claim?

Use these questions to help interpret the source and link your findings to the question.

- When was it produced? Does the date make it more or less reliable? Why?
- Why was it produced? What was its purpose? You will have to use your historical skills to infer why it was produced from its content. How are people presented, and who can you identify?
- Who is the intended audience? Is it aimed at German people or those in other countries?
- What is the central focus of the painting (who is portrayed in the middle)?
- What does the portrayal of people or events show about the nature of the German empire?
- Are there symbols or messages in the portrayal? Are features or clothing emphasized for effect? Why?
- What is the context? What do you know from your contextual knowledge about what was happening when this source was created?

Using these types of questions to analyse sources will help you build your evaluation skills. Once you have considered these points, think about your contextual knowledge of events and the people you have studied. Consider whether this knowledge and your opinion about the messages in the source and its nature, origin, motive, and audience have a positive or negative impact on its value as evidence.

Essay questions

Writing an introduction and writing essays analytically

Writing an introduction

Having planned your answer to the question, as described in the previous chapter (page 69), you are now in a position to write your crucial opening paragraph. This should set out your main line of argument and briefly refer to the issues you are going to cover in the main body of the essay. Analytical essays will require you to reach a judgment about the issue in the question, and it is a good idea to state in this vital opening paragraph what overall judgment you are going to make.

It might also be helpful, depending on the wording of the question, to define in this paragraph any key terms mentioned in the question.

Avoiding descriptive answers, writing analytically, and the crucial importance of the opening sentence of each paragraph

Causal essay questions

Causal essay questions are not asking you to describe events or developments; instead, you have to explain causes. Very good answers will distinguish between the relative importance of different causes.

Look at these two extracts from answers. One describes, and one explains.

Explain why the Frankfurt Parliament collapsed. [10 marks]

Extract A

The Frankfurt Parliament which was elected in 1848 was an attempt to create a national parliament and included representatives from all over Germany. It consisted largely of middle-class Germans who wanted a united Germany. It debated a new constitution and offered the throne of a new German state to the king of Prussia. There was a discussion about whether Austria should be included. The Frankfurt Parliament did not last, and by 1849 the experiment was over.

Extract B

The Frankfurt Parliament was a bold attempt to create a new united Germany, but its composition did not reflect the whole nation. It was dominated by the urban middle class, and this was a long-term weakness. The working classes and the rural communities were under-represented. This led to divisions, and the middle classes were afraid of the unrest among the urban workers, weakening the unity of the movement for a new Germany. Another major weakness was the failure of the parliament to produce strong leadership. The major power which sent representatives was Prussia, but the Prussian King Friedrich Wilhelm IV refused to accept the throne of Germany because it would have meant accepting change brought about by his subjects and went against his idea of monarchy. The parliament could not agree on whether Germany should include Austria with its extensive eastern lands or just be a "kleindeutsch" nation of German speakers. Thus, a new constitution could not be brought in before the victories of Austrian forces against rebels in the east meant that Prussia and other German princely states began to restore the power of the traditional rulers. The revolutionaries who had brought about the new parliament were not willing to take up arms to defend it and preferred the restoration of the old Confederation to social upheaval and further repression by military force. Though a lot has been made of long-term weaknesses and divisions, the key element was the lack of support of the Prussian king because the loyalty of the Prussian army was to him, and in the end the power of the armed forces was too much for the liberals.

Extract B not only avoids telling the story but makes a distinction between long- and short-term causes and begins to argue about the relative importance of different explanations.

Analytical essay questions

These types of questions require an analytical answer and not a narration of events. This means you must focus on the key words and phrases in the question and link your material back to them, which is why your essay plan is crucial, as it allows you to check you are doing it. You can avoid a narrative answer by referring back to the question, as this should prevent you from just providing information about the topic. To keep focused on the question, ensure that the last sentence of each paragraph links back directly to the question.

Let us consider the following analytical essay question:

To what extent was German unification the result of Bismarck's actions?   [20 marks]

In order to answer this question, you would need to consider the following issues about Bismarck:
- Did he enable unification by allowing the army reforms to go ahead?
- Did his diplomacy ensure that the other powers did not support Denmark, Austria, and France and so allow him to use these wars to unify Germany?
- Did he bring the South German states into a new German Empire by provoking and winning a war against France?

Then, you would need to consider other factors such as:
- the economic impact of Prussian economic growth and the *Zollverein*, which gave Prussia its strength and influence
- the weaknesses of Bismarck's opponents both inside and outside Germany
- the diplomatic situation which led other powers not to interfere and made Bismarck's diplomacy possible.

A very strong answer will weigh up the relative importance of each factor as it is discussed; a weaker answer will not reach a judgment until the conclusion, and the weakest answers will either just list the reasons or, worst of all, just describe them.

The following is part of a descriptive answer for the question above:

> Bismarck became Minister President in 1862 and achieved success in getting army reforms by ignoring the Prussian parliament. He made an agreement with Russia in 1863 and fought successful wars against Denmark and Austria. In 1867, he formed the North German Confederation, increasing the power of Prussia. Relations with France declined from the good terms he had negotiated in 1865 to war in 1870. The defeat of France led to the proclamation of the German Empire in 1871.

The paragraph offers a lot of factual material but does not explain how these developments led to unification or how they show Bismarck's role or the role of other factors. Why was it so important for unification that Bismarck pushed through army reforms? What was the significance of the agreement with Russia, and did Russian neutrality just depend on Bismarck? Why did the wars lead to unification, and were the victories entirely the work of Bismarck?

> This paragraph outlines some of the facts about war and is quite well informed, but there is little explanation. Was Moltke a good leader, and why? What was the significance of the withdrawal of Metz and the capture of the emperor? The reader is having to do a lot of work to find the actual explanation.

The Franco Prussian war began in 1870. Prussia had the support of the South German states, and their leader was Moltke. Prussia brought their troops to the French frontier and invaded rapidly. There were battles in which France resisted the advance. The French leader, Bazaine, decided to fall back on the fortress of Metz, which was besieged. A large French force was at Sedan, but this was encircled and during the battle the French emperor was captured. The French government decided to go on with the war, but the Germans besieged Paris.

The opening sentence of each paragraph

One way that you can avoid a narrative approach is to focus on the opening sentence of each paragraph. A good opening sentence will offer a view or an idea about an issue relevant to the question, not describe an event or a person. With a very good answer, you should be able to read the opening sentence of each paragraph and see the line of argument that has been taken in the essay. It is therefore worth spending time practicing this skill.

ACTIVITY

"Economic and social discontent were the main reasons for the outbreak of revolutions in Germany in 1848." How far do you agree? [20 marks]

Look at the following ten opening sentences. Which of these offer an idea which directly answers the question above, and which simply give facts?

1. Revolution was widespread in Germany in 1848.
2. The poor harvests and unemployment were a key reason for revolution in 1848.
3. Some revolutionaries preferred a *kleindeutsch* solution.
4. There was widespread discontent about Metternich's policies by 1848.
5. The revolutionaries had different aims. Some wanted a new constitution; others wanted economic reform.
6. The revolutions were most successful in urban areas which had social and economic discontent.
7. The 1848 revolutions had many causes, but national feeling was more important than economic discontent.
8. There was a great deal of enthusiasm for revolution in 1848, and hopes for change were very high.
9. There were uprisings in many cities such as Berlin and Dresden in 1848.
10. 1848 was the year of revolutions throughout Europe.

3 Russia from autocracy to revolution, 1881–1924

Introduction

This chapter looks at developments within Russia as the state changed from the absolute rule of a tsar to the establishment of the world's first communist regime. It will consider how and why revolutionary events developed and why the regime was unable to prevent its overthrow. Finally, it will examine the reasons why there was so much instability and how the Bolsheviks were able to emerge as the ruling power. This chapter examines these developments through the following questions:

▶ What challenges faced the Tsarist regime between 1881 and 1894?
▶ What were the causes and outcomes of the 1905 Revolution up to 1914?
▶ How and why did the Bolsheviks seize power in October 1917?
▶ How were the Bolsheviks able to consolidate their power up to 1924?

▶ KEY DATES

1881	Alexander III becomes tsar after assassination of Alexander II
1885	Creation of Peasants' Land Bank
1887	Proposed Constitutional reform Failed attempt to assassinate Alexander III
1889	Land Captains introduced
1891	Famine
1894	Nicholas II comes to the throne
1904	War with Japan
1905	Revolution October Manifesto
1906	Fundamental Laws First *Duma* meets
1906–11	Stolypin is prime minister
1911	Stolypin assassinated
1912	Lena Goldfield Massacre
1914	Russia enters First World War
1915	Nicholas II takes personal command of his forces
1916	Brusilov offensive
1917	February Revolution Abdication of Nicholas II Establishment of Provisional Government Return of Lenin July Days Kornilov Mutiny October Revolution

(Continued)

> ## KEY DATES (Continued)
>
> | | |
> |---|---|
> | 1918 | Civil War |
> | | Constituent assembly meets |
> | | War Communism |
> | | Murder of Tsar Nicholas and royal family |
> | 1921 | Kronstadt Rising |
> | 1921 | New Economic Policy introduced |
> | 1922 | USSR comes into existence / formed |
> | 1924 | Death of Lenin |

1 What challenges faced the Tsarist regime between 1881 and 1894?

Russia was an enormous country, covering 21 million km² by 1900, and stretching across two continents – Europe and Asia. Its size made it very difficult to rule effectively. Most of the population lived in European Russia, where the two largest cities, Moscow and the capital, St. Petersburg, were situated. Its capital was nearer to New York than to Vladivostok. The country was made up of a wide range of different peoples, nationalities, and religions, which made controlling the country even more difficult.

Figure 3.1 Map showing the Russian Empire

The state was ruled by one person, the tsar, who by both law and tradition was an **absolute** or **autocratic ruler** (see page 141). The tsar treated the country almost as his personal estate, which meant that the chances of major reforms or modernisations were very unlikely. The tsar's position was further supported by the Russian Orthodox Church. It was deeply conservative and was determined to preserve the Tsarist system and saw it as its duty to teach the people obedience to the tsar. Although there were official bodies such as the Imperial Council, the Cabinet of Ministers, and the Senate, which gave the tsar advice, his word was final.

KEY TERM

Absolute/autocratic ruler One person who rules with complete control over their subjects.

KEY TERM

Peasants Peasants is the term used for the majority of people in Russia, who lived in rural villages. They worked on the land, growing crops and rearing animals. Some peasants worked for landlords, and others lived in rural communes. Some peasants were known as "state peasants" and paid taxes to the Tsarist state directly, and they had more freedom. Living conditions for all peasants were harsh, and few owned any land, even after reforms were made. Almost all peasants had to pay taxes.

KEY FIGURES

Alexander II (1818–81) was welcomed to the throne following the harsh rule of his father, and many were pleased with his reforms. However, more radical groups wanted further change and the ending of autocracy. Alexander was assassinated by the People's Will, a terrorist group, having just signed an agreement which would have brought about very limited constitutional change.

Russia was a rural state, with some 80 per cent of the population living in the countryside. The peasants lived in single-room wooden huts along with any animals they possessed. Life expectancy was estimated at 40 years for males because of the awful working conditions, disease, and starvation. Women's life expectancy was shorter, estimated at 30 years, due to a lack of healthcare for mothers, and poor nutrition. There were signs of urban and industrial growth, but in 1881 industrial enterprises were small-scale.

How Russia was ruled in the period from 1881 to 1894

Throughout the period from 1881 until 1917, Russia was ruled by two tsars, Alexander III, 1881–94, and Nicholas II, 1894–1917. They were both autocrats who used a mixture of reform and repression to enforce their will. This was reinforced through manifestos, speeches, and policies. The introduction to the Fundamental Laws of 1832 had stated the tsar was an autocratic and unlimited monarch. Although Alexander III's father, **Alexander II**, is often described as a willing reformer, even he was determined to uphold this autocracy, while Alexander III himself is often associated with a period of repression, following the assassination of his father in 1881. Therefore, even when reforms were made, there was no question of the tsar relinquishing any control.

By the start of the 1880s, Alexander II had become more isolated from the people and unpopular with the more educated in society. He became more and more conservative in outlook. However, the death of his first wife in 1880 and his marriage to the much younger and more liberal-minded Princess Dolgoruky resulted in a confused policy with the appointment of Loris-Melikov as Minister of the Interior. Not only did Melikov abolish the Third Section (secret police), but he also removed the reactionary Tolstoy at the Ministry of Education. Most importantly, Melikov took the government towards the most significant political reform of the reign. During Alexander II's reign, changes were made to local government, including the introduction of the *Zemstvos*. These were rural councils established across the country. They had members voted for by landowners and peasants, weighted in the favor of the nobility. *Zemstvos* had powers over local issues. By 1881, plans were in place for the summoning of a national assembly, in part made up of nominated

ALEXANDER III (1845–1894)

1881	Becomes tsar following the assassination of his father, Alexander II
	Immediately issues Statute Concerning Measures for the Protection of State Security and the Social Order. Starts program of Russification.
1884	Education brought more closely under state control
1885	Peasants' Land Bank established
1889	Land Captains appointed
1891	Famine
1894	Dies of kidney disorder

Alexander III was the second son of Alexander II, best known for his height and physical strength. From an early age, he was prepared for a military career, but in 1865, at the age of twenty, he became heir to the throne when his older brother, Nicholas, died suddenly. Alexander's military background may explain his staunch belief in autocracy. His rule is seen as one of repression and often contrasted with that of his father. Alexander III believed that his policies would restore stability and preserve autocratic rule. His reign was largely peaceful and witnessed a series of successful economic reforms under his finance minister, Sergei Witte.

> **KEY TERMS**
>
> **Zemstvo** A form of local government in Russia. Introduced by Tsar Alexander II, they were run by elected officials called Land Captains.
>
> **Paternalistic** Describes a fatherly but controlling concern for the welfare of the people.
>
> **Liberal democracy** A system in which the people vote for national assemblies or parliaments to whom governments are responsible. Governments must keep to the laws approved by assemblies and respect the rights of citizens to free speech and freedom from punishment without trial.

members, but also including elected representatives from *Zemstvos* and town councils. Alexander had just given his personal approval to it when he was assassinated. It was a limited move away from autocracy. It did not aim to establish a constitution, but it did represent a move towards a more representative body.

Autocracy

There were several elements to Russian autocracy.

The role of the tsar

Autocracy meant that all policymaking and decision-making was in the hands of the tsar. As head of the Russian Orthodox Church, the tsar (and many others) believed he was appointed by God and accountable only to him, and not the Russian people. However, this also meant that he was responsible for the spiritual and physical well-being of his people. As a result of his divine appointment, many believed that he had semi-divine powers and that it was his duty to set moral standards while protecting the people from evil. Although his edicts were law and he was free to choose his own advisors, he was seen as a **paternalistic** figure, with most Russians viewing him as the "little father." Most of the population, some 80 per cent, were illiterate peasants, and therefore it was believed they lacked the ability to reason and make decisions which would be needed in a **liberal democracy**. Many believed any move towards democracy would bring chaos.

The role of the State Council and key ministries

Although the tsar was all-powerful, the task of ruling and defending such a vast country which lacked natural defences was not an easy one. In practice, he was unable to make all decisions, and there were a variety of organs of government with specific roles. Alexander III inherited a central government structure dating back to the early nineteenth century, and it would remain largely unchanged until 1905, when revolutionary events appeared to bring about change. Government was highly centralized and hierarchical, with the tsar at the top and the other elements of government answerable to him, not the people. Under Tsarist rule, there was:

- the Council of Ministers. This was the main lawmaking and administrative body which discussed draft legislation. It acted as the link between the other elements of government and the tsar. It was not used by Alexander III after 1882.
- the Imperial Council of State, established in 1810. It advised the tsar on finance and legal issues, but he did not have to follow its advice.
- the Committee of Ministers, established in 1861. Each minister had specific responsibility for a particular aspect of the administration. The most important were the Minister of the Interior, responsible for domestic affairs, particularly law and order; the Minister for War; the Minister for Finance; and the Chief Procurator of the Holy Synod, responsible for religious affairs.
- the Senate. This was the Supreme Court, and its main duty was to act as the final court of appeal on legal issues.

Alexander III also relied on a number of close advisors, in particular Konstantin Pobedonostsev, who was the chief minister in the government from 1881 to 1905 and also Chief Procurator of the Most Holy Synod, the governing body of the Russian Orthodox Church. He was extremely conservative and had developed a deep dislike for anything which appeared to be liberal or democratic, dismissing the idea of representative government as "the great lie of our time." He had been the personal tutor to Alexander III and would also act as tutor to the future tsar, Nicholas II, and therefore did much to shape their outlooks. His opposition to any reform and his upholding of repressive policies led to him being known as "the Grand Inquisitor." It was his belief in the absolute autocracy of the tsar which held great weight in the political development of Russia in this period.

> ### KONSTANTIN POBEDONOSTSEV
>
> Best known for his reactionary attitude and policies, Konstantin Pobedonostsev (1827–1907) was a civil servant and professor of civil law at Moscow University. He was appointed tutor to the future Alexander III following the death of his brother, as Alexander II believed his son needed support because he had been prepared for a role in the army, not to rule Russia. His autocratic and conservative beliefs would have a major influence on the future Alexander III. Pobedonostsev was devoutly religious and was appointed Chief Procurator of the Most Holy Synod. This post was a civil role which meant he had a huge influence over education and censorship, as well as directing religious policy. He was an opponent of liberal democracy and supported autocracy. He held antisemitic views.

The role of the army

The Russian Imperial Army played an important role in enforcing autocracy. The tsar was the supreme commander of the army and could deploy units wherever and whenever he wished. Russia had the largest army in Europe, comprising over 900,000 men, and although the army was only rarely used domestically, it was an effective deterrent against any opposition to the tsar.

Russia's army was comprised mostly of peasants, who were conscripted for 25 years. There were frequent church services at which priests would often bless the soldiers' bayonets and tell them that to die fighting for the tsar was a holy experience. Officers came from the cadet corps. This was a military training organization for young people, but only those from the nobility. The system was one of patronage and privilege, based around birth and promotion rather than merit. The tsar himself selected the higher officers as a reward for loyal service. In theory, therefore, those serving in the army would support autocracy and enforce it militarily. However, despite its imposing size, the Imperial Army had many weaknesses and problems (see page xx).

The role of the Church

The Russian Orthodox Church was also one of the main supports for the autocracy and played an important role in the government of the country. It was closely connected to the regime, promoted the idea of divine right, and greatly influenced the superstitious peasants who formed most of the population. Its importance ran from the very top of the Church, as seen with the influence of the reactionary Konstantin Pobedonostsev, who was appointed to the non-clerical role of Chief Procurator of the Holy Synod in 1880 and played a key role in advising Alexander III. The influence of the Church was also seen at a local level. Priests had close ties to their villages. They read out government decrees and informed the police of subversive activity, acting as the "eyes and ears" of the government in the local area. The Church also exercised censorship controls, and punishments for social and moral crimes, thereby having an influence over the daily lives of the people and helping ensure that traditional values were upheld, even in areas far away from the centre of power.

The effectiveness of the system

This system did appear to work effectively, but changes in Russian society and the economy led to political groups emerging who wanted political reform and constitutional changes, while as the period progressed some radical elements called for the complete overthrow of the Tsarist system.

Alexander III was determined to uphold the principle of autocracy, believing that his father had been too liberal in his rule. Konstantin Pobedonostsev encouraged the tsar to reassert the principle of autocracy and abandon his father's reforms. Alexander III announced, "I shall be sole and absolute ruler, for a kingdom cannot be ruled without an iron hand. Only absolute power can safeguard Russia." This approach was characterized by many of his policies, which were repressive in nature.

Reform and repression

Although the tsars were not willing to countenance a dilution to the autocracy, reform and repression were both used to control the population. When reform was introduced, be it political, social, or economic, it was usually as a means of appeasing opposition and making sure that the Tsarist system worked more efficiently and effectively by modernising the institutions over which it presided. During Alexander II's reign, he undertook reform for precisely these reasons, passing a series of reforms, the main ones of which were as follows:

1861	The Emancipation of the Serfs
1862–75	Army reforms
1863–64	Education reforms
1864	Introduction of new legal system
1864	*Zemstvos*, or local councils, established
1870	*Dumas*, or municipal councils, established

Key issues for Alexander III and the legacies of his father's reforms

Of all Alexander II's reforms, it was the Emancipation of the Serfs edict, announced in 1861, which had the most long-lasting consequences. There were political, social, and economic impacts of the Emancipation, many of which would last into the reign of Alexander III and beyond.

Before the edict, peasants were attached to the land, were subject to the authority and jurisdiction of the landlords, and worked under the system known as "serfdom." This meant they were under the total control of the landowner. In return for a family allotment, the serfs had to work the land and undertake military service. However, there was growing disquiet among the peasantry, who wondered why they had to pay for land their families had farmed for generations. They were, after all, the very people who worked to feed the Russian population. As a result, unrest grew and Alexander II and others were concerned that the regime could face serious challenges.

The Emancipation edict laid down a number of terms:
- Privately owned serfs were freed. (State serfs followed in 1866.) They could now own property, run businesses, and marry whom they chose.
- The former serfs received land from the estates of the nobility.
- The state compensated the nobles for the loss of land and income.
- The peasants had to help pay the compensation to the nobles through **redemption payments**. These payments were spread over 49 years, and former serfs gained the legal right to the land only when these had been paid.
- The administration of the system was carried out by the members of the village council, or *mir*, who held the land collectively and were responsible for the payment of taxes and redemption payments.

This reform has led to Alexander II being called the "Tsar Liberator." However, many peasants and nobles did not like the terms, and there was considerable opposition.

The lasting impacts of emancipation

Emancipation impacted peasants in many ways. Firstly, the allocation of land did not satisfy the peasants' desire for land, and that failure would eventually play a role in the collapse of the Russian Empire. Much of the land they were given was of poor quality, and they usually received about four-fifths of what they farmed before. Peasants were often unable to meet the redemption payments, as they could not earn enough from the land they had been given.

It has been argued that peasants were free only in theory; practice was very different. Their lives were now effectively controlled by the *mir*, a peasant assembly which had the authority to redistribute land, determine what was to be grown, and ensure that the principle of subsistence farming remained intact. The *mir* organized the payment of taxes and was also responsible for redemption payments. It could prevent peasants who were in arrears from travelling over 20 miles by withholding passports.

However, peasants were at least now able to regulate their private lives, bring actions through self-governing peasant courts, and engage in trade.

KEY TERM

Serfs Agricultural labourers bound to the lands or estates they worked on. They belonged to their landlords. Serfs had to work on the land, pay rent for their homes and land taxes, and were legally tied to the landowner's estate. They were "freed" from this status by Alexander II's "Emancipation of the Serfs" in 1861, but most remained poor and with limited freedom.

Redemption payments The repayment of loans which had been used to purchase land following the Emancipation edict of 1861.

There were very limited benefits to agriculture. Agricultural productivity rose by 20 per cent by the end of the century, but Japan's, in comparison, doubled. Many agricultural problems remained after emancipation. The *mir* being in control discouraged peasants from trying different methods which could have further raised production levels. As they still did not really own the land, most peasants made very few attempts to improve it. To meet redemption payments, the peasants were forced to sell most of their grain, which meant they had little seed for the following year and little money to invest in improving their land. Many of the worst elements of the pre-Emancipation farming system remained in place. The strip system limited attempts to increase crop yields as much land was wasted. The strip system and the three-field system (where land was divided into thirds, and one third was left to rest each year) both discouraged innovation and seriously limited improvements in productivity. Also, modernization also slow; peasants who had relied on subsistence farming could not suddenly become modern agriculturalists.

Emancipation did bring other, more positive, changes. Lack of jobs, and difficulties in making a living, drove many peasants to the towns and cities. This increased the industrial workforce and helped develop the industrial economy. Emancipation ended the hold of the nobility on administration and policing; therefore, a new institution, the *Zemstvo*, was needed (see page 145). Emancipation meant that changes to the judiciary were needed too, as peasants were no longer subject to the jurisdiction of the nobility.

Emancipation also brought change to the lives of many nobles, and many lost their status. Before the edict, many nobles had struggled to maintain their estates and had therefore taken out loans to cover their costs. After Emancipation, many of these loans had to be repaid as nobles had received compensation. However, as they had lost land, their struggles increased. Many were unable or unwilling to adapt to the new system and so moved to towns and rented out their land. By 1905, the land owned by the nobility had been reduced by 40 per cent.

Army and education and legal reforms

Under Alexander II, there were a number of other key reforms.

Army reforms: Alexander II attempted to modernize the army after its defeat in the Crimean War (see page 146). Conscription was widened to all classes, not just the peasantry. Service length was reduced to 15 years.

Education reforms: Alexander's education edict of 1864 established a system of primary and secondary education for all children. The number of university students was increased, and lectures on European government were permitted.

Legal reforms: A jury system was introduced for criminal cases, and a system of local, provincial, and national courts set up. Better pay for judges was implemented to reduce corruption, and public attendance at court was permitted.

The nature of Alexander III's rule

If Alexander II's rule is often associated with "reform," then that of his son, Alexander III, is closely linked to "repression." This is usually explained as Alexander III's reaction to his father's assassination in March 1881 at the hands of a terrorist group known as "the People's Will" (see page 154).

Repression was carried out through a number of groups and measures:
- the Secret Police (the Third Section and later the *Okhrana*)
- the Army
- propaganda
- censorship.

The more liberal ministers, such as Loris-Melikov, were removed and replaced by more conservative ministers, such as Nikolai Ignatiev and, later, Dmitri Tolstoy. The aim was to restore the nobility to the position they held before Emancipation. In 1889, the position of the justice of the peace was abolished in local government and replaced by the Land Commandant or Captain, a position held by members of the nobility. The *Zemstvo* was attacked, and the franchise was restricted. Education was also a victim of these more conservative policies. At the heart of these changes was Russification, whereby the local characteristics of regions within the Empire were suppressed.

> **ACTIVITY**
>
> Make a list of the political, social, and economic outcomes of the Emancipation of the Serfs which were still an issue during Alexander III's reign. Construct a diagram which shows how these different outcomes overlap. Decide on the best type of diagram to illustrate this.

Repression under Alexander III

Soon after coming to power, Alexander III had 150 members of "the People's Will," the group responsible for the assassination of his father, arrested and publicly hanged as a warning to others. He followed this by increasing the powers of the police, making the Department of the Police, which supervised the *Okhrana*, responsible to the Ministry of Internal Affairs. As a result, the *Okhrana* could be monitored, and spies and counterspies were used to scrutinize activities, particularly of the growing opposition.

> What can we learn from Source 3.1 about Alexander III's attitude to the government of Russia?

SOURCE 3.1

An extract from Alexander III's *Manifesto on unshakable autocracy*, April 1881

The base and wicked murder of a Russian Sovereign by unworthy monsters from the people, done in the very midst of that faithful people, who were ready to lay down their lives for Him – this is a terrible and shameful matter, unheard of in Russia, which has darkened Our entire land with grief and terror. But in the midst of Our great grief, the voice of God orders Us courageously to undertake, in deference to Divine intention, the task of ruling, with faith in the strength and truth of autocratic power. We are summoned to reaffirm that Power and preserve it for the benefit of the people from any encroachment.

The Statute of State Security was also introduced in 1881. This allowed the government the power to carry out extreme measures when it was deemed necessary during "emergencies." This included the power to declare martial law, make gatherings of more than 12 people illegal, close schools and universities, and increase censorship of newspapers. Special courts were set up to process people charged with political crimes very quickly.

A series of measures followed throughout Alexander III's reign which would further strengthen the repressive nature of the regime:
- 1882: any region of the empire could be declared an "area of subversion." This meant that anyone could be arrested, imprisoned, or even exiled simply on the grounds of suspicion.
- 1885: the reintroduction of closed court sessions, where trials were held in secret without juries.

Local government

Perhaps the greatest changes in policy by Alexander III were in local government. Under the rule of Alexander II, there had been moves toward some form of representative government at a local level, which provided a forum for debate and even criticism of government policies. He introduced the *Zemstvo*, a rural council established at district and provincial levels. Although it was an elected system voted for by landowners, urban dwellers, and peasants, electors were chosen by property qualification, which weighted the system in favour of the nobility. They were given power to deal with local issues, such as public services and the development of industry and did make significant improvements in both welfare and education. However, as they were dominated by nobles and lacked power in many areas, the *Zemstvos* did little to undermine the power of the autocracy, giving only a semblance of power to the people and certainly not introducing democracy.

The most significant change in local government under Alexander III occurred in 1889, with the appointment of **Land Captains**. Chosen from among members of the nobility, they replaced local magistrates and had a number of functions and powers which included:
- overseeing the rights of the peasantry
- preserving public order, safety, and decency
- acting as judges in certain civil and lesser criminal cases
- the power to impose fines of up to five roubles
- the power to imprison individuals for up to seven days
- the power to suspend court officials and recommend their dismissal
- the power to override *Zemstvos* decisions.

> **KEY TERM**
>
> **Land Captains**
> Landowners who were appointed to oversee the work of the *Zemstvos* and ensure that moderate policies were followed. They had numerous functions and powers, including overseeing the rights of peasants, preserving public order and safety, imposing fines of up to five roubles, imprisoning individuals for up to seven days, suspending court officials and recommending their dismissal, and acting as judges in certain civil and lesser criminal cases.

Their creation served to add a further cause for peasant discontent as they replaced peasant officials in the village and were little more than bureaucrat-administrators who were there to implement the wishes of the tsar and, given their noble background, were more likely to be supporters of the autocracy and pleased to recover some of the influence they had lost following the Emancipation edict.

Further conservative legislation followed, with reforms to the *Zemstvo* in 1890 and 1892. In 1890, the peasant vote to the *Zemstvos* was reduced to obtain a more subservient body. In St. Petersburg, the size of the electorate was reduced from 21,000 to 7000. The more liberal members of both the *Zemstvos* and judiciary, who were critical of the government, were removed. At the same time, many proposals put forward by the assemblies were obstructed or undermined as the government was fundamentally opposed to the principle of elected assemblies.

Education

Another area which was particularly impacted by the more repressive measures was education. Alexander II's reforms had aimed to raise both literacy and numeracy levels so that Russia could modernize. Free primary education was made available to all and was placed under the control of the *Zemstvos*, not the Church. New secondary vocational schools were established, and universities became self-governing and could therefore introduce more liberal courses. Censorship was also relaxed, and therefore more newspapers, pamphlets, and books were available.

However, under Alexander III, attitudes to education changed. The Minister of Education from 1882 to 1898, I.V. Delyanov, opposed many of Alexander II's reforms. As a result, he brought in a range of measures to undo earlier progress, particularly in universities. Their administrative autonomy was limited in 1884, and tuition fees were raised in 1887, which limited the numbers who could attend. Education was also a useful means of preventing social mobility; the raising of fees in primary and secondary education ensured that "children of coachmen, servants, cooks, washerwomen, small shopkeepers, and persons of similar type should not be brought out of the social environment to which they belong."

Russification

The policy perhaps most closely associated with the reign of Alexander III was that of **Russification**, as the tsar followed Pobedonostsev's dictum of "Autocracy, Orthodoxy, and Nationality." The policy of Russification had started during the reign of Alexander II with the Polish Revolt of 1863 and the resulting Milyutin Plan, which reduced the level of autonomy that the Polish people had been allowed before the revolt. It also imposed Russian as the official language for administration and prevented the Catholic Church from communicating with the Vatican. However, under Alexander III the policy reached new levels, as the influence of national minorities within the Empire was severely restricted.

In practice, this meant imposing the Russian language on other nationalities and minority ethnic groups within the Empire and attacking their cultures. This was achieved by:
- enforcing Russian as the first official language
- imposing Russian as the language to be used in local government and trials
- forbidding those who could not speak Russian fluently from holding public office
- encouraging adherence to the Orthodox Church
- closing Catholic monasteries
- forbidding non-Orthodox groups from building new places of worship
- suppressing any resistance to these measures.

This meant that it was in the interest of officials to maintain the dominance of Russian values at the expense of other national cultures. Discrimination against non-Russians, which had previously been hidden, now became a feature of Russian public life and was certainly more open and vindictive. State interference in administration, education, and religion was more frequent.

> **KEY TERM**
>
> **Russification** A policy to transform the non-Russian people of the Empire into pure "Rus."

> **ACTIVITY**
>
> Create a list of similarities and differences between the policies of Alexander II and Alexander III. Then, consider which part of the Tsarist system controlled the policy and was needed to enforce it.

> Explain in your own words what Ilyminsky sees as the problem facing the Russian government in integrating the non-Russian peoples, according to Source 3.2.

▶ SOURCE 3.2

Ilyminsky, who saw himself a protector of the nationalities (non-Russians) yet also stood for Russification, writing to Pobedonostsev in 1891

This is the dilemma: If, from fear of the separate nationalities, we do not allow the non-Russians to use their language in schools and churches, on a sufficient scale to ensure a solid, complete, convinced adoption of the Christian faith, then all the non-Russians will be fused into a single race by language and faith. But if we allow the non-Russian languages, then, even if their individual nationalities are thus maintained, these will be diverse, small, ill-disposed, and united with Russian people by the unity of their faith. But I believe the that such diverse nationalities cannot have any solid existence, and in the end will cause them to fuse with the Russian people.

Where there was resistance to these measures, opposition was often suppressed by the military. This was particularly evident in Poland, the Baltic States, Ukraine, and Finland. Although the aim had been to unite and strengthen the country, it had the opposite effect. National feeling among the repressed groups increased and the policy encouraged some to join opposition groups.

The 5 million Jewish people who lived in western Russia suffered the most from the policy of Russification. Alexander II had lifted a number of restrictions on Jewish people to aid economic growth; however, under Alexander III a harsher policy of repression was followed, and laws were passed restricting Jewish people's rights and movement, while they were also restricted to living in certain areas, or ghettoes. However, perhaps the most disturbing aspect of the policy was the **pogroms** which took place, most notably in the years 1881–84. The government often failed to intervene or suppress them. As a result, many Jewish people were attacked, raped, or even murdered, and the destruction of their property was common. Consequently, a significant number of Jewish people emigrated, while others, similarly to the persecuted nationalities, joined revolutionary groups.

KEY TERM

Pogrom An organized attack, often encouraged by the state, on Jewish people.

What can we learn from Source 3.3 about how the Commission believed that Russian Jews should be treated? Use your contextual knowledge to assess how far the suggestions of the Commission were implemented under Alexander III.

SOURCE 3.3

Commission Report on "the revision of current laws concerning Jews," in 1883

The whole five million Jewish population of Russia, unattractive though it may appear to certain groups and individuals, is yet an integral part of Russia. We are not dealing with foreigners, whose admission to Russian citizenship might be conditioned by their usefulness or uselessness to Russia. The Jews of Russia are not foreigners. For more than one hundred years, they have formed a part of the same Russian Empire which has incorporated scores of other tribes, many of which count by the millions.

The development of the Russian economy in the period from 1881 to 1894

In the years following the death of Alexander II, Russia experienced a period of rapid industrial development. However, agriculture remained the most important sector throughout the period 1881–1894, with most of the population employed in farming, despite moves to industrialize. Despite this, agriculture was subservient to the needs of industry, with the government concerned with increasing food production so that enough food was produced to feed a growing industrial **proletariat**. As industries developed, cities struggled to provide adequate housing, sanitation, and public services to keep up with the growing population of people working in factories. The Crimean War had shown how economically backward the country was, and there was an urgent need to catch up with the West economically, particularly if Russia were to be considered a great power. It was evident that Western powers had based their economic progress and wealth creation on the development of the iron, steel, and coal industries. As a result, Russian leaders believed they needed to copy the industrial revolutions which had taken place in the West if they were to restore their military status, which seemed even more essential given the power struggles in Europe.

KEY TERM

Proletariat Workers who do not own businesses or factories but earn a living working in manual, industrial, or service jobs.

EXTENSION

Crimean War (1853–56)

This was the first major European War since the time of Napoleon. Russia claimed to protect Slavs who lived in the Ottoman (Turkish) Empire and was also concerned about the growing weakness of the Turkish Empire and what would happen if it collapsed. War was provoked by the French government, who backed the Catholic monks over rights to the Holy Places in Jerusalem, ruled over by Turkey, while Russia supported the Orthodox monks. The tsar's minister was eager to show Russia's power over Turkey, but Britain and France backed Turkey and war broke out. Russia raised large forces but was unable to dislodge Britain and France from Russian soil. Nicholas I died while the war was still continuing and was succeeded by Alexander II, who made peace with the Treaty of Paris in 1856, but had to agree to the continued closure of the Mediterranean to Russian ships.

Bunge's policies

Although **Nikolay Bunge** is not as well known as the later finance minister, Sergei Witte (see page 160), he laid the foundations for much of Witte's work. Bunge was Minister of Finance from 1881 to 1886, when he became Chairman of the Cabinet of Ministers. He adopted a **laissez-faire** approach, significantly reducing taxes in order to establish a prosperous peasantry who would have spending power. This would create the demand for goods which in turn would help stimulate Russia's industry. He was also concerned about the threat of socialism and the potential for revolution and introduced some measures to protect industrial workers. It was the first time that the government had intervened on such a scale in the economy, and it would help create the industrial growth seen later in the period and can be contrasted with many of the more repressive measures that Alexander III introduced.

Bunge introduced a number of significant tax changes:
- 1881:   Salt tax was reduced.
- 1886:   Poll tax was abolished.

He also introduced the first form of income tax to Russia in 1885 and introduced an inheritance tax. These reforms reduced the tax burden on the peasantry to one-third of the 1860 levels, but despite this, the peasantry was still responsible for paying about 90 per cent of the tax burden.

Bunge also introduced the Peasants' Land Bank in 1883, which allowed the peasantry to borrow money at low rates of interest in order to purchase further land. Then, in 1885, he brought in the Nobles' Land Bank to help many of the members of the nobility who were struggling to maintain their estates. At the same time, he consolidated the banking system, and these reforms helped to stabilize the Russian currency. By creating a trading balance, Russia was able to borrow money from abroad to invest in industrial projects.

Russian industry was in its early stages, and Bunge introduced a series of protectionist tariffs to protect Russian industry from foreign competition, giving industries the opportunity to develop. Although later periods saw much greater railway development, Bunge bought up a number of failing private lines and not only built some new ones, but also standardized Russian rolling stock.

While the Land Bank of 1883 aided the peasantry, Bunge also took steps to improve the working conditions of industrial laborers because of his fear that they might become revolutionary because of the state's repressive intervention in the economy, and exploitation. He believed that protecting the workers was more likely to prevent the growth of revolutionary ideas among the workforce. As a result, between 1882 and 1885, he introduced legislation to improve the working conditions of women and children. These labor laws created a system of factory inspectors to enforce them, but in practice there were 267 inspectors for the whole of Russia, which made them less than effective. In 1886, a system for the hiring and firing of workers, as well as paying wages and regulating workers' fines, was also introduced. Bunge likewise planned other reforms to improve living conditions; legalize trade unions; provide training for industrial workers; provide accident insurance; construct workers' houses and other facilities, such as cafes; and set up a system to investigate disputes between workers and factory owners. However, these ideas came under criticism in a period when repression was the more typical response to threats and, under pressure from conservatives, he resigned in January 1887. This repressive approach was reflected in the appointment of Vyshnegradsky as his successor. He, while following the financial elements of Bunge's policies, ignored the social reform elements. He also continued the policy of protection, so that tariffs on some goods reached 33 per cent by 1891 but increased government income by 50 per cent.

It is therefore correct to see Bunge as creating the conditions for Russian industrial growth, which enabled the securing of foreign loans from France after 1888 and brought about a surplus for the first time in 1892. It was these achievements which were built on by Witte later in Alexander's reign.

KEY TERM

Laissez-faire In French this means "allow to do." A doctrine where a government has minimal interference in the economy, with few laws or rules controlling individuals or businesses.

KEY FIGURE

Nikolay Bunge (1823–95) was a professor of political economy who was known for his writings on serfdom and finance. He was appointed Rector of Kyiv State University in 1859, before being summoned as a Deputy Minister in 1880, and was made Finance Minister in 1881. As Finance Minister, he is often seen as the architect of Russian capitalism, but his reformist policies angered conservative deputies, and he was forced to resign.

KEY TERM

Staple industries The main or basic industries needed by a state, such as coal, iron and steel, and textiles.

Economic developments

There had been significant changes in economic policy under Alexander II. The result was the growth of the **staple industries**, but also some newer ones, such as oil. This was particularly noticeable in western Russia, where the traditional manufacturing industries, such as textiles, grew as a result of the introduction of new machinery. Similar developments were seen under Alexander III's rule in both coal and pig-iron production, as is shown in the table below:

Table 3.1 Russian coal and pig-iron production (1 pood = 36 lb = 16.3 kg)

Date	Coal (poods) in millions	Pig-iron (poods) in millions
1880–84	225.4	29.2
1885–89	302.6	37.6
1890–94	434.4	66.9

[From: M.E. Falkus, *Industrialisation of Russia*]

Alexander III continued the huge expansion of railway construction started under Alexander II. This growth was vital for the industrial sector as it meant that raw materials and finished products could be moved at far greater speed. This played a considerable role in increasing industrial output in this period.

Table 3.2 The development of Russia's railway system, 1861–90

Date	Kilometres constructed
1861–65	443
1866–70	1378
1871–75	1660
1876–80	767
1881–85	632
1886–90	914

[From: M.E. Falkus, *Industrialisation of Russia*]

The result was that industrial output expanded at an annual rate of 8 per cent throughout the 1890s, so that by the outbreak of the First World War, Russia was the world's fifth largest economy.

SOURCE 3.4

What can we learn about industrial development in Russia during the reign of Alexander III from Source 3.4?

The oil fields of Baku, Azerbaijan, which was part of the Russian Empire, photographed sometime in the 1880s

Economic problems including taxation and famines

Although the period witnessed economic growth, there were a number of problems facing the Russian economy and society. The most serious problem was rural overpopulation, which was not solved by the movement of peasants to the growing industrial towns and cities. The proportion of the labor force working in agriculture declined from 74 per cent to only 72 per cent between 1877 and 1905. Population growth was quite dramatic, but agricultural output did not rise sufficiently, despite grain production in Russia rising by an annual average of 2 per cent between 1881 and 1913. Such growth did not overcome the land problems and rural poverty.

The most serious problem associated with this was shortage of land for peasants. The increase in population, which rose by some 25 per cent between 1877 and 1905, put an enormous strain on the availability of cultivatable land. Although the amount of land owned by the peasantry did increase, the average size of their land holdings decreased from 35 acres in 1887 to 28 acres by 1905. As a result, the peasantry overworked the land they had, and this often exhausted it so that yields declined. The lack of land also meant that rent and the purchase price of land rose above their real value. As a consequence, many peasants were forced to sell as much grain as possible to pay for essential goods and meet the tax demands of the government. Even after Bunge's taxation reforms, peasants still paid about 90 per cent of Russia's taxes. This pressure left them with little disposable income to buy non-essential goods, hindering growth in consumer goods.

The shortage of grain was made worse by foreign debts, which led to Russia selling grain abroad and this continued even when there were severe shortages at home. This happened particularly in 1891 and 1892, when famine and an outbreak of cholera led to the deaths of up to 400,000 people. Many peasants were unable to meet their financial commitments to the state. In the period 1896–1900, direct tax arrears averaged 119 per cent of expected collections, and arrears on redemption payments reached 138 per cent. Social tensions were not helped by the government dispatching punitive expeditions to rural areas to coerce people to pay. Although not every peasant lived in poverty, there were many who did, and it helped create unrest. The 1890s witnessed a number of rent and labor strikes, while the illegal seizure of land by peasants from the nobility increased.

> **ACTIVITY**
>
> Create a chart showing the reasons for Bunge's industrial and financial policies and the results of each.

Social change in the period from 1881 to 1894

Although the population of Russia grew quite dramatically during this period, it is very difficult to be precise, as the first official census was not taken until 1897, and even then, the inconsistent methods used to collect the information means the results are not completely trustworthy. An estimate suggests that the population in 1885 was 98 million, with it reaching some 116 million by 1897. The growth was certainly rapid in the period after 1870, and this was due to increasing birth rates rather than decreasing death rates. Rising birth rates were the result of industrialization, which provided greater employment opportunities, increased real income, and encouraged couples to have more children. On the other hand, increased industrialization created poor living conditions and therefore public health problems, which resulted in an increasing death rate.

Urban growth

There was also a change in the distribution of the population. Although Russia was still a predominantly agricultural state in 1894, there were more people living in towns and cities than in 1881. Although the urban population had grown most rapidly between the 1850s and 1870s, from about 6 per cent to 12 per cent, growth continued. Around 15 per cent of the population lived in towns by 1897. The growth in the numbers living in urban areas was the result of many peasants moving from the countryside, made possible by the Emancipation edict of 1861. This created more unequal layers in society, with a growing urban population living in poor conditions.

Despite this, Russia remained an agricultural society, and even at the end of the nineteenth century some 80 per cent of the population relied on agriculture for their livelihoods, with the result that the economy was still underdeveloped compared with the rest of Europe,

which had much larger populations engaged in industrial activity. However, it is important not to see the peasants as all the same, and this is made apparent in the census, which included the following categories:
- peasants in rural areas, in scattered communities
- peasants in towns
- cossacks, who at the time were understood to be peasants from southeast Russia, known for their horse-riding skills
- settlers
- foreigners
- others.

Development of the middle class

An important development was the emergence of a middle class. Although the number of middle-class citizens was small, perhaps some 2 million by 1914, it was significant as they were industrialists, professionals, and business owners. Their emergence presented a challenge to the traditional order as they were the creators of wealth and began to feel that they should have a say in how the country was run.

In direct contrast to the emergence of the new or rising middle class were the nobility. Many were struggling at the start of the period with their estates failing to yield a profit and their often-extravagant lifestyles, which led to them borrowing funds secured on their property to settle outstanding debts. Some even sold off land to the peasantry after 1861, to help with repayments of loans they had taken out. Despite this, they still owned about 200 million acres of land in the 1870s, but by 1914, this had fallen to 140 million acres, with over 90 per cent of that reduction being the result of sales to peasants. However, there was still a core of nobility remaining, and it was in their interests to ensure that the tsar maintained his position. The tsar also sought to conserve and improve the nobility's position. In 1885, the Nobles' Land Bank was created to give loans at preferential rates to members of the nobility who wanted to buy land. The nobles also regained their influential powers in the *Zemstvos* through the role of Land Captains, which returned local governance to more autocratic principles, as they could overrule peasant-led courts and officials.

Although the period was characterized more by continuity, there were signs of change, particularly with the growth of a middle class and the emergence of an intelligentsia, which would lead to demands for political change and reform.

ACTIVITY

Complete a chart on the changing position of each social group in Russia in this period.

Social group	What changed?	What stayed the same?

The role of opposition

Although Alexander III's reign is often described as "the Reaction," it did not destroy opposition to the regime, but merely repressed it. Despite much closer supervision from the police, opposition became more organized, with a range of political groups emerging and developing. Opposition ranged from those who wanted to bring about moderate reform to radicals who wanted to overthrow the regime. Opponents of the regime welcomed the repressive policies, believing that these would actually encourage revolutionary activity.

> What impression of Tsar Alexander II's assassination is given in Source 3.5?

SOURCE 3.5

An engraving from 1881 depicting the assassination of Tsar Alexander II in St Petersburg in the same year

Alexander III's reign saw success in reducing terrorist organizations, driven by the desire of the new tsar to avenge the death of his father. Terrorist movements declined after 1881 and by the end of Alexander III's rule, virtually ceased to exist. There was still some localized peasant unrest, but no popular rising against the tsar until 1905. Organized Marxist groups did emerge and grew in popularity but were still a very small minority. Instead, there was widespread support for the regime and its measures, while many revolutionaries had become disillusioned.

The development of opposition from peasants and urban workers

Alexander II's reforms and a general discontent with living and working conditions had led to the emergence of opposition. His relaxation of censorship had led to more radical works being published, while his education reforms had encouraged more freedom of thought. A number of political parties had emerged in the later part of his reign, with the more radical groups wanting an end to Tsarist rule. There had also been opposition from a number of individuals, such as the philosophers Nikolai Chernyshevsky and Alexander Herzen in addition to the anarchist Mikhail Bakunin. They began to influence the young, educated Russians to adopt socialist ideas.

Russia was undergoing a period of rapid population and economic growth, and this, along with the repressive policies and Russification pursued by Alexander III, created a situation in which many political and national groups became frustrated and angered by the policies of coercion that accompanied the Tsarist system.

The industrial growth, particularly in the latter part of Alexander III's reign, brought a large number of peasants to the cities, attracted by the prospect of work in the new factories. However, conditions and pay in the new factories were often poor and this created a group of angry and disillusioned workers who were a potential threat to social order. Many of the new industrial workers found adapting to the discipline of factory life difficult, while working and living conditions, such as the long hours in dangerous conditions, only added to their discontent and provided a breeding ground for socialist ideas.

> **KEY TERMS**
>
> **Radical** The term derives from the Latin *radix*, which means root. Radical ideas are very different than mainstream ideas and often call for fundamental change.
>
> **Socialist** Describes a policy or an idea that adheres to the values of socialism. Also, a person who believes in the values of socialism (see page 87).

What can we learn from Source 3.6 about living conditions for workers in Alexander III's Russia?

SOURCE 3.6

An inspector describing conditions in barracks for unmarried men at the Bryansk metallurgical factory in 1892

These dwellings can be compared without any exaggeration with the quarters of domestic animals: their unwashed and filthy condition cannot recall a human living-place. Even in summer, when the windows and door are ajar, the air in them is stifling; on the walls and the bunks are traces of slime mould, and the floors are barely visible for the filth which sticks to them.

In the countryside, the peasantry was also becoming increasingly angry. The land question had not been resolved, and the growing peasant population meant that, despite the size of Russia, there was a land shortage. Redemption payments which followed Emancipation were an increasing burden that many were unable to meet. The land they now farmed was also often less than that they had had before Emancipation, and it did not belong to them until they had completed all the redemption payments. If peasants wanted to buy more land, they had to borrow from the Land Bank, but this burdened them with large **mortgage** repayments which would take generations to repay. As a result, most peasant families had just a few acres which often became divided into small strips so that every household in the family had some land. The resentment caused by the lack of land was only added to by the role of the *mir* and Land Captains. If the peasantry had hoped that Emancipation would bring much greater freedom, they were mistaken. Their lives were now controlled by the *mir* rather than the nobility, while the creation of Land Captains only added to their sense of frustration and anger as they were appointed from and by the nobility, meaning that in practice there was little change for the peasantry. Despite anger over these developments, it was the famine of 1891–92 which really brought about opposition in the countryside. Attempts by the People's Will (see page 153) during the reigns of Alexander II and Alexander III had seen little success, but support for this and other opposition groups grew as a result of the central governments' failure to give help to the peasantry, particularly as it was these groups who tried to bring in humanitarian aid to the countryside.

Political opposition

Zemstvos

The introduction of *Zemstvos* in 1864 by Alexander II had brought a measure of self-government to local affairs. However, it raised hopes of wider public participation in central affairs and therefore created disappointment when this did not follow. Furthermore, the electoral arrangements angered the peasantry, as the nobility held about 40 per cent of the seats, while the peasants, despite being vastly more numerous, slightly less than 40 per cent, with the townsmen and clergy holding the rest. The government also placed restrictions on the *Zemstvos'* powers of local taxation, and they were also required to carry out some tasks with their own money which had previously been carried out by central government. Despite this, they were largely successful and showed that the people were capable of looking after their own affairs. They did a good job in public education, health and welfare, local economic development, and road building. However, this very success created disappointment, as their success in these areas was not followed up by the opportunity for the public to take part in central government.

Populism

During Alexander II's reign, attempts by writers such as Nikolai Chernyshevsky to arouse the peasantry and turn them into the leaders of revolutionary change had failed. However, these ideas formed the basis of the Populist (*Narodnik*) movement, which attempted to spread socialist ideas into the countryside. At this point, revolutionary opposition had had little success, but after 1874, it began to make significant gains in terms of support.

In 1877, a small group of Populists formed a new organisation, Land and Liberty. They had similar aims, but were also committed to the high-profile technique of political assassination and made several attempts to kill the tsar. In 1879, the organization split into two factions, the Black Partition Group and a larger group, the People's Will.

KEY TERM

Mortgage A loan used to purchase real estate, such as a house or land. The property itself serves as security for the loan, which means if the borrower fails to repay the loan according to the agreed terms, the lender can take the property to recover the money lent.

The People's Will

It was the People's Will (*Narodnaya Volya*) which was the most effective of the opposition groups. Its members made several attempts on the tsar's life in 1879 and 1880. Tsar Alexander II made concessions to some of the group's demands, while at the same time ordering police operations, which resulted in numerous arrests. These forced the People's Will to take desperate measures, and the group planned a further attempt on the tsar's life.

On March 13, 1881, the tsar agreed to some of the proposals for administrative and economic reforms. He then went on parade, and on his return to the palace, a bomb was thrown at his carriage. It did not injure him, but it seriously hurt some in his escort. When Alexander got out of his carriage to help, another bomb was thrown which ultimately resulted in his death. Ironically, on the very day that he had agreed to reforms, the terrorists finally assassinated him.

As we have seen, Alexander III responded to his father's murder with heavy repressive policies towards the People's Will. He arrested 150 members of the group, which virtually ended its existence. However, by 1886 the organization had reformed and re-emerged, despite the continuation of repressive policies. In 1887, members of the group who had been making bombs to assassinate Alexander III were arrested. This group included Alexander Ulyanov, Lenin's brother, and he, along with four others, were hanged. Once again, the group's actions failed to spark enthusiasm among the peasantry, and its activity declined after 1887. The People's Will came to prominence again during the famine of 1891–92, when it organized humanitarian aid, which won it some support.

The group's preference for violence over other forms of protest such as strikes contributed to its failure, as oppression under Alexander III had simply increased. However, in the longer term it did have some influence on the development of the revolutionary movement. Towards the end of the century, several of its members were released from jail, and they helped form the Socialist Revolutionaries in 1901, reviving many of the methods of *Narodnaya Volya*.

The growth of Marxism

Karl Marx, a German revolutionary thinker, had published his *Communist Manifesto* in 1848. He and his co-writer, Friedrich Engels, argued that human society was shaped by social conventions based on economics, especially the labor process, resulting in class struggles between those who did the work and those who controlled the system and benefited most from it. He argued that only under classless communism could humanity be liberated. In a capitalist society, the developing working class would ultimately replace the bourgeois (middle class) controllers of labor.

It took time for Marxism to take root in Russia. The revolutionary movement had grown during Alexander II's reign, but fundamental changes took place in the period after 1881. The old "Populist" belief that the Russian peasantry, through the commune, would lead Russia to socialism became discredited. It had become obvious that the peasants had little interest in revolutionary activity, and the rapid industrialisation created conditions which did not fit this model. Intellectuals turned to Marxism because it highlighted the developing industrial working class (proletariat) as the potentially revolutionary group, rather than the peasantry, which had proved so disappointing in this respect.

The first Marxist revolutionary who had an influence on Russia was **Georgi Plekhanov**, organizer of the Black Partition group. Exiled to Geneva in 1880, he had translated Marx's writings into Russian. Perhaps, most surprisingly, the Russian authorities allowed his translation of Marx's writing to enter Russia, believing that these ideas would distract the people from what the authorities believed to be the more dangerous views of the People's Will, who had assassinated Alexander II. Although he remained in exile until a brief return to Russia in 1917, he founded the Emancipation of Labor group in 1883. This group would later merge to form the Russian Democratic Labour Party (Social Democratic Party) in 1898, during the reign of Nicholas II. However, although he was involved in the foundation of the party, many considered him too theoretical in his approach, and the party's appeal was limited. It needed a much more practical and revolutionary program if it was to win mass support. This view was put forward by Vladimir Ulyanov, better known as Lenin (see page 182).

KEY FIGURES

Karl Marx (1818–83) was a German revolutionary. He believed that society operated according to scientific principles. He argued that human behaviour was determined by class struggle, a process which continued throughout history. He believed that human history was about to reach its culmination with the revolutionary victory of the workers (proletariat) over the bourgeoisie. This would lead to a dictatorship of the proletariat, and once all classes had been destroyed, conflict would end, and there would be a peaceful, classless society.

Georgi Plekhanov (1856–1918) Born into a minor noble family, Plekhanov became a populist and later a leader of the Black Partition group. To avoid arrest, he moved to Geneva in 1880. Plekhanov promoted the idea of a proletarian revolution, believing that Russia would undergo industrial development and therefore follow Marx's model of a class struggle between the industrial proletariat and factory owners. He also believed that this was the best way to destroy the Tsarist autocracy. He returned to Russia in 1917 but opposed revolutionary leaders and left for Finland, where he died in 1918.

KEY TERM

Bourgeoisie A term used to describe the middle and upper classes in society, who typically own businesses and property. They have wealth, influence, and control over the means of production, such as factories and companies.

The first organized Marxist group formed in St. Petersburg in 1883. Initial groups were just intellectual discussion groups, but from the early 1890s, Marxism was taken up by an increasing number of young student radicals, and a number of small Marxist cells emerged in some cities, such as St. Petersburg and Moscow. Most importantly, for Russian revolutionaries, the "Great Spurt" of the 1890s (see page 160) was the beginning of the final stage of the class struggle. The revolutionaries believed it had created conditions which would produce a politically conscious workforce, who could make a successful revolution possible. In this final stage, the workers would overthrow the **bourgeoisie** and take power in a revolution. Initially, in the early 1890s, they rejected terror as a method to achieve their goals, instead focusing on propaganda in an attempt to win support for their ideas. It was after 1894 that Marxists really began to make an impact. They were involved in strikes in St. Petersburg, and formed the Social Democratic Party in 1898.

Although Alexander III had been able to keep opposition under control, it had not been destroyed. It was largely his determination and strength of will which had prevented revolutionary activity from developing further, and it would take only a weaker figure as tsar, such as Nicholas II, for this to explode into full-scale revolution.

> What is the message of Source 3.7? It is produced by the Social Democratic Party. What knowledge do you have which supports or challenges the message of the source?

SOURCE 3.7

A Social Democratic Party propaganda poster showing the social structure of the Tsarist state. The text reads, from top to bottom: "We rule you; We fool you; We eat instead of you; We shoot you; We work for you."

KEY DEBATE

WAS ALEXANDER III'S REGIME MERELY REPRESSIVE?

At first sight, it seems very difficult to argue against the view that the regime of Alexander III was anything but repressive. Historians have used the term "the Reaction" to describe his reign. This is hardly surprising, given his reaction to the assassination of his father by the People's Will and his issuing of the Statute of State Security in 1881, which increased government powers. In support of this view, historians have stressed the importance of his tutor and chief advisor, Pobedonostsev, an extreme conservative, as playing a key role. These historians have also considered the restrictions which were placed on any liberal developments which had taken place during the reign of Alexander II. In particular, this view has been supported by considering the restrictions placed on the *Zemstvos* franchise, the introduction of Land Captains, and the removal of legal officials who were sympathetic to any liberal ideas. Some have also argued that further repression was seen with the extended powers given to the *Okhrana* and the increased censorship which followed the more liberal regime of Alexander II.

However, other historians have argued that this focus on a simply negative and repressive regime is misleading. They argue that this ignores, in particular, the economic developments of the 1890s, which was a period of industrial expansion. Bunge and Vyshnegradsky's financial policies had given a boost to the Russian economy, with government income increasing by 50 per cent as a result of applying tariffs on imports and increasing grain exports by 20 per cent. This made a dramatic improvement to the Russian economy and government budgets. However, the policies had also resulted in horrific hardships and famine, and some have challenged this argument and suggested that, despite the growth, the changes were made not solely for economic motives, but also to improve Russia's military might, which could be used not just against foreign challenges, but also domestic unrest.

It would be difficult to argue that the regime was not repressive, but there is certainly an argument to be made that industrial development did take place, even if ultimately it played a significant role in bringing about the fall of the Tsarist regime.

ACTIVITY

Write a brief explanation of the following terms: autocracy, socialism, Marxism, radical, liberal democracy.

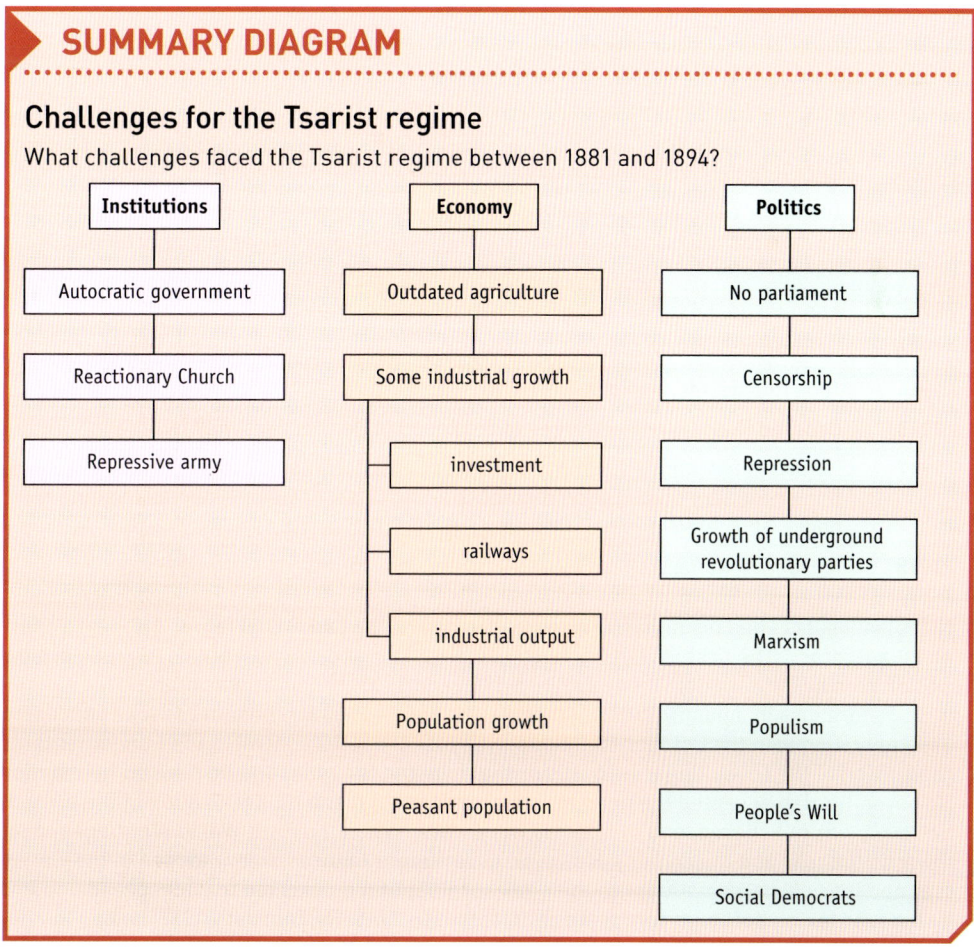

SUMMARY DIAGRAM

Challenges for the Tsarist regime

What challenges faced the Tsarist regime between 1881 and 1894?

2 What were the causes and outcomes of the 1905 Revolution up to 1914?

In 1905, Russia experienced popular unrest and revolution following a build-up of social and political tensions and military failures in a war against Japan. The tsar had to make concessions to divide the different revolutionary groups, but he was able to restore his authority in 1906. Nevertheless, the revolution led to major changes, with the introduction of a national elected assembly and economic reforms.

The causes of the 1905 Revolution

The 1905 Revolution was caused by many factors.

Discontent with the regime of Nicholas II

When Nicholas II became tsar of the Russian Empire in 1894, he faced many problems which prevented Russia from being a modern state, particularly the political and social structure and its economic condition. Nicholas II's personality and characteristics suggest that he was not suited for such a role. It may even be argued that it was his personality which would ultimately lead to the downfall of the dynasty in 1917. Historians have often seen him as weak-willed, lacking in confidence, and a poor judge of people, and more interested in his family than in governing the country. However, he did have an enormous sense of duty and saw it as his job to keep the autocracy intact. Therefore, at the very time that Russia faced serious political, social, and economic challenges, its ruler was reluctant to reform the country, prioritizing the maintenance of the dynasty and its powers.

▶ NICHOLAS II

1868	Born into the Romanov dynasty
1894	Took over as tsar on the death of his father, Alexander III. In the same year, he married the Princess Alexandra, the German granddaughter of Britain's Queen Victoria.
1905	Announced the October Manifesto and new constitution
1906	Introduced the first *Duma*
1914	Took Russia into the First World War
1915	Ordered Russian armed forces to be placed under his personal command
1917	Return to Petrograd (formerly St. Petersburg) but was halted by rebels. Senior military officials and members of the *Duma* advised Nicholas to stand down. Abdicated to "save" Russia.
1918	Murdered, along with his family, in Ekaterinburg

Nicholas II succeeded his father, Alexander III, in 1894. He lacked his father's decisive character but shared his views about autocracy. The first part of his reign saw Russia make considerable economic progress, but the tsar's authority was shaken by military defeats by Japan in 1904 and 1905. Nicholas was blamed for a massacre of demonstrators in St. Petersburg in January 1905, and the Revolution of 1905 forced him to make concessions and accept a national assembly (*Duma*) in the October Manifesto. He reasserted his control in the Fundamental Laws (1906). He accepted the repression of the revolutionaries by his prime minister, Stolypin, and he himself held nationalistic and antisemitic views. However, he also accepted the need for reform of the land and modernization of the armed forces. Political power, however, was not shared, and the *Dumas* were weak. When the First World War began, people initially felt patriotic towards the tsar and the country. However, government failures, heavy losses in the war, and resentment towards the tsar and tsarina's association with their advisor Rasputin quickly led to widespread unpopularity. This was made worse by the tsar taking personal command of his forces in 1915. By February 1917, he had lost the respect of many leading figures in government and the armed forces. A wave of demonstrations in the capital and a refusal of troops to support the tsar led to his abdication in March 1917. He and his family were killed by revolutionaries in 1918.

Under autocratic rule, any measures to tackle the problems that the country faced would have to come from the tsar. However, he would not bring in reforms which would undermine his position. There was also disagreement within government over the direction the country should follow. The Westerners wanted Nicholas to bring in measures similar to those of western European states, while the Slavophiles argued that Russia should preserve its Slavic culture and traditions.

Nicholas II continued many of the repressive policies of his father. He relied heavily on his tutor, Pobedonostsev, who was his chief advisor. Like Pobedonostsev, Nicholas believed that Tsarism and religion were closely linked, stating in 1906, "The All-Russian emperor possesses the supreme autocratic power. Not only fear and conscience, but God himself commands obedience to his authority." He believed it was his duty to "uphold the principle of autocracy as firmly and as unflinchingly as did my ever-lamented father," and therefore his priority was the maintenance of the Romanov dynasty. Pobedonostsev also encouraged Nicholas to continue the policy of Russification, whereby Russian ways and values were imposed on the people.

Political opposition

Tsar Nicholas II's commitment to maintaining the autocracy and the lack of political reform caused resentment from some in society. Lack of change ensured that the opposition which developed under the previous regimes would continue and evolve into two main groups which wanted to overthrow Tsarism.

The Socialist Revolutionaries

The Socialist Revolutionaries (SRs) developed from the Populist movement of the 1870s. They wanted to improve the living conditions of the poorest in society, including the growing urban proletariat. The Populists had attempted to win the support of the peasantry, but economic growth and industrial development had led to a development of interest in political and social issues among the rapidly growing urban workforce, and the Populists saw an opportunity to gain support among this new group. The aim was to widen the concept of **the "people,"** so it included not just the peasantry, but all those who wanted to bring about an end to Tsarism. The key figure in reshaping Populist ideas and strategy which would become those of the Socialist Revolutionary Party was **Victor Chernov**. He played a significant role in the founding of the party in 1901 and became its leader.

The Social Democrats

In the 1890s, Marxism attracted a small but growing number of followers, particularly among students in the main cities (see pages 154 in previous section). This led to Marxists forming the Social Democratic Party in 1898. Many of these followers believed that the "Great Spurt" (see page 160) should be making industrial workers more politically aware. In reality, very few workers had time to engage with complex Marxist theory, and they had little interest in overthrowing the Tsarist system. At the Social Democratic Party's inaugural meeting, only nine delegates attended.

Support for the party grew slowly, as did divisions between followers over what should be the focus and how change should be achieved. While most focused on the political system, others were more concerned with improving the pay and working conditions of the workers. Some believed the party should consist of those working full-time for revolution, while others wanted a party to attract as many people as possible. This led to the development of two groups within the Social Democrats.

One group would become known as the Mensheviks (from the Russian *menshe*, meaning "less"), and the opposing, larger group became known as the Bolsheviks (from the Russian *bolshinstvo*, meaning "majority"). Both believed it was possible to politically educate the working class and create a revolutionary force to overthrow the Tsarist system. However, the Bolsheviks, led by Lenin, believed in a radical, complete revolution led by a small party of professional revolutionaries which could use violence to achieve its aims. Mensheviks believed in more progressive change, involving as many people as possible, including the middle class and the bourgeoisie. They believed that change could be achieved through non-violent methods, such as strikes.

> **KEY TERM**
>
> **The people** The part of the population, separate from the ruling elite, that the Socialist Revolutionaries believed embodied the will of the Russian nation.

> **KEY FIGURE**
>
> **Victor Chernov** (1873–1952) was the son of a former serf. Chernov was particularly interested in land reform. He was the main theorist behind the policies of the Socialist Revolutionaries and led the party after its formation. He became a minister in the 1917 Provisional Government and was elected president of the constituent assembly in 1918. He left Russia in 1920 and lived the rest of his life in exile.

Economic problems

There were economic problems in both the towns and countryside. The agricultural economy was not well developed. Farming had remained the same for decades, with many still using wooden ploughs, while standards of living were very low. The situation was made worse as grain continued to be exported; furthermore, its impact was felt in the growing towns and cities as prices rose, and workers, who earned barely enough to buy their bread at normal prices, suffered severely when the price virtually doubled.

Although industry was developing, Russia was a long way behind its international rivals, and the growth was largely the result of small-scale enterprises rather than large-scale production. Where there was large-scale production, it was concentrated in the old "staple" industries, such as iron and steel, mining, and textiles. Russian technology also lagged behind that of the West. As a consequence, industry and agriculture were both undeveloped, with the result being that Russia could not compete economically with the major European economic powers of Britain, France, and Germany.

The economic position of both the peasantry and industrial workers created a range of social problems. For the peasantry:
- Living standards remained very low, despite the creation of the Land Bank in 1883 and the abolition of the peasant poll tax in 1886.
- Problems in agriculture caused by land shortages and lack of innovation and investment meant that bad harvests, when they occurred, often devastated peasants' incomes, as well as leading to food shortages and even famine. The poor harvests of 1902 were widespread throughout much of the country.
- The population was growing rapidly, and this contributed to rural unemployment, underemployment, and famine, as seen in 1891–92.
- The poll tax was hated by the peasants, but its abolition did not satisfy them, as their income had fallen given how much they had to spend on their plots, which had also decreased in size.

The situation in the fast-growing towns and cities was little better.
- The industrial workforce grew rapidly, from 1.4 million in 1890 to 2.9 million by 1912. This brought about the rise of a new class, the industrial worker. Some industrial workers developed a political awareness due to their geographical proximity to fellow workers and their common working and living conditions. As we have seen, this led to the development of socialist organizations and political parties.
- The rapid growth of towns created public health problems. Housing was poorly built, there was a lack of sanitation, and water supplies were inadequate. Diseases, including cholera, spread rapidly.

As Nicholas gave the impression of not being interested in either reform or modernization, many people began to feel alienated from their ruler.

The policies of Sergei Witte

Sergei Witte was a supporter of industrialization, but he was conservative in his political views. He was the first minister to focus on industry rather than agriculture, part of the so-called substitution effect where investment capital was substituted or directed from agriculture to industry. This concerned many of Russia's elite, who had a more traditional outlook on the economy and still believed that agriculture should be the basis of growth and development, with Witte even commenting that "all thinking Russia was against me," a clear indication that his policies were viewed as radical. There were five main elements to Witte's approach:
- He brought back a policy from the time of Alexander II and invited foreign experts in different industries to Russia to share their knowledge.
- The use of foreign loans returned, and taxes were raised to provide capital for industrial investment.
- The Russian rouble was placed on the **Gold Standard** in 1897 to help achieve financial stability.
- State investment was focused on heavy industry and railway construction.
- Protectionism was increased, with the aim of protecting domestic industries by putting high tariffs on foreign imports.

> **KEY TERM**
>
> **Gold Standard** When the value of a unit of currency (e.g., one dollar) is linked to a specific weight of gold.

KEY TERM

Great Spurt A name given to a period of rapid industrial growth, encouraged by the finance minister Witte by direct government support of trade and industry, railway construction, and a stable currency which encouraged foreign investment.

As Minister of Finance, Witte oversaw the **Great Spurt**:
- Coal production doubled from the 1890s to 1905.
- Steel production rose sevenfold over the same period.
- Russia became the world's fourth largest producer of iron.
- New technologies, such as oil and chemical industries, were developed.
- The amount of railway track rose from 29,183 km in 1891 to 52,612 km in 1901, and the Trans-Siberian railway was constructed.
- Income from industry increased from 42 million roubles in 1893 to 161 million by 1897.
- There was an average growth rate of 7.5 per cent in industrial production.

This growth appeared to be evidence that Russia had become a major power, and it gained international prestige as a result.

Despite the evidence of economic growth, there were some shortcomings in his policy:
- Witte focused on heavy industry and neglected other industrial sectors, such as engineering and textiles.
- The reliance on foreign loans was dangerous as they could be recalled at short notice.
- The reliance on foreign experts limited the opportunities for home talent.
- The development of the rail network was expensive, yet in 1914 it had eleven times fewer kilometres of track than Germany. The Trans-Siberian railway was not only poorly built but was also unfinished.
- Many industrial policies came at the expense of agriculture, which was paid little attention. Increased demands for grain exports to fund industrialization led to food shortages, especially after bad harvests. Increased taxation made peasants' lives even harder, which caused widespread discontent.

ACTIVITY

Copy and complete a chart like the one below to summarize the measures taken by Witte. Assess the effectiveness of those measures: what changed, and what stayed the same?

Measure	Evidence of success	Evidence of failure	Judgment on impact

SERGEI WITTE

Sergei Witte (1849–1915) was born in Tbilisi in Georgia. His father was of Dutch origin, and his mother came from high Russian nobility. An economic expert, he had organized rail transport during the Turkish War (1877–78). As Minister of Finance under Alexander III from 1892, he had pursued a policy of developing transport and industry. Nicholas II kept him in post until 1903, so he largely oversaw the "Great Spurt" in Russian industry. In 1905, he negotiated the peace treaty with Japan and drafted the October Manifesto, setting up a national *Duma*, of which he became prime minister. He resigned as the tsar moved to greater repression. He urged Nicholas II not to go to war in 1914, but by then had lost all influence.

1849	Born
1871–74	Studied railway administration in Odesa
1875	Put in charge of the Odesa railway
1877–78	Organised rail transport during the war with the Ottoman Empire
1889	Asked to establish a railway department in the Ministry of Communication
1892	Became Minister of Finance
1903	Appointed as Chairman of the Committee of Ministers
1905	Appointed chief Russian negotiator to conduct peace negotiations with Japan
1905–06	Prime minister
1915	Died in Petrograd

Defeat in the Russo-Japanese War

The 1905 Revolution was not a sudden event. There were several areas of grievances, including the repressive nature of the regime and the political, social, and economic problems which were discussed in the last section. These were added to by the disastrous Russo-Japanese War of 1904–05, which showed Nicholas's inability to manage the country. Opposition within the country had continued to grow, with increasing support for groups which were influenced by Populism and Marxism, as well as student unrest, protests about poor harvests in 1902, strikes at factories, and anti-war protests once the war with Japan began. This culminated in the revolutionary events of 1905.

War with Japan in 1904 was hardly surprising. The two countries had quarrelled for some time over Manchuria, in northeast China and Korea. Russia still hoped to increase its influence in Asia, following the relative decline in its position in Europe. Russia also wanted to obtain an ice-free port, such as Port Arthur, as most of its major ports on the northern coastline were frozen for some part of the year, while the Treaty of Paris in 1856 had prevented Russian ships from having access to the Mediterranean from the Black Sea. According to the Interior Minister, Vyacheslav von Plehve, Russia needed "a small, victorious war to avert a revolution" as it would distract from the domestic problems, but it was Witte who was particularly keen on war, as he wanted Russia to expand economically into Asia.

However, the war was a shambles. The Japanese defeated the Russians at the battle of Yalu in southern Manchuria, forced Russia to surrender Port Arthur, sank much of the Russian fleet in the battle of Tsushima Strait and then inflicted a humiliating military defeat at Mukden. As a consequence, Russia lost Manchuria, Korea, and Port Arthur.

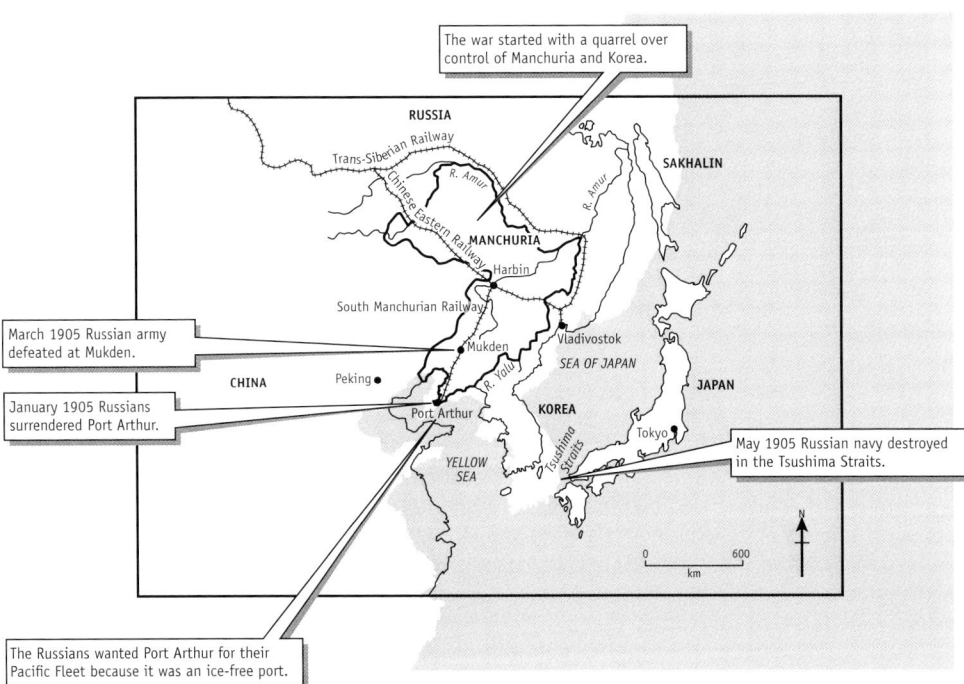

Figure 3.2 The Russo–Japanese War, 1904–05

The consequences of the war

The Russians had underestimated Japan's strength and had failed to prepare adequately for the conflict. Russia's performance led to concerns being expressed about the tsar's ability to maintain Russia's position as a major power and the effectiveness of his rule and autocracy. Most importantly, the military incompetence was linked to the tsar himself. The war also revealed the limited effectiveness of many of the earlier reforms, particularly in terms of transportation and communications. The unfinished Trans-Siberian railway was unable to solve the logistical problem of getting troops and supplies to the front quickly. This led to more investment in transportation, but this resulted in rapid urbanization and the further deterioration of living and working conditions.

The war also sparked social unrest at home, and Nicholas was forced into making a number of reforms, but these failed to solve the problems. Economic growth did not appear to bring the workers any benefit, and the poor conditions and defeat in the war simply encouraged the workers to challenge their employers with strikes, and there were even riots. The war also encouraged political challenges from the masses with the formation of **Soviets**, and the All-Russian Union of Peasants. There was also growing disquiet from the emerging middle class and intelligentsia. In response, Nicholas introduced an element of democracy by establishing the *Duma* and hoped that such actions would show the people that he was more willing to be accountable for his actions.

Defeat had contributed considerably to the growing tensions, and by 1905 Nicholas was faced with opposition from a combination of the peasantry, industrial workers, and the growing middle class. Previous unrest had been largely caused by industrial downturns and poor harvests but 1905 was different, as it was largely caused by government policies.

> **KEY TERM**
> **Soviets** Russian word for councils, made up of elected workers.

> What is the message of Source 3.8? How is the Russian army depicted? Use your knowledge of events to explain what the Russians wanted to portray with this image of the army.

SOURCE 3.8

A Russian propaganda poster, *The breakfast of the Cossack* **from 1904**

The events and consequences of the 1905 Revolution

The 1905 Revolution started in St. Petersburg but spread throughout the empire, forcing the tsar to make some concessions.

Bloody Sunday

The revolution began with Bloody Sunday on January 22, 1905, although there had already been a strike at the Putilov steelworks in St. Petersburg, which led to a wave of strikes across Russia. The protest on January 22 was led by a priest, **Father Georgy Gapon**. He attempted to lead a peaceful protest of workers and their families to the tsar's Winter Palace to present a loyal petition calling on him to improve their conditions (see Source 3.9).

KEY FIGURE

Father Georgy Gapon (1870–1906) was a *Zemstvo* official who became a priest and tried to help workers in St. Petersburg. However, although he founded a trade union organization, he was also working for the secret police, whose policy was to infiltrate workers' organizations. He led a march in January 1905 to petition the tsar for better conditions, but this led to deaths (Bloody Sunday). He fled to England but returned to Russia at the end of 1905 and resumed contact with the police and workers' organizations, but he was killed by revolutionaries as a traitor in 1906.

> What are the key points of the petition in Source 3.9? What additional knowledge could you use to consider whether this view of reasons for the 1905 Revolution was justified?

SOURCE 3.9

From a petition intended to be delivered by the marchers to Tsar Nicholas II on Sunday, 22 January 1905

We working men and inhabitants of St. Petersburg, our wives and children, and our parents, helpless and aged men and women, have come to You, our ruler, in quest of justice and protection. We have no strength at all, O Sovereign. Our patience is at an end. We are approaching that terrible moment when death is better than continuance of intolerable sufferings.

Our first request was that our employers should discuss with us, but this they refused to do. They regard as illegal our other demands: reduction of the working day to eight hours, the fixing of wage rates in consultation with us, and investigation of our grievances against the factory managements. We have been in slavery with the help and cooperation of Your officials. Anyone who dares to speak up in the defence of the interests of the working class and ordinary people is jailed or exiled. Is this, O Sovereign, in accordance with the laws of God, by whose grace You reign?

However, the march created panic among the police, who opened fire and sent in the cavalry. This led to the death of some 200 protestors, with many more injured. This was seized on by Tsarist opponents and used to show the brutal and uncaring nature of the regime. Although Nicholas was not in St. Petersburg, the events did much to damage the ideal of the tsar as the "little father."

Strikes and unrest in 1905

In response to the events of Bloody Sunday, disorder spread. There were strikes in the major towns and cities. Government officials were attacked, Grand Duke Sergei and Plehve were assassinated by Socialist Revolutionaries, and unrest spread to the countryside, where landlords were targeted. Public buildings were seized, and peasants squatted in landlords' houses. The workers organized themselves into trade unions, and sailors on the ship *Potemkin* mutinied. As the government struggled to contain the unrest, the non-Russian minorities seized the opportunity to assert themselves: Georgia declared its independence, the Polish leaders demanded self-government, and the Jewish leaders asked for equal rights. Finland became autonomous and set up a democratic parliament. Meanwhile, the *Kadets*, led by Paul Milyukov, persuaded other liberal groups to form the Union of Unions in an attempt to organize an alliance with workers and peasants to force the government to establish a **Constituent Assembly**.

KEY TERMS

Potemkin A battleship named after the aristocratic favorite and lover of the eighteenth-century Empress Catherine the Great. While stationed in Odesa on the Black Sea, its crew mutinied in 1905.

Kadets The party which supported a constitutional liberal democracy. Its membership was largely middle class, and it never achieved mass support.

Constituent Assembly An elected body whose task is to draw up a new constitution, or a set of rules under which a country is to be run.

What impression of the 1905 Revolution is given by Source 3.10?

SOURCE 3.10

Photograph of street barricades in St. Petersburg during 1905

ACTIVITY

Draw a diagram to show all the causes of the 1905 Revolution. How are the causes in your diagram linked? Annotate the causes to show the links.

The reactions of Nicholas II to the 1905 Revolution

Nicholas turned to Witte to help restore order. Firstly, Witte secured peace with Japan. Nicholas then appointed him chairman of the Council of Ministers. Witte advised the tsar to issue a new declaration of his policy, or manifesto, in August 1905.

The October Manifesto

The October Manifesto offered concessions, most notably the promise to create an assembly of elected representatives, in an attempt to reduce tensions. But the limits to the concessions, with the tsar stating that he reserved "to ourselves exclusively the care of perfecting the organization of the Assembly," failed to restore order, and more strikes followed. By October 1905, the unrest had grown into a general strike, and workers in the cities of St. Petersburg and Moscow formed themselves into Soviets, demanding better conditions. This united opposition was a serious threat, and the government was forced to act to try to divide it.

In October, Nicholas issued a new manifesto. This went further than August and offered:
- a legislative *Duma* or parliament
- freedom of speech, assembly, and worship
- the legalization of political parties and trade unions.

This seemed to be a dramatic change for Russia, as it appeared as if autocracy was being abandoned to be replaced by a Western-style constitutional monarchy. However, it did not satisfy the demands of the workers and peasants, despite the promise of greater freedoms. As a result, another general strike occurred in St. Petersburg, and rioting had to be suppressed by troops. In the countryside, there was peasant unrest, but the peasants were calmed by the promise of a reduction and eventual abandonment of redemption repayments.

The formation of the Duma

The *Duma* appeared to offer an element of democracy as it was an elected body, and it was hoped that it would show the tsar was willing to be more accountable. However, such a view was soon destroyed, as the first meeting of the *Duma* coincided with Nicholas issuing the Fundamental Laws. The electoral process also ensured that any changes would be minor, as elections for the first *Duma* in 1906 were based on the following rules:
- Only men over the age of 25 had the right to vote.
- Members of the armed forces could not vote.
- Electoral districts within provinces were not equally represented.
- A second chamber, appointed by the tsar, had the right to veto measures.

KEY TERMS

Laborists The SRs had boycotted the first election but stood as Laborists.

Octobrists A liberal-reformist monarchist party whose members believed in moderate constitutional reform but not revolution.

Progressists Made up of businessmen who wanted moderate reform.

Rightists Not a party, but represented conservative views.

KEY FIGURE

Petr Stolypin (1862–1911) was the son of a general. He studied agriculture and became interested in land reform. Rising in state service, he became governor of Grodno province in 1902 and by a mixture of repression and reform kept the province under control in 1905. A conservative, he was rewarded by being appointed Minister of the Interior and then Prime Minister in the same year, 1906. His main aim was to strengthen the position of the tsar, and this was seen in his suppression of the unrest which followed the Vyborg Manifesto. His views had been affected by his family being injured in a bomb attack, and his response to terrorism was to increase police repression. However, the unrest peaked by 1907, and Stolypin was ordered to reconsider government policy over land distribution, where he now followed a reforming policy to control the peasantry. Faced with feuds within government, he resigned in 1911 and was subsequently assassinated.

Although the electoral rules did mean that there were representatives from a broad range of opinions and political groups, it also ensured that the body was highly critical of Tsarist policy. The first two *Dumas* were in session for only a short period of time and achieved little.

Table 3.3 *Duma* election results, 1906–07

Party or group	First *Duma* 1906	Second *Duma* 1907
SDs (Mensheviks)	18	47
SRs		37
Laborists	136	104
Kadets	182	91
Octobrists	17	42
Progressists	27	28
Rightists	8	10
National parties	60	93
Others		50
Total	448	502

The first Duma, April–July 1906

The first *Duma* was dominated by two political groups, the Laborists and the *Kadets*. However, the hopes of the moderate liberals were dashed by the issuing of the Fundamental Laws and by the government securing a loan from France, which meant it did not need to go to the *Duma* for money. The Fundamental Laws also stated that the *Duma* would have two chambers: the elected lower house, and a second house consisting of a state council whose representatives were largely chosen by the tsar. This second chamber ensured there was little reform as it had the right of veto. Furthermore, it was stated that no law could be put in place without the approval of the tsar. The *Duma* soon discovered how limited its powers were when discussing the issue of land redistribution. The government stated it was not an option, which angered the *Duma* and led to Nicholas claiming its actions were illegal and dissolving it.

In despair, some members of the *Duma* reassembled at Vyborg, in the neighbouring province of Finland, close to St. Petersburg, where they drew up the **Vyborg Manifesto** or Vyborg Appeal, calling on the people of Russia to oppose their government. This led to some violence and gave the government the excuse it needed for retaliation. The government appointed **Petr Stolypin** as Chief Minister. Not only were the Vyborg deputies arrested, but **martial law** was introduced, and military courts were set up to crush unrest, with some 2500 executed between 1906 and 1911.

KEY TERMS

Vyborg Manifesto Drawn up by 200 *Kadets* and Laborists, it urged the people to defy the government by refusing to pay taxes and disobeying conscription.

Martial law A situation, usually following a crisis, when the government temporarily places the military in charge of maintaining order and enforcing laws.

The second Duma February–June, 1907

The repressive policies of Stolypin had an impact on the composition of the second *Duma*, with the *Kadets* losing half of their seats. However, they were replaced by more radical and anti-tsar SDs and SRs. On the other hand, the more conservative right also gained seats, and this made the *Duma* even more fractious. Despite this, Stolypin tried to work with it, but the *Duma* opposed his land programme. However, the breakdown between the government and the *Duma* was caused by its attack on the way the imperial army was organized and deployed. The SR and SD deputies were accused of subversion, and the tsar dissolved the *Duma* and proceeded to change the electoral system.

The survival of the Tsarist regime

Having survived the challenge to his authority, the tsar was soon able to reassert his power.

The Fundamental Laws

Nicholas made it clear that he was unwilling to see his absolute power decline in discussions prior to the issuing of the Fundamental Laws (see Source 3.11).

> **What is the view of the writer of Source 3.11 towards autocracy? Note down specific details from the source to support your answer.**

SOURCE 3.11

Tsar's statement, April 1906.

If I were convinced that Russia wanted me to abdicate my autocratic powers, I would do that, for the country's good. But I am not convinced this is so, and I do not believe that there is need to alter the nature of my supreme power. It is dangerous to change the way that power is formulated. I know, too, that if no change is made, this may give rise to agitation, to attacks. But where will these attacks come from? From so-called educated people, from the proletariat, from the Third Estate? Actually, I feel that eighty per cent of the people are still with me.

In April 1906, he announced the Fundamental Laws. These stated that: "The Sovereign Emperor possesses the initiative in all legislative matters. No law can come into force without his approval." Source 3.12 gives details on other aspects of the Fundamental Laws.

> **What does Source 3.12 say about the Russian government's attitude towards law and power in 1906? Note down specific details from the source to support your answer.**

SOURCE 3.12

From the Fundamental Laws, April 1906

4. The Emperor of All the Russias possesses Supreme Sovereign Power. Obedience to His authority, not only out of fear but in good conscience, is ordained by God Himself.
5. The person of the Lord Emperor is sacrosanct and inviolable.
7. The Sovereign Emperor exercises legislative power in conjunction with the State Council and State *Duma*.
8. The initiative in all legislative matters belongs to the Sovereign Emperor. Only upon His initiative may the Fundamental Laws be subject to revision by (in) the State Council and the State *Duma*.
9. The Sovereign Emperor ratifies laws and without His ratification (approval) no laws can go into effect.
10. Total administrative power belongs to the Sovereign Emperor throughout the entire Russian State. At the highest level of administration, His authority is direct; at subordinate levels of administration, he entrusts a certain degree of power, in conformity with the law, to the proper agencies or officials, who act in His name and in accordance with His orders …

Repression

It was clear the tsar was determined to maintain control even if there was a legislative assembly. He would control how the *Duma* worked and ultimately decide what laws would and would not be approved. It appeared as if 1905 had changed nothing as Nicholas reasserted his autocratic powers. Stolypin as Chief Minister acted quickly to control the unrest and outbreaks of violence that followed. Field court martials for civilian rioters were continued, resulting in quick trials.

Table 3.3 The number of victims of unrest and the number of death sentences handed out to those held responsible for the uprising

Year	Killed	Wounded	Sentenced	Executed
1905	233	358	72	10
1906	768	820	450	144
1907	1231	1312	1056	456
1908	394	615	1741	825

KEY TERM

Stolypin's necktie The name given to the hangman's noose following 2500 executions between 1906 and 1911, when Stolypin was Chief Minister.

A further 2000 were executed after being tried by the ordinary courts between 1905 and 1908, with the hangman's noose becoming known as **Stolypin's necktie**.

Repressive measures were enacted through a combination of the police, the army, and the *Okhrana* to target revolutionary groups. As well as the thousands executed, thousands more were exiled to Siberia or deported to other countries. In the countryside, soldiers used violence, including beatings and rape, as well as executions, to suppress peasant unrest.

The third and fourth Dumas

Despite the difficulties of working with the *Dumas*, the tsar did not dispense with them. Instead, the unrest led to Stolypin changing voting rights so that those elected were more likely to come from the nobility and therefore be more conservative and less critical of the tsar. Voting was limited to members of the propertied class, with peasants and workers losing the right to vote, changing the composition of the *Duma* from the first two, as can be seen in the chart below.

Table 3.4 *Duma* election results, 1907–17

Party/Group	Third *Duma* 1907–12	Fourth *Duma* 1912–17
SDs (Mensheviks)	0	0
SDs (Bolsheviks)	19	15
SRs	0	0
Laborists	13	10
Kadets	54	53
Octobrists	154	95
Progressists	28	41
Rightists	147	154
National parties	26	22
Others	0	42
Total	441	432

As a result, the third and fourth *Dumas* were more submissive to the tsar and his government. They introduced a series of reforms to the army and navy, and in the judicial system, and an insurance scheme for workers. This has led some to suggest that it was only the government's attitude which prevented the *Dumas* from bringing about even more significant change (see Source 3.13).

How does Source 3.13 explain the problems in government? Is this argument convincing?

SOURCE 3.13

Comment made by Mikhail Rodzianko, chairman of the *Duma*, 1913

We are accustomed to think that part of the executive power of the crown is delegated to ministers and to the nominated members of the council. But what do we see? Your Majesty will agree that members of the government either do not wish to execute your will, or do not take the trouble to understand it. The population does not know where it is. Each minister has his own opinion. The cabinet is for the most part split into two parties, the state council form a third, the *Duma* a fourth, and your own will is unknown to the nation; this is not a government, it is anarchy.

The third Duma, November 1907–June 1912

As a result of a conservative-dominated third *Duma*, Stolypin was able to pursue his land reforms (see page 169) without serious opposition. However, the *Duma* did not simply support the regime:
- It exercised its right to question ministers.
- It discussed state finances.
- The committee system was used to make proposals to modernize the army.

- Schools for children of the poor were established.
- National insurance for workers was introduced.

These achievements were possible as the regime placed far more trust in the *Duma*.

The fourth Duma, *November 1912–February 1917*

The fourth *Duma* was dominated by politicians from the right. Despite this, they were appalled by the killings in the Lena Goldfields massacre of 1912. Although there were clashes with the government, this *Duma* did carry out several reforms, providing the beginnings of a welfare state. However, as politicians on the left were ignored, there was little change in the nature of the Russian state, and it can therefore be argued that major problems were left unresolved.

The nature and extent of opposition to Tsarist rule

The first two *Dumas* had clearly shown that there was political opposition to the tsar, with both the Social Democrats and Socialist Revolutionaries gaining support. However, the changes to the electoral rules saw their support in the *Dumas* decline. The liberal members, or *Kadets*, were disappointed by developments but were unwilling to openly oppose the tsar. Radical beliefs, such as Marxism, did attract some support, as did **anarchism**. However, many of the radicals, such as Lenin, had been forced into exile, and therefore the radical groups lacked enough support to offer a serious challenge to the regime. They did send revolutionary material into Russia, which evaded censorship, but its impact was limited. As a result, it appeared, at least on the surface, as if the country was politically stable.

This does not mean that there was not disquiet, with the most notable example occurring at the Lena Goldfields in 1912. Here, the miners worked very long days under extremely difficult conditions. They complained about the meat they were forced to buy from the company shop, but the company ignored their complaints, and so a month-long strike started. This ended in violence. The employers asked the authorities to break up the strike, and on April 4, troops were sent in to disband the strikers and ended up firing on them. They killed between 200 and 300 strikers and injured as many as 500, which led to other solidarity strikes elsewhere, culminating in a general strike in July 1914.

Industry continued to grow, but the conditions in the factories were often appalling. This led to many disaffected workers on the streets of the major cities in protest between 1911 and 1914. Government policy following the assassination of Stolypin in 1911 was one of repression, but this caused more disorder. The number of strikes that the Ministry of Trade and Industry described as political rose from 24 in 1911 to 2401 in 1914. Workers were faced with rising inflation and static wages, while growing class consciousness led to the potential for workers to challenge the authority of the tsar.

Strikes and unrest became more common. There was unrest among the peasantry who were unable to keep up their payments for land they had bought. In towns, poor living conditions added to the disquiet. By 1914, only 200 out of over 1000 towns had piped water, and just 38 had a sewerage system. In 1910, there was an outbreak of cholera in St. Petersburg which killed over 100,000. Therefore, even if there was not political unrest as such, there was widespread dissatisfaction with the system.

However, when the police moved in, a considerable number of strikers were killed or injured, a clear indication of the willingness of the regime to enact brutal policies of repression. This seemed to have an impact throughout the country (see Source 3.14).

SOURCE 3.14

A Secret Police agent describing the situation in St. Petersburg, 1912

There has never been so much tension. People can be heard speaking of the government in the sharpest and most unbridled tones. Many say that the "shooting" of the Lena workers recalls the "shooting" of the workers at the Winter Palace of January 9, 1905. Influenced by questions in the *Duma* and the speeches which they called forth there, public tension is increasing still

---

ACTIVITY

Create a table of similarities and differences between the four *Dumas*. How different were the first and second *Duma* compared to third and fourth?

KEY TERM

Anarchism A belief that all government is oppressive and should be abolished.

What is the attitude to public tension in Source 3.14? Consider the author of the source. From your knowledge, do you think this agent would be a reliable source? What might affect the reliability of their message?

more. It is a long time since even the extreme left have spoken in such a way, since there have been references in the *Duma* to "the necessity of calling a Constituent Assembly" and "overthrowing the present system by the united strength of the proletariat."

Union militancy continued when a general strike brought St. Petersburg to a halt in July 1914 and was probably prevented from developing further only due to the outbreak of the First World War. Industrial development had created problems that the government seemed unable to deal with, adopting ever-more brutal methods of repression, which caused further disquiet and protest. Although the police and army might be able to crush unrest, they could not eliminate it.

> ### ACTIVITY
>
> Draw a diagram to show the groups who supported and opposed the tsar by 1914. Add the most important reasons for support or opposition.

The extent of changes in Russia between 1905 and the start of the First World War

Nicholas's attitude towards the *Dumas* had shown he was unwilling to support major change. However, their reforms, although limited, did lead to some economic improvements, and by 1914 Russia was beginning to develop into a modern industrial state.

Stolypin's agrarian reforms and their impact

Stolypin was ordered to reconsider government policy over land distribution, which had caused disquiet in the early *Dumas* (see page 165). His aim was to de-revolutionize the peasantry, many of whom had supported the 1905 Revolution, and create a separate class of better and more prosperous peasants. This policy, known as "the wager on the strong," was aimed at creating a class of peasants who would be more likely to support the Tsarist regime. The Policy consisted of a number of elements:
- Unused or poorly used land was made available to the Peasants' Land Bank.
- Peasants could buy the land on favorable terms.
- Peasants who still farmed strips under the authority of the *mir* were given the opportunity to leave the *mir* and consolidate this land into smallholdings (small-scale farms) which were more efficient.

It was hoped that these moves would create numerous small peasant farms run independently from the *mir*, while their independence would lead to innovation and enterprise, which would help to increase crop yields. Stolypin also hoped that those who benefited would create a class of peasants loyal to the tsar and thereby help increase stability in the countryside.

Although some 2 million peasant households, from between 10 and 12 million people, had moved into small-scale farming by 1914, many preferred the security of communal farming as they were very conservative and resistant to change. Many who did consolidate sold up and moved to the growing towns and cities. The policy also failed to tackle one of the major complaints of the peasantry: noble ownership of land. The peasantry believed that only a redistribution of it would solve the problem of land hunger, while others resented the appearance of the independent peasant farmer who, they argued, had been given the best land, which undermined the traditional values of the commune. Despite this, there was an expansion in the numbers joining the wealthier class of peasants, reflected in the number paying increasingly higher taxes. But it would be a slow process to transform the peasantry, and the outbreak of war in 1914 brought it to a halt, making any judgment on its success difficult.

Developments in industry and their impact

The drive for industrial growth continued under Nicholas II, led initially by the Finance Minister, Sergei Witte. He believed that industrial growth would further help reduce revolutionary activity. As a result, economic growth averaged 8 per cent in the period to 1914.

Having lagged behind the rest of the world in terms of railways, Russia had the second largest extent by 1914, with some 70,000 kilometres of track. This growth helped stimulate the heavy industries of coal, iron and steel, and oil (Table 3.5). Railway growth also reduced transport costs and allowed both raw materials and finished products to be moved more quickly.

Table 3.5 Production in key industries, 1880–1910 (production in millions of metric tons)

	1880	1890	1900	1910
Coal	3.2	5.9	16.1	25.4
Pig-iron	0.42	0.89	2.66	3.0
Crude oil	0.5	3.9	10.2	12.1

[Taken from, M. Scott-Baumann, *Tsarist and Communist Russia*]

As a result, Russia had the world's fifth largest economy by the outbreak of the First World War. However, this growth came at a high cost. Russia remained dependent on foreign investment, and rapid industrialization had a significant social impact. Although Russia continued to be a rural-based society, industrial development led to the rapid growth of towns. The population of St. Petersburg grew from one million in 1900 to 2.25 million by 1914. There was a sudden movement of workers into cities without adequate housing and services, which created huge discontent. Conditions in the factories were often dangerous, and there were health problems associated with pollution. Workers were paid low wages and had to pay high taxes, only adding to unrest and strikes. For many, industrial work represented a vast change in their lives as they had to follow disciplines they had not had in the rural world. Industrial growth led to greater communication with the West, and this led to the spread of political ideas, which could spread easily among the workers in poorer areas of cities, resulting in the growth of an urban proletariat. Many of these problems were outlined by Alan Monkhouse, a British engineer, who went to work in Moscow in 1911 (Source 3.15).

SOURCE 3.15

What additional knowledge could you use to consider whether this view of events in Source 3.15 was justified?

A British engineer describes conditions in Moscow in 1911

The sanitary conditions existing in these districts were appalling. In these working-class suburbs of the cities, typhoid and infantile diarrhoea took their toll. As I drove to work daily, I usually saw four or five pathetic little processions. Two children usually took the lead carrying an ikon, the other the lid of a small coffin. A bereaved parent plodded behind holding the little open coffin. A weeping mother dragged her feet along the hot and dusty cobbles. Not surprisingly, drunkenness was common.

The human impact of industrialization was far from positive. Immigration into the cities pushed wages down; depressions led to unemployment; and working hours were long, with many doing an 11.5-hour day and then going home to crude two-storey wooden buildings which were overcrowded and without either drainage or water supply. The census of 1896 revealed that four to six people had to share a bed or, in some instances, workers were housed in dormitories. It is not surprising that this provided the ideal breeding ground not only for the spread of disease, but also for the spread of revolutionary ideas.

What can we learn from Source 3.16 about how stable Russia was in 1913? What knowledge do you have which either supports or challenges that view?

SOURCE 3.16

Tsar Nicholas II and Tsarina Alexandra at the Winter Palace, St. Petersburg, during the 300th anniversary of the House of Romanov celebrations in 1913

ACTIVITY

Create a table like this. Look back over the section to fill in as many factors as you can to explain why the tsar managed to remain in power after the 1905 Revolution to 1914.

Possible reason	How it contributed	Evidence against	Link to other factors

When you have completed the table, decide which is the most significant reason or combination of reasons and attempt some synthesis. This means bringing together different elements in an analysis. Reflect on these conclusions: do current political, social, or economic issues influence your views? What is the key evidence that has led you to your latest conclusion?

Despite the many issues that remained, by 1914, Russia was relatively stable. The economy was improving, and Russia was beginning to develop into a modern industrial state because of Witte's reforms. There was rising production in both heavy industries and some of the new technologies, while there was also a growing labor force. Although that created its own problems, there was little evidence to suggest that the regime would collapse within three years. However, it must not be forgotten that the tsar was unwilling to change, and this made the system vulnerable to a severe challenge. After all, in 1914, Russia was still largely an unreformed autocratic state.

ACTIVITY

Complete a chart on the changes in Russia in the period 1905–14.

Factor	What improved?	What did not improve?

> **KEY DEBATE**
>
> **WAS THE PERIOD FROM 1905 TO THE OUTBREAK OF THE FIRST WORLD WAR ONE OF STABILITY OR INSTABILITY?**
>
> Some historians claim that in 1914, Russia was stable, with a developing industrial strategy and improving economy. Opponents of the regime had been controlled by mild political reforms. Despite the upheavals of 1905, the imposition of the Fundamental Laws meant that despite the reforms and introduction of the *Duma*, the tsar still retained absolute authority. The nobility and army played a crucial role in supporting the Tsarist autocracy, dominating the civil service and army command. The tsar retained a large army, which supported him and which he was able to use however he wanted. During civil unrest, elite Cossack cavalry regiments were dispatched to quell uprisings, and the *Okhrana* infiltrated radical groups to keep opponents under close scrutiny. The Orthodox Church continued to support the tsar's authority. Many still saw the tsar as "the little father," and there were widespread celebrations and a nationwide tour in 1913 for 300 years of Romanov rule, something which would have been unlikely a few years before.
>
> However, other historians emphasize the fragility of the state, still divided by internal tensions. They argue that the underlying problems which had caused uprisings continued to cause discontent. The blocking of Stolypin's reforms by the nobility, threatened by the idea of losing power in the countryside, meant that concerns of the peasantry and their representation in local government remained an issue. Industrial militancy continued to increase, seen most clearly at the Lena Goldfields in 1912, as did simmering peasant discontent, as many felt conditions had become even worse after supposed reform. They argue that by 1914, the Tsarist regime was extremely weak due to civil unrest, unpopular reforms, and increased suppression.

> ▶ **SUMMARY DIAGRAM**
>
> **Outcomes of the 1905 Revolution**
>
> What were the causes and outcomes of the 1905 Revolution up to 1914?
>
> | Causes | Outcomes |
> |---|---|
> | Defeat by Japan | *Duma* reforms |
> | Lena Goldfields strikes | Growing economy |
> | Opposition from *Dumas* | Romanov celebrations |
> | | Support for war 1914 |
> | | Fundamental Laws |

3 How and why did the Bolsheviks seize power in October 1917?

The long-term weaknesses of the Russian regime were made worse by the strains of war, and in February 1917, unrest in the capital led to the government losing control and the abdication of the tsar. This led to an unstable situation where power was shared between a parliamentary provisional government and a workers' and soldiers' council (Soviet) in St. Petersburg (now known as **Petrograd**) leading to a second revolution in October.

The impact of the First World War on Tsarist rule

On July 28, 1914, just a month after the assassination of the Austrian Archduke Franz Ferdinand on June 28 by a Serbian terrorist group, Austria, encouraged by Germany, declared

> **KEY TERM**
>
> **Petrograd** The name of the Russian capital was changed from St Petersburg in 1914, as it was thought to sound too "German." Petrograd's name was again changed to Leningrad in 1924 to honor Lenin after his death.

war on Serbia, a Slav nation. Russia saw itself as the protector of the Slav peoples of the Balkans and considered it Russia's duty to ensure that they did not fall under the control of a "hostile" power, such as Austria. This ultimately forced Nicholas II to mobilize the Russian army, which led to Germany, and later Austria–Hungary, declaring war on Russia. Nicholas had hoped that the mobilization of Russian forces would deter action by Austria, which was not unrealistic given the size of the Russian army and the manpower it had in reserve. Throughout July, attempts were made to reduce tension and avoid conflict. Nicholas II was cousin to the German *Kaiser*, and a series of personal telegrams were exchanged to try to diffuse the situation.

However, Russia faced a difficult problem. It had two mobilization schemes, one partial, which was based on a limited war against Austria–Hungary; the other full-scale mobilization based on a war against both Austria–Hungary and Germany. Whichever plan was followed, it relied on precise railway timetabling to move troops, but the complexity of the timetables also meant that the use of one type of mobilization prevented the other from being implemented. Russia's fear was that if it mobilized partially, it would leave its Polish border defenceless if attacked by Germany, while a full mobilization might provoke Germany. As a result, on July 30, after much hesitation, Nicholas signed the full mobilization order. He had intended this to be a diplomatic move to discourage war. However, on July 31, Germany demanded Russia stop its mobilization, and when it received no response, Germany declared war on Russia on August 1. Austria–Hungary followed four days later.

These events would ultimately lead to the downfall of the Tsarist autocracy. However, the outbreak of war seemed to improve the position of the tsar. The *Duma* voted to agree on war credits, which allowed the raising of taxes and loans to finance the war. Patriotism led to popular demonstrations in support of war and an upsurge in support for the tsar, who was seen as a symbol of that patriotism. Only the Bolsheviks seemed to oppose the war. They were seen by most as traitors, and many were forced to flee. Lenin was already in exile in Austrian Poland, but with Austrian help, went into exile in neutral Switzerland.

The First World War played a crucial role in Russia's drift to revolution. The war showed that politically, economically, and socially the country was not equipped to face the challenges of a modern war.

The *Duma* voted in August 1914 for its own suspension for the duration of the war. This was because a wave of patriotic feeling and support for the tsar led to a belief that the *Duma* might only hinder the war effort. However, Russia's poor military performance led to it demanding its own recall less than a year later. Nicholas finally agreed to this in July 1915. However, his ministers failed to work with non-governmental bodies, such as the Union of *Zemstvos* and the Union of Municipal Councils, which joined to form the **Zemgor**. The success of this body was important, as it suggested that there were ways to govern other than the tsar.

The tsar also refused to listen to the *Duma* and refused its demands to dismiss his cabinet and replace it with a "Ministry of National Confidence." This was the last chance that Nicholas would have of maintaining the support of moderate parties, as many *Duma* members now established the **progressive bloc**. This grouping tried to persuade him to make concessions, but the tsar was unwilling to listen, and it turned previous supporters into opponents. Meanwhile, the tsar simply changed his ministers, but they were not up to the task and so government slipped further into chaos.

KEY TERMS

Zemgor (from *Zemstvo* and the Russian for "town" – *gorod*) A union of representatives of local government members, businessmen, and influential townsmen set up to support the war effort in 1915. Its first chairman was Prince Lvov, later the first leader of the provisional government of 1917 after the tsar's abdication.

Progressive bloc A loose union of moderate and liberal members of the *Duma*.

> **ACTIVITY**
>
> What were the main reasons why the First World War had an impact on the tsar's position? Which one do you think was the most important reason?

The impact of defeats in the First World War on the tsar's position

The best chance for Russia to win the war was probably a quick victory, but there were early defeats at Tannenberg, at which some 300,000 Russian soldiers were killed or wounded, and at the Masurian Lakes, where a further 100,000 men were lost, of whom 50 per cent were taken prisoner. Russia lost twice as many troops as the enemy during these early campaigns. These defeats lowered the morale of the Russian troops, who were let down by poor commanders, such as Generals Samsonov and Rennenkampf, who made poor strategic decisions. By 1915, there was a **shell crisis** and a lack of guns at the front. In part, this was due to administrators who did not have the abilities to cope with the logistical challenges, but it was also due to transport failings and the vast distances that supplies needed to be moved, so that in the same year the **Great Retreat** was underway.

The Russian armed forces were suffering setbacks for several reasons. Firstly, there was the problem of the administration of supplies, which left troops short of food, ammunition, and medical equipment. Secondly, commanders continued to use outdated tactics and did not change them despite soldiers being ill equipped, with shortages meaning that ordinary Russian soldiers were forced to take weapons and shoes from dead colleagues to be able to continue to fight. They had lost twice as many men as the enemy during these early campaigns, and hopes of victory declined, leading to a loss of morale at home. The Russian army was largely composed of peasant soldiers who were conscripts with minimal military experience, and by 1916, initial enthusiasm for the war had turned to pessimism. Soldiers began to desert in ever-increasing numbers.

The defeats during 1915 and the lack of strong leadership that the war needed led to Nicholas II taking direct command of the Russian forces in August 1915. Although the tsar attempted to inspire the troops, it was a disastrous decision. Nicholas had been trained as a soldier, but he was not a natural commander, and he had to rely on his generals. He did not know enough about the actual fighting, and did not bring any new ideas of strategy. Also, departure from Petrograd left a vacuum at the centre of government. Nicholas was based at the Military Headquarters at Mogilev, a supply centre rather than the actual front. Therefore, he was cut off from how the war was progressing and was also unaware of developments in the capital city. His military appointments were weak, favoring high social status over actual military skills. The situation was not helped as senior officers were reluctant to tell him the truth of what was happening. However, the biggest problem for Nicholas was that now he was directly in command, all the defeats were blamed on him.

Despite these problems, 1916 did appear to offer some respite. There was a more successful campaign led by General Brusilov, but this did not bring victory, as gains were not followed up and did not justify the high rate of casualties. A million men were lost in the year. The failure of the Brusilov offensive and the development of a **war of attrition** showed that the tsar was incapable of bringing the war to a successful conclusion.

The longer the war went on, the more apparent the Russian military weaknesses were (see Source 3.17).

> **KEY TERMS**
>
> **Shell crisis** The logistical problem faced by Russian commanders at the start of the war in supplying troops at the front with sufficient ammunition.
>
> **Great Retreat** The name given to the withdrawal of Russian forces in 1915 to a new front line inside Russian territory.
>
> **War of attrition** A war where both sides try to wear down the enemy by killing more soldiers and exhausting the enemy's resources rather than winning decisive victories.

What is the view of the writer of Source 3.17 about the Russian army?

SOURCE 3.17

A report on the Russian army, January 1917

When this mass is at last demobilized and poured out over the country, it will wash away old landmarks and destroy barriers which have kept back the flood. All will join in one general demand: that the government should answer for bringing the country to the state it is in. To what extent the Government is really responsible will not concern them. Everyone agrees there will be a revolution. On this occasion, the Army will be on the side of the people.

Among the better class of officers, I note a great change of late. It daily grows greater and franker, daily more freely expressed. That is their attitude towards the Emperor. From time immemorial, they have abused the Government. In the last year, I have noticed a new and sinister trend of feeling towards the Emperor. One by one they have fallen away from him, louder and louder they declare the existing state of affairs to be impossible. They condemn the Emperor as being weak and vacillating, ruled by the Empress, and keeping in office Ministers not only utterly incompetent, but with pro-German tendencies.

Weaknesses in the government during the war

The tsar's departure for the front left the situation open to baseless rumors that civil government was in the hands of his wife, **Tsarina Alexandra**, and **Rasputin**. Rasputin had influence over the tsarina because of his apparent ability to lessen the **hemophilia** from which the tsar and tsarina's son suffered. Alexandra was an object of suspicion among Russian people because she was German. The tsar's advisors and ministers despised Rasputin and distrusted the tsarina as she was thought to take his advice. It was therefore difficult for even the most ardent supporters of the tsar to defend a system whereby, at Russia's darkest hour, they believed the country was ruled by a pair whom many thought of as "that German woman" and a "mad monk." There was a vicious cycle at work. Falling faith in the tsar made the rumours more credible, which increased the loss of support for the tsar.

On December 30, 1916, Rasputin was murdered by a group of aristocrats who thought they would help the tsar by getting rid of the problem. He was poisoned, shot at close range, and battered, and was still alive when he was thrown into the icy river Neva, where he finally died of drowning. By this stage, most supporters of the tsar had deserted him. In November 1916, the leader of the *Kadet* party outlined the divisions within Russia (Source 3.18).

KEY FIGURES

Tsarina Alexandra (1872–1918) was a German princess – Alix of Hesse and granddaughter of Queen Victoria of Britain. She met Nicholas in 1884, and they were married in 1894, when she became empress. Shy, nervous, and reclusive, she was unpopular in Russia and was ready to give Nicholas extreme advice. She was devoted to her family and to Rasputin, which made her popularity sink lower. She was killed with her husband and children by the Bolsheviks in 1918.

Grigori Rasputin (1869–1916) was a Siberian peasant who established himself as a self-professed holy man. Mystics were a common feature in Russia and were widely revered. He met the tsar in 1905 and captivated the royal family. The tsarina believed he could cure their son's hemophilia. His views became influential on the tsarina before and during the war. Many also mistakenly thought he was her lover. Intensely unpopular, he was assassinated in December 1916, possibly with secret help from the British.

KEY TERM

Hemophilia A genetic condition in which the blood does not clot. It can lead to severe bruising and internal bleeding, and has the potential to be life-threatening.

> What does Source 3.18 say about the condition of the Russian government? What does that tell the reader about attitudes to this issue? Note down specific details from the source to back up your answer.

SOURCE 3.18

Paul Milyukov, leader of the *Kadet* party, speech to the Fourth *Duma*, November 1916

This present government has sunk beneath the level on which it stood during normal times in Russian life. And now the gulf between us and that government has grown wider and become impassable. Today, we are aware that with this government we cannot legislate, and we cannot, with this government, lead Russia to victory. We are telling this government, as the declaration of the Progressive Bloc stated: We shall fight you, we shall fight you with all legitimate means until you go.

There had been challenges to Nicholas II before, most notably in 1905. However, by the start of 1917 things were very different. This time the range of opposition to the tsar was much greater. There were rumors of serious unrest breaking out in Petrograd and this was confirmed by the *Duma* president in early February, when he told the tsar, that serious protests were imminent. This seemed to confirm the reports of the *Okhrana*, who had reported in January 1917 that the industrial workers were on the verge of revolution (Source 3.19).

> Who was the intended audience of Source 3.19? What impact might this have on the content and attitudes shown in the source?

SOURCE 3.19

An official report written by a member of the tsar's secret police, the *Okhrana*, January 1917

The mass of industrial workers are quite ready to let themselves go to the wildest excesses of a hunger riot. The working masses, led in their actions and sympathies by the more conscious and already revolutionary-minded elements, are violently hostile to the authorities and protest with all means and devices against a continuation of the war. Thus, left-wing revolutionary circles are convinced that a revolution will begin very soon.

But it was not just the workers who had deserted the tsar; even his traditional supporters had. At the front, soldiers were mutinying, and news of their hardships spread back home. Many soldiers deserted, fearful that their families would die if they did not return home, and it was they who provided a focal point of dissatisfaction in many of the cities where unrest developed. The scale of the dissatisfaction became apparent when soldiers were ordered to restore order in the cities and refused to fire on protestors.

> **ACTIVITY**
>
> Make a list of the political, social, and economic consequences of the First World War for Russia. Construct a diagram which shows how they overlap.

The causes and effects of the February Revolution

The impact of the First World War was felt not only in the military and government; it also caused huge economic and social problems which, along with discontent with the Tsarist system highlighted by the war, led to revolution in February 1917.

Economic and social problems on the home front

The Russian economy was unable to cope with the demands of total war. Although there were attempts to adapt both agriculture and industry to the demands of war, it was simply unable to cope, and this had a massive impact on the lives of ordinary Russians.

Inflation and food shortages

The economic impact of the war was seen most clearly in rising inflation and prices. The cost of the war was some 3 billion roubles, whereas peacetime expenditure was 1.5 billion roubles. To meet the shortfall, the government borrowed from overseas and at home and raised taxes and printed more money. The result was rampant inflation. By 1917, prices had risen 400 per cent since the start of the war, while average wages had only doubled.

There were also food shortages despite the average output of cereals being higher than it had been before the war. With prices rising, peasants and grain producers withheld stocks from the market to get a higher price. In addition, government inefficiency in deploying railway resources seriously hampered food distribution. In the northern cities, far away from the southern grain-producing areas, the suffering was severe. By 1917, Petrograd was receiving less than a quarter of the amount of grain which had been available in 1914. In addition, the military had priority in using the transport system. It took control of both the railways and roads so that moving food supplies to civilian areas became increasingly difficult. Despite the growth in the railway system in the years before the war, it simply was not enough, and it became chaotic as the military attempted to move troops and armaments. As the system broke down, trucks could not be moved, and food often rotted in them. In Moscow, which required 2200 wagons of grain per day, only 700 were reaching the city by February 1917.

Social problems

The disruption to food supplies made living and working conditions very difficult. In desperate times, many workers turned to alcohol, especially vodka. Nicholas II had introduced a prohibition on alcohol at the start of the war, but alcohol taxes made up a third of government revenue, which was hard to lose. By 1916, it was clear the ban was not working, as workers found illegal ways to make alcohol. When the ban was lifted, the damage was already done, and illegal vodka production in home-made stills was widespread.

Land seizures

The redistribution of land was a major issue among the peasantry, and, as order on the home front began to break down, a few peasants simply began to seize land from the nobility. Once news of this reached the front, it encouraged soldiers to desert, determined that they would not miss out. In some instances, the redistribution was organized, but in many instances, peasants simply smashed down fences and took the land.

Events of February 1917, leading to the abdication of the tsar

According to the Russian dating system, which follows the older Julian calendar rather than the Gregorian one, the revolution lasted from February 18 to March 4, 1917.

Table 3.6 Events of the February Revolution

February 18	Strike begins at the Putilov steel works in Petrograd
February 19	Rumors that bread rationing is to be introduced
February 23	International Women's Day. This leads to marchers and workers from the Putilov plant joining to protest for female equality and improved conditions.
February 25	General strike. Troops fire on workers.
February 27	The Petrograd Soviet is formed. Some members of the *Duma* establish a Provisional Committee.
February 28	Nicholas II is prevented from returning to Petrograd
March 1	Soviet Order Number 1 passed. This gives the Petrograd Soviet control over the military.
March 2	The Provisional Committee declares itself the Provisional Government. Nicholas signs abdication decree.
March 3	Provisional Government declares a revolution has taken place
March 4	Abdication of Nicholas announced

Given the situation in the major cities, unrest and protests began again at the Putilov Steel works, the largest factory in Petrograd. Over the next few days, the numbers on the streets increased dramatically. This was initially encouraged by rumors that there would be further cuts in the bread supply. Although this was not true, the tensions within the city led to it being believed. International Women's Day brought more people out onto the streets. Many of the women were demanding equality, but they joined with other protestors who were demanding an end to the war and an improvement in food supplies and in their living and working conditions.

Within two days the protests had grown, and a city-wide strike had started. Workers occupied factories, and the authorities were unable to disperse them due to the sympathy among many of the police. This led to troops firing on protestors. While serving as the president of the *Duma*, Rodzianko, a conservative, and loyal supporter of the tsar, urged him to change his ruling methods. The events were still largely chaotic. Many of the protests appeared to be about food shortages and problems created by the war. Few seemed to be politically driven or call for the removal of the tsar.

The tsar was still at the front, some 650 km away, while the tsarina remained in Petrograd. It was Alexandra who provided her husband with details of the developments within the capital city. He ordered the commander of the Petrograd police to restore order but was told that some members of the police and militia had joined the demonstrators and that some military units were disobeying orders. The breakdown in law and order within the city was such that martial law could not be declared, as the loyalty of the army was uncertain. However, the most important development was the desertion of the garrison.

The Provisional Committee and the Petrograd Soviet

The desertion of the garrison prompted Rodzianko to inform the tsar that the only way to save the situation and preserve his position was if major concessions were made. Nicholas's response was to dissolve the *Duma*. However, a group of twelve defied the order and established a special committee, which would later be the Provisional Government. This was a significant moment, as it marked the first unconstitutional defiance of the tsar and was soon followed by a call from Alexander Kerensky, a member of the *Duma*, for the tsar to stand down.

▶ ALEXANDER KERENSKY

Alexander Kerensky (1881–1970) was the son of a teacher. He studied law and history at university and became associated with radical opposition groups, defending 1905 revolutionaries in trials.
A prominent socialist in the *Duma*, he spoke against the government. After the February Revolution, he was a member of both the Provisional Government and the executive committee of the Petrograd Soviet. He was Minister for War and in July 1917 became the Prime Minister. Wavering between supporting the radical revolutionaries and a military coup, he lost support and was overthrown by the Bolsheviks in October. He lived in exile until his death in the USA in 1970.

1881	Born
1904	Graduated from St Petersburg University
1905	Joined the SRs and became a lawyer
1912	Elected to the fourth *Duma* as part of the Labor group
1917	Campaigned for the end of monarchy in Russia, then became vice chairman of the Petrograd Soviet and in July Prime Minister in the Provisional Government
1918	Emigrated to western Europe
1940	Emigrated to the USA
1970	Died in New York

KEY TERM

Suffrage The right to vote; "universal suffrage" is the right of all adults to vote.

At the same time, another important event took place. This was the formation of the "Petrograd Soviet of Soldiers', Sailors', and Workers' Deputies." Together, these groups became the unofficial government of Russia, as they believed the tsar was unfit to rule. This marked what would later be called the start of Dual Power, whereby the two powers came to an agreement. The Soviet forced the Provisional Government to agree, among other things, to call a Constituent Assembly which would be elected on the basis of universal **suffrage**.

The abdication of the tsar

As the situation deteriorated, most ministers abandoned the government and left Petrograd. This led to Rodzianko informing the tsar that only his abdication could save the crown and resulted in Nicholas's decision to return to his capital city. He believed that returning would help calm the situation, but his train was intercepted and forced to divert to Pskov, some 260 km from Petrograd. The members of the old *Duma* and high command of the army informed him how bad the situation was and advised him to abdicate. He accepted their advice and renounced the throne, not only for himself but for his son as well. The abdication document he signed named his brother, the Grand Duke Michael, as the new tsar. However, Michael refused to accept it, realising the extent of anti-Tsarist feeling.

Michael's refusal left the Provisional Government responsible for ruling Russia. The rule of the Romanovs was over, and Nicholas's formal abdication was announced.

The abdication of Nicholas had been brought about by events in the capital, with very few instances of unrest elsewhere. The Bolsheviks, the most revolutionary of the political parties, played little direct part in the regime's downfall, with many of their leaders still in exile. What is also noticeable is that there were no groups willing to defend the autocracy. Indeed, several elite groups were actively plotting against the tsar, in effect to make him the scapegoat for failures and thereby protect their own privileged positions.

The overthrow of the autocracy was not completely bloodless, and up to 2000 people were killed or wounded. Whether the events which took place in the capital should be seen as overthrowing the monarchy is another question. An examination of the timeline at the start of this section suggests that developments were haphazard and there was no real plan. Perhaps the most important reason for the eventual downfall was that those in power lacked a plan. While almost all involved wanted to remove Nicholas, they had not expected the monarchy itself would disappear. It was the desertion of high-ranking officers and the refusal of members of the *Duma* to disband which brought it down. Once Nicholas lost the support of the army, it was virtually impossible for him to remain in power. It was this loss of support which was very different from 1905. Nonetheless, few had foreseen the refusal of Grand Duke Michael to take up the reins of power, a decision which ended Tsardom itself.

The First World War also played an important role in the downfall of Tsardom. War had tested the nation, revealing the strengths and weaknesses of all its institutions. The prolonged duration and extensive scale of the conflict ultimately led to the regime's downfall. A short war which did not end in victory, such as the Russo-Japanese War, might not have been fatal for the regime, but the cumulative impact of several factors, such as 3 million deaths, rapid inflation, collapse of the transport system, hunger, ineffectual ministers, and an incompetent tsar were more than the system could withstand.

ACTIVITY

Copy and complete the table to show the causes of the February Revolution. Rate each cause 1–5 to show how important it was.

Cause	Explanation	Importance on scale of 1–5	Reasons for importance score

Formation and aims of the Provisional Government

Although the tsar had gone, the new government had extensive challenges. In fact, it still faced the problems that the tsar had faced:
- continuation of the war
- land redistribution
- economic dislocation.

Added to these issues was the problem that the Provisional Government lacked real authority as it was not an elected body and had come into being because of the refusal of some members of the old *Duma* to disband. It also faced challenges from the Petrograd Soviet, which would further limit its authority.

However, it was the task of the Provisional Government, initially led by **Prince Lvov**, to take charge. It was provisional, or temporary, as it was only to hold power until elections could be held for a Constituent Assembly, which was to be elected based on universal suffrage and a secret ballot.

Some have argued that the Provisional Government was weak because it was not democratically elected and was made up of old *Duma* members. However, this was not a major issue since its main task was to set up a Constituent Assembly. A far greater challenge was presented by the existence of the Petrograd Soviet, which, although it did not set out to be an alternative government, was soon opposing virtually everything that the Provisional Government attempted to do. This was particularly the case over the big question of the war. The Provisional Government was keen to continue Russia's involvement and push for a decisive victory, while the Soviet wanted "peace without annexations or indemnities" (meaning a peace settlement without losing any Russian land and without paying any money to the victors). This division would be crucial and would play a major role in the failure of the government.

The issuing by the Petrograd Soviet of Order Number 1 also created problems for the Provisional Government, as it meant that army orders were not binding unless they were approved by the soldiers' committees, meaning that they did not have complete control over the armed forces. The Order also placed control of the armed forces in the hands of the Soviet, which further restricted the power of Provisional Government (Source 3.20).

> **KEY FIGURE**
>
> **Prince Lvov** (1861–1925) was a member of an eminent noble family who became a liberal and joined the *Kadets* after 1905. He was prominent in the opposition in the *Duma* after 1915 and was the first prime minister of the Provisional Government after the fall of the tsar. Lacking support, he resigned in July. Imprisoned by the Bolsheviks in 1918, he was deported and lived in exile until his death in France in 1925.

> Rewrite Source 3.20 in your own words.

SOURCE 3.20

The Petrograd Soviet of Workers' and Soldiers' Deputies Order Number 1, March 14, 1917

The Soviet of Workers' and Soldiers' Deputies has decided:

- In all companies, battalions, squadrons, and separate branches of the military service of all kinds and on warships, committees should be chosen immediately.
  - All orders issued by the State *Duma* shall be carried out, except those which run counter to the orders and decrees issued by the Soviet of Workers' and Soldiers' Deputies.
  - All kinds of arms, such as rifles and machine guns, must be under the control of the company and battalion committees and must in no case be handed over to officers even at their demand.
- The addressing of officers with titles such as "Your Excellency," "Your Honor," etc., is abolished, and these are replaced by "Mr. General," "Mr. Colonel," and so on.

These orders meant that compromise with the Soviet was now essential. The Provisional Government had little choice but to agree to the eight conditions of support that the executive committee of the Petrograd Soviet presented to them as its conditions for support of the government:

1. Amnesty for all political prisoners
2. The right to speak, assemble and strike
3. Equality for all nationalities, religions, and social origins
4. Convocation of the Constituent Assembly
5. Police organs to be replaced by militia whose officers were elected

6 New elections to the Soviets
7 Military units which participated in the revolution not be sent to the front
8 Off-duty soldiers to receive temporary status as civilians.

Until April, when the Bolshevik leader Lenin returned, the relationship between the government and the Soviet appeared to work. Leon Trotsky, who was highly involved in the Soviet and became its Chairman in September 1917, saw this relationship rather differently than the moderate socialists and suggested that the Soviet was the dominating force (see Source 3.21).

> How useful is Source 3.21 as evidence of the importance of the Soviet in the period after the abdication of the tsar?

SOURCE 3.21

Leon Trotsky, A History of the Russian Revolution, 1932

From the moment of its formation, the Soviet, in the person of its Executive Committee, begins to function as a sovereign. It elects a temporary food commission and places it in charge of the mutineers and of the garrison in general. The tasks and functions of the Soviet grow unceasingly under pressure from the masses. The revolution finds here its indubitable centre. The workers, the soldiers, and soon also the peasants, will from now on turn only to the Soviet. In their eyes, the Soviet becomes the focus of all hopes and all authority, an incarnation of the revolution itself.

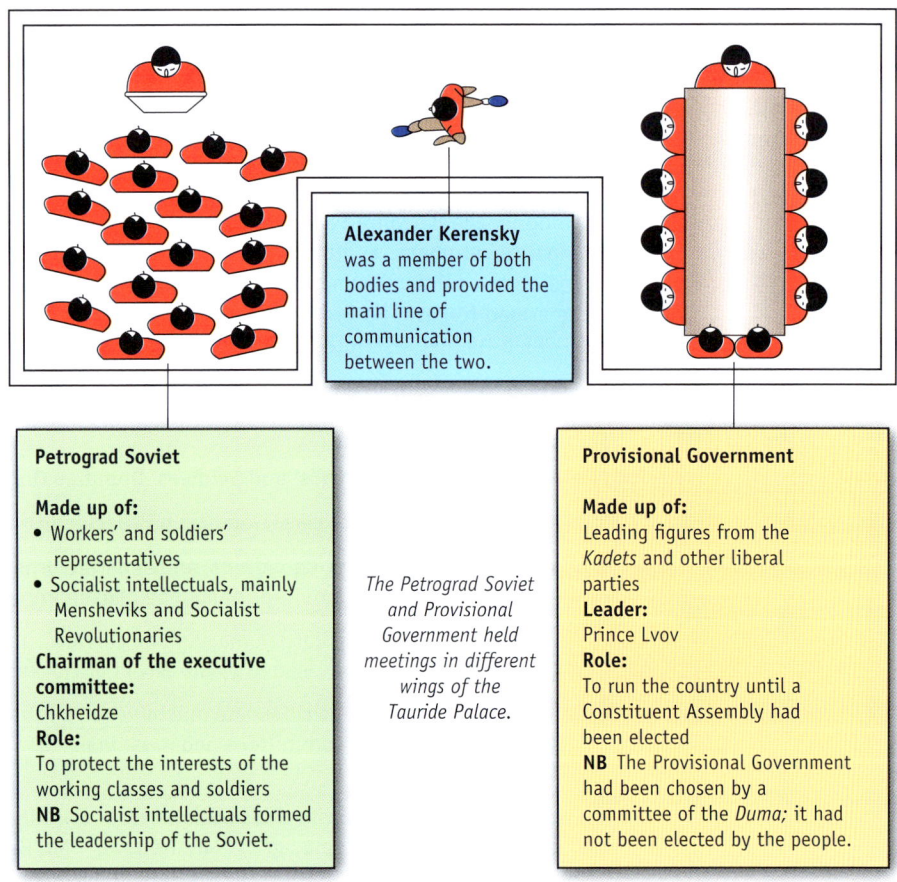

The Petrograd Soviet and Provisional Government held meetings in different wings of the Tauride Palace.

Alexander Kerensky was a member of both bodies and provided the main line of communication between the two.

Petrograd Soviet

Made up of:
- Workers' and soldiers' representatives
- Socialist intellectuals, mainly Mensheviks and Socialist Revolutionaries

Chairman of the executive committee:
Chkheidze

Role:
To protect the interests of the working classes and soldiers

NB Socialist intellectuals formed the leadership of the Soviet.

Provisional Government

Made up of:
Leading figures from the *Kadets* and other liberal parties

Leader:
Prince Lvov

Role:
To run the country until a Constituent Assembly had been elected

NB The Provisional Government had been chosen by a committee of the *Duma*; it had not been elected by the people.

Figure 4.1 The membership and role of the Petrograd Soviet and the Provisional Government

VLADIMIR ULYANOV (LENIN)

1870	Born as Vladimir Ilyich Ulyanov, to a minor aristocratic family of partly Jewish ancestry
1897	Exiled to Siberia; took the alias Lenin
1900	Joined the Social Democratic Party
1903	Led the Bolshevik breakaway movement in the SDs
1900–17	In exile abroad apart from November 1905 to December 1907, when he was in Russia and Finland
1917	Returned to Petrograd in April to lead the Bolsheviks in the October Revolution
1917–22	Led the Bolsheviks in consolidating their hold on Russia
1921	Introduced the New Economic Policy
1924	Died

Vladimir Ulyanov (1870–1924), better known to history as Lenin, turned against the Tsarist regime following the execution of his brother in 1887. In his writing, he adapted Marxist theory to fit Russian conditions. He argued the Bolshevik party would direct a revolution based on the support of the working class. He returned to Russia after the abdication of Nicholas II, writing his April Theses, and after the July Days, he urged his party to take advantage of the power vacuum created by the Kornilov affair and lead a Soviet-based insurrection to overthrow the Provisional Government in October 1917. He, along with Trotsky, and others, led the drive for the creation of the new state, overcoming armed opposition both from foreign powers and within Russia. He was forced by peasant resistance to slow the pace of transition to socialism and restore limited market relations in the New Economic Policy in 1921. From 1922, he suffered from ill health following a series of strokes. He withdrew from direct involvement in politics and died after being incapacitated for two years.

LEV BRONSTEIN (TROTSKY)

1879	Born into a Ukrainian Jewish family
1905	Became Chairman of St. Petersburg Soviet
1907–17	Lived in various European countries and in the USA
1917	Principal organizer of the October coup
1918	Negotiated the Treaty of Brest-Litovsk
1918–20	Created the Red Army
1924–27	Out-manoeuvred in the power struggle with Stalin
1940	Assassinated in Mexico

Trotsky (1879–1940) was originally a Menshevik, and it was in this role that he was appointed Chairman of the St. Petersburg Soviet in 1905. He was exiled between 1907 and 1917 but used that time to develop his theory of "permanent revolution," emphasizing that Russia could pass directly to socialism without having to undergo an era of capitalism. He returned to Petrograd after the February Revolution and joined the Bolsheviks, becoming Chairman of the Petrograd Soviet, using the position to help organize the October Revolution. He became Commissar for Foreign Affairs in the first Soviet Government and was chief negotiator in the peace talks with Germany. He was responsible for the organization of the Red Army in the Civil War. However, having been a Menshevik, he was never fully accepted by some Bolsheviks and lost out to Stalin in the struggle for power following Lenin's death. He was exiled in 1929 and in 1940 was assassinated by an agent of Stalin's.

Reasons for the failure of the Provisional Government

In February 1917, when the Tsarist autocracy fell, very few people would have thought that by the end of October 1917, the Bolsheviks would have been able to seize power. They lacked mass support, most of their leaders were in exile, and most expected that a Constituent Assembly would establish a new form of government for Russia. However, a series of mistakes, as well as the leadership of Lenin and skill of Trotsky, meant that by October, the Bolsheviks were in a position to stage a successful **coup**.

Challenges facing the Provisional Government

Despite the challenges it faced, the Provisional Government did have some early successes:
- Political prisoners were released from jail.
- There were improvements in working conditions as trade unions were recognized and an eight-hour day was brought in.
- Full civil rights were granted.
- Religious freedom was allowed.

It did appear as though Russia was moving toward a more liberal and modern state with the adoption of these progressive measures.

However, the Provisional Government made a series of mistakes in the period from March to October 1917. Changes it made allowed political groups such as the Bolsheviks to develop. Firstly, Stalin and **Kamenev** returned to Petrograd from exile in Siberia in March, and then Lenin returned from exile in Switzerland in April. It was Lenin's return which was particularly significant. His call for "no support for the Provisional Government" drove a wedge between the two powers and undermined the initial cooperation. An attempt was made in May 1917 to heal the divisions with the formation of a coalition government, with Lvov inviting six members of the Soviet to join it. However, this did not satisfy the more radical members of the Soviet, and problems continued.

> **KEY TERM**
>
> **Coup** From the French "*coup d'etat*," or "blow to the state." A forceful takeover of power.

> **KEY FIGURE**
>
> **Lev Kamenev** (1883–1936) returned from Siberian exile after the abdication of the tsar. He held various positions in government and was a leading member of the *Politburo* under Lenin. However, he was a victim of Stalin's purges and was executed in 1936.

SOURCE 3.22

A painting of Lenin's arrival at Finland Station in Petrograd on April 16, 1917 by Russian artist Mikhail Sokolov

What impression of Lenin's return to Russia is given by Source 3.22? This was painted by Sokolov in 1930. How does this affect the reliability of the source as information for Lenin's arrival? Consider who is portrayed, and why, in your answer.

The day after his return, Lenin set out his ideas in the April Theses. Lenin:
- condemned the Provisional Government for being bourgeois and said it should not be supported
- called for cooperation with other political parties to be ended
- called for Soviet power and a workers' and peasants' government.

This message led to two very important propaganda slogans to emerge:
- "All power to the Soviets"
- "Peace, Land, and Bread"

These were very important, as they reinforced Lenin's call for the Soviets to take political power and for Russia to withdraw from the war and deal with food shortages and the land issue. Such calls would win large-scale support among the workers and peasants.

Failure to end the war

Lenin's call to end the war was in complete contrast to the Provisional Government. In an attempt to win support for the Provisional Government, Lvov ordered a new offensive in the war. This was organized by the Minister of War, Alexander Kerensky, and proved to be a disaster. There were heavy losses and mass desertions, which led to further protests against the war. This led to a loss of support for the Provisional Government and increasingly radical demands from the Soviet, so that by June its members were demanding an even greater say in national government. The protests culminated in July, when sailors at the naval base of Kronstadt mutinied.

The July Days

These events led to what have been called the July Days, when the Kronstadt sailors and allies attempted to overthrow the government. However, they were not supported by the main political parties, and the government was able to summon enough loyal troops to put down the protests. The successful crushing of the unrest was credited to Kerensky, who, despite the failings of the offensive, was appointed Prime Minister. He then launched a political attack against the Bolsheviks, whom he accused of being behind the July Days and of being German agents. Neither charge was true. Leading members of the party either went into hiding, like Lenin, who fled to Finland, or were arrested, like Trotsky. Their newspaper, *Pravda*, was closed down, and their party was forced to operate in secret. It appeared as though Bolshevik hopes of taking power were over.

However, the Bolsheviks had an extraordinary change of fortune because of the political machinations of General Kornilov (see Source 3.23 on page 184).

Need for land reform

The Provisional Government faced mounting discontent in the countryside, largely due to land ownership. The issue was very complex. The best solution suggested was to wait for an elected assembly to resolve it. This displeased the peasantry and led to more land seizures, which increased quickly from September. This also encouraged soldiers to desert as they did not want to miss out on land seizure, further weakening the armed forces. National elections to a Constituent Assembly were postponed.

The Kornilov Revolt

The Provisional Government also faced a challenge from General Kornilov. Kornilov brought his troops to Petrograd with the intention of closing the Soviet and then hoped to replace the Provisional Government with a military-style dictatorship, which might even restore Tsardom. He made a patriotic appeal to the people of Russia for support, claiming that he was saving the country (Source 3.23).

Read Source 3.23. What additional knowledge could you use to consider whether this view of events in the summer of 1917 is justified?

SOURCE 3.23

Kornilov's declaration to the people of Russia, August 26, 1917

People of Russia! Our great motherland is dying. The moment of death is near. I, General Kornilov, declare that the Provisional Government, under pressure from the Bolshevik majority in the Soviet, acts in full accord with the German General Staff, and concurrently with the imminent landings of the enemy forces on the coast of Riga, destroys the army and convulses the country from within.

I, General Kornilov, declare to each and all that I personally desire nothing but to save Great Russia. I swear to lead the people through victory over the enemy to the Constituent Assembly, where it will decide its own destiny and choose its new political system.

His plan collapsed, in part because railway workers refused to transport his troops, but also because the Bolsheviks and other Soviet parties prepared quickly to resist him. Kerensky, who may have been allied with Kornilov at first, broke with him after some confused communications, resulting in Kerensky thinking Kornilov was going to overthrow him. Kerensky armed the Soviet and called on all loyal citizens to defend Petrograd. Trotsky and other Bolsheviks were released from prison, while others came out of hiding and took the weapons being offered by the Provisional Government to defend the city, although Lenin remained in Finland. Their response turned the Bolsheviks into heroes as they were willing to defend the revolution and Petrograd. This gained them more support, but it also showed how weak the Provisional Government was, as it had been forced into arming the population to prevent a potential counter-revolution. There was a considerable shift in the position of the Bolsheviks from the low point of the July Days, and this was reflected in Bolshevik resolutions gaining majorities in both the Petrograd and Moscow Soviets in early and mid-September respectively.

ACTIVITY

How quickly did support for the Provisional Government decline? What affected the pace of change?

KEY DEBATE

WHY DID THE PROVISIONAL GOVERNMENT FAIL?

Historians argue that the Provisional Government failed for a number of reasons. Some have argued that it was doomed from the very start and stood no chance of surviving, as it contained only liberals whose support came from Russia's small middle class. Others have suggested that it failed because it made some bad decisions. Although the Provisional Government lacked legitimacy as it was unelected, it was accepted at the start and contained some popular members, and it might have survived had it called a Constituent Assembly.

Those who argue that it faced considerable challenges point to the fact it had to share its authority with the Petrograd Soviet, which had popular support from workers, peasants, soldiers, and sailors. The Soviet disagreed with the Provisional Government over Russia's involvement in the war. The Soviet wanted to start peace negotiations, while the Provisional Government wanted to continue Russia's involvement in the war until victory.

Some historians have taken this further and argued that it was war which was crucial in bringing about the fall of the government. Although Russia faced problems before the war, with many social groups wanting major changes, this downplays the role of the First World War, which was the first global total war and therefore had a massive impact. Popular support for the war was continually declining, and there was an increasing number of deserters. By continuing the war, the Provisional Government lost further support as war-induced inflation cut living standards and increased food shortages.

Other historians have focused on the issue of the redistribution of land. Even before the war, the peasantry had been angered by the failure of the government to redistribute the

(Continued)

> **KEY DEBATE (Continued)**
>
> land of the nobility. The Provisional Government failed to tackle this problem and argued that only a properly elected government could deal with the issue, but this did not satisfy the peasantry. The peasantry therefore turned against the government and continued to seize land regardless.
>
> Finally, some have seen August 1917 as a turning point in the fortunes of the Provisional Government. The Kornilov affair showed just how weak the government was, particularly Kerensky. He was seen as suspect, even sympathetic, in dealing with Kornilov's attempted coup, and was not trusted by either the workers or peasants. The Provisional Government survived because of the Bolsheviks, who were now seen as heroes and gained support, taking control of both the Petrograd and Moscow Soviets. It was this which allowed them to overthrow the government in October. This therefore suggests that August 1917 was a turning point in the Provisional Government's failure, rather than its being doomed from the very start.

Methods used by the Bolsheviks to seize power in October 1917

There were multiple factors involved in facilitating the Bolsheviks' rise to power.

Bolshevik promises

The Bolshevik promises of "All power to the Soviets" and "Peace, Land, and Bread" were easy for people to grasp and remember, and were in direct contrast to what the Provisional Government was doing.

Lenin's leadership

Although Lenin had spent long periods in exile, most notably from 1906 to 1917, he was a major influence on the Bolshevik Party and would play a crucial role in its seizure of power. Even from his exile, his writings had given the Bolsheviks a sense of direction, and his oratory skills had been seen when he returned in April 1917 and issued the April Theses. However, his greatest significance was in the events of autumn of 1917.

Lenin had been continually appealing to the party to prepare for the overthrow of the Provisional Government. His call became more intense as the government failed to solve the problem of the war or the land question and appeared to be more reactionary in its outlook. Lenin argued that the Bolsheviks must seize the moment and on September 12 wrote, "History will not forgive us if we do not assume power."

Lenin was concerned that if the Bolsheviks did not act, they would lose their chance. In particular, he was concerned by two events which were due to take place:
- the meeting of the All-Russian Congress of Soviets in late October
- the elections to the Constituent Assembly.

Lenin was convinced that it was essential for the Bolsheviks to seize power before either of these events happened (see Source 3.24).

SOURCE 3.24

> What is the purpose of Source 3.24? Note down ideas from your own knowledge of events which might be useful to explain its purpose.

A letter by Lenin to the Central Committee, October 24, 1917

The situation is critical in the extreme. In fact, it is now absolutely clear that to delay the uprising would be fatal. With all my might, I urge comrades to realize that everything now hangs by a thread. We are confronted by problems which are not to be solved by conferences but only by the masses and by the struggle of the armed people. We must at all costs, this very evening, this very night, arrest the government, having first disarmed the officers. We must not wait! We may lose everything!

Under no circumstances should power be left in the hands of Kerensky and his group, not under any circumstances. The matter must be decided without fail this very evening, or this very night. History will not forgive we revolutionaries for delaying when we could be victorious today (and we certainly will be victorious today), while we risk losing much tomorrow, in fact, risk losing everything.

It would be an infinite crime on the part of the revolutionaries if we let the chance slip, knowing that the salvation of the revolution, the chance of peace, salvation from famine, and the transfer of the land to the peasants depend upon them. The government is shaky. It must be given the death blow at all costs.

He believed that if they overthrew the Provisional Government before the Congress of Soviets met, then they could claim authority as the coup would have been carried out in the name of the Soviets and handed them power.

However, Lenin faced considerable opposition from within the Bolshevik Central Committee. To overcome this opposition, Lenin secretly returned to Petrograd on October 7 and spent a lot of time trying to convince opponents that this was the correct course of action. On October 10, the Central Committee agreed to put an armed rising on the agenda but did not agree on a date. It was the actions of the Provisional Government which forced the Bolsheviks to act.

Rumors that the Bolsheviks were about to act had been spreading around Petrograd for some weeks. However, it was an article written by two members of the Bolshevik Central Committee, Grigory Zinoviev and Lev Kamenev, which appeared to provide the Provisional Government with the proof it needed. Zinoviev and Kamenev argued that it would be a mistake to attempt to seize power (Source 3.25), showing the divisions there were within the Bolshevik party.

KEY FIGURE

Grigory Zinoviev (1883–1936) was a close colleague of Lenin following the formation of the Bolshevik party. He was executed during Stalin's purges.

> Study sources 3.24 and 3.25. Compare the views in both sources about attitudes to a Bolshevik seizure of power. Find one similarity and one difference between the sources.

SOURCE 3.25

Article by L. Kamenev and G. Zinoviev, October 11, 1917

We are most profoundly convinced that to declare at once an armed uprising would mean to stake not only the fate of our party, but also the fate of the Russian and international revolution. There is no doubt that there are such historical situations that an oppressed class has to acknowledge that it is better to join battle and lose than to surrender without a fight. Is the Russian working class in such a position now? No, and a thousand times no.

This convinced Kerensky that a date had been set and, rather than waiting, he decided to act first. On October 23, the Bolshevik newspapers were closed, and attempts were made to arrest the leading Bolsheviks. This left Lenin with no choice; he called for the rising to begin.

The role of Trotsky, the Petrograd Soviet, and the Military Revolutionary Committee (MRC)

Trotsky's role in events went back to 1905, when he was appointed Chairman of the Petrograd, or as it was called then, St. Petersburg, Soviet. Although he was subsequently exiled, he resumed his role as Chairman in September 1917. In this role, he persuaded the Petrograd Soviet to establish the Military Revolutionary Committee (MRC). However, even more important was his appointment as one of three coordinators of the MRC, which had been established on October 9 to organize the defense of the city against a possible German attack or a Kornilov-style coup. It was Trotsky who organized the rising. He realized that by having control of the MRC, the Bolsheviks would control Petrograd. By having control over the MRC, it meant that he controlled the only effective military force in the city, as the Petrograd garrison did not back the government, and Bolsheviks had infiltrated key divisions in the army. Not only that, but any actions it took would be viewed as legitimate because it acted on the authority of the Soviet.

KEY TERM

Red Guards A force of about 10,000 men, largely recruited from those who worked in the factories.

It would be Trotsky and the MRC who would direct the **Red Guards** and organize the seizure of the key strategic points in Petrograd, namely the telegraph offices, bridges, the main railway station, and the power stations.

The events of the October Revolution

There were a number of short-term reasons for the October Revolution. The Provisional Government had become discredited. Its policies were unpopular, particularly its decisions to continue the war and delay the Constituent Assembly and its failure to tackle the major peasant grievance of land redistribution. Not only had Kerensky failed to bring about reform, particularly over land, but also his handling of the Kornilov Revolt showed him to be weak and further increased opposition. The continuation of the war resulted in food shortages, inflation, and demonstrations. The Provisional Government had lost the trust of the people, and therefore by October, there were serious doubts as to whether it could succeed.

The Bolsheviks had been calling for a revolution for some time, but it was Kerensky's decision to close down their newspapers and attempt to arrest their leaders which triggered it. The Bolshevik Revolution started on October 24, and it took just three days for Petrograd to be under Bolshevik control, during which time there was very little fighting.

Table 3.7 Key events of the October Revolution

October 7	Lenin returns from exile after the July Days.
October 9	Petrograd Soviet establishes the Military Revolutionary Committee.
October 10	Bolsheviks start to plan the revolution.
October 11	Kamenev and Zinoviev oppose the idea of a revolution.
October 23	Kerensky closes down Bolshevik newspapers and attempts to arrest Bolshevik leaders.
October 24–25	Soviet takes control of Petrograd strongpoints.
October 25–26	Evening of October 25: first session of the Congress of Soviets opens. Night of 25–26 October: Members of the Provisional Government arrested, Kerensky flees, Red Guards and left-wing military units seize the Winter Palace. Soviet power declared, and Congress of Soviets elects a Soviet Government with Lenin as chairman and mainly Bolshevik members, as leading opponents boycott proceedings. Soviet Government issues Decrees on Peace and Land.
October 27	Soviet power begins to be declared in cities and towns in the provinces. Civil conflict begins escalating to a civil war.

The seizure of power was relatively straightforward for the revolutionaries. They faced virtually no military opposition, as the Provisional Government lacked a military force. The Petrograd garrison did not come to the Provisional Government's aid. Even the seizure of the Winter Palace faced little opposition, and the Red Guards did not have to storm the gates, as is often shown in films, as there were hardly any defenders (Source 3.26).

SOURCE 3.26

> What is the view of the writer of Source 3.26 about the Bolshevik seizure of power?

A report from the British newspaper the *Manchester Guardian*, November 10, 1917 (western calendar)

Towards five o'clock on Wednesday the Soviet, which has become master of the whole city, began to isolate the Winter Palace, where practically the whole of the Government remained. Detachments occupied all routes giving access to the Palace. Barricades were erected haphazard, made of logs taken from neighbouring wood depots, and planks from works under construction. Traffic was gradually stopped, and in the area isolated, only troops, armoured cars and two anti-aircraft guns placed near the police headquarters on the Nevsky Prospekt remained. Trams were stopped on this part of the route, but a short distance beyond they are running as usual, and the ordinary service will be maintained. The disturbances which the actions of the Committee [MRC] have occasioned are therefore purely local and temporary. Ordinary life is going on with almost a tinge of indifference.

Once they had entered the building, those who were supposed to be defending it simply gave up and lay down their weapons. On the Neva river, the ship *Aurora* fired its guns, which was the signal for the revolutionaries to begin their assault on the Winter Palace, where the Provisional Government was located. Members of the Provisional Government who remained there tried to escape.

The Soviet seizure of power had been easy, in part because there was a power vacuum and power simply fell into its hands.

Compare and contrast Source 3.26 and Source 3.27 in their view of the Bolshevik seizure of power in October 1917. Why are they different? Consider the date and purpose of each source.

SOURCE 3.27

A painting made in the 1930s by Sokolov-Skalya showing the storming of the Winter Palace

Why were the Bolsheviks successful in seizing power?
- They were viewed as heroes because they had defeated Kornilov.
- They refused to work with other parties and were therefore not associated with unpopular policies, such as the continuation of the war.
- They rejected the creation of the Constituent Assembly.
- The Provisional Government had made mistakes, particularly allowing leading Bolsheviks to return from exile.
- Bolshevik use of propaganda; slogans such as "Peace, Land, and Bread" were very popular promises.
- Kerensky failed to crush the Bolsheviks after the July Days and then armed them to defeat Kornilov.
- The skills of Lenin and Trotsky allowed them to conceal their own seizure of power behind the mask of the Petrograd Soviet.

On the night of October 27, Lenin told the Second All-Russian Congress of Soviets that the Bolshevik-led Petrograd Soviet had taken power in their name. He then read out a list of ministers, or commissars, of the new government. At the head of the *Sovnarkom* (government) was Lenin. The majority of SRs and Mensheviks walked out, protesting that this was just a Bolshevik coup, though arguably their response made such an outcome inevitable, as no other major party supported the new government. Trotsky's response to them was blunt (Source 3.28), arguing that seizure of power was a popular uprising, while other parties had abandoned the ideals of the revolution.

KEY TERM

Sovnarkom Council of People's Commissars, or a governing cabinet for the new Russian state, set up by Lenin in October 1917.

> How does Trotsky in Source 3.28 explain the Bolshevik seizure of power? Is this argument convincing?

SOURCE 3.28

Trotsky, speech to the Second All-Russian Congress of Soviets, October 26, 1917

The insurrection of the masses stands in no need of justification. What is taking place is not a conspiracy but an insurrection. We molded the revolutionary will of the Petrograd workers and soldiers. The masses gathered under our banner, and our insurrection was victorious. But what do they, the other socialists, offer us? To give up our victory, to compromise, and to negotiate – with whom? With whom shall we negotiate? With those miserable cliques which have left the Congress or with those who still remain? But we saw how strong those cliques were? There is no one left in Russia to follow them. And millions of workers and peasants are asked to negotiate with them on equal terms. No, an agreement will not do now. To those who have left us and to those proposing negotiations we must say: You are a mere handful, miserable, bankrupt; your role is finished, and you may go where you belong – to the garbage heap of history.

Although the Bolsheviks had taken power in Petrograd, they faced a harder struggle elsewhere, even in Moscow. In Kyiv, there was much fighting between Ukrainian nationalists and Ukrainian Bolsheviks, with the former gaining the upper hand and declaring autonomy within the Russian state. The major naval port of Odesa, on the Black Sea, declared for a coalition socialist government, while in the Cossack region continued to maintain its independence. Bolshevik control over the rest of Russia would have to be fought for, and this would eventually lead to a civil war which would last until 1921.

ACTIVITY

How similar were the February and October revolutions? Create a table of similarities and differences between the two revolutions.

SUMMARY DIAGRAM

October 1917
How and why did the Bolsheviks seize power in October 1917?

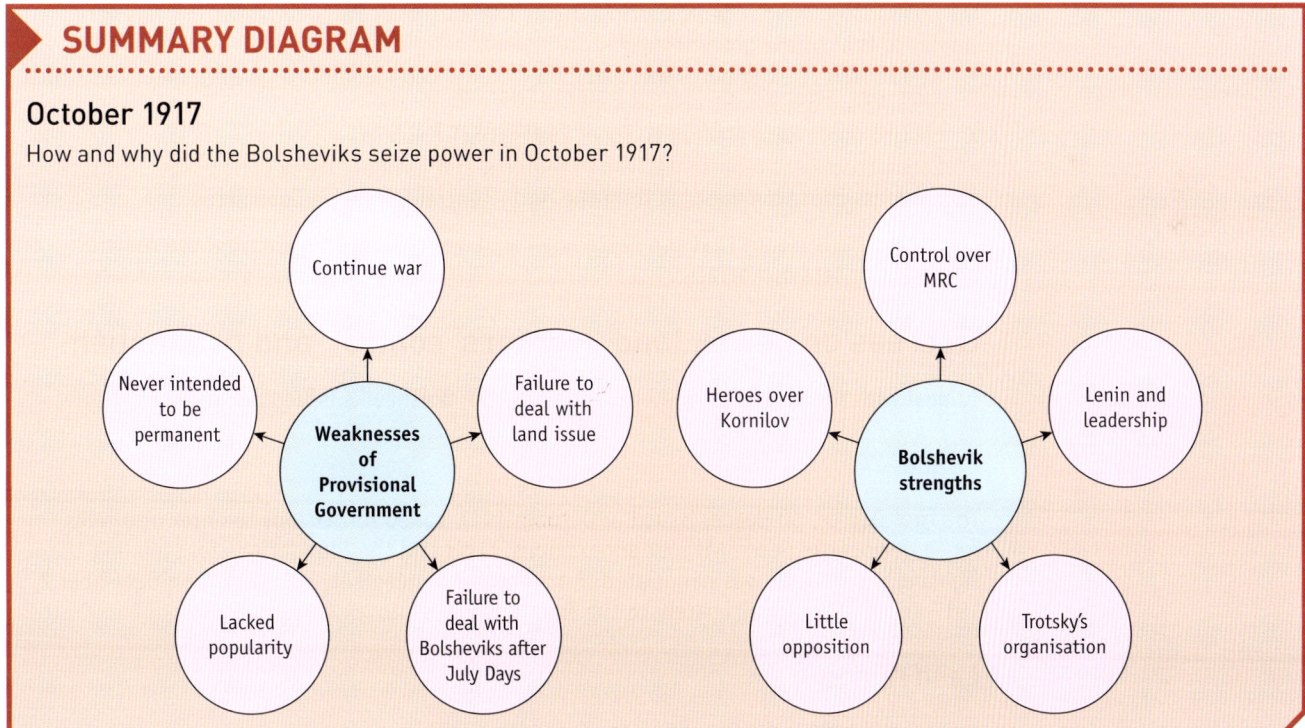

4 How were the Bolsheviks able to consolidate their power up to 1924?

Although the Bolsheviks had taken power in the October Revolution, their authority did not extend much beyond Petrograd and Moscow. It would therefore be very difficult for them to introduce the revolutionary policies that some of their supporters wanted and expected. They also faced a number of problems, most notably the question of the First World War. It was this, the issue of land, and the elections to the Constituent Assembly which had to be addressed first.

Bolshevik policies

Before the Bolsheviks could enact their policies and start to address Russia's problems, they had to set out how the new government of Russia would work.

Establishment of *Sovnarkom*

The Bolsheviks soon established a new government structure at the Second All-Russian Congress of Soviets. A Council of People's Commissars (*Sovnarkom*) was set up, nominally responsible to the Congress. This was made up of people's commissars, ministers who had specific responsibilities. Its chairman (Prime Minister) was Lenin, who claimed that it could pass laws independently between Congresses, thereby giving it ultimate power. This system appeared to be democratic as members of *Sovnarkom* were the result of a chain of elections:
- Village soviets chose representatives for district soviets.
- District soviets elected members for provincial soviets.
- Provincial soviets elected the All-Russian Congress.

However, as the Soviets were increasingly dominated by the Bolshevik Party, it meant that they dominated government, particularly as the Bolshevik Party organization was very similar to that of the government:
- At a local level, the party was made up of cells. Cell members organized meetings which encouraged grass-root involvement.
- Cell members were elected to town and district committees.
- Committees sent representatives to regional and national Party Congresses.
- Congress chose members to form the party central Executive Committee.

In practice, this meant that the Bolshevik Party was the government, and the regime became even less democratic.

Decrees on peace, land, workers' control, and nationalism

To deal with the problems created by the war, the Bolsheviks issued a number of decrees.

Peace

The first Decree, on Peace, issued in October 1917, called for nations to enter into talks for "a democratic peace without annexations." This laid the foundations for stopping the fighting while peace was negotiated. An armistice (agreement) was signed on December 2, 1917 and would lead ultimately to the Treaty of Brest-Litovsk (see page 192).

Land reform

In November 1917, the Decree on Land was issued. This accepted the seizure of private land by the peasants and gave authority to a process which had already started. However, it did state that the division and redistribution were to be carried out by the village Soviets. In many ways, it was similar to the proposals that the SRs had been putting forward and therefore helped in winning over some SRs, mainly the Left SRs, who split from the rest of the party.

KEY TERM

Vesenkha (The Supreme Soviet of the National Economy) The government body responsible for overseeing the national economy.

ACTIVITY

Consider the Bolshevik decrees. Which one would you choose as the most important in strengthening Bolshevik control? Why should this decree have greater prominence than the others?

Workers' control

The same month also saw the Decree on Workers' Control. As with the Decree on Land, this largely authorized what had been taking place. It accepted the takeover of factories by workers, but due to the decrease in output, it also ordered the workers' committees to maintain "the strictest order and discipline."

Economic changes

The government, despite lacking control of the whole country, also began to establish state control of the economy and, in December 1917, established **Vesenkha**, which nationalized the banks and railways, cancelled foreign debts, and began to develop the transport network. There was also a Decree on Nationalization issued in June 1918, which brought nearly all the major industrial enterprises under central government control.

Treaty of Brest-Litovsk

The rule of both Nicholas II and the Provisional Government had fallen, largely because they had failed to bring the war to a satisfactory conclusion. Lenin was determined that the same fate would not befall the Bolsheviks. However, even within the party there were disagreements as to how this was to be achieved, with Lenin arguing for immediate peace and Trotsky for a delay, in part to transform the war between nations into a revolutionary war uniting the workers of all nations to fight their elites.

Lenin was aware that the war had exhausted Russia. He realized that it was impossible to bring the war to a successful conclusion and therefore there was little point in continuing at the risk of defeat. Although Trotsky did not want to continue the war and agreed with Lenin's view that Russia had no chance of emerging victorious, he did adopt a slightly different view. He hoped that German forces would collapse in the west and that there would be a revolution in Germany and therefore wanted to extend negotiations in the hope that such developments would occur.

Trotsky's approach angered the German government, who failed to understand that the Bolsheviks were not concerned by national defeat. They were international revolutionaries, whose first concern was to spread the revolution, but Lenin was also aware of the practical situation, with Germany willing to advance on Petrograd. However, Sokolnikov, who signed the Treaty on March 3, 1918, did argue that the peace was a *diktat* enforced on a defenceless country.

The treaty gave up large amounts of Russian territory (see Figure 4.2), and Russia had to pay reparations of 3 billion roubles for the damage it had caused.

Divisions within the Bolshevik party over the Treaty

The treaty created opposition within the party, as many wanted a revolutionary war against what they saw as imperialist Germany. Lenin, however, argued that peace was the only realistic option, and that Russia simply could not continue the struggle and needed time to recover. Lenin felt that the new Soviet Republic needed to survive as the only defence against capitalist imperialism. He did, though, argue that Russia would, later, be strong enough to reverse the humiliating treaty. Lenin thought that there would be continuing rivalry between capitalist powers which would weaken them and allow Soviet Russia to promote revolution in the future. Despite this, there was a fierce debate in the Central Committee, and the treaty was approved by only one vote. It is important to understand why Lenin was willing to give up such large amounts of Russian land. It was not simply that Russia was too weak to continue to fight, but that both Lenin and Trotsky believed that a worldwide workers' revolution would begin, which was of far greater significance than the peace terms.

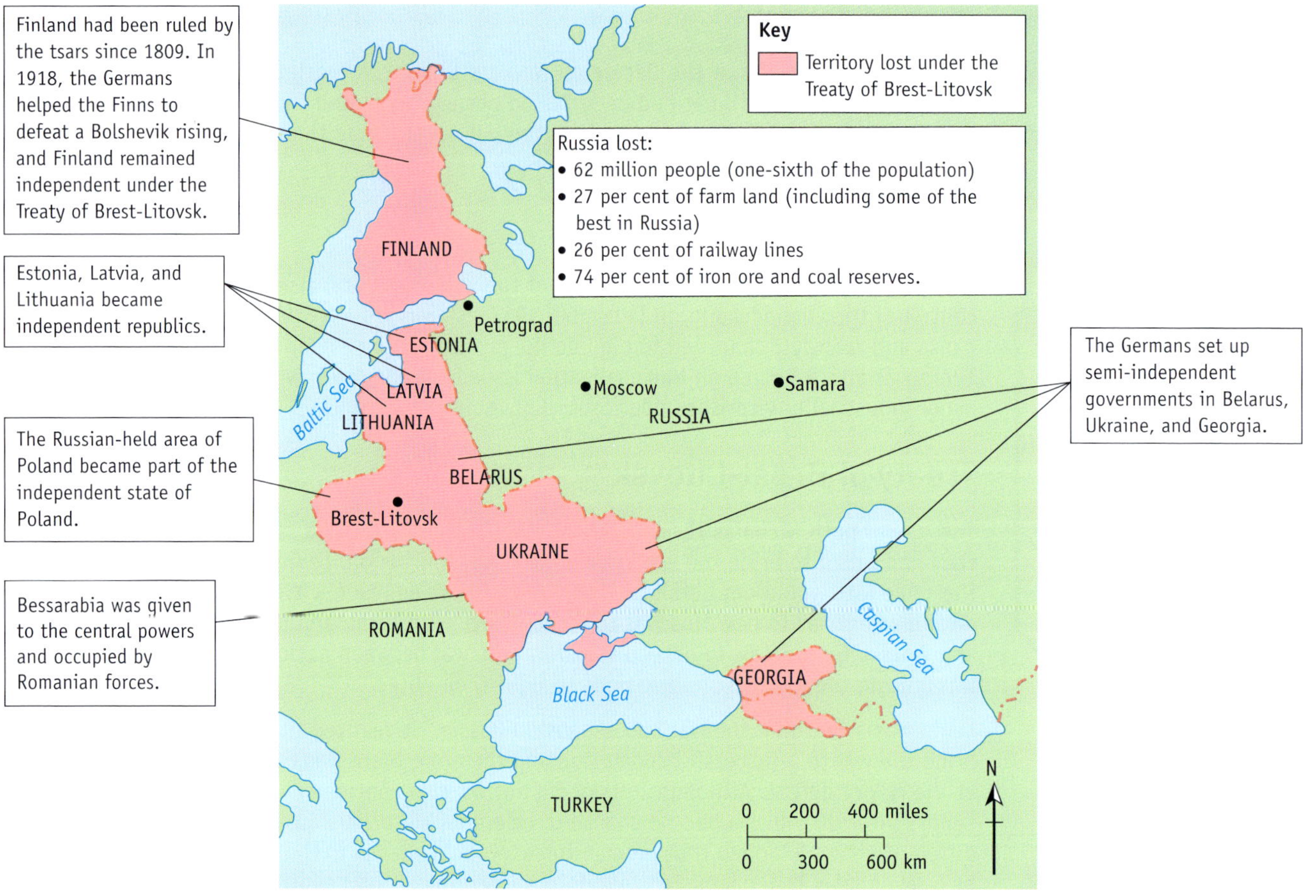
Finland had been ruled by the tsars since 1809. In 1918, the Germans helped the Finns to defeat a Bolshevik rising, and Finland remained independent under the Treaty of Brest-Litovsk.
Estonia, Latvia, and Lithuania became independent republics.
The Russian-held area of Poland became part of the independent state of Poland.
Bessarabia was given to the central powers and occupied by Romanian forces.
Key
Territory lost under the Treaty of Brest-Litovsk
Russia lost:
• 62 million people (one-sixth of the population)
• 27 per cent of farm land (including some of the best in Russia)
• 26 per cent of railway lines
• 74 per cent of iron ore and coal reserves.
The Germans set up semi-independent governments in Belarus, Ukraine, and Georgia.
FINLAND
Petrograd
ESTONIA
LATVIA
LITHUANIA
Baltic Sea
Moscow
Samara
RUSSIA
BELARUS
Brest-Litovsk
UKRAINE
ROMANIA
Caspian Sea
GEORGIA
Black Sea
TURKEY
0 200 400 miles
0 300 600 km
N

Figure 4.2 The terms of the Treaty of Brest-Litovsk

KEY TERM

Left Communists
A group of Bolsheviks, led by Nikolai Bukharin, who in 1918 opposed Lenin's more pragmatic measures. Rather than make peace with Germany, they hoped to spread revolutionary war to Europe.

ACTIVITY

Create a list of the key consequences of the Treaty of Brest-Litovsk. Which is the most important result? Explain your choice.

Not all of the party agreed, particularly the **Left Communists**. It was the developments on the Western Front in August 1918 that allowed Lenin to triumph. The German collapse in the West and the total withdrawal of German forces from Russia meant that the treaty was meaningless. More importantly, it strengthened Lenin's hold over the party as its Left SR allies were horrified by the treaty and in late spring 1918 conducted an ill-conceived coup against the Bolsheviks. It collapsed, allowing Lenin to expel the Left SRs from government and ban them as an organization.

The establishment of a dictatorship

The Bolsheviks faced several problems in consolidating their power. There was opposition to them from much of the population, and the outcome of the elections to the Constituent Assembly reflected this (see Table 4.1). These issues would be dealt with through a variety of methods.

The *Cheka* (the All-Russian Extraordinary Commission for Combatting Counter-revolution and Sabotage)

The *Cheka* had been established by the Bolsheviks in December 1917 and was the successor to the *Okhrana*, which ended with the fall of the tsar. Its specific role was to deal with counter-revolutionaries. Under Trotsky and its founder, Felix Dzerzhinsky, any controls which were needed to maintain power were implemented, and any resistance was met with force. After the attempted assassination of Lenin by an SR terrorist in August 1918, the *Cheka* implemented a reign of terror, whereby people were subdued through the threat of arrest, imprisonment, exile, or execution.

Answerable only to Lenin, the *Cheka* operated as a law unto itself and was given virtually unlimited powers, which were used brutally, with 8500 being killed in the first year. The tsar and his family were shot without trial at Ekaterinburg in July 1918, though this was not a *Cheka* operation.

> **SOURCE 3.29**
>
> **A speech by Felix Dzerzhinsky, Head of the *Cheka*, December 1917**
>
> This is no time for speech making. Our revolution is in serious danger. We are ready to do all to defend the attainments of our revolution. Do not think that I am on the look-out for forms of revolutionary justice. We have no need for justice now. Now, we have need of a battle to the death! I propose, I demand the use of the revolutionary sword, which will put an end to all counter-revolutionaries. We must act not tomorrow, but today at once. Do not demand evidence to prove that the prisoner has opposed the Soviet government; your first duty is to ask him to which class he belongs, what are his origins. These questions should decide the fate of the prisoner.

> What is the message of Source 3.29? Why do you think the writer might hold this view?

> **KEY TERM**
>
> **Red Army** Short for "the Workers' and Peasants' Red Army." Formed from Kronstadt sailors, Red Guard, workers who volunteered, and soldiers from the collapsing Imperial Army.

As part of this process, the *Cheka* would also enforce the requisitioning of grain, and "enemies of the revolution" were sent to carry out hard labor. There was also a show trial of the leading members of the SRs. At the same time, the **Red Army** imposed its authority over the population.

The *Cheka* was particularly active in pro-White areas during the Civil War and arrested many who were deemed to be "enemies of the people," with 150,000 likely to have been executed between 1918 and 1921, though estimates go as high as half a million. Many others were sent to labor camps in inhospitable regions, such as Siberia. It can therefore be clearly seen that terror was used as a political weapon in the battle for control.

The closure of the Constituent Assembly

A problem that the Bolsheviks faced was the elections to the Constituent Assembly. The Provisional Government had organized the election from mid-November 1917. Although the Provisional Government was no longer in power, the Bolsheviks allowed the election to go ahead, hoping they would win a majority as this would further legitimize their power. As the table below shows, this did not happen.

Table 4.1 Results of the election to the Constituent Assembly

Party	Votes	Seats
Socialist Revolutionaries	17,490,000	370
Bolsheviks	9,844,000	175
National minority groups	8,257,000	99
Left SRs (pro-Bolshevik)	2,861,000	40
Kadets	1,986,000	17
Mensheviks	1,248,000	16
Total	41,686,000	

These results were a clear indication that there was considerable opposition to Bolshevik rule. Aware that they would not be able to consolidate power through future elections, Lenin decided to use military force to end the Assembly, and it was closed down after just one day. Lenin justified his actions by arguing that the elections had been conducted using the old system, which had not fully considered the split in the SRs. In any case, Lenin believed that the only way to eradicate exploitation was to crush capitalists who resisted. He argued that it was necessary to destroy the bourgeoisie in order to give power to the people (Source 3.30).

Rewrite Source 3.30 in your own words so that its meaning is clear.

SOURCE 3.30

Lenin, speech, January 1918

Those who point out that we are now "dissolving" the Constituent Assembly although at one time we defended it are not displaying a grain of sense, but are merely uttering pompous and meaningless phrases. At one time, we considered the Constituent Assembly to be better than Tsarism and the republic of Kerensky with their famous organs of power; but as the Soviets emerged, they, being revolutionary organizations of the whole people, naturally became incomparably superior to any parliament in the world, a fact that I emphasized as far back as last April. By completely smashing the bourgeois and landed property and by facilitating the final upheaval which is sweeping away all traces of the bourgeois system, the Soviets impelled us on to the path that has led the people to organize their own lives.

Our cry was, "All power to the Soviets;" it is for this we are fighting. The people wanted the Constituent Assembly summoned, and we summoned it. But they sensed immediately what this famous Constituent Assembly really was. And now we have carried out the will of the people, which is – All power to the Soviets.

The closure of the Constituent Assembly was agreed in January 1918 by the Third All-Russian Congress of Soviets, which also announced the establishment of the Russian Soviet Federative Socialist Republic.

However, the dissolution of the Assembly did create unease, and this was added to by Lenin's desire to take Russia out of the war and reach peace with Germany. This led to many, particularly among the SRs, arguing that Lenin had not only betrayed the revolution but was also was a German agent. Even some of Lenin's own supporters were worried about this. There was criticism of his methods, and some believed that he was destroying democracy. Lenin, however, argued that the country was faced with challenges on all fronts and therefore harsh measures were needed. He stressed the concept of democratic centralism, whereby party members obey the leadership.

Reasons for the Bolshevik victory in the Civil War

The origins of the Civil War, which would last for four years, can be traced back to the October Revolution. Some groups saw this as a chance to launch a counter-revolution against the Bolsheviks, while others saw it as an opportunity to gain national independence. The dissolution of the Constituent Assembly, the Bolshevik monopoly of power, and the weakness of the Bolshevik state only added to the likelihood of war. Lenin himself did not want a war, but he considered it almost unavoidable that the elites would fight to protect their privileges and property. He was prepared to use the war as an opportunity to destroy the counter-revolution.

The events of the war

The war was complex because it involved multiple groups. It was not just the Bolshevik Reds against the elite Whites. National minorities such as Ukrainians and Georgians were fighting for independence. There were also peasant forces, called the Greens, who were fighting against forced requisitioning of grain.

The actual date of the start of the war is debatable. Some have argued that it began when Kornilov made his bid for power; others that the first phase began in October 1917. Kerensky launched an offensive to try to retake the capital, and White forces gathered in the south of Russia, well away from the big cities, which were being taken over by the Bolsheviks in the months after October. By the spring of 1918, Lenin thought the civil war was all but over, but it reignited on an even bigger scale when, in May, Czech troops trying to leave Russia through Siberia opened fire on Red Army forces. This second phase lasted until 1920, and smaller battles were ongoing until 1922.

The Bolshevik Red Army controlled most of central western Russia and the main cities and industrial centres. Their opponents, the Whites, were attacking from different directions and could not concentrate their forces. They got some help from foreign powers: Britain, France, the USA, and Japan. Finnish, Turkish, and Polish forces also fought against the Red Army. French assistance was important in preventing the Red forces taking Warsaw in 1920, but generally foreign intervention tended only to make the Reds more popular by exposing the Whites as "false" nationalists, dependent on foreigners. Both sides fought with considerable brutality. In 1918–1920, there were over 1500 horrific pogroms in which 250,000 Jewish people were murdered. These violent, organized attacks were mostly perpetrated by the White forces, but the Red Army also carried out violent pogroms during the civil war. The Whites could not create a strong political base or gather enough forces at one front to win. They also struggled to coordinate because they were competing with each other for leadership in the anti-Bolshevik movement.

Table 4.2 The main events of the war

January 1918	Red Army established
March 1918	Treaty of Brest-Litovsk. British and other Allied troops arrive in the Arctic north (Murmansk and Archangel).
Spring 1918	Opposition from the Cossacks defeated
April 1918	Kornilov's army defeated in south Russia (Rostov and Krasnodar), and Kornilov himself is killed in the fighting. Lenin announces the war is about to end. Foreign intervention to support Bolshevik opponents.
May 1918	Czech Legion revolts and becomes a focus for those fighting the Reds in Siberia. Conscription into the Red Army introduced.
June 1918	The tsar and his family murdered
August 1918	Trotsky executes deserters. USA sends troops to aid the Whites and establish anti-Bolshevik government in the Russian Far East (Vladivostok).
September 1918	Opposition government of former members of the Constituent Assembly is established at Ufa
November 1918	Admiral Kolchak becomes Supreme Ruler of White Armies
December 1918	French army lands at Odesa
February 1919	Denikin assumes command of White forces in southeast
March 1919	Kolchak's forces cross the Urals but driven back by Red Army
April 1919	French evacuate Odesa. Red Army counterattacks on Volga near Kazan, and Kolchak's forces go into months of rapid retreat.
June 1919	Denikin and southern Volunteer Army take Kharkiv
July 1919	Denikin takes Tsaritsyn
August 1919	Red Army counterattacks and drives the Volunteer Army back to the south
September 1919	British and Allies evacuate Archangel
October 1919	Red Army defeats General Yudenich at Petrograd
January 1920	Admiral Kolchak resigns
February 1920	Kolchak captured and executed by Bolsheviks
April 1920	Polish forces attack Russia and reach Kyiv. Reds counterattack, but are then pushed back from the approaches to Warsaw. Denikin is succeeded by Wrangel.
October 1920	Russo-Polish armistice
November 1921	White troops under Wrangel driven from southern Russia (Sevastopol)

KEY TERM

Czech Legion A force of some 35,000 men, largely composed of Czech soldiers who had been fighting for the allied cause on the Eastern front in the First World War. Their attempts to leave for Vladivostok were stopped, and so they rose up against the Bolsheviks.

KEY FIGURES

Admiral Alexander Kolchak (1873–1920) was the former commander of the Russian Black Sea Fleet.

General Anton Denikin (1872–1947) was an ex-Tsarist general who supported Kornilov and succeeded him as head of the Volunteer army when Kornilov died.

General Nicolai Yudenich (1862–1933) was an ex-Tsarist general who fought in the Russo-Japanese War.

Baron Pyotr Wrangel (1878–1928) had served in the army during the Russo-Japanese War and First World War. He had been decorated for bravery.

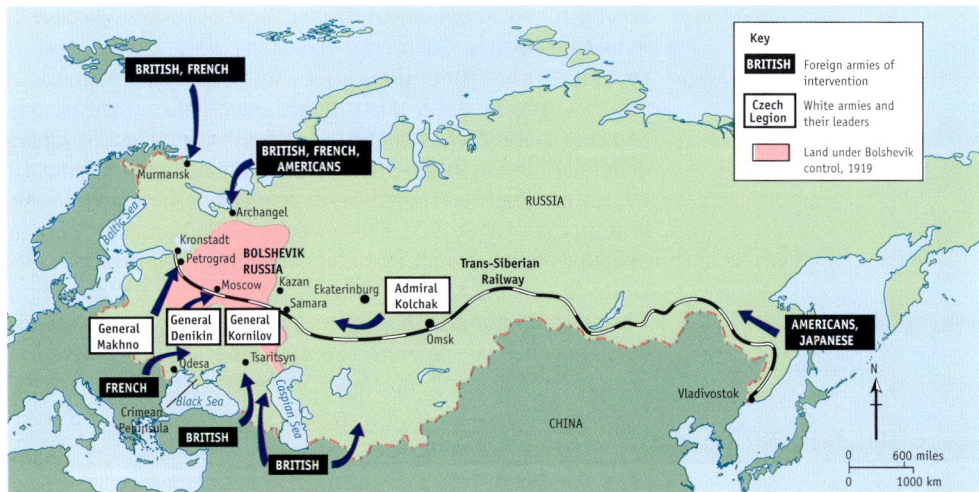

Figure 4.3 The Civil War, 1918–21

The strengths of the Bolsheviks

Bolshevik strengths were a major factor in their victory in the Civil War, and these can be organised under four headings:
- Leadership
- Unity and organization
- Popular support
- Geographical factors.

Leadership

The leadership of Lenin, and particularly Trotsky, was crucial in the Bolshevik victory. While Lenin helped maintain a united belief in the socialist cause, it was Trotsky who, as war commissar, was skillful in managing the Red Army. He organized the defense of Bolshevik internal lines of communication, denied the Whites any opportunity to gather a large, concentrated force in one area, and disrupted their supply lines. All of this was based on his realization of the importance of controlling the Russian rail network, shown in that Trotsky had his own armored train so that he could move from front to front. He traveled some 65,000 miles during the war. Trotsky was also prepared to be brutal when required, as seen in the policies of War Communism (see page 198) or the use of the death penalty for soldiers who retreated. Although he was extreme in his measures, he also realized the importance of morale, and he conveyed a sense of inevitable victory to his troops, which helped sustain them. He led by example, showing considerable bravery, taking his special forces to areas where the fighting was fiercest.

Unity and organization

The Bolsheviks had a single, unified command structure. Not only was the Red Army well organized and well led by Trotsky, but he turned the Red Army of workers and peasants into a well-disciplined force. By 1920, the Red Army had some 3 million under arms. Trotsky also used experienced former Tsarist officers to counter the experience of the Whites' officers. Similarly, he created cavalry units to counter the Cossacks in the South.

The morale of the Red Army was sustained by Trotsky and Lenin and the army's political commissars. They used propaganda trains to spread the Bolshevik message. The imposition of brutal measures by the *Cheka* (see page 193) allowed strict wartime measures, such as War Communism (see page 198) and the militarisation of labor, to be enforced and, although there were desertions, the use of **Red Terror** helped maintain discipline. The Reds also offered captured White troops the choice of enlistment or execution. Trotsky and Lenin

> **KEY TERM**
>
> **Red Terror** The deliberate Bolshevik policy of gaining control by brutality and the killing of suspected and actual opponents.

planned for links between the Red Army forces to be secure and ensured the defence of the two most important centres of industrial production: Petrograd and Moscow. As a result of their tactics, they were able to exhaust the Whites' ability to attack, wear them down, and then drive them back on the major fronts until they surrendered. Undoubtedly, the Red Army showed a far greater sense of purpose and had high morale, sustained in part by Bolshevik propaganda. The Bolsheviks used propaganda to argue that peasants would lose land if the Whites were victorious, and they offered a much better alternative for peasants and workers.

Popular support

The Reds were able to claim that they were fighting for Russia and the nation against the Whites, who were "in league with foreigners." They also claimed that it was a class war and that the peasants and industrial workers would benefit from a Bolshevik victory, whereas the Whites would restore some form of aristocratic rule. Most of the peasantry showed little enthusiasm for either side and were just as willing to desert from the Reds as the Whites. However, it was the issue of land which won the Bolsheviks some support as Lenin legitimized their right to land, while the Whites stated it would be restored to its former owners. Some workers and soldiers did support Bolshevik ideas, but there was not mass support for them because of food shortages and the implementation of War Communism. Despite this, in comparison to the Whites, the Reds did offer them a better chance of maintaining what the workers and peasants had gained from the revolution and therefore seemed a better option.

Geographical factors

The Bolsheviks retained control of the key cities of Moscow and Petrograd, which were major administrative and industrial centres. Most of their support was in the industrial areas, which gave them supplies as they had control over the main armament factories. They also had control over a concentrated area of land in the west of Russia, which they were able to supply, helped by maintaining control over much of the rail network. Moscow was at the hub of the rail network and made it much easier to transport both men and weaponry to the front. The central area of Russia, controlled by the Bolsheviks, was also much more heavily populated than other areas, and therefore they were able to conscript larger numbers to fight, often resulting in them outnumbering the White opposition.

> ### ACTIVITY
> Consider the key reasons for the victory of the Reds in the civil war. Which is the most important? Consider the impact of all the different reasons and their effect on the people, the progress of the war, and the control of each side.

War Communism

In 1918, Lenin introduced very restrictive economic measures, known as War Communism. The key features of this were:
- nationalization of major industries
- the forced taking or requisitioning of grain and agricultural products and the abolition of the market.

Every part of people's lives was subjected to winning the Civil War. However, the measures of War Communism had a devastating impact on both agricultural and industrial production. Peasants refused to hand over grain and refused to produce more food until the government was willing to pay a reasonable price for it. This led to the *Cheka* sending out requisition units to seize food. However, the result was that even less food was available. By 1921, this policy, along with a drought, led to a major famine as less than half the grain produced in 1913 was harvested. The situation was very similar in industry. Nationalization had not led to an increase in production, and the Civil War made matters worse as military needs took priority. Manpower was reduced as men were conscripted to fight, and **hyperinflation** only added to the problems. Also, being cut off from international trade led to many difficulties, such as problems in sourcing spare parts for factory and railway machinery.

KEY TERM
Hyperinflation A very rapid rise in prices, and the resulting decrease in the value of money.

Despite these difficulties, the Bolsheviks were able to impose their control and terror, and political mobilizatoin appeared to work to some extent. Lenin was able to destroy some of his opponents, perhaps supporting the view that he wanted a civil war for just such a purpose. Not all opposition was eliminated. In 1920, a peasant army formed in Tambov province and attacked requisition squads, taking over large areas. Uprisings such as this one and others in West Siberia occurred only after the White threat was eliminated, showing the civil war had helped prevent opposition within Soviet areas and focused it against the foreign powers. After the Whites were defeated, peasants fought their cause against the Bolsheviks. The peasant army grew to some 20,000, and the Red Army was able to take back control of the area only with the greatest difficulty by the summer of 1921.

The summary on page 203 clearly shows the importance of Trotsky in the Red victory. In particular, he had a simple strategy which allowed the Reds to emerge victorious. This was based around maintaining Bolshevik internal lines of communication, denying the Whites the opportunity to concentrate their forces and maintain their supplies. All of this depended on control of the railways, which Trotsky saw as crucial, and it is therefore not surprising that most of the decisive battles took place near railway junctions and depots.

Weaknesses of the Whites

On the other hand, the Whites suffered from a number of weaknesses. Most importantly, they had very little popular support and, in addition, they were not united and were fighting for a range of causes and fought as separate detachments.

SOURCE 3.31

A Bolshevik propaganda poster called *The capitalists unleashing their dogs*

> What are the messages of sources 3.31 and 3.32? Use details from the sources to support your answer. Explain why they put forward such different views of the Reds and Whites.

SOURCE 3.32

A pro-Whites Russian civil war poster showing the Red Army forcibly taking grain and possessions from peasants

Leadership and organization

The Whites did not possess a leader with the same skills and ability as Trotsky. Many of the White commanders treated their soldiers with contempt, displaying the worst aspects of the behavior of former Tsarist commanders. This did little to boost morale and encouraged desertions. There was a lack of discipline but also widespread corruption, with uniforms and munitions sold on the black market, which helped to fund the extravagant lifestyle in which many of the officers lived. The Whites were unwilling to form a united front, and this allowed the Bolsheviks to attack each army separately.

A lack of a common aim was also a considerable weakness. There were divisions between socialists, liberals, and the dominant monarchists which further weakened their cause, with officers going so far as to suppress the Socialist Revolutionary assembly of former Constituent Assembly members in Ufa in the eastern Urals. The officers gave Kolchak the title "Supreme Ruler," which was approved by the allies and the coordinating center of the Whites on the fringe of the First World War's Peace Conference in Paris. He then had hundreds of SR activists arrested; some were executed. As a result, the SRs staged revolts against Kolchak, further weakening the White cause.

The White leaders, in expectation of the rapid collapse of Bolshevism and their own success, were more concerned with their individual interests and were reluctant to give them up to form a united or coordinated front. In any case, the coordinating center was over 1500 kilometres away in Paris. This made it much easier for Red armies to tackle each White army separately and would play an important role in events in the Volga region in 1919. Although many of the White commanders had considerable military experience, men such as Wrangel and Yudenich had been trained in traditional methods of warfare and were unable to adapt to more modern methods and technology, compared to Bolshevik skill in conducting political warfare.

Use of conscription and support

The Reds were able to portray the Whites as supporters of the tsar and the old form of government, which had brought little benefit to the masses, and therefore many were reluctant to support them. The Whites also lost the support of minority nationalist groups as they wanted to restore the Russian Empire's pre-1917 borders, angering Ukrainians and Georgians, Armenians, and others who wanted greater autonomy or independence. As a result, separatists would not support the Whites when they were based in their territory, further weakening their support. This can be seen with the Cossacks, whose sole concern was autonomy for their own region, and although some were willing to fight against the Bolsheviks, they kept their units separate from the Volunteer Army as a whole and would not always obey orders from White central command. Once they had secured their homeland, they were unwilling to go further into Central Russia. Denikin might have been able to win their support if he had promised them autonomy, but he would not agree to this. There were others who would not make concessions to national groups, such as the *Kadets*, who wanted a "Russia Great, United and Indivisible." This certainly did not help the White cause, as some of their armies were in the south, where demands for greater independence were strong and where a willingness to make concessions might have won them greater support.

The peasants were also reluctant to support White armies because of their brutality. This was, again, particularly noticeable in the south, where the Cossacks drove out thousands of non-Cossack peasants. Outside their own lands, the behavior of the Cossacks was even worse, conducting looting, rape, and pillaging against peasants, and massacres against Jewish people. It is therefore hardly surprising that many people in the area gave their support to the Reds.

The main source of soldiers for the Whites was peasants who were conscripted into the army. They deserted in their thousands, largely because commanders, such as Denikin, helped landlords regain their estates. The Whites were closely identified with the old order, and although they talked about democracy, many really wanted to restore Russia to its pre-1917 position, but the peasants and workers had gained too much since then to support such a development. Therefore, the Whites could raise only 500,000 soldiers, while Trotsky's Red Army numbered some 3 million and even peaked at over 5 million at the end of the war.

Issues of supply

The Whites were heavily reliant on supplies and support from abroad because they did not control the main industrial regions. As a result, the Bolsheviks could portray them as anti-Russian. The Whites also faced problems in that supplies from abroad were often late arriving, did not arrive in sufficient quantities for an offensive to be launched, or arrived at the wrong place.

Geography

The Whites were geographically scattered, with armies in the northwest, south, and southeast. This meant that they could not put together a sufficiently large force to challenge the Red Army. Their nominal political center was in Paris, and communication links were very unreliable.

Foreign intervention

The Allied powers were initially concerned that the Bolshevik seizure of power would free German forces from the war in the East and allow them to turn all their might onto the West. This became evident following the Treaty of Brest-Litovsk and resulted in the Allied occupation of the ports of Murmansk and Archangel. After the war in Europe ended, the Allied powers considered a full attack on the Bolsheviks. This seemed more urgent as communist revolutions briefly emerged in parts of Germany (Berlin and Bavaria) and in Hungary, where Bela Kun's regime lasted five months. The Bolsheviks had also announced that they would not honor foreign debts and nationalized a number of foreign companies, which was seen as theft. An international campaign against the Reds followed, involving British, French, Japanese, American, Italian, Czech, Finnish, Lithuanian, Polish, and Romanian forces.

However, it did not help the White cause, as the intervention was not coordinated, and there was no serious attempt to remove the Bolsheviks. The intervention was easily resisted, aided by the fact many of the nations had little desire for another long campaign after the First World War. The campaign was also weakened by the unwillingness of trade unionists to load goods which would be delivered to White forces to fight the new workers' state. Intervention was successful in the Baltic: foreign intervention forced Lenin to recognize the

independence of Estonia, Latvia, and Lithuania, while Finland gained independence due to local resistance. However, this was not repeated in other areas, and gradually foreign troops were withdrawn:
- 1919: French and American troops withdrawn.
- 1920: Remaining Western forces leave.
- 1922: Japanese troops leave – the only force to remain for the whole war.

Although the withdrawal of foreign forces was not a military victory for the Bolsheviks, it was portrayed as such and was a propaganda triumph. Lenin was shown to have saved the nation from foreign and imperial domination. As well as helping the Reds to recover the prestige they had lost with the signing of Brest-Litovsk, it allowed the Bolsheviks to portray the Whites as agents of foreign powers.

The importance of the Kronstadt Mutiny

Lenin upheld War Communism for as long as possible, but peasant resistance and refusal to grow and sell grain meant that changes were needed. The anti-Bolshevik rising in Tambov was followed by growing opposition to War Communism and strikes in Petrograd in early 1921.

Causes, events and impact

The most serious challenge occurred in February 1921, when mutinying sailors and workers from the dockyard and naval base in Kronstadt demanded greater freedom. This was particularly worrying, as the protestors had been ardent supporters of the October Revolution and Soviet power. The protestors demanded:
- new and free elections to the Soviets
- elections to be held using a secret ballot
- freedom of assembly
- rights for trade unions
- the ending of the right of the Communists to be the only permitted socialist party
- freedom for the press
- freedom to bring in food from the countryside.

As their demands increased, Trotsky ordered General Tukhachevsky to recapture Kronstadt. Between 50,000 and 60,000 troops were sent across the ice, but the cost of their success was the deaths of some 10,000 Red Army soldiers. The leaders of the rising were condemned as Whites and shot, while those who escaped were hunted down by the *Cheka*.

Lenin argued that the brutality of the Red Army was justifiable as the rising had been the work of enemies of the revolution.

> **ACTIVITY**
>
> Write an organized summary of reasons for the defeat of the Whites. Make sure you include a supported judgment about which was the most significant factor in the defeat of the Whites.

> **KEY DEBATE**
>
> **WHY DID THE BOLSHEVIKS FOLLOW A POLICY OF TERROR?**
>
> Historians have long debated the nature of Bolshevik rule between 1917 and 1921. Some have argued that it was the particular circumstances in Russia during this period which meant there was no alternative but to follow a policy of terror. The Bolsheviks faced not only opposition to their rule from within Russia, but also foreign intervention. These historians have also argued that such policies could be justified by considering their success: political and social stability, which had been absent from Russia for some time, was restored, and foreign intervention was defeated. This argument has been further developed by historians arguing that it was civil war which forced Lenin to abandon the idea of moving toward democracy and follow a policy of terror.
>
> Other historians have argued that terror was essential to consolidate the power of the Bolshevik party over Russia. They have argued that Lenin believed the defeated groups or parties would not give up their power without a fight, as seen in the civil war, and therefore, to prevent this happening, the Bolsheviks had to use every means to prevent the reactionaries from winning back the power they had lost. In contrast to the other historians, these have therefore argued that violence was implicit in the form of communism that Lenin had developed.

The introduction and impact of the New Economic Policy

Lenin's decision to introduce the NEP was largely intended to tackle the problem of food shortages and looming famine and reduce opposition to the Bolsheviks. Lenin told the Party Congress in 1921:

> What additional knowledge could you use to consider whether the view of the reasons for the introduction of the NEP in Source 3.33 was justified?

SOURCE 3.33

Lenin's speech to the party congress, March 15, 1921

We must try to satisfy the demands of the peasants who are dissatisfied, discontented, and cannot be otherwise. In essence, the small farmer can be satisfied with two things. First of all, there must be a certain amount of freedom for the small private proprietor; and, secondly, commodities and products must be provided. The effect will be the revival of capitalism, but the proletarian regime is in no danger as long as the proletariat firmly holds power in its hands. We must not be afraid of Communists "learning" from bourgeois specialists, including merchants, small capitalist cooperators, and capitalists.

The measure was purely economic, and there was no indication that Lenin was willing to reduce his political control; if anything, it would be tightened.

The NEP was intended to persuade farmers to grow more food. Requisitioning was ended, and peasants were allowed to sell surpluses at local markets. Small-scale enterprises were denationalized so that small-scale workshops could flourish. However, the state retained control over heavy industry – what Lenin described as "the commanding heights." Internal trade was encouraged, as restrictions on the sale of private goods and services were lifted and a new rouble was introduced to try to restore confidence in the currency and end inflation. Foreign trade and investment were also to be encouraged.

Although there were objections to these measures within the party, the disastrous economic situation and famine ensured that the measure was approved unanimously even though it was a clear retreat from the principle of state control of the economy. To persuade opponents, Lenin made it clear that it was a temporary measure.

Even though it was a success economically, with industrial output increasing rapidly, opponents objected to the emergence of private traders, or *nepmen*, whom they viewed as enemies of the revolution.

> **KEY TERM**
>
> ***Nepmen*** The name used to describe those who gained from the New Economic Policy as a result of the free trade and the ability to sell their products.

Table 4.3 Growth under NEP

Output	1921	1922	1923	1924
Grain harvest (millions of tonnes)	37.6	50.3	56.6	51.4
Value of factory output (millions of roubles)	2004	2619	4005	4660
Electricity (millions of kW hours)	520	775	1146	1562
Average monthly wage of urban worker (roubles)	10.2	12.2	15.9	20.8

The policy disagreements threatened to split the party. To prevent this, Lenin introduced the "On Party Unity" measure at the 1921 Tenth Party Congress. This measure banned factionalism to stop criticism of government decisions. Lenin also banned all other socialist parties, thus completing the suppression of opposition which had started in 1918. It was now very difficult for any members of the party or others to question policy as they would be seen as challenging the party.

By the end of 1921, Lenin had been able to increase his control. The party was more centralized and less democratic. All the key government posts were held by senior Bolsheviks, and the administration was dominated by the top members of the party. However, given the weak position they were in after the October Revolution, their survival was a remarkable achievement. However, at what cost had it been achieved? Had they upheld the ideals of the revolution? These are issues to think about now that you have completed your study of this period in Russian history.

> **ACTIVITY**
>
> Write a list of key similarities and differences between War Communism and the NEP.

> What is the purpose of Source 3.34? Which details on the poster were chosen to influence the viewer? Make a list of ideas from the images on the poster.

SOURCE 3.34

NEP poster. The text reads: The result of NEP in Russia will be a socialist Russia – Lenin.

> **SUMMARY DIAGRAM**
>
> **Consolidation of power**
> How were the Bolsheviks able to consolidate their power up to 1924?

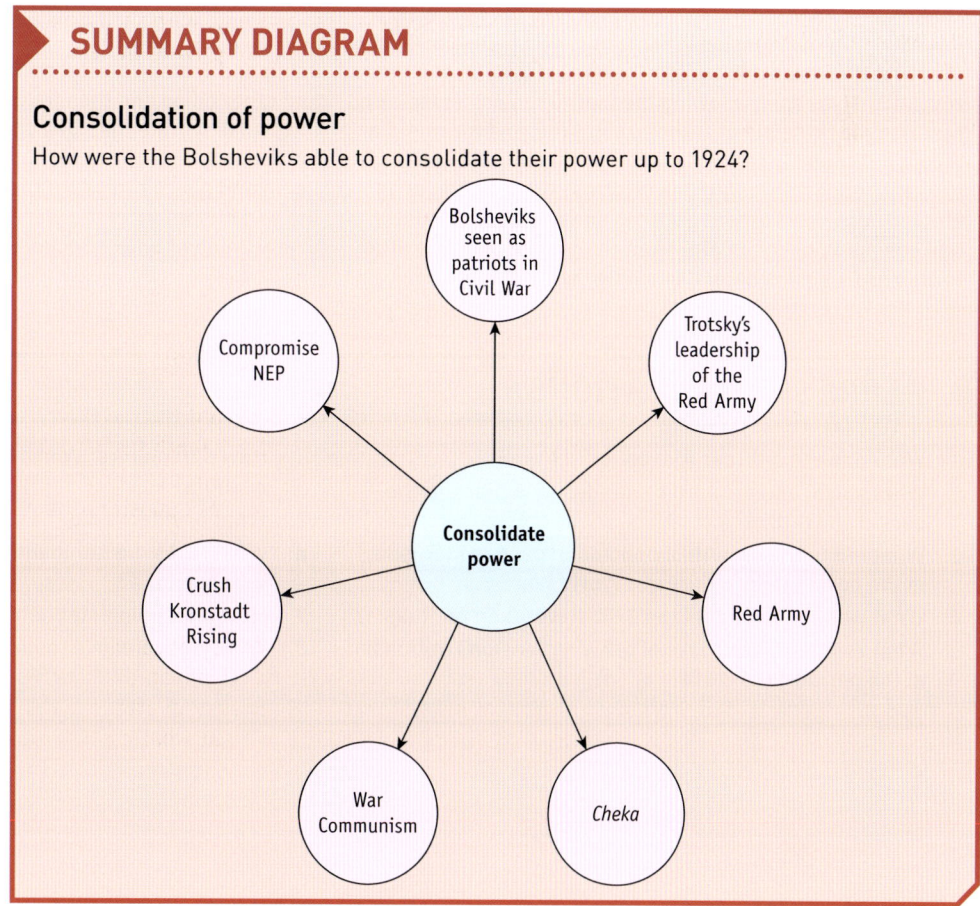

ACTIVITY

How much did life change for the Russian people in the period 1917–1924? List evidence to support both sides of the argument – that there was much change or that there was little change. If possible, you could then hold a class debate on the question. Each group should use cards with clear debating points on one side and supporting evidence on the other.

CHAPTER SUMMARY

The centuries-old Tsarist system was coming under pressure at the start of this period as a result of the impact of economic change, the desire for political change, and defeat in war. The countryside was restless because of population growth and land hunger. Alexander II attempted to address the problems through a series of reforms, particularly in the early part of his reign. These reforms tackled some of the major issues, such as serfdom and land ownership, political and judicial reform, and the army. Despite these reforms, there were a growing number of radical and revolutionary groups, though these were not extensive. However, they were able to carry out assassination attempts on Alexander II's life, and this resulted in a return to more repressive measures. His assassination in 1881 saw his son, Alexander III, follow a policy of harsh repression of discontent and control of the countryside, and a policy of peace.

Nicholas II unwisely went to war in 1904, and the poor performance of Russian forces, losses, and inflation created the conditions in which longer-term discontents could erupt into revolution. This was the most serious challenge to Tsarism in modern times, and the tsar was forced to offer concessions in October 1905. These divided the revolutionaries and the middle-class liberals, and the revolutionaries split, allowing the tsar to regain control. He restated the principle of autocracy in 1906, and his minister Stolypin ruthlessly repressed the opposition while gaining peasant support through land reforms. The creation of an elected quasi-parliament gave the semblance that Russia had changed politically. However, the regime could do little to stop growing discontent, and only the outbreak of war in 1914 prevented further disturbances as the nation was gripped by patriotic feelings. However, the initial defeats in 1914 and the retreat of 1915 brought criticism of the tsar and his government. A progressive bloc in the *Duma* was formed, and it criticized the tsar's inefficient ministers. The influence of the disreputable holy man Rasputin made matters worse. Despite a military resurgence in 1916, the war did not look winnable, and there were increasing shortages, rising prices, and casualties. Discontent erupted in February 1917, and the tsar lost control of the capital and could no longer rely on the loyalty of his army. He abdicated, and for the first time Russia became a republic. However, the continuation of the war and the failure to bring in rapid measures to solve social and economic problems and set up a new constitution allowed radical forces to take their chance. The new Provisional Government was fatally weakened by a dual authority of a parliamentary government and a Soviet of workers and soldiers. Though a seizure of power failed in July, the disruption caused by Kornilov's failed military coup gave Lenin and the Bolsheviks a window of opportunity in October 1917, despite limited support in the country as a whole and not being the biggest revolutionary party.

Lenin and Trotsky masterminded the takeover of Petrograd and other cities and then fought a successful war to defend the socialist state that they created. Their opponents were too divided to be effective, and the ruthless efficiency of Lenin and his commissars resulted in victory by 1920 and the establishment of the world's first communist state and a new Union of Soviet Socialist Republics.

REFRESHER QUESTIONS

1. What powers did Tsar Alexander III have?
2. What social and economic changes took place in the period 1881–1894?
3. What led to the growth of opposition parties in Russia in the period before the First World War?
4. What was the impact of the 1905 Revolution on Russia?
5. What evidence was there of growing tensions in Russia in the period 1906–1914?
6. How did the First World War damage the Russian economy?
7. What problems did the Provisional Government face?
8. What roles did Lenin and Trotsky play in the events of October 1917?
9. How did Lenin establish Bolshevik control of Russia?
10. What were Lenin's main achievements?

Study skills

Source questions

Using contextual knowledge effectively

Using contextual knowledge to explain similarities and differences

In some source questions, you will need to use your own knowledge to explain the similarities and differences between the sources. Consider the following question:

Read sources A and B. Compare these two sources as evidence about reasons for the unrest in St. Petersburg in 1905. [15 marks]

Firstly, read the sources carefully and identify the similarities and differences between the attitudes in each source.

SOURCE A

Sire,

We working men of St. Petersburg, our wives and children, and our parents, helpless, aged men and women, have come to you, O Tsar, in quest of justice and protection. We have been beggared, oppressed, and over-burdened with excessive toil. We are not recognized as normal human beings, but are dealt with as slaves who have to bear their bitter lot in silence. Patiently we endured this; but now we are being thrust deeper into the slough of rightlessness and ignorance, are being suffocated by despotism by employers and their arbitrary whims, and now, O Tsar, we have no strength left. The awful moment has come when death is better than the prolongation of our unendurable tortures. Therefore, we have left work, and informed our employers that we shall not resume it until they have fulfilled our demands.

St. Petersburg Workingmen's Petition to Tsar Nicholas II January 22, 1905

SOURCE B

The government is on the brink of bankruptcy. It has reduced the country to ruins. The people, worn out by suffering and hunger, are incapable of paying taxes. Factories and plants are stopped by strikes. Banks are failing. All trade exchanges have been reduced to the barest minimum. The government's struggle against revolution is causing daily unrest. For many years the government has spent all its state revenue on the army and navy. There is a shortage of schools. Roads have been neglected. In spite of this, there is not enough money even to keep the troops supplied with food. The war was lost partly because military supplies were inadequate. Mutinies of the poverty-stricken, hungry troops are flaring up all over the country. Only the Constituent Assembly, after the overthrow of the autocracy, can halt this financial ruin. It will carry out a close investigation of the state finances and will draw up a detailed, clear, accurate, and certified balance sheet of state revenue and expenditure.

Extract from the Manifesto of the St. Petersburg Soviet December 1905, a workers' council initially formed to coordinate strikes

The following chart outlines the similarities and differences between the two sources, A and B, about the reasons for unrest. Each point is backed up with specific details from the sources, using short quotes which can be used as evidence. Remember to keep evidence precise and concise; writing out long quotations will waste valuable time.

Similarities	Differences
Both agree that factories have stopped because of strikes by workers. A: "we have left work, and informed our employers that we shall not resume it until they have fulfilled our demands" B: "Factories and plants are stopped by strikes"	B wants the overthrow of the government and autocracy: "Only the Constituent Assembly, after the overthrow of the autocracy, can halt this financial ruin;" but A is appealing to the Tsar for change, with deference to their divinely appointed leader: "Sire ... have come to you, O Tsar, in quest of justice and protection."
Both agree that people are suffering in poverty and with poor working conditions A: "beggared, oppressed, and over-burdened" B: "worn out by suffering and hunger"	A sees the actions of employers as the reason for unrest, but B sees the government as the reason for problems. A: "suffocated by despotism by employers and their arbitrary whims" B: "The government is on the brink of bankruptcy. It has reduced the country to ruins."

ACTIVITY

Write a paragraph explaining the differences between the two sources using the provenance of the two sources together with your understanding of the historical context.

Then, consider why these sources have differences about the reasons for unrest.

Examine the provenance of each source – and identify the date of each source.

Think about the nature, origin, and purpose of each source, and its intended audience – why would this change the views displayed in the source?

What details of the historical context do you know which might explain the difference? Consider the date of each source and of key events which have taken place – "Bloody Sunday," the October General Strike, and the October Manifesto. Which of these events may have changed attitudes towards the Tsar, the government, and employers between January and December 1905?

Analyzing sources to reach a judgment

In this type of question, there will be a statement, and you will need to decide how far the sources support or challenge this view. The sources will always give you opportunities to both support and challenge the statement. Sometimes, a source will be more complex, partly supporting and partly challenging the view. You should aim to decide what each source tells you about the statement in the question, considering the nature, origin, and purpose of the source in its historical context. Then, you need to reach a judgement which addresses the "How far" element of the question. Which side of the argument is stronger? Consider this question and its view of Bolshevik use of propaganda in the civil war. Then read the sources.

Read all the sources. "The Bolsheviks won the civil war because they used propaganda that presented them as defenders of the revolution against the old order." How far do these sources support this view? [25 marks]

SOURCE A

A telegram sent from Lenin to the People's Commissar for Education and Culture, Anatoly Lunacharsky. From *Collected Works*, by V.I. Lenin.

September 18, 1918

People's Commissar Lunacharsky
Petrograd

I have heard today Vinogradov's report on the busts and monuments, and am utterly outraged; nothing has been done for months, to this day there is not a single bust, the disappearance of the bust of Radishchev is unacceptable. There is no bust of Marx on public display, nothing has been done to distribute propaganda by putting up inscriptions in the streets. I reprimand you for this criminal and carelessly lazy attitude and demand that the names of everyone responsible should be sent to me for prosecution. Shame on the saboteurs and thoughtless loafers.

Lenin
Chairman, Council of People's Commissars

SOURCE B

Yakov Okunev, *A New Way for Culture Propaganda* (1919). From *Soviet Russia*, a "Weekly [magazine] Devoted to the Spread of Truth About Russia" in the USA, published by the Russian Soviet Government Bureau. Yakov Okunev was an author who wrote books imagining ideal societies in the far future.

Lenin's train – that is what the peasants and workers call the train; it now carries the name of Lenin and recently returned to Moscow after a trip around the western part of the Soviet Republic.

This train consists of 15 cars, decorated with paintings in bright colours, with forceful and unmistakably revolutionary inscriptions. It contains a cinema, a bookshop, and a branch of the telegraph bureau, which posted the latest news at every station.

During its trip the train circulated books, papers, and pamphlets worth more than a half-million roubles, gave away more than 150,000 proclamations and leaflets, posted more than 15,000 posters, and supplied 556 organizations with various publications. About 90,000 workers, peasants, and soldiers from the Red Army attended the lectures, meetings, and conferences; about sixty lectures were organized on all sorts of important questions. Agitators will reach the most hidden corners of Soviet Russia, there to keep the fire of Revolution, to spread leaflets and pamphlets, and to waken the great masses of the peasants and the poor.

SOURCE C

An image from a 1920 poster by Bolshevik artist Viktor Deni (Denisov), portraying Trotsky as Saint George fighting the dragon of counter-revolution. After the revolution, Deni worked designing propaganda posters for the government publisher and as a cartoonist for *Pravda*.

SOURCE D

From *Hunted Through Central Asia* (1932), by Pavel Stepanovich Nazarov, a White Russian geologist. He was caught plotting against the bolsheviks in Tashkent and was imprisoned by the Cheka. This book is about his escape from prison in 1919 and what happened during the year he spent as a fugitive.

He spoke very well on the necessity of the "universal arming of the people" for the support of the "universal social revolution." The former army of the Tsars had been created by the Imperialists for international bloodshed for the protection of the interests of the capitalists and landowners," he said, "but the present army, the Red Army was organized for the protection of the working people."

As I listened to it seemed to me every now and then that the speaker was not always being serious. He hardly suppressed his smiles at his own words at his audience and at all the precious rubbish and ridiculous jargon which the Soviet authorities made him learn.

> This comedy was played by an excellent fellow, a former captain in the Tsar's army who was in command of the parade.
>
> Then to the tune of the "Internationale" they marched past in straggling order, a handful of red soldiers, disgracefully turned out, a few young soldiers who were just children, and in front marched a little girl with a red flag. I was very sorry for the small crowd of peasants who gazed at the parade without understanding and were not interested in the Bolshevik nonsense.

> **ACTIVITY**
>
> How might a response look? The following paragraph provides an example of how you might evaluate one of the sources, Source A.

Source A supports and challenges the view.

Lenin, who is now the Chair of the council, says that "nothing has been done in the way of propaganda" and "nothing has been done for months" to replace busts and monuments. This shows how important Lenin felt it was to promote revolutionary heroes and historical figures such as Marx. However, this source suggests this was not being prioritised in 1918 and challenges the idea that propaganda helped the Reds win. However, this source is nuanced and supports the view that propaganda was important because of Lenin's attitude to it. Lenin's tone and language suggest that he is extremely angry – "utterly outraged" – and he calls this a "criminal" attitude, demanding names of those not dealing with propaganda, suggesting they should be prosecuted. This shows Lenin sees propaganda as vital to gain popular support by showing the people that the old regime was definitely finished, to undermine any support for the White forces who wanted to stop the revolution. I know from my knowledge that the Bolsheviks quickly replaced Tsarist symbols in major cities – for example, double-headed eagles at the Kremlin and were replaced with Bolshevik red stars.

This source is particularly useful as it was written just after the start of the civil war which started in June 1918. It shows the view of Lenin, one of the key Bolshevik leaders, that propaganda was extremely important as it is written directly from him to one of his commissars, showing his personal views. As this source was dated from the beginning of the civil war, it could be used to support the idea that the Bolshevik leaders knew propaganda would be important from the start, but it was not prioritized enough by others at the start of the civil war. Overall, it does not support the view that the Bolsheviks "won the civil war" due to propaganda as it shows only failure, but it does help to show the importance Lenin placed upon it from the start.

Write a similar paragraph for one of the other sources.
- Explain what view is given by the source on the view in the question – that the Bolsheviks won because of their use of propaganda.
- Explain any other factors the source mentions.
- Use contextual knowledge to support or challenge the view in the source.
- Consider the provenance of the source, including its date, and nature, origin, and purpose, and how this impacts the validity of the view.
- Reach a judgment as to whether, in light of its provenance, the source supports the view.

Glossary

Absolute monarchy Rule by a monarch with complete freedom to pursue any policy without accountability to an elected assembly or the people. Many absolute monarchs claimed "divine right," believing they were chosen by God.

Absolute/autocratic ruler One person who rules with complete control over their subjects.

Active citizens French men over the age of 25 who contributed enough through taxes to be thought worthy of a share in the running of the country. They had the right to vote for the deputies of the Assembly.

Anarchism A belief that all government is oppressive and should be abolished.

Ancien Régime A term used in the revolutionary period in France from 1789 to describe the old type of political and to show disrespect for the old French monarchy.

Antichrist A biblical figure that some Christians believe would be sent by the Devil to oppose Jesus. There was a belief that he would take the shape of a tyrannical ruler, and some believed this was Napoleon.

Bill of rights A legislative guarantee to citizens of a country that their liberties will be respected and that they will not be subject to arbitrary rule.

Bourgeoisie The middle and upper classes in society, who typically own businesses and property. They have wealth, influence, and control over the means of production, such as factories and companies.

Bread riots A common feature of French life was riots by poor and often hungry people to seize corn or take bread from bakers.

Brigands People who attack and rob others, especially in mountains and forests.

Civil Constitution of the Clergy The name given to the new official position of the Church in the French Revolution, which placed it under state control.

Confederation of the Rhine A union of all German states except for Austria and Prussia, created by Napoleon in 1806.

Conscription Enforced military service required by the state.

Constituent Assembly An elected body whose task is to draw up a new constitution, or a set of rules under which a country is to be run.

Constitution A set of rules by which a country is governed.

Constitutional monarchy A form of government in which a monarch shares power with an elected assembly and is bound by a written constitution, or rules.

Consul for life Napoleon Bonaparte was made First Consul after the coup of 1799. In 1802, he declared himself the ruler of France, or Consul for Life. The term "consul" derives from a title used in the ancient Roman Republic.

Corvée The obligation in pre-revolutionary France to work on public roads or the king's highways. It was unpopular, and, as the nobles and clergy were exempt, it caused a lot of resentment. Abolished during the revolution.

Coup From the French "*coup d'etat*," or "blow to the state." A forceful takeover of power.

Crimean War (1854–56) A war in which Britain, France, and the Ottoman Empire fought against Russia with the aim of controlling Russian territorial expansion into the Ottoman Empire.

Cult of the Supreme Being The official religion of France between May 7, 1794 and July 28, 1794. Founded by Robespierre to respect God while linking faith with republican virtues.

Czech Legion A force of around 35,000 soldiers, predominantly Czech, who had fought for the allied cause on the eastern front in the First World War.

Diet The name given to the assemblies of parliaments of the German states.

Diocese In Christianity, an area under the care of one bishop.

Direct taxes Taxes levied on personal income or property.

Enclosure The enclosing of land by hedges or fences in order to divide up large, open fields.

Enlightenment The growth of scholarly and intellectual writing on many aspects of philosophy, science, the arts, economics, government, religion, and politics in the eighteenth century. These writings often questioned established religion, the monarchy, and social inequality.

Feudal dues Payments made to lords by peasants based on traditional privileges.

Franchise The right to vote. See also: Suffrage.

Germinal The seventh month in the French revolutionary calendar.

Gold Standard When the value of a unit of currency (e.g., one dollar) is linked to a specific weight of gold.

Great Retreat The withdrawal of Russian forces in 1915 to a new front line well into Russian territory.

Great Spurt A period of rapid industrial and economic growth in late-nineteenth-century Russia.

Guerrilla war A war fought not by big armies on battlefields but by smaller, often improvised, groups attacking enemy forces and communications.

Hemophilia A genetic condition in which the blood does not clot. It can lead to severe bruising and internal bleeding, and has the potential to be life-threatening.

Hébertists A group in revolutionary France who supported the journalist Jacques Hébert and his newspaper *Père Duchesne*. They wanted an increase in the Terror.

Holy Roman Empire A central European empire which had its origins in the coronation of Charlemagne in 800. From the fifteenth century, the title of Holy Roman Emperor was held by the royal family of Austira, the Habsburgs. Formally dissolved by Napoleon Bonaparte in 1806.

Hyperinflation A very rapid rise in prices, and the resulting decrease in the value of money.

Indemnity Bill An 1866 bill granting Bismarck "indemnity," meaning that he was freed from all responsibility or blame for having ignored the constitution.

Junker The term for a Prussian landed aristocrat, often seen in names by the use of the word "von" (of).

Kadets The party in Russia in the early 1900s which supported a constitutional liberal democracy. Its membership was largely middle class and it never achieved mass support.

Kaiser German word for "emperor."

Kamarilla The Prussian king's courtiers or favorites, the inner circle.

Laborists The SRs had boycotted the first election but stood as Laborists.

Laissez-faire French, meaning "allow to do." A doctrine where a government has minimal interference in the economy, with few laws or rules controlling individuals or businesses.

Land Captains Landowners in Tsarist Russia who were appointed to oversee the work of the *Zemstvos*. They had numerous functions and powers.

Left Communists A group of Bolsheviks, led by Nikolai Bukharin, who opposed Lenin's more pragmatic measures in 1918.

Liberal democracy A system in which the people vote for national assemblies or parliaments, to whom governments are responsible. Governments must keep to the laws approved by assemblies and respect the rights of citizens to free speech and freedom from punishment without trial.

Martial law A situation, usually following a crisis, when the government temporarily places the military in charge of maintaining order and enforcing laws.

Mortgate A loan used to purchase real estate, such as a house or land. The property itself serves as security for the loan, which means if the borrower fails to repay the loan according to the agreed terms, the lender can take the property to recover the money lent.

National Guard An armed force of French citizens formed in July 1789 to keep order.

Naval blockade A naval warfare strategy in which ships are used to prevent vessels from leaving and entering an enemy port to prevent delivery of supplies, movement of troops, and trade.

Neo-Jacobins Groups in revolutionary France who were radically opposed to the to the Directors and who saw the regime as betraying the core principles of the revolution.

Nepmen Those in the Soviet Union who gained from the free-trade opportunities of the New Economic Policy (NEP, 1921–1928).

Noblesse d'épée French, "nobles of the sword" in reference to the swords used by medieval knights who earned their titles for military service. These nobles were seen as more prestigious than the *noblesse de robe*.

Noblesse de robe French, "nobles of the robe." Nobles who obtained their titles for public service. "Robe" refers to robes worn by judges and other public officials.

Octobrists A liberal-reformist monarchist party in late imperial Russia. They believed in moderate constitutional reform but not revolution.

Paris sections Paris was divided into electoral districts known as "sections." These were run by their own officials and committees.

Paternalistic Describes a fatherly but controlling concern for the welfare of the people.

Peasants Primarily farmers, often working small plots of land, or tenant farmers paying rent to landlords. Their standard of living was generally poor.

Peasants (Russia) The majority of people in Russia, who lived in rural villages, were peasants. Some peasants were known as "state peasants" and paid taxes to the Tsarist state directly, and they had more freedom.

Petrograd The name of the Russian capital was changed from St. Petersburg in 1914, as it was thought to sound too "German." Petrograd's name was again changed to Leningrad in 1924 to honor Lenin after his death.

Pogrom An organized attack, often encouraged by the state, on Jewish people.

Police state A country where the activities of people are very strictly controlled by the government with the help of a police force, often working secretly against supposed enemies. The level of power and control is very great.

Potemkin A battleship named after the aristocratic favorite and lover of the eighteenth-century Russian Empress Catherine the Great. While stationed in Odessa on the Black Sea, its crew mutinied in 1905.

Prairial The ninth month in the French revolutionary calendar.

Progressists Made up of business men who wanted moderate reform.

Progressive bloc A loose union of moderate and liberal members of the *Duma*.

Proletariat Workers who do not own businesses or factories but earn a living working in manual, industrial, or service jobs.

Protestants Followers of Christian religious reforms begun in the sixteenth century.

Provenance The origin or source of a document or artifact.

Radical Extreme, usually in reference to extreme change or extremist beliefs.

Realpolitik Politics which focuses on national interests rather than ideals.

Red Army Short for "The Workers' and Peasants' Red Army." Formed from Kronstadt sailors, Red Guard members, workers who volunteered, and soldiers from the collapsing Imperial Army.

Red cap of liberty A soft conical hat based on the headgear of an ancient eastern European people called the Phrygians. It came to symbolize revolutionary liberty and was often worn by the *sans-culottes*.

Red Guard A force of about 10,000 men, largely recruited from those who worked in the factories.

Red Terror The deliberate Bolshevik policy of gaining control by brutality and the killing of suspected and actual opponents.

Redemption payments The repayment of loans which had been used to purchase land following the Emancipation edict of 1861.

Refractory clergy French clergy who refused to swear the oath to the Constitution. Also known as "non-juror priests," from to the French "jureur," or "swearer." Later organized resistance against the revolution and were objects of hatred and vengeance for the radicals.

Reign of Terror A period during 1793 and 1794 when people were arrested and executed throughout France for being enemies of the revolution.

Representatives on mission These were deputies sent to ensure that armies and their leaders were loyal to the ideas of the revolution.

Revolutionary Wars The collective term for the wars in which France fought European powers which opposed the revolution.

Rightists People who held conservative views. Not a political party. In this book, the word is used in a Russian context.

Russification A policy to transform the non-Russian people of the Empire into pure "Rus."

Sans-culottes French, literally "those without breeches." Richer men wore breeches and stockings but poorer men wore pants – so they were literally "without breeches." Thes *sans-culottes* were politically active and often not the very poorest of the people of Paris but small shopkeepers and artisans who resented the rich and were influenced by the radical ideas of clubs such as the Jacobins. They took a key role in many of the political disturbances of the revolution in Paris.

Serfs Agricultural labourers bound to the lands or estates they worked on. They belonged to their landlords. Serfs had to work on the land, pay rent for their homes and land taxes, and were legally tied to the landowner's estate.

Seven Years' War A prolonged war fought by France in 1756–63. France had limited success and increased its national debt considerably.

Shell crisis Shortages of ammunition at the start of the First World War. This book refers to the Russian Shell Crisis, but Britain experienced similar problems.

Socialism The political belief that the state should own major means of production and operate them for the benefit of workers, rather than landowners or business investors who profit by exploiting workers.

Socialist A person who believes in the values of socialism. Also describes a policy which adheres to the values of socialism.

Sorbs A Slavonic minority ethnic group, also known as *Wends*. By the mid-nineteenth century, there were about 165,000 *Sorbs* with their own languages, customs, and cultures living in the border areas between modern-day Germany and Poland.

Soviet The Russian word for a council made up of elected workers.

Sovnarkom Council of People's Commissars, or a governing cabinet for the new Russian state, set up by Lenin in October 1917.

Stolypin's necktie The name given in Russia to the hangman's noose following 2500 executions between 1906 and 1911, when Stolypin was Chief Minister.

Staple industries The main or basic industries needed by a state, such as coal, iron and steel, and textiles.

Suffrage The right to vote; "universal suffrage" is the right of all adults to vote. See also: Franchise

The people The part of the population, separate from the ruling elite, that the Socialist Revolutionaries believed embodied the will of the Russian nation.

Thermidor The eleventh month of the French revolutionary calendar. Also, the name for the reaction against the Reign of Terror which began with Robespierre and his supporters' executions.

Three-tier system A voting system used in Prussian elections until 1918. Its structure made sure that the wealthiest voters had the most voting power.

Total war War which involves using all the resources of a country and includes not just armies but the entire population.

Vendémiaire The first month in the French revolutionary calendar.

Vesenknu (The Supreme Soviet of the National Economy) The government body responsible for overseeing the national economy.

Vyborg Manifesto Drawn up by 200 Kadets and Laborists, and urged the people to defy the government by refusing to pay taxes and disobey conscription.

War of attrition A war where both sides try to wear down the enemy by killing more soldiers and exhausting the enemy's resources rather than winning decisive victories.

War of the Austrian Succession A prolonged war fought by France from 1740 to 1748. France had limited success and increased its national debt considerably.

Watch committees Surveillance committees whose role was to watch for people suspected of plotting or carrying out anti-revolutionary activities. They played a major role in the Terror.

Zemgor Russian, from "*Zemstvo*" (a type of local government) and "gorod" meaning "town." A union of representatives of local government members, businessmen, and influential townsmen set up to support the war effort in 1915.

Zemstvo A form of local government in Russia. Introduced by Tsar Alexander II, Zemstvos were run by elected officials called Land Captains.

Zollverein German, meaning "customs" (*Zoll*) "union" or "association" (*Verein*). A group of countries which have agreed to trade without paying tariffs when goods are moved from one area to another.

Further reading

Chapter 1 France, 1774–1814

D. Andress, *The French Revolution and the People* (Hambledon, 2004)

D. Andress, *The French Revolution. A Peasants' Revolt* (Head of Zeus, 2019)

T. Blanning, *The Pursuit of Glory* (Penguin, 2007)

M. Broers, *Napoleon, Soldier of Destiny* (Faber, 2015)

M. Crook, *Revolutionary France* (OUP, 2002)

R. Darnton, *The Revolutionary Temper in Paris 1748–1789* (Allen Lane, 2023)

W. Doyle, *Origins of the French Revolution* (OUP, 1980)

G. Ellis, *Napoleon Profiles in Power* (Longman, 1997)

S. Englund, *Napoleon, a Political Life* (Harvard, 2005)

E. Hazan, *A People's History of the French Revolution* (Verso, 2014)

A. Horne, *The Age of Napoleon* (Modern Library, 2006)

C. Jones, *The Great Nation, France from Louis XV to Napoleon* (Columbia UP, 2002)

C. Jones, *The Fall of Robespierre*, (OUP, 2023)

P.M. Jones, *The French Revolution, 1787–1804* (Longman, 2003)

M. Lyons, *Napoleon and the Legacy of the French Revolution* (Palgrave, 1994)

P. McPhee, *Liberty or Death* (Yale, 2016)

J. Popkin, *The History of the French Revolution, A New World Begins* (Basic Books 2021)

D. Rees and D. Townson, *Access to History, France in Revolution* (Hodder, 2016)

J.M. Robert, *The French Revolution* (OUP, 1997)

A. Roberts, *Napoleon the Great* (Allen Lane, 2014)

J. Tulard, *Napoleon, the Myth of the Saviour* (Weidenfeld and Nicolson, 1984)

S. Waller, *France in Revolution* (Heinemann, 2002)

M. Wells, *The French Revolution and the Rule of Napoleon* (Hodder, 2018)

M. Wells, *The Real Story of the French Revolution: Separating Myth from Reality* (Pen and Swords, 2024)

A. Zamoyski, *Napoleon, the Man behind the Myth* (William Collins, 2019)

Chapter 2 Liberalism and nationalism in Germany, 1815–71

D. Blackbourn, *The Fontana History of Germany 1780–1918: The Long Nineteenth Century* (Blackwell, 1997)

J. Breuilly, *The Formation of the First German Nation-state* (Palgrave, 1996)

J. Breuilly, *Austria, Prussia and the Making of Germany 1806–1871* (Routledge, 2014)

R. Chrastil, *Bismarck's War* (Penguin, 2024)

C. Clarke, *The Iron Kingdom: The Rise and Downfall of Prussia 1600–1947* (Allen Lane, 2006)

C. Clarke, *Revolutionary Spring. Fighting for a New World 1848–1849* (Penguin, 2024)

G. Craig, *Germany 1866–1945* (OUP, 1980)

E. Crankshaw, *Bismarck* (Macmillan, 1981)

E. Feuchtwanger, *Bismarck* (Routledge, 2002)

M. Fulbrook, *A Concise History of Germany* (CUP, 2004)

M. Kitchen, *A History of Modern Germany, 1800 to the Present* (Wiley-Blackwell, 2011)

G.R. Malleson, *The Re-founding of the German Empire, 1848–1871* (Legore Street Publishing, 2023)

H. Schulze, *The Course of German Nationalism* (CUP, 1991)

H. Schulze, *Germany, a New History* (Harvard UP, 2001)

L.D. Steefel, *Bismarck, the Hohenzollern Candidature and the Origins of the Franco-Prussian War of 1870* (Borodino Books, 2018)

J. Steinberg, *Bismarck, A Life* (OUP, 2011)

A. Stiles, *Access to History, The Unification of Germany 1815–90* (Hodder, 1986)

A.J.P. Taylor, *Bismarck, the Man and the Statesman* (Hamish Hamilton, 1958)

V. Ullrich, *Bismarck, the Iron Chancellor* (Haus Publishing, 2022)

M. Wells, *Bismarck* (Collins, 2004)

M. Wells, *Unification and Consolidation of Germany and Italy, 1815–90* (CUP, 2013)

D.G. Williamson, *Bismarck and Germany, 1862 to 1890* (Longman, 2011)

Chapter 3 Russia from autocracy to revolution, 1881–1924

A. Beevor, *Russia, Revolution and Civil War 1917–1924* (W and N, 2023)

E.H. Carr, *The Russian Revolution from Lenin to Stalin 1917–1929* (Palgrave, 2004)

D. Christian, *Imperial and Soviet Russia* (Macmillan, 1997)

R.W. Davies, *From Tsarism to the New Economic Policy* (Cornell University Press, 1991)

O. Figes, *A People's Tragedy* (Pimlico, 1997)

G. Hosking, *Russia and the Russians* (Allen Lane, 2001)

D. Lieven, *Nicholas II: Emperor of All the Russias* (Pimlico, 1993)

C. Merridale, *Lenin on the Train* (Penguin, 2017)

S. McMeekin, *The Russian Revolution, a New History* (Profile, 2018)

C. Mieville, *October* (Version, 2018)

R. Pipes, *Russia Under the Bolshevik Regime 1919–24* (Collins Harvill, 1994)

R. Pipes, *Russia Under the Old Regime* (Penguin, 1995)

R. Pipes, *The Russian Revolution 1899–1919* (Collins Harvill, 1990)

C. Read, *From Tsar to Soviets: The Russian People and their Revolution* (Routledge, 1996)

C. Read, *Lenin: A Revolutionary Life* (Routledge, 2005)

V. Sebestyen, *The Russian Revolution* (Apollo, 2023)

R. Service, *Lenin: A Biography* (Macmillan, 2004)

R. Service, *The Penguin History of Modern Russia: From Tsarism to the Twenty-first Century* (Penguin, 2009)

R. Service, *Blood on the Snow, the Russian Revolution 1914–1924* (Picador, 2023)

S.A. Smith, *Russia in Revolution 1890–1928* (OUP, 2017)

S.A. Smith, *The Russian Revolution: A Very Short Introduction* (OUP, 2002)

M. Steinberg, *The Russian Revolution 1905–1924* (OUP, 2017)

A. Wood, *The Origins of the Russian Revolution* (Routledge, 2003)

Index

A

agriculture
    Austria 102
    France 6
    Germany 86
    Russia 142, 143, 146, 155, 158–9
Alexander III, Tsar 139, 142–6, 150–2
Alexander II, Tsar 139, 142–4
Alexandra, Tsarina 156, 174, 177
aristocracy
    Austria 76
    France 3–4, 52–3
Arndt, Ernst 76, 80
Austria
    and Bismarck 104
    economy of 102
    and the German Confederation 74–8, 80, 85, 89, 110, 113, 115, 117
    and German unification 104
    and the Holy Roman Empire 72
    and Italy 103
    and Prussia 100
    Schleswig-Holstein 110–3, 115, 117
    War of Austrian Succession (1740–63) 6

B

Babeuf, François-Noel (Gracchus) 43
banks 55, 101, 191, 205
Barras, Paul Vicomte de 47–8
Battle of Leipzig (1813) 61–2
Battle of Trafalgar (1805) 57
Bismarck, Otto von 98, 104, 108–9, 113, 118
    and the Austro-Prussian War 110–1, 113, 124
    Biarritz, meeting at 114
    EMS telegram 123
    and the Franco-Prussian War 123–4, 126–7
    and the German Empire 98, 129–30
    and German unification 119
    Hohenzollern Candidature 121–2
    Luxembourg Crisis 121
    and North German Confederation 121
    and the Prussian Parliament 104–5, 108
    Schleswig-Holstein 111–2
    see also Prussia
    Zollparlament 120
Bolsheviks 137, 171, 185, 188, 190–2
    Cheka 192–3
    Civil War 194–8
    consolidation of power 19–4, 203
    Lenin's leadership 181, 185
    October revolution 181, 186–7, 190
    policy of terror 201
    Red Army 195–6
    The Red Terror 196
Brest-Litovsk, Treaty of (1918) 181, 191–2, 195, 200–1
Brienne, Etienne-Charles de Loménie de 8
Brissot, Jacques-Pierre 18–9, 26
Brittain 57
    see also Coalition allies
    Coup of Brumaire (1799) 1, 48–9
Bundesrat 129–30
Bunge, Nikolay 147

C

Calonne, Charles de 8
capitalism 147, 181, 202
censorship
    France 2, 17, 43, 50–1
    Germany 86, 107
    Prussia 90–1, 103
    Russia 141, 143–5, 155
    Saxony 93
Chernov, Victor 157
Chouans 20
coal 101, 148, 159, 169
Confederation of the Rhine 57, 73, 83–4
Congress of Châtillon (1814) 61
Congress of Vienna 74
constitutional monarchy 17–9, 23, 92
Convention of Gastein (1865) 112
Crimean War 103, 113, 146

D

Danton, Georges-Jacques 17, 19, 26, 34
Declaration of Pilnitz (1791) 26
Declaration of the Rights of Man and of the Citizen (1789) 14–15
Declaration of the Rights of Women (Olympe de Gouges) 24
Denmark
    Schleswig and Holstein 95–6, 110–13
Desmoulins, Camille 17, 19, 37
d'Herbois, Collot 37, 40
Diderot, Denis 5
Ducos, Pierre 48
Dzerzhinsky, Felix 192–3

E

Emancipation of the Serfs (edict) (1861) 142
Enlightenment 2, 5–6

F

Feuillants 17, 19, 26–7
First World War 171–6, 199
food shortages
    France 6, 13, 41–2
    Germany 159
    Russia 158, 175–7
Fouché, Joseph 37, 51
France
    active citizens 21, 23
    Ancien Régime 2, 4
    Assemblies
        Legislative 21, 26
        National 11–15, 17, 21
        National Constituent 21, 23
    assignats 21, 34, 40
    Brumaire, Coup of (1799) 1, 48–9
    Champs de Mars (1791) 25
    Civil Constitution of the Clergy 22
    Committee of Public Safety (CPS) 34
    conscription 59
    Constituent Assembly 15, 21, 23
    constitutions 17, 21, 23–4, 33, 49
    counter-revolutionary groups 20–1
    Consulate 50, 52, 56
    corvée 8
    Council of State (Conseil d'État) 50
    Cult of the Supreme Being 20, 37
    Declaration of the Rights of Man and of the Citizen (1789) 14–15
    Declaration of the Rights of Women 24

the Directory (1795-99) 25,
    42–4, 48
  Coup of Brumaire 48
  financial reforms 55
  and the Revolutionary wars 44
direct taxes 3–4
economic problems 6–7, 27, 32,
    39–40, 44, 48
education, Napoleonic France 55
effects of war 32
émigrés 20–1, 26
Estates General 2–3, 7–16, 20–1, 25
and Germany 74, 95–6
food riots 7, 9, 39
Girondins 18–20, 27, 32–3
margouilis national 44, 48
and Napoleon 46
National Convention 30, 32
National Guard 14
passive citizens 21
Paris sections 34
parlements 2, 3, 14, 21
police state 51
Revolutionary Calendar 31, 39, 42
revolutionary groups 17–20
Revolutionary Wars 27, 44, 72
sans-culottes 27–9, 31, 33, 35
Second Coalition 44, 48
Second Coalition, War of the
    (1798) 27
September Massacres 30
and Spain 44, 57, 59–61
the Terror 31, 35–7
the White Terror 40
see also the Directory (France);
    Revolutionary Wars (France)
Vendémiaire, uprising of (1795) 42
see also Louis XVI, King of
    France; Napoleon Bonaparte;
    Revolutionary Wars (France)
franchise 93
Franco-Prussian War 124, 126–7
Franz Josef, Prince 99
Frederick August II, king of Saxony 93
Frederick William IV, king of Prussia 26
  see also Friedrich Wilhelm IV, king
    of Prussia
French Revolution (1789) 2–16
  constitution 12
  March of the Women 15
  October Days 16
  Storming of the Bastille 13–14
  Third estate 3, 6, 10, 11, 12
  Tennis Court Oath 12
Friedrich Wilhelm IV, king of Prussia
    90–1, 98, 128–9

G

Gagern, Heinrich von 89, 96
Gapon, Father Georgy 161–2

Germany
  bill of rights 93
  and Bismarck 89, 98, 105, 110,
    119, 120, 121
  Carlsbad Decrees (1819) 77
  Confederation of the Rhine 73–4
  culture and the arts 80, 84
  economic growth 79, 101
    railway expansion 85
    steam power 79, 101
  French émigrés in 25–6
  German Confederation (the Bund)
    74
    Constituent Assembly
      (*Volparlament*) 94–5
    Frankfurt Parliament 94–7
    Schleswig-Holstein 95, 103,
      110, 112
    social and economic problems
      86–8
    Zollverein 84–5, 102
    Zollparlament 120
  German Empire 106, 108,
    124, 127–8
  German Progressive Party (DFP)
    107
  Holy Roman Empire 72
  Indemnity Bill (1866) 118
  industrial development 119
  liberalism 103
  and Metternich 75–6, 99
  Metternich system 75, 78, 82, 86
  middle class, growth of 79, 85
  National Association
    (Vaterlandsverein) 82
  nationalism 75, 76, 80–2, 84
  National Society 103
  North German Confederation 98,
    117, 121, 127–8, 131
  parliaments 74, 78, 98
    Diets 74, 76
  Reich 129–30
  Reichstag 129–30
  revolutions of 1848 88–9, 97, 105
  unification 119, 130
  see also Prussia
Gramont, Comte de 122

H

Hohenzollern Candidature 121–3
Holy Roman Empire 72
Hungary 91, 99, 116, 124, 172, 200

I

Ilyminsky, Alexander 145–6
iron industry 146, 148, 159, 169
Italian War of Independence (1859)
    103–4
Italy 44, 46–7, 57, 59, 75, 99, 100

J

Jacobins 17–19, 27, 31, 32, 40, 43
Japan 156, 159, 163
  Russo-Japanese War (1904–5)
    160–1

K

Kadets 162, 164, 166, 179
Kamenev, Lev 182, 186–7
Kerensky, Alexander 177, 183–8, 194
Kolchak, Admiral Alexander 195, 199
Kornilov, General 183–4, 194–5
Kronstadt Rising 138, 183, 201, 203

L

Laborists 164, 166
Leipzig, Battle of (1813) 61–2
Lenin, Vladimir
  April Theses 181, 183, 185
  and the Civil War 194, 201
  death of 138
  leadership of the Bolsheviks
    185–6, 196
  NEP (New Economic Policy) 202
  and the October Revolution 181,
    187, 202
  and War Communism 197, 201
  see also Bolsheviks
Leopold, Prince von Hohenzollern-
    Sigmaringen 122
liberalism 103
  Germany 71, 75, 78–9, 86, 97,
    100, 103–4
  Prussia 79–80
Louis XIV, king of France 2, 128
Louis XVI, king of France 1–3, 7, 23,
    30, 32
  constitutional monarchy 17–19
  flight to Varennes 25
  overthrow and execution 29, 91
  policies and reform attempts 7
  and the Revolutionary Wars 27
Louis Philippe, king of France 91, 115
Ludwig I, king of Bavaria 93
Lützow, Adolf von 80
Luxembourg Crisis 121
Lvov, Price Georgy 179

M

Marat, Jean-Paul 19, 33, 35
Marie Antoinette, queen 5, 26,
    27, 37
Marie-Louise of Parma 54
Marmont, August de 62
martial law 164
Marx, Karl 87, 153
Marxism 153–4
Méricourt, Théroigne de 24

Metternich, Prince Clemens von 73–5, 77, 90–1
   Metternich's system 75–6, 78–9
middle class
   France 3–4. 72
   Germany 79–81, 84–9, 93, 104–5
   Russia 150, 161
Moltke, Helmut 116, 125
Montagnards 32–3

N

Napoleon Bonaparte 1, 27, 31, 46–9, 50, 52, 62–3
   battles 57, 60–2
   and the Continental System 57
   domestic reforms 50–6
   Empire 52–4
   and enslaved people 58
   fall from power 56–63
   Holy Roman Empire dissolved 72
   marriages of 46–7, 54
   and Metternich 73
   wars 57, 60–1
Napoleon III 114–15, 120–1
Necker, Jacques 7
Nicholas II Tsar 139–40, 156–7, 165
   abdication 178
   and the First World War 172–3
   Fundamental laws 137, 139, 156, 163–5, 171
   industrial growth 168–9
   opposition to tsarist rule 175
   police state 51
   reform 142
   and the Revolution of 1905 156, 163
Nogaret, Dominique-Vincet Ramel de 44

O

Octobrists 164, 166
Okhrana 143–4, 155, 166, 175
Olmütz, humiliation of 100, 107, 131
Ottoman Empire 27, 44, 58, 113

P

paternalistic 140
peasants (Russia) 140–4, 147, 149–53, 158–9, 161–3, 166, 176, 183–186
   and Cossacks 200
   Decree on Land (1917) 190
   New Economic Policy 202
   Red Army 193, 196–8
   Stolypin's agrarian reforms 168
Peninsular War (1808–14) 1, 57
Pilnitz, Declaration of (1791) 26

Plekhanov, Georgi 153
Pobedonostev, Konstantin 141
population growth
   France 59
   Germany 86–7, 102
   Russia 6, 149, 155, 203–4
Potemkin 162
Progressivists 164
proletariat 87, 146
Prussia
   Bismarck as Minister President of 98, 104–5, 108, 118–9
   Brunswick Manifesto 29
   Carlsbad Decrees 77
   constitution 97
   constitutional monarchy 92
   economy 91, 101–2
      railways 85–6
   1848 revolutions 90–2, 94, 97
   Franco-Prussian War 124, 126
   and the Frankfurt Parliament 96
   Friedrich Wilhelm IV, king of Prussia 90, 91, 93, 97–8, 128–9
   and the German Confederation (the Bund) 74, 83
   and the German Empire 101, 106, 124, 128, 131
   and German Unification 118–9
   Hohenzollern Candidature and war with France 121–4, 127
   Holy Roman Empire 72
   Junkers 91
   Kamarilla 91
   Landwehr 107
   liberalism 79–80, 103
   Luxembourg Crisis 121
   March Days 89–91
   nationalism 80, 84
   and the North German Confederation 121, 125, 127–8, 131
   Olmütz, humiliation of 100
   Pilnitz, Declaration of (1792) 26
   Revolutionary Wars 27, 44, 72
   Schlesswig-Holstein 95, 97, 111–12, 115
   Sorbs/Wends 84
   three-tier system 92
   urbanization 87
   Von Lützow, Adolf 80
      Black Troopers (*Frei Korps*) 80
   war with Austria 98, 113–4, 116–8, 120
   Wilhelm I, king of Prussia 103, 106
   Zollverein 84–5, 102, 115
   see also Bismarck, Otto von; Germany

R

Radowitz, General Joseph von 100
railways
   Germany 78, 84–5, 101
   Prussia 85–6, 125
   Russia 169, 176, 191, 198
Rasputin, Grigori 174
realpolitik 108
religion
   France 2, 3, 5, 22
      the Concordat 56
      Cult of the Supreme Being 20, 37
      religious terror 37
   Russia 157
Revolutionary Wars (France) 27, 44
   and Germany 72
Robespierre, Maximilien 17–20, 31, 33–5, 37–8
Roon, Albrecht von 107
Rousseau, Jean-Jacques 5
Russia
   and Austria 171–2,
   autocracy 140–1
   Cheka 192–3, 197
   Civil War 138, 194–5, 200–1
      see also Bolsheviks
   Communists, Left 192
   Dumas (parliaments) 142, 163–4, 166–7, 172, 177, 178
   economy and economic growth 146–50, 158, 169
      banks 147
      "Great Spurt" 157, 159–60
      industrialization 169
      middle class development 150
      New Economic Policy (NEP) 202
      railways 148, 169
      social problems as result of 158
   education 145
   February Revolution 137, 175–6
   and the First World War 172–3, 175–6
   and France 60–1
   and Germany 172, 181, 191, 194
   industrial developments 146–8, 151, 169, 191
   industrial workers 143, 146–7, 153, 157–8, 175
      wages 147, 167, 169, 175
      strikes 161–3, 167, 169
   Fundamental Laws 139, 156, 163–5, 171
   Kadets (liberals)
   Kronstadt Mutiny 138, 183, 201
   July Days 183
   Lena Goldfield Massacre 137
   Lenin, Vladimir

April Theses 181, 183, 185
and the Civil War 194, 201
death of 138
leadership of the Bolsheviks 185–6, 196
NEP (New Economic Policy) 202
and the October Revolution 181, 187, 202
One Party Unity policy 202
and War Communism 197, 201
Marxism 153–4
New Economic Policy (NEP) 202
Nicholas II, Tsar 139, 142, 156–7, 165, 178
October Manifesto 156, 159, 163
October Revolution 187–8
Okhrana 144
Peasants 140–4, 147, 149–53, 158–9, 161–3, 166, 176, 183–186
and Cossacks 200
Decree on Land 190
and the New Economic Policy 202
Red Army 193, 196–8
Stolypin's agrarian reforms 168
People's Will 143–4, 152–3
Petrograd Soviet of Soldiers', Sailors', and Workers' Deputies 178–80, 186
pogroms 146
population growth 149–51
Populism 152
Provisional Government 177–9, 181–4
Revolution of 1905 137, 156, 161–4
Red Army 193, 195

Red Guards 186
Russification 143, 145, 151
and Jewish people 146
Russo-Japanese War (1904) 160–1, 163
serfs, emancipation of 142–3
mir 143
Social Democratic Party 154, 157
socialism 87, 153, 181
Socialist Revolutionaries 157
Soviets 161
trade unions 147, 162–3, 182, 201
Treaty of Brest-Litovsk (1918) 191
Tsarist regime 137, 138, 155, 165, 178
impact of First World War on 171–2
opposition to 167
Whites 198–200
Vyborg Manifesto 164
Zemgor 172
Zemstvos 139–40, 142–5, 152
see also Bolsheviks; Nicholas II; Tsar
Russo-Japanese War (1904–5) 160–1

S

Schleswig - Holstein 95, 103, 110, 112
Convention of Gastein (1865) 112
Seven Week's War 116
Seven Year's War (1756–63) 6
Sieyés, Emmanuel 44, 48
Stolypin, Petr 164, 166, 168
suffrage 117, 178

T

tax farmers 6
Tennis Court Oath 12
Thermidor 31, 38
Thermidor, Coup of (1794) 1
Thermidorian Reaction 40–41
Thermidorians 40–2
Thiers, Adolphe 126
Treaty of Chaumont (1814) 63
Trotsky, Leon 180–1, 186, 189

V

Vienna, Congress of (1815) 74
Vienna, Treaty of (1864) 71, 111
Vyborg Manifesto 164

W

War against Austria 60, 113
War of Liberation 71
War with Denmark 110
Bismarck's involvement 111–12
Wilhelm IV, King of Prussia 90–1, 94
Witte, Sergei 147, 158–9, 163, 168–70
women 5, 14, 24, 43, 55, 78, 86, 147
International Women's Day 177
"March of the Women" 15
Wrangel, Baron Pyotr 195

Y

Yudenich, General Nicolai 195

Z

Zemstvo 140
Zinoviev, Grigory 186

Photo credits

The Publishers would like to thank the following for permission to reproduce copyright material.

p.2 © Shutterstock / Everett - Art; **p.9** © Josse Christophel / Alamy Stock Photo; **p.12** © Niday Picture Library / Alamy Stock Photo; **p.18** © Sunny Celeste / Alamy Stock Photo; **p.20** *t* Image courtesy of the Miriam and Ira D. Wallach Division of Art, Prints and Photographs: Print Collection, The New York Public Library; **p.20** *b* © The Picture Art Collection / Alamy Stock Photo; **p.21** © PWB Images / Alamy Stock Photo; **p.22** © National Library of France, Prints and Photography Department, RESERVE FOL-QB-201 (121); **p.28** *t* © Pictorial Press Ltd / Alamy Stock Photo; **p.28** *b* © Classic Image / Alamy Stock Photo ©Historical Images Archive / Alamy Stock Photo; **p.34** © The Granger Collection / Alamy Stock Photo ; **p.35** © Album / Alamy Stock Photo; **p.36** © World History Archive / Alamy Stock Photo; **p.39** © ClassicStock / Alamy Stock Photo; **p.41** © The Picture Art Collection / Alamy Stock Photo; **p.46** Image courtesy of National Gallery of Art, Washington, Samuel H. Kress Collection 1961.9.15; **p.46** © Zuri Swimmer / Alamy Stock Photo; **p.48** © The Print Collector / Alamy Stock Photo; **p.53** © Painters / Alamy Stock Photo; **p.58** © PRISMA ARCHIVO / Alamy Stock Photo; **p.75** © https://www.metmuseum.org/art/collection/search/436887, https://creativecommons.org/publicdomain/zero/1.0/; **p.81** © INTERFOTO / Alamy Stock Photo; **p.83** © Yogi Black / Alamy Stock Photo; **p.90** © The Print Collector / Alamy Stock Photo; **p.90** © Alfredo Dagli Orti / REX / Shutterstock; **p.92** © The History Collection / Alamy Stock Photo; **p.94** © The Picture Art Collection / Alamy Stock Photo ; **p.95** © The Picture Art Collection / Alamy Stock Photo; **p.97** © ARTGEN / Alamy Stock Photo ; **p.98** © Allstar Picture Library Ltd / Alamy Stock Photo; **p.106** © ARTGEN / Alamy Stock Photo; **p.109** © INTERFOTO / Alamy Stock Photo; **p.109** © Granger Historical Picture Archive / Alamy Stock Photo; **p.112** © INTERFOTO / Alamy Stock Photo; **p.114** © Sueddeutsche Zeitung Photo / Alamy Stock Photo; **p.115** Public Domain. https://commons.wikimedia.org/wiki/File:Napoleon_III._of_France.jpg; **p.129** © Pictorial Press Ltd / Alamy Stock Photo; **p.139** © Historic Images / Alamy Stock Photo; **p.148** © ARTGEN / Alamy Stock Photo; **p.151** © The Granger Collection / Alamy Stock Photo; **p.154** © Chronicle / Alamy Stock Photo; **p.156** © Everett Collection Historical / Alamy Stock Photo; **p.159** Image courtesy of Library of Congress **p.161** © CPA Media Pte Ltd / Alamy Stock Photo; **p.163** © CBW / Alamy Stock Photo; **p.170** © GRANGER - Historical Picture Archive / Alamy Stock Photo; **p.174** © IanDagnall Computing / Alamy Stock Photo; **p.177** © Heritage Images / Hulton Archive via Getty Images; **p.181** © Photos.com via Getty Images; **p.181** © Illustrated London News; **p.182** © Album / Alamy Stock Photo; **p.188** © A. Burkatovski / Fine Art Images / SuperStock; **p.198** © Heritage Image Partnership Ltd / Alamy Stock Photo; **p.199** © Heritage Image Partnership Ltd / Alamy Stock Photo; **p.203** © Heritage Image Partnership Ltd / Alamy Stock Photo; **p.208** © Album / Alamy Stock Photo;